JUST AS HOMER IS UNIQUE AMONG POETS,
SO STANDS ROME AMONG OTHER CITIES, AND ROME'S EMPIRE
AMONG ALL OTHERS IN THE WORLD.

W. H. VON HUMBOLDT

TEXT BY

BARRY CUNLIFFE

PROFESSOR OF EUROPEAN ARCHAEOLOGY, U??? OF OXFORD

ROME AND HER EMPIRE

WITH THE COLLABORATION OF PHOTOGRAPHERS

BRIAN BRAKE

AND

LEONARD VON MATT

DESIGNED BY

EMIL M. BÜHRER

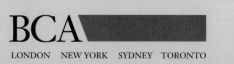

LONDON NEW YORK SYDNEY TORONTO

This edition published 1994
by BCA by arrangement with
Constable and Company Ltd
A Production of EMB-Service for Publishers
Copyright © 1994 by EMB-Service for Publishers
Printed in Italy

CN 8529

THE CHAPTERS

IN THE BEGINNING
pages 30–51

Shepherd tribes, three thousand years ago, settled the seven hills at the crossroads of the Etruscan and Greek cultures. Legend and art trace their struggles with foreign despots, their rise from hamlet to city-state.

PATRICIANS AND PLEBEIANS
pages 52–97

The Republic: five centuries of conquest and expansion which strained the democratic structures to the breaking point. Carthaginian territory and Greek art enriched Rome, while civil strife and a new army prepared the way for one-man rule.

THE IDEA OF THE CITY
pages 98–173

A blueprint of the urban model that Rome imposed far and wide—the city-plan, religion, water supply, transport, trade. The Romans are overheard and observed in their stadiums, their baths, their mansions, and their slums.

EXPANSION OF THE EMPIRE
pages 174–209

Roman armies thrust their way forward in every direction, in campaigns against the peoples of Germany, the Sahara, Britain, and the Persian Gulf. Romanization followed. The steady growth from Caesar to the full Empire in A.D. 138.

LIFE IN THE PROVINCES
pages 210–265

A tour of the Empire, with studies of each important province. Africa became Rome's breadbasket, Iberia was mined for precious ores, the Danube served as trading post. Each province had its unique character, and its role to play in the vast Roman economy.

ROME IN RETREAT
pages 266–307

Barbarian invasions, economic collapse, and government chaos led to the downfall of Rome and the dismembering of her Empire. Along with the rise of Christianity there came the emergence of a new capital and a new empire in the east.

THE THEMES

Before the Roman military conquests, the Mediterranean was already a crossroads of diverse cultures dominated by the maritime trade and expansion of the Phoenicians and, above all, the Greeks. Phoenician relief of a ship, Beirut.

INTRODUCTION

In history you have
a record of the infinite variety
of human experience
plainly set out for all to see;
there you can find
for yourself and your country
examples and warnings;
fine things to take as models,
and base things, rotten
through and through, to avoid.

Livy

The Roman world has always held a particular fascination. The men and women of those times, their achievements and their motivations have been pored over by generation after generation, each one interpreting the great saga in their own way and drawing from it everything from moral enlightenment to simply the enjoyment of a really good story. In the eighth century A.D. a Christian monk who probably lived for a while in the abbey at Bath wrote a poem, known as 'The Ruin', about the decaying remains of the old Roman temple and baths which he would have seen daily. For him these gaunt ruins, 'the works of Giants', were a stark reminder of the frailty of hu-

the transience of his puny humanity. Later generations responded to their Roman past in different ways. In early medieval times British historians tried to link the origins of the British to the Trojan myth in classical mythology, which accounted for the foundation of Rome. In doing so they were seeking a legitimacy for their race.

By Tudor times, when Shakespeare was writing, many of the surviving Latin texts had been published and disseminated throughout Europe and the outlines of Roman history were becoming widely known at least among the educated classes. To writers like Shakespeare they were a source of wonderful stories peopled by charac-

The unity of the immense Empire depended on engineering and construction achieve- ments (such as the aqueduct between Zaghouan and Carthage, in Tunisia) that far surpassed anything accomplished in earlier times.

mankind when seen against the consistent power of God. 'Wondrous is this masonry, shattered by the Fates. The fortifications have given way, the buildings raised by giants are crumbling...the owners and builders are perished and gone, and have been held fast in earth's embrace, the ruthless clutch of the grave, while a hundred generations of mankind have passed away.' Here barely 400 years after Roman rule in Britain had ended was a man trying to understand something of the past and to learn from it about

ters larger than life who were tormented by all the uncertainties and conflicting loyalties that are a part of the human condition. By telling the story of Caesar's murder at the hands of his friend Brutus and the others Shakespeare could make his audience ponder the whole complex moral problem of regicide which had recently troubled Britain.

The development of overseas trading enterprises, and the empires which inevitably followed from them in the eighteenth and nineteenth centuries,

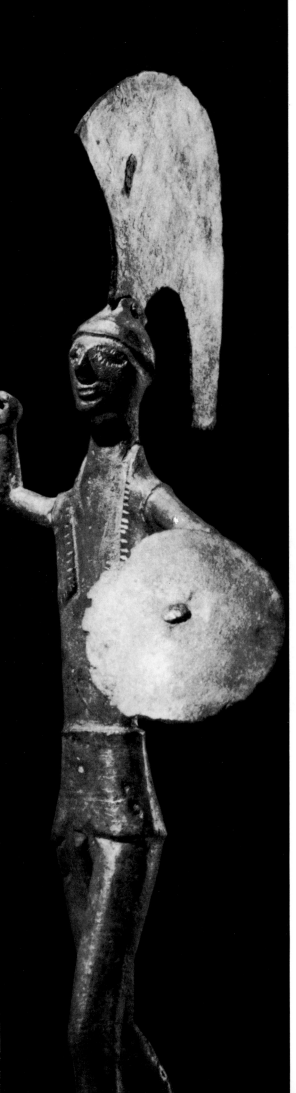

In the marvels
of her buildings, the city has
almost surpassed
the brilliant successes won by Roman
arms....a second world
has sprung up in our midst.

Pliny the Elder

provided a new context within which Roman history could be re-examined and used as justification. After all was not the subjugation of Africa, with all the hideous barbarity of the slave trade, merely a re-enactment of the Roman conquest of temperate Europe? And the opening up of America was not unlike the Roman colonization of great tracts of North Africa. A colonial administrator serving the British Raj in Calcutta or a commander patrolling the North West Frontier would have had no difficulty justifying the Empire which he was serving by reference to the Roman history he had learnt in his public school. It was the same belief in repetitive history that

new areas of interest have developed more in tune with the concerns of the modern world. The integration of native political and economic systems into the fabric of the empire so as to allow them a continuing sense of ethnic identity is a vast area for study—and for admiration. Another area is the question of demography. The rapid increase, and later the crippling decrease in population within the empire, its causes and its disastrous effects, have much to tell us about our modern world. And then there is the whole question of the Roman attitude to harnessing natural energy and controlling the landscape for productive purposes—how did the empire sustain its

Myths of Romulus and Remus conjure up a Trojan ancestry belied by archaeological evidence such as this early Etruscan hut-shaped urn. A later legend (right): Marcus Curtius (in the fourth century) rides into a crevasse as a sacrifice to save Rome.

underpinned Mussolini's vision of a new Roman empire in the 1930s. Against such a background of imperial expansion it is easy to see why the study of the Roman empire became central to a proper education and why the emphasis of the study focused around the nature of the Roman administration, and, of course, the army. In the post-war, post-colonial era things have changed. This is not to say that the genius of the Roman administrative and military machines have lost their fascination—far from it—but

growth over so long a period with so little recourse to fossil fuels? These are just some of the subjects which show why the study of the Roman empire is of direct relevance to our contemporary concerns.

On the intellectual level, then, one can see why a fascination with the Romans has endured and will continue to do so. The Romans were human beings living in a complex and fast changing society: they were subjected to many of the same pressures and worries as ourselves and enjoyed many of the same

11

things. Their individual responses and the trajectory of their history help us better to understand ourselves and our current situation.

Yet there are other ways in which the world of the Romans forces itself into our consciousness. Perhaps most dramatic is the sheer enormity of the territory over which Rome dominated. This was borne home to me a year or two ago when, within the space of a few months, I spanned the empire visiting, in rapid succession, the Roman baths at Bath in the west of Britain, the ruins of the city of Volubilis in the province of Mauritania, now Morocco, and the streets of Jerash in Jordan. A few weeks later in the National Museum in

at finding shards of Italian wine amphorae and Arretine drinking cups on the east coast of India at Arikamedu near Pondacherry—exactly the same types of vessel he had excavated a few years earlier at a native British *oppidum* at Wheathampstead near St. Albans. The activities of Roman entrepreneurs pervaded the known world.

How Rome came to dominate so vast an area is our theme but before we

The Celts, a threat to Rome for centuries, were conquered by Julius Caesar between 58 and 49 B.C. Caesar's strategic genius, supported by an ever more efficient military machine, gave Rome vast new territory and firm control of Gaul. Mask from the Pyrennees, third-second century B.C., Museum of Tarbes, France.

rior of Italy and the main route between the powerful, metal-rich area of Etruria and the fast-developing city states of Magna Graecia in the south. By about 500 B.C. Rome had freed itself from Etruscan domination and was poised to extend its influence within the peninsula. That it did so with such success is in part due to the dour,

LANDMARKS IN A THOUSAND-YEAR HISTORY

The Roman debt to Greece, a Hellenistic temple in the heart of Rome.

Julius Caesar and Cleopatra: the growth of Rome's dominance and of Caesar's personal power at home.

His heir, Augustus, first emperor, who brought a strong centralized administration, stability, prosperity.

Copenhagen I was able to see a collection of ornate Roman silver vessels found in a barbarian grave at Hoby on the Danish island of Lolland. They had reached this remote spot, well beyond the northern frontier of the empire, either by trade or as spoils from a raid—a reminder that though the empire stretched from 3200 miles east to west to 2000 miles north to south its influence reached out far beyond its formal frontiers. Sir Mortimer Wheeler made the point in a particularly vivid way when he described his excitement

begin to embark upon the detail of the epic let us stand back and see the whole in perspective.

Why it was that the inhabitants of the seven hills of Rome were able to come together to forge a city that could dominate the civilized western world is a complex question for which there is no simple monocausal explanation. Rome owed its ascendancy to many factors. To begin with its location was favourable. Sited on the river Tiber within easy reach of the sea, it commanded both an easy way to the inte-

serious nature of the people, a temperament pervaded by a distinct thread of cruelty. From the outset the social system was based on military prowess. Competition among the elite was externalized so that status was gained and enhanced by success in campaigns against neighbouring enemies. Thus external warfare became essential to the maintenance of internal social order.

To begin with the conflicts were restricted to the Italian peninsula and inevitably they led to territorial gains

The empire comprehended
the fairest part of the earth,
and the most civilized
portion of mankind. ... The gentle
but powerful influence
of laws and manners had
gradually cemented
the union of the provinces.
Their peaceful inhabitants enjoyed
and abused the advantages
of wealth and luxury.

Edward Gibbon

but after the middle of the third century B.C. Rome was drawn into taking sides in the escalating hostilities between the Greek settlers of Magna Graecia and the Carthaginian sphere of influence. The First Punic War (264–241) which ensued left Rome master of Sicily. Sardinia and Corsica were soon to follow. Gradually the conflict widened drawing Rome into a further war with Carthage in Spain (the Second Punic War, 218–201).

By the end of the third century Rome's economy was beginning to become dependent on territorial expansion and the command of the Mediterranean trade routes. It now became imperative to destroy rivals and this was effec-

wish to return. Thus there was land to spare and this was bought up by the elite to be worked by slaves. The overall result was that Italians gravitated to the cities creating an increasingly unstable mob while the land came increasingly under the control of the senatorial class who derived much of their income from its efficient exploitation. The kind of monoculture practised—most frequently vine produc-

that the growing empire lay within a zone of territories broadly similar in their ecological make-up but once the limits had been reached, as they had by the beginning of the second century A.D., further expansion was impossible. The Emperor Hadrian bowed to the inevitable by effectively sealing the boundaries of empire with systems of continuous frontier works intended to be permanent. By this time the empire was bounded on the south and east by desert, on the west by ocean and on the north by the treacherous forests and marshes of the North European Plain. Inhibited from further expansion the economic system began to totter. Add to this population decline in many re-

The paved-road network that linked the empire and aided further conquests. Roman road, Syria.

Arch of Septimius Severus, Rome, commemorating victories at a time when triumph followed triumph.

Barbarian invasions (in a third-century relief) and popular rebellions weakened Rome's control.

Constantinople: a new capital in the east (A.D. 330), successor to the shaken western empire.

tively done in a single year, 146 B.C., when, within the span of a few months, Rome destroyed Carthage in the west Mediterranean and Corinth in the east. Seven years later, in 133 B.C., the collapse of native resistance in Spain and the gift of the kingdom of Pergamum in Anatolia left Rome as effective master of the Mediterranean.

Almost continuous warfare for several centuries had greatly affected the Roman economic and social systems. In Italy men left the land to serve in the army and on retirement had little

tion—created surpluses which could only be turned to reasonable profit in foreign markets. To maintain any degree of stability it was necessary to ensure both an inflow of manpower (slaves) and raw materials and an outflow of agrarian surpluses, principally wine. This imperative gave a new impetus to military campaigning abroad. Put another way, for the social and economic systems of Rome to survive it was necessary for the empire to expand continuously.

Expansion was possible all the time

gions and a growing barbarian pressure building up against the northern and eastern frontiers and the spectacular collapse of the early fifth century was inevitable. Though the Byzantine world of the east was a phoenix—and a very splendid one—arising from the ashes of Rome, the Greek-speaking, Christian beast with its oriental plumage was a very different creature to old Rome—Latin-speaking, essentially pagan and retaining to the end something of the traditional values of gravity, piety and simplicity.

THE EVIDENCE

Evidence of Rome is everywhere apparent, embedded in our languages and our scripts, reflected in architecture, woven into the fabric of our literature, and frequently, though less obviously, buried beneath our feet. There was no time when ancient Rome was not being actively studied; indeed even the Romans were fascinated by their past. Livy, piecing together the origins of the city from folklore and other scraps; Claudius, studying the Etruscans through sources no longer available to us; and Constantine, collecting a group of antique reliefs to include in his triumphal arch—all were caught up in a nostalgia for the past and a desire to understand their roots. The traces which remain of Roman civilization are plentiful, and the picture that can be reconstructed is vivid in its detail, vast in its extent, and remarkable for the precision of its focus.

A study of the contemporary written record is perhaps the most direct way to begin to understand the past. Fortunately the Romans were prolific recorders. Not only was their literature copious, but they also took delight in monumentalizing their achievements with inscriptions. Their coins too were regularly used to transmit news of major events or to instill into the populace the need for piety for the gods and reverence for their emperor. When, in the third century, the Empire

The money that the Romans left behind is among the best historical evidence we have. From their first real coinage (ca. 275 B.C.) until the Empire's collapse, mintings were frequent, with up-to-date inscriptions and revealing details. Coins became a communication channel from government to people, to mark important events such as victories or food hand-outs, to show portraits of the emperors, and to rally support. Even a coin's metallic composition is informative, indicating relative solvency.

Coins can bring Roman ruins back to life. *Above:* The Colosseum, completed in A.D. 80, on a coin issued by the emperor Titus in 79–81, is shown packed with spectators. Especially interesting are the topmost stories, which no longer exist, and the sense of how the structure looked when in use. Several less famous buildings are known to us primarily from coins: the two-story meat market of Nero, the elaborate Circus Maximus, the Basilica Aemilia in the Forum, the wharfs of Ostia.

The emperors stamped their profiles on the money they issued (see pages 194 ff.), and often showed themselves engaged in government duties and ceremonies. *Above:* The homely Caligula addresses the army, A.D. 37–38. The coin shows us the soldiers' uniforms, equipment, and the eagle standards they carried, and captures a political ceremony that must really have occurred. *Below:* In a quasi-religious rite, Emperor Lucius Verus (A.D. 161–169), speaks from the sacred *Sella Curulis.*

Opposite: A quadriga, or four-horse chariot, on an early two-drachma piece (205 B.C.), provides further historical testimony. Using such coins as a guide, specialists have been able to reassemble fragments of stone quadriga statuary from many Roman triumphal arches. The goddess Victory, at left, holds the reins; beside her stands Jupiter with scepter and lightning bolts. This was a popular theme on Roman coins for several centuries; Jupiter, the protector, stood beside Rome or Victory.

ROMA

In stone, on metal, and on tablets, the Romans left an enduring written record. Manuscripts such as this third-century A.D. copy of Virgil's *Georgics (right)* transmit histories, chronicles, diaries, speeches, letters, and literary works. We learn about military victories, boundaries, ceremonies, dates, and important individuals from stone inscriptions like the commemorative text *(below)* from a monument in Timgad, Algeria. *Opposite:* Stone calendar from Aviternum, Italy.

Overleaf: Roman art as evidence. *Left:* A Pompeian wall painting, 60 B.C., illustrates the customs of the wealthy classes. White-clad youths are shown serving and entertaining guests at a banquet. *Right:* Our best information on Roman clothing, military uniforms, and accessories comes from statues such as this torso of a provincial official from second-century A.D. Djemila in Algeria. Mosaics (as in the background) cover an enormous range of subject matter.

was engulfed in an economic and political crisis, coins came into their own as a propaganda medium bearing reassuring messages like "Happiness of the Age" and "Peace Everywhere"—when really peace and prosperity were fast slipping away. In the absence of mass media, coinage fulfilled an important function.

Other forms of writing such as monumental inscriptions, altars, or simple tombstones are of vital importance to

ity rate within particular social classes. Without such evidence our knowledge of the Romans would be much the poorer, but there are lesser grades of inscription which are equally fascinating. The inscribed lead curse from Bath which begins, "May he who carried off Vilbia from me become as liquid as the dumb waters...," reminds us of real human suffering, while the graffiti on the walls of Pompeii, bawdy and political alike,

written on papyrus or wood-backed wax tablets, which by some accident of preservation, either in waterlogged conditions or in the dry desert climate, have survived for archaeologists to discover. They present an intimate wealth of human detail. A young soldier writes home to his mother in Egypt: "Dear Mother, I hope this finds you well. When you get this letter I shall be much obliged if you will send me some money... send me a riding coat, some oil, and above all my monthly allowance." Or a brother to his sister in Egypt: "If you come across any mustard-relish, buy it and make some pickle. If you make anything good, make an extra amount for your brother's house." Or the wooden tablet from London, sent by a master to his servant Epillicus: "I believe you know I am very well. If you have made the list, please send. Do look after everything carefully. See that you turn that slave girl into cash." Fragments like these echo the authentic voices of the people stripped of their grandeur.

Roman literature, or that small part of it which survived transcribed, often many times, in the monasteries of medieval Europe, adds another dimension. The great historical writings of Livy provide an essential background, full of detail, to the early history of the Republic without which a narrative history would have been difficult to reconstruct. Later come the tough, pithy accounts of the Gallic Wars written largely by Caesar himself, partly to project his own image to the Roman world. Caesar's writings give an invaluable insight into the anthropology of the northern barbarians, as do the works of the historian Tacitus (late first century A.D.). Tacitus, however, was inclined to present the northerners in the somewhat idealized guise of the

our study. An inscription from a building might indicate its date of construction; a group of altars would name not only the gods worshipped at a particular location but also the type of people who traveled there and their places of origin; while tombstones provide a wealth of detail, from the disposition of troops to the mortal-

present the Romans as flesh and blood. The individual who scrawled on a Pompeian wall, "The emperor's mother is only a human being," was indulging in a rare but dangerous wit.

Whether on coins, carved in stone, or daubed on walls, these words were meant for public view. Another, much rarer, source is the private letters

Archaeological evidence continues to come to light. As recently as 1960, an accidental discovery by a ditch-digger in Fishbourne, England, led to the excavation of a major palace complex from the late first century A.D. Specialists are shown here restoring a mosaic floor, one of the many splendid mosaics contained in the palace of the British king Cogidubnus at Fishbourne. These excavations have completely changed our notions of Roman Britain.

Right: Aerial photograph of a Roman town in present-day Tunisia, where the Romans had more than fifty important settlements. Excavations from all over Europe and the Mediterranean area show the great versatility of Roman building, a remarkably skillful adaptation to different conditions and natural sites. The regular grid pattern of this layout shows that the town was of Roman origin (no older than the first century B.C.).

noble savage—a direct reaction against the enervating times in which he was writing. With the writings of Tacitus the historical tradition enters the time of the Empire and is continued by Dio Cassius and Herodian to the time of Ammianus Marcellinus—the historian of Rome in decline.

The natural and practical worlds are also extensively covered by contemporary writers. Pliny the Elder's *Natural History* is encyclopedic; Lucretius, an epicurian, attempts to explain natural phenomena in terms of philosophical concepts; and Vitruvius lays down his rules of architecture—everything from mixing mortar to establishing the harmonics of a theater—and Apicius presents a series of cooking recipes telling us, for example, how to prepare such delicacies as stuffed sow's udder.

At a different level the speeches and letters of Cicero and the letters of Pliny the Younger greatly enliven the day-to-day workings of the late Republic and the early Empire: here we see

powerful, thinking men react to the responsibilities of public life according to their personal code of conduct even though, in the case of Cicero, it could lead to violent death and mutilation. Nor is creative literature lacking; the epic poetry of Virgil, the lesser poems of Horace and Ovid, the plays of Terence and Plautus all have their place in filling out and enriching our picture of Roman life.

Numismatics, epigraphy, and the study of ancient literature are all old established disciplines. Petrarch (1304–1374) had already amassed a fine collection of classical texts and regularly used coins as historical sources, while his contemporaries engaged in the study of inscriptions. The first corpus of all known Roman inscriptions was published in Ingolstadt in 1534. The study of surviving monuments did not lag far behind. Indeed it is fair to say that by the beginning of the sixteenth century practically all the major academic approaches to the appreciation of Roman culture had

been established, with one exception—archaeological excavation.

Excavation did not begin to emerge as a full-fledged discipline until the end of the nineteenth century, and as a science it is only during the last fifty years that it has come of age, no longer being considered a poor relation to its sister disciplines. Admittedly the removal of dirt from around buried or partially buried monuments is an age-old pursuit. Such procedures became immensely popular after the discovery of Pompeii and Herculaneum in the eighteenth century, and in the nineteenth century missions from all the major European powers were engaged in uncovering the ancient cities of the then underdeveloped regions and shipping all the movable antiquities back to their own national museums: the Germans at Priene, Miletus, and Pergamum in Asia Minor, the British at nearby Ephesus, and the French in the great cities of Tunisia and Algeria. At home campaigns of excavation were being undertaken designed to explore the European Roman past. In France Napoleon III sponsored work to elucidate Caesar's campaign, in Germany the frontier zone was actively explored, and in Britain the mosaics of rich countryside villas like Bignor and Woodchester were being exposed to an admiring public. But this was not excavation in a modern sense—it was little more than site clearance. Yet for all its shortcoming this work began to add a new dimension to knowledge and, more important, to point to the considerable potential of the method. The aims and aspirations of the modern excavating archaeologist are very different from those of his predecessors. The uncovering of structures and their reconstruction, albeit usually on paper, is indeed one aim common to both,

as is the desire to place them in an historical context, but there the similarities with the past end. Nowadays the archaeologist concerns himself with recovering the entire picture of the past insofar as the surviving data and his techniques of recovery and analysis allow. He studies the physical environment in which the site lies and the dynamic relationship between that environment and man; he attempts to discover the economic base upon which the community subsisted; and he examines the mechanisms by which one community related to another. In other words, the questions asked are concerned with the complexities of human behavior, much of the evidence for which lies embedded in the soil itself. Thus it is no longer acceptable to shovel the soil away from a monument. It has to be minutely examined and its contents extracted, analyzed, and quantified. Preserved insect wing cases can give an amazing insight into the living conditions experienced by peasant farmers who camped out during the summer with their herds on the flood plain of the Thames near Oxford. In the same way fragments of nuts, seeds, and other organic refuse recovered from the mud in Carthage harbor can be used to describe the conditions under which the Carthaginians lived in the decades immediately preceding the destruction of their city by the Roman general Scipio.

These examples may seem trivial when viewed against the vastness of the Empire, and in many ways they are; but like the poems of Virgil, the market of Trajan, or the mosaics from Piazza Armerina, the insects from the Oxfordshire mud, in their different way, are contributing to our fuller understanding of Rome and her Empire.

KOPKYP

THE LEGENDARY ORIGINS OF ROME

There are moments in the growth of a nation when the people need to pause to take stock and examine their past in order to reassure themselves of their oneness—to catch their breath before surging ahead to greater achievements. For the Romans such a time came at the end of the third century B.C. in the period of exhaustion and exuberance following the defeat of their deadly enemy Carthage. The city of Rome was poised to control the universe. "Be magnanimous as masters of the world," Livy wrote later, "and lay down your strife with mortals: like the gods, care for and spare the human race." In this time of reassessment the victors had to show themselves, through a respectable ancestry, to be fit to assume the mantle of leadership. At such a moment a nation's scholars naturally turn their attentions to discovering or inventing history.

For Roman historians like Fabius Pictor and those who came after him the task was difficult, not least because, they claimed, all early records had been destroyed when the Gauls sacked Rome in 390 B.C. Little factual material remained, except lists of magistrates and perhaps temple records, together with a wealth of tradition embedded in the religious customs, the myths, and the folktales of the people. From this varied base an official "history" was created.

It was widely accepted that the foundation of the Republic began at the end of the sixth century (traditionally 509 B.C.), from which time an historical framework, albeit rudimentary, could be constructed. Before that date there were no fixed points although everyone knew that the foundation of the city went back much earlier. The historians' explanation of the city's origins was based on two separate traditions: the story of the Trojan Wars recorded in Greek mythology, and the local Roman folktale of Romulus and Remus. By conflating these two accounts, historians created a highly respectable foundation myth that provided Rome with an ancestry rising directly from the heart of Greek culture. The key figure in this genealogy was the Trojan nobleman Aeneas, who, as the son of Venus and a mortal father, was semidivine. According to one version of this story, Aeneas and his followers, fleeing from the destruction of Troy, eventually landed in Latium in central Italy. It was the grandson of Aeneas, Romulus, who founded the city in 753 B.C. and so became the first of the seven kings to reign in the 240 years or so before the creation of the Republic. Thus Greek mythology, folk tradition, and dim memories of the period of monarchy were neatly brought together in the single reassuring story of a people descended from a goddess. When later it became known that Greek historians placed the fall of Troy in the twelfth century B.C. (a date borne out by archaeological evidence), Roman writers found no embarrassment in overcoming the chronological problems thus presented: they inserted a dynasty, the kings of Alba Longa, between Aeneas and Romulus to cover the missing four hundred years. Such was the flexibility of the legendary tradition.

Mother-goddess of the Roman people: Julius Caesar claimed descent from Venus *(left)*, legendary mother of the Trojan Aeneas. According to myth and literature, Venus protected Aeneas in his flight from Troy and guided him to Italy, where his descendants founded Rome. As their power grew, the Romans saw their past in increasingly exalted terms: gods mixed with men, myth with history.

REMUS

Remus: Son of Rhea Silvia and Mars. He contested his brother Romulus's right to found a city. In the ensuing conflict he was killed. His body was buried on the Aventine.

Romulus: Having killed his brother, he founded the city of Rome on the Palatine. To provide his growing city with women, he had Sabine maidens abducted. One, Hersilia, became his wife.

MARS

RHEA SILVIA

ROMULUS

Rhea Silvia: Daughter of King Numitor of Alba Longa. Her uncle Amulius forced her to become a Vestal Virgin in order to prevent her from having children. But while she was fetching water from a sacred grove (or, as another story has it, in a dream) she was raped by the god Mars and bore twin boys. She was imprisoned by her uncle Amulius and died, or was freed, or was thrown into the Tiber, according to the different traditions.

Proca: A king of Alba Longa, twelve generations after Ascanius/Iulus. Proca's two sons divided the legacy upon his death: Numitor became king, while Amulius received the treasure.

JULIUS CAESAR

AMULIUS

Amulius: Usurped the throne from his brother Numitor and forced Numitor's daughter to become a Vestal Virgin so that no rightful heir to the throne could be born. Was later slain by Romulus and Remus.

Ascanius: Son of Aeneas, succeeded his father as king of Lavinium. After thirty years he founded a new city at Alba Longa—the mother city of Rome. He was called Iulus by the Romans and was claimed to be the ancestor of the Julian family.

PROCA

NUMITOR

Numitor: Older brother of Amulius and father of Rhea Silvia. His throne, usurped by Amulius, was later restored to him by his twin grandsons Romulus and Remus.

Julius Caesar, to enhance his prestige, repeatedly drew attention to his family's ancient roots, claiming to descend from Iulus (Ascanius) and therefore from Venus. He could thus show himself to be a true patrician, and also prove his right to hold the powerful office of chief priest, or *pontifex maximus*. This religious post, which Caesar won in 63 B.C., was a lifelong appointment that had great political weight.

ASCANIUS/IULUS

Creusa: Daughter of King Priam of Troy, Aeneas's wife, and mother of Ascanius. Separated from Aeneas during the sack of Troy, she disappeared in the melee. Her spirit returned to console Aeneas and urged him to flee with their son.

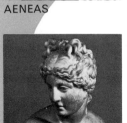

CREUSA

AENEAS

Aeneas: Son of Anchises and Venus, fled with his father and son from the flames of Troy where his wife died. After his journeys across the seas he landed in Latium, where he married the king's daughter Lavinia and founded the town of Lavinium.

Anchises: Found one night on Mount Ida by the goddess Venus and seduced by her. Jupiter was so angered by the boasting of Anchises that he threw a thunderbolt at him causing him to limp.

ANCHISES

VENUS

Venus: Goddess of love, born from sea foam. She instigated love affairs between the gods and mortals. Jupiter in retribution caused her to fall in love with Anchises, to whom she came adorned in flowers and accompanied by wild animals.

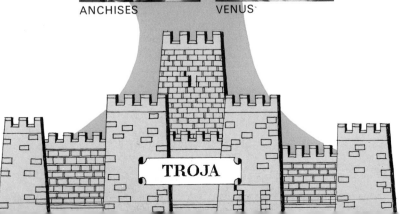

TROJA

THE ROMAN ODYSSEY

Virgil (70–19 B.C.), shown on a mosaic from Tunisia, holding a scroll of the *Aeneid*. He sits between the muses of Epic and Tragedy. By taking a collection of familiar myths and presenting them in an epic style so markedly influenced by Homer, Virgil sought to create a Latin odyssey to stand beside the great Greek epics.

The *Aeneid*, the last and probably the greatest poem written by Virgil, late in the first century B.C., presents the poet's personal version of the many traditional stories surrounding the travels and struggles of Aeneas as he journeyed from the burnt-out remains of Troy eventually to settle in the land of the Latins.

Virgil's story begins when Aeneas, sailing in the Mediterranean, is shipwrecked and driven ashore in North Africa by the mischievous gods. Here he meets Queen Dido who had recently fled from her hometown of Tyre, on the east coast of the Mediterranean, and had founded the city of Carthage. At a great feast prepared in his honor Aeneas tells his hostess of his adventures—his escape from Troy with Anchises his father and Ascanius his son, his attempts to settle in Thrace, and his visit to Delos where the oracle advised him to "seek their ancient mother." Believing this to

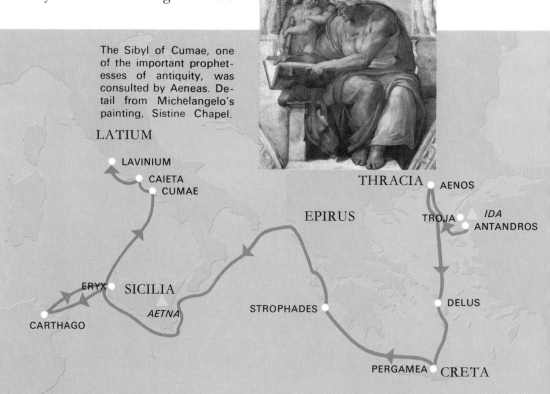

The Sibyl of Cumae, one of the important prophetesses of antiquity, was consulted by Aeneas. Detail from Michelangelo's painting, Sistine Chapel.

LATIUM

LAVINIUM
CAIETA
CUMAE

THRACIA   AENOS

EPIRUS   TROJA   *IDA*
ANTANDROS

ERYX   SICILIA

AETNA   STROPHADES   DELUS

CARTHAGO

PERGAMEA   CRETA

Right: Dido and Aeneas: "The sky connived at the union; the lightning flared; on the momentous peak nymphs raised their cry. On that day were sown the seeds of suffering and death." Fourth-century mosaic.

Left: "Pious Aeneas" carries his elderly father Anchises from the flames of Troy. Terra-cotta figure found at Veii: fifth century B.C.

Next Evander showed Aeneas
a thick wood which the forceful Romulus
was to adopt as his sanctuary
and, under a dank crag, the Wolf's Cave.
He conducted him to the Capitol,
which is now all gold,
but was once wild and ragged, covered
with woodland undergrowth.
Even in those old days the spot
held a sinister awe
of its own, which used to inspire
fear and alarm into the country folk.
Evander continued:
"The Arcadians believe that here
they have often seen
Jupiter himself shaking the dark aegis
to awake the clouds of storm.
And you can also see two hill-towers.
Father Janus founded the one,
and Saturn the other."

mean that he had to visit the homeland of the Trojans, he sailed to Crete, but here he was told in a dream that the oracle meant he was to settle in Italy whence one of his ancestors had come. The first part of the story, full of dramatic incident and excitement, reaches its climax when Aeneas and Dido fall in love. The gods object and Aeneas is forced to leave Africa; his last vision as he sails away is of the flames from Dido's funeral pyre. Her suicide—from grief at losing her lover—symbolizes the beginning of

After a brief return to Sicily where a colony was founded, Aeneas begins the last stage of his journey. He stops to visit the Sibyl at Cumae before finally landing on the shores of the Tiber.

Aeneas finds the land ruled by Latinus, whose daughter Lavinia was expected to marry Turnus, a young prince of a neighboring tribe. The oracle, however, had said she would marry a stranger and Latinus knows it must be Aeneas. In the inevitable conflict which ensues Turnus is killed and

Journey's end: Aeneas and his followers landing in Italy at the kingdom of Evander. Fresco by Pietro da Cortona (1596–1669), in the Palazzo Doria Pamfili, Rome. In legend, Evander, son of Hermes, arrived in Italy sixty years before the Trojan War, having traveled with his followers from Arcadia. He settled at the future site of Rome. When Aeneas arrived in Italy, Evander greeted him and provided troops for his battles against the Latins.

The tradition was known to Emperor Antoninus Pius, who honored Rome's legendary links with Arcadia by granting tax concessions to the town from which Evander was supposed to have come.

the unbridgeable rift between Carthage and Rome. "The Trojans knew how bitter are the agonies when intense love is outraged and the extremity to which a woman in distraction will go; and the knowledge started a train of thought somber with presentiment."

They approached Evander's home,
the house of a poor man,
and saw cattle herds lowing everywhere
about the sites
of the present-day Roman Forum.

Aeneid, from Book VIII

the Latins and Trojans are reconciled. Aeneas marries Lavinia as the oracle had predicted, and founds a town named after her. Finally, after the death of Latinus, Aeneas succeeds to the throne, and in accord with the wishes of the goddess Juno, the name of the Trojans passes from history.

THE SHE-WOLF

A symbol much loved and much copied in the Roman world:
Right: The earliest known statue of the she-wolf, Etruscan bronze from around 500 B.C. The twins were added much later, after 1471.
Below left: Shepherds discover Romulus and Remus with the she-wolf: stone altar relief, central Italy.
Below right: A provincial view, Avenches (Switzerland).

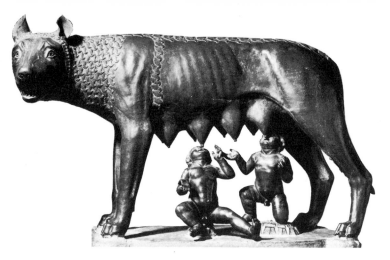

The foundation myth tells how after many generations of obscure rulers there emerged two brothers, Romulus and Remus, children of Rhea Silvia and the god Mars. The children, condemned to death by their great-uncle Amulius, were set afloat on the Tiber by kindhearted servants and were eventually washed ashore on the Palatine Hill near the cave of Lupercal where there grew a fig tree sacred to the goddess Rumina. Rumina was the tutelary goddess of rearing children, and it was no doubt under her guiding hand that a she-wolf appeared to suckle the infants. Eventually the boys were found by a shepherd who took them home and reared them as herdsmen. Some years later the young men found themselves in dispute with neighboring

herdsmen as a result of which their true identity was revealed.

Another story describes how the brothers decided to found a city by leading a colony from Alba Longa but failed to agree where the site should be. Romulus favored the Palatine Hill, Remus the Aventine. Accordingly the gods were consulted and at their advice each brother settled down on his favorite hill to watch the auspices. One

story has it that Remus saw a flight of six white vultures while Romulus saw twelve. Undecided as to how the sign should be interpreted, they quarreled and Remus was killed. According to another version, when Romulus saw twelve vultures he began to build his city wall but Remus mocked him by jumping over it—a profane act which was punished by death. Thus, in violence and fratricide, according to the legends, the city of Rome was born. The earliest official recognition of the story of the twins known to us was in 296 B.C. when two Roman officials set up statues of the twins and the she-wolf in the Comitium, a structure in the Roman Forum. Thereafter the symbolism of Rome's origin became widespread.

The legend is evidently very old. Although the constituent elements can no longer be untangled, the story of the she-wolf must reflect an ancient totemic wolf cult, of the kind one might expect to have developed among shepherding communities. Some historians believe that the story of the two brothers symbolizes a duality, either racial or political, in the early history of the city. Theories and explanations of this kind only deepen the fascination of the legend.

IN THE BEGINNING

Italy, lying between the North and the South, combines the advantages of each, and her preeminence is well founded and beyond dispute. She can repel the assaults of the northern barbarians, she can defeat the ploys of the southerners. A divine intelligence placed the city of the Roman people in an excellent and temperate country, so that she might acquire the right to rule over the whole world.

Vitruvius

Two views of Apollo, by two rival Mediterranean powers—the Etruscans and the Greeks. In their fight for supremacy in Italy, they both left their mark on the developing Roman civilization.

Above: *Detail of the famous statue of Apollo from Veii. This major piece is almost certainly the work of the Etruscan sculptor Vulca. It dates to about 500 B.C.*

Right: *Archaic bronze statue of Apollo from Piraeus, Greece, made about 525 B.C. Originally he held a bow in his left hand and a vessel for pouring libations in his right.*

Map: *Rome developed, between 800 and 600 B.C., in the power vacuum between Etruria (yellow) and Greece's colonies (brown). The Carthaginians (green) were already a major Mediterranean power.*

THE ROOTS
OF ROMAN CULTURE

Throughout the Late Bronze Age (1300–800 B.C.) the whole of the Italian peninsula shared a broadly similar culture linked, during the thirteenth and twelfth centuries, by trading contacts to the Myce-

naean world of the Aegean. It is possible that dim folk memories of the period of trade lay behind the myth of Aeneas and the Trojan origins of Rome.

Before about 600 B.C. Latium was of little significance: power lay with the Etruscan confederacy whose control spread south as far as Campania. It was in Campania that the Etruscans eventually came into contact and conflict with Greek colonists—a conflict which culminated in the Greek victories at Cumae in 524 and 474. Etruscan expansion was thus checked.

The peasant peoples of the seven hills learned much from their neighbors and benefited from the lively trade which passed through their territory. Eventually, within a few years of the first Etruscan defeat in the south, the growing city of Rome threw off its Etruscan kings and began to compete for power in central Italy.

...in the rich and fertile plain of Sele,
in this vast plain
rises as Venus from the shell
Paestum, shining with its magnificence and art.

Strabo

Poseidonia (Paestum), on the west coast of Italy, was probably founded from Sybaris in southern Italy to challenge the trading monopoly which the Euboean colonies of Cumae and Pithecussae held with the Etruscans.

The town is dominated by the remains of its three great Doric temples which stand now in grand isolation magnificently preserved.

The temple of the goddess Hera (below)— once thought to be dedicated to Neptune— was built in the fifth century B.C. by an architect who probably gained his inspiration from the Temple of Zeus at Olympia, which it closely resembles. It is a striking reminder both of the close cultural ties which were maintained between the colonies and Greece, and of the richness and vitality of the new towns of "Greater Greece," southern Italy.

GREEK COLONIZATION

CUMAE

POSEIDONIA

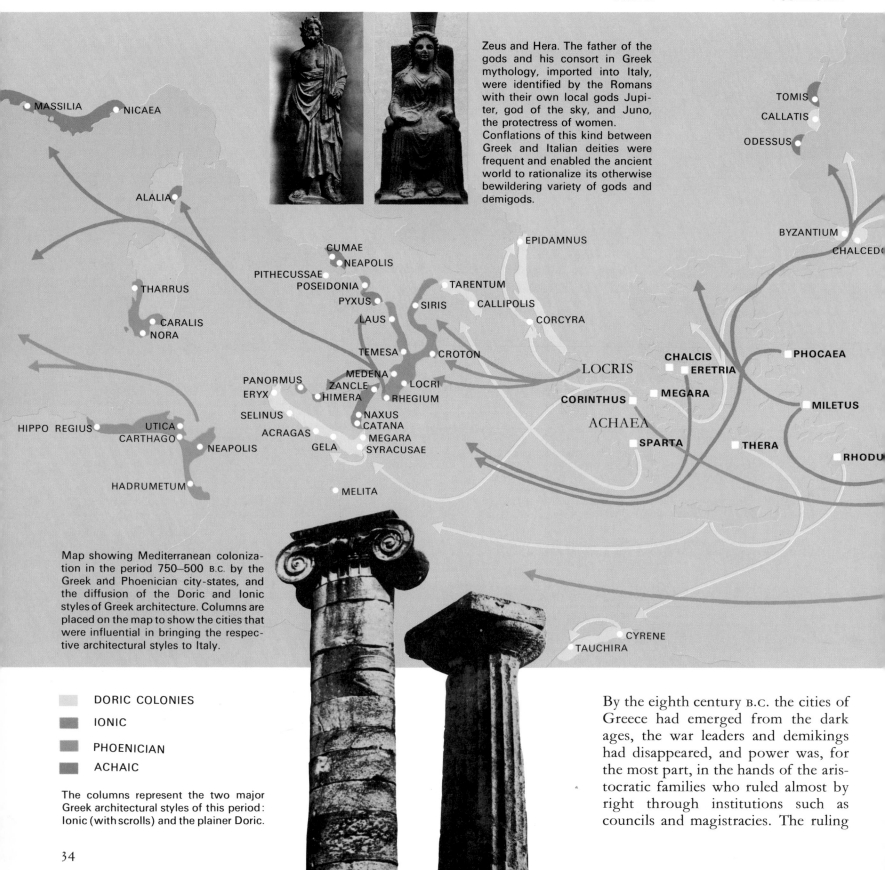

Zeus and Hera. The father of the gods and his consort in Greek mythology, imported into Italy, were identified by the Romans with their own local gods Jupiter, god of the sky, and Juno, the protectress of women. Conflations of this kind between Greek and Italian deities were frequent and enabled the ancient world to rationalize its otherwise bewildering variety of gods and demigods.

MASSILIA
NICAEA
ALALIA
THARRUS
CARALIS
NORA
HIPPO REGIUS
UTICA
CARTHAGO
NEAPOLIS
HADRUMETUM

CUMAE
NEAPOLIS
PITHECUSSAE
POSEIDONIA
PYXUS
LAUS
TEMESA
MEDENA
PANORMUS
ERYX
ZANCLE
HIMERA
SELINUS
ACRAGAS
GELA
NAXUS
CATANA
MEGARA
SYRACUSAE
MELITA

SIRIS
TARENTUM
CALLIPOLIS
CROTON
LOCRI
RHEGIUM

EPIDAMNUS
CORCYRA

LOCRIS
CHALCIS
ERETRIA
CORINTHUS
MEGARA
ACHAEA
SPARTA
THERA

PHOCAEA
MILETUS
RHODU

TOMIS
CALLATIS
ODESSUS

BYZANTIUM
CHALCEDO

CYRENE
TAUCHIRA

Map showing Mediterranean colonization in the period 750–500 B.C. by the Greek and Phoenician city-states, and the diffusion of the Doric and Ionic styles of Greek architecture. Columns are placed on the map to show the cities that were influential in bringing the respective architectural styles to Italy.

- DORIC COLONIES
- IONIC
- PHOENICIAN
- ACHAIC

The columns represent the two major Greek architectural styles of this period: Ionic (with scrolls) and the plainer Doric.

By the eighth century B.C. the cities of Greece had emerged from the dark ages, the war leaders and demikings had disappeared, and power was, for the most part, in the hands of the aristocratic families who ruled almost by right through institutions such as councils and magistracies. The ruling

There flourished in Italy
powerful, noteworthy Greek cities
which altogether
came to be called by the name
Magna Graecia: Greater Greece.

Cicero

TARENTUM   CROTON   SYRACUSAE

The Greek colonies of Italy issued their own coins, each with their own easily recognizable symbols. *Left to right:* The city of Cumae, showing the sea monster Scylla (ca. 430 B.C.); Poseidonia (Paestum), the god Poseidon with his trident (530–510 B.C.); Tarentum, with Taras sitting astride a dolphin (380–345 B.C.); Croton, showing Apollo shooting the python (400 B.C.); Syracuse, woman head with hair in sphendone (410-400 B.C.).

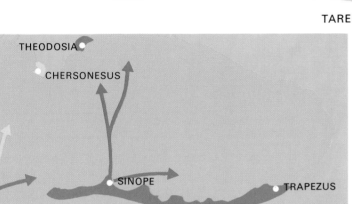

Part of the sculptured frieze from the Treasury of Siphnos at Delphi (ca. 525 B.C.) gives a vivid impression of armor and fighting methods towards the end of the period of colonization. The men, armed with short swords, fight in close formation protected by round shields and helmets of bronze.

The power of Carthage was based on its mercantile fleets. *Below left:* Ships depicted on the wall of the palace of Sennacherib (705–681 B.C.) at Nineveh. The historical scene records the flight from Tyre of Luli, the king of Tyre and Sidon, in 701. Ships of this kind would have been used in the Phoenician colonization of the west Mediterranean.

cities was shipped off to the barbarian world, to found new cities. These "colonies" were, however, truly independent since they were tied to their mother cities only by trading agreements and by those elements of the constitutional pattern which they chose to adopt. Soon successful colonies set up new colonies of their own. The movement began in the middle of the eighth century, and by the mid-sixth century Greek cities had sprung up all over the Mediterranean and extended as far east as the Black Sea. Although the new cities controlled enough land to be self-sufficient, the "colonization" movement was not an act of imperial aggression—there was no attempt to create an empire. Each city was essentially a self-contained trading post providing the mechanism by which products from the barbarian hinterland could be drawn into the civilized Mediterranean world. In exchange Greek products, principally fine pottery, metalwork, and wine, and, more important perhaps, the example of Greek culture were rapidly disseminated throughout the neighboring territories.

In Italy the earliest colonies were founded by the Euboeans in locations chosen to facilitate trade with the Etruscans. Cumae near Naples was established just before 750, and Pithekoussai on the isle of Ischia probably came into being at about the same time. Foundations in southern Italy and Sicily, designed to control and protect trade routes between the east and west Mediterranean, followed sometime after with the establishment of Syracuse in 733 and then Sybaris about 720. There was much inner colonization, and by the middle of the seventh century B.C. most of southern Italy had become an extension of the Greek world.

families dominated the political arena while at the same time controlling the best and most productive land. Inevitably, as the population increased so too did social strife.

For some while overseas colonization provided a vital safety valve. Surplus population from individual Greek

THE LAND
OF THE ETRUSCANS

The Etruscans were a civilized people who controlled much of central and nothern Italy in the period from the eighth until the fourth century B.C. From their homeland, in modern Tuscany, their influence spread south into Campania and north across the Apennines into the Po valley, until a number of factors—the territorial interests of Greek trading colonies from the south, the growing power of Rome, and the barbarians' inroads from the north—eventually combined to wipe them from the map.

Etruscan civilization had its roots in the rich and well-developed Bronze

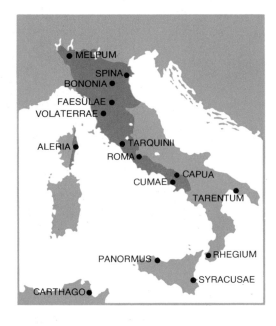

Age culture of northern Italy. Throughout this period, and in particular after the collapse of Mycenaean power in Greece in the twelfth century, close links were maintained with central Europe. From there it is possible that the knowledge of ironworking was acquired sometime in the ninth century. A high degree of cultural uniformity (known archaeologically as the Villanovan culture) existed at this

Left: Bronze was a favorite medium in Etruria, where ample copper and tin were available. This late example is a stylized votive figure of a warrior (26 cm high), fourth-third century.

Head of a youth, bronze, third century B.C., unknown provenance.

Right: Greek-style red-figured painted bowl showing Apollo riding a mule. From southern Etruria, fourth–third century.

Below: Tomb fresco of Trojan Prince Troilus, Tarquinia, late sixth century B.C.

The arch, an Etruscan invention, proved essential to Roman architecture and engineering. An outstanding Roman example is the Gateway of Jupiter (see head at top), from Falerii Novi, late fourth–early third century.

Right: Canopus (cinerary urn in human shape), a typical product of Clusium. Terra-cotta, sixth century B.C.

Right center: Detail from the terra-cotta sarcophagus of a wealthy husband and wife who are shown here reclining on a couch at their funerary banquet. From a sixth-century tomb at Cerveteri.

time across much of nothern Italy, but the communities of Etruria began to distinguish themselves by a marked increase in prosperity, based upon the exploitation of the important mineral wealth of the area accompanied by a growth in population. Large permanent settlements began to develop, frequently on hilltop locations, which were later to develop into regular Etruscan towns.

Sometime soon after the middle of the eighth century, Etruscan communities underwent an "orientalizing" phase as eastern ideas and styles were absorbed into their art and culture. Some writers prefer to see this as the result of new immigrants coming in from the east, but the majority now agree that the most likely cause was the opening up of the rapidly developing Etruscan towns to influences transmitted by Greek traders working from the Greek colonies of southern Italy. These influences, partly oriental, partly Greek, were avidly received and absorbed and, mixed together with indigenous barbarian styles, gave rise to the distinctive "Etruscan" culture.

The prosperous Etruscan towns soon attracted Greek immigrant craftsmen. The Roman writer Pliny records the story of one Demaratus, a nobleman driven out of his hometown of Corinth by political troubles, who decided to settle in the Etruscan town of Tarquinia. He took with him a painter and three clay-modelers who introduced the technique of clay statuary to the Etruscan audience. The story may well be true. There are a number of examples, attested archaeologically, of the setting up of similar workshops in a range of media including pottery and bronze casting. Increases in population and prosperity led inevitably to the emergence of a well-defined aristocracy who could afford to patronize the craftsmen producing luxury items such as fine metalwork for the table or sculpture and painting for their tombs. Styles of burial too showed change. From about 700 B.C. the old burial rite of cremation began to be replaced (at least in the more developed coastal cities) by inhumation and, for the rich, elaborate rock-cut tombs were constructed, sometimes adorned with paintings of high quality and usually fitted out with all the items the dead aristocrat would need in the afterlife.

Developed Etruscan culture was essentially city-based, but it is wrong to think of it as politically unified. Although each city had a degree of independence, all the major cities—traditionally there were twelve of them—were loosely bound together in a confederacy. Originally the cities were ruled by kings, but at the end of the sixth century Etruria, like its neighbors, suffered a constitutional crisis—kings were deposed, to be replaced by regularly elected magistrates. The political and social development of Etruria was closely similar to that of other communities in central Italy; what served to set the Etruscans apart was their prosperity and the brilliant flourishing of art and culture which it brought with it.

Vase with bull's head and equestrian figure, from Bologna, seventh century B.C., showing Oriental influence.

THE CAULDRON

LIGURES
GENUA

ETRUSCI
BONONIA
VOLATERRAE
RUSELLAE
CLUSIUM
VULC
TARQUINII
PANORMUS
CARTHAG.
SELINUS

The varied art and architecture found in Italy between the sixth and the third centuries illustrates the great diversity of its peoples. Primitive crafts were pursued in some areas while elsewhere there arose sophisticated models of Greek architecture.

Left: A sixth-century canopus from Clusium with a stylized suggestion of the human form.

The sixth and fifth centuries B.C. were a time of rapid social and political change in Italy. The two great powers, the Greeks and the Etruscans, lived in a state of uneasy equilibrium with each other—they were interdependent and yet rivals. Both maintained considerable fleets to keep the shipping lanes open for profitable trade. In the south the Greeks were dominant, but in the north an alliance between the Etruscans and the Carthaginians ensured effective control of the ocean between Etruria, western Sicily, and North Africa. Soon after 600 B.C. the Greeks began seriously to challenge Etruscan naval supremacy by opening up a passage west beyond Sardinia and Corsica. The turning point came in about 540 when, off the east coast of Corsica, the Greeks won a costly victory over the combined Etruscan and Carthaginian fleets. Further confrontations followed. On land an Etruscan attempt to gain control of the Greek colony of Cumae in 524 failed in spite of the vast force they assembled, and fifty years later, after a series of unprovoked piratical attacks against towns in Sicily and Lipari, the Etruscan fleet was destroyed off Cumae by Hiero of Syracuse.

The battle of Cumae, 474, marked the effective end of Etruscan sea power. Thereafter the Etruscans established new trading routes northward through the Apennines and into the Po valley.

While this struggle for power between the Greeks and the Etruscans was taking place, other tribes of the Italian peninsula were beginning to emerge from their archaeological obscurity. In the north, in spite of Etruscan expansion, the Veneti maintained control of the Po River delta. They belonged, culturally, to a group of closely linked tribes who by this time

Four bronze statuettes from Broglio in Etruria. The style is purely native, showing little Greek influence. Sixth century B.C.

The Siculian necropolis of Pantalica, Sicily, built before 800 B.C.

Among the earliest Roman money to be issued is this coin of 250 B.C.

In small-scale products such as this bronze farmer figure, the Etruscan craftsmen followed popular local traditions.

Carved stone loom weight, Calabria, eighth century B.C.

Left: The Greek theater at Syracuse (begun 475 B.C.; expanded about 335), where Aeschylus probably watched his own plays.

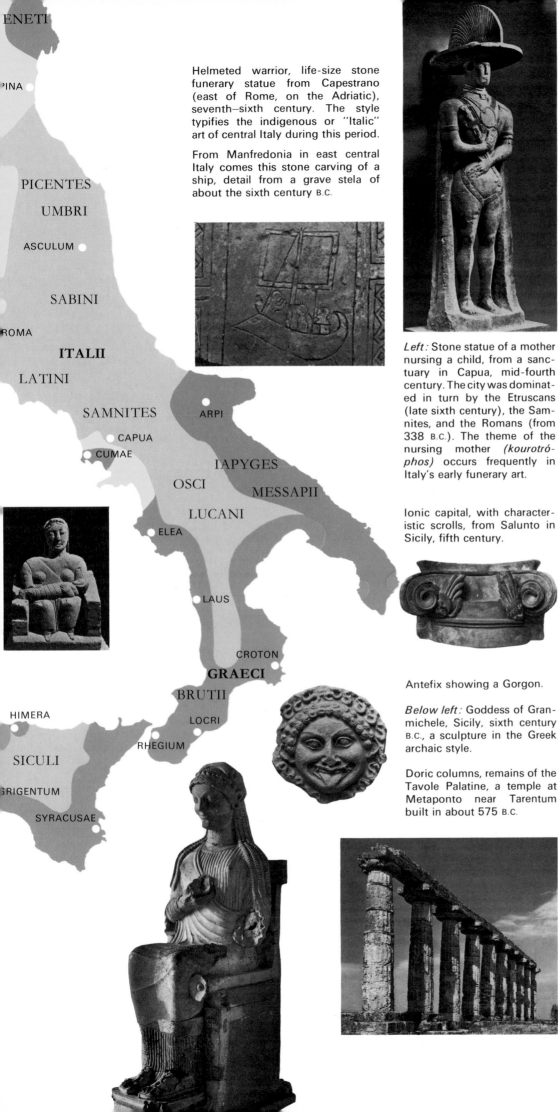

Helmeted warrior, life-size stone funerary statue from Capestrano (east of Rome, on the Adriatic), seventh–sixth century. The style typifies the indigenous or "Italic" art of central Italy during this period.

From Manfredonia in east central Italy comes this stone carving of a ship, detail from a grave stela of about the sixth century B.C.

Left: Stone statue of a mother nursing a child, from a sanctuary in Capua, mid-fourth century. The city was dominated in turn by the Etruscans (late sixth century), the Samnites, and the Romans (from 338 B.C.). The theme of the nursing mother *(kourotró-phos)* occurs frequently in Italy's early funerary art.

Ionic capital, with characteristic scrolls, from Salunto in Sicily, fifth century.

Antefix showing a Gorgon.

Below left: Goddess of Granmichele, Sicily, sixth century B.C., a sculpture in the Greek archaic style.

Doric columns, remains of the Tavole Palatine, a temple at Metaponto near Tarentum built in about 575 B.C.

had grown rich from exploiting the trade routes along the eastern fringes of the Alps. On the other side of the peninsula, around the Gulf of Genoa, were the Ligurians, living for the most part in strongly defended hilltop forts in the Maritime Alps.

Further south, along the spine of Italy, were groups of hill farmers, culturally backward by comparison with the Greeks and Etruscans, and sometimes fierce in their attempts to acquire the wealth of their civilized neighbors. The Umbrians occupied a territory east of the Tiber, the Sabines came next, with Samnites further to the south and the Osci beyond. The essentially pastoral nature of their economy and the rugged territory in which they lived created a restlessness which often erupted as bands of warriors poured down from the hills.

At the southern tip of the peninsula the different tribes seem to have been in a state of almost constant migration. The Lucani were spreading southward and coming into contact with the Greek towns of the coast, while tradition has it that the Siculi of Sicily had migrated from the toe of Italy forcing the indigenous Sicani into the extreme western tip of the island.

It was against this background of movement, change, and conflict that Rome emerged. The Latini, in whose territory the city lay, were an indigenous people whose ancestry can be traced back in the archaeological record to the Bronze Age. A simple farming people, they lived in modest timber huts arranged in villages and buried the cremated remains of their dead in urns modeled like their houses. There was little to set them apart from their neighbors; yet within a few centuries these people were to lead the world.

THE SEVEN HILLS

The site of Rome lay near the mouth of the River Tiber where its wide marshes narrowed and firm banks allowed an easy crossing to be made. It is hardly surprising, therefore, that the hills which were to become the city were occupied far back into the distant past by communities able to control

the movement of people and goods which inevitably converged on this point.

The abrupt landscape must have had many attractions for the early settlers. The marshy valleys and steep hills provided natural protection, while on the wooded slopes flocks and herds could browse in peace. Archaeological evidence recovered from deep below the levels of the later city suggests that the earliest villages had begun to develop sometime before 800 B.C. on the Palatine, Quirinal, Viminal, and Esquiline hills, while the cemeteries of these communities occupied the valley slopes below. These early villages, divided from each other by deep ravines and marshy valleys, tended to develop in isolation, producing their own individual styles of ornaments and having distinctive burial fashions.

Below: Model of part of the Early Iron Age settlement on the Palatine Hill. Excavations on the hill have exposed the foundations of early houses cut into the bedrock. Using these as evidence of the ground plan, and the funerary hut-urns to give some idea of the superstructures of the buildings, an accurate picture of the early village can be built up. The Palatine settlements, which began sometime before 800 B.C., are among the earliest on the seven hills. This hill became the center of Republican Rome, the site of important palaces and temples.

Right: The seven hills of Rome and the Tiber River, around 1000–800 B.C. The hills were at most about 50 meters high (55 yards), but with steep slopes that rose abruptly above the flat marshland. Several small streams flowed between the hills. At the western foot of the Palatine Hill was the Lupercal Spring, where the wolf is said to have nursed Romulus and Remus.

Latin tribes from the south and Sabines from the north settled in the eighth century B.C. in small circular villages on the hilltops. Traces of their burial grounds have been found in the valleys.

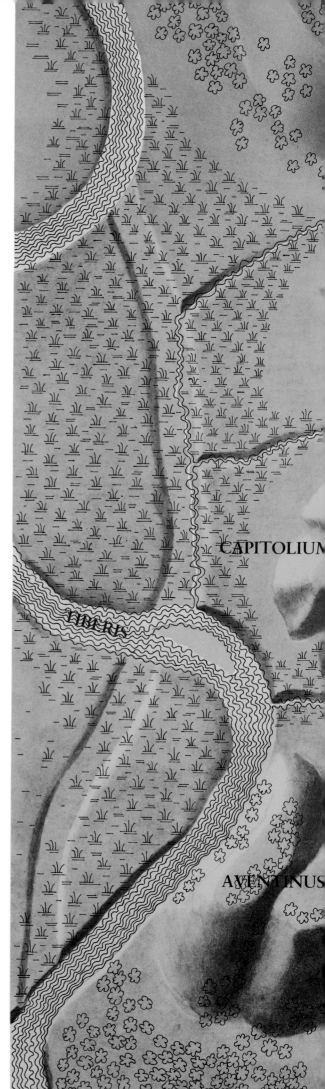

CAPITOLIUM

TIBERIS

AVENTINUS

QUIRINALIS

VIMINALIS

ESQUILINUS

PALATIUM

CAELIUS

Gradually as the population increased, after about 700 B.C., settlements began to spread down the hillsides, sometimes extending over older cemeteries, and by about 625 B.C. huts were being constructed in the valley between the Capitol and Palatine—the area destined to become the Roman Forum.

The separate communities did not remain isolated. The first stage in their coming together was, in all probability, represented by the ancient festival of *Septimontium*, held every year on 11 December, when each of the communities offered sacrifices in honor of the hill on which they lived. The fact that the same day was chosen suggests that now, for the first time, the separate villages were beginning to feel a degree of unity.

Traditionally two of the hills of Rome, the Quirinal and the Capitol, were said to have been colonized by the Sabines while the rest were occupied by the Latini. Such a distinction cannot be recognized in the archaeological evidence. Some archaeologists, however, believe that it was on the Esquiline, where cemeteries of inhumed warriors have been found, that the Sabines lived. Whatever the answer, tradition and archaeology combine to demonstrate a cultural, and no doubt political, variety among the earliest settlers of the seven hills.

Overleaf: Legendary rape, or abduction, of the Sabine women by followers of Romulus, one of the dramatic events of his reign. The story symbolizes the centuries of close but stormy relations between the Romans and their Sabine neighbors, who were finally conquered in 290 B.C. and granted full Roman citizenship in 268. Oil painting (ca. 1635) by Nicolas Poussin, Metropolitan Museum, New York. The theme has also inspired famous paintings by Carracci, da Cortona, Rubens, and David as well a statue by Giambologna.

THE SEVEN KINGS

The period of monarchical rule, which traditionally lasted for 244 years (753–509 B.C.), is known only through myths and legends, which were brought together in a single narrative by the historian Livy who compiled his great history of Rome during the reign of Augustus. For Livy the kings played a vital part in the growth of the state. The people were at this time "a rabble of vagrants, mostly runaways and refugees [who], unrestrained by the power of the throne, would no doubt have set sail on the stormy sea of democratic politics." He saw the kings, then, as providing the necessary constraints while the disparate mass of citizens groped its way towards political maturity. It was the story of this development he attempted to tell when he wrote of the seven kings.

According to the Roman legends the city of Rome was founded by Romulus on 21 April 753 B.C. It was he, so the story goes, who instituted the festival of *Septimontium* that united the separate villages. Fugitives were offered asylum in Rome during his reign and were settled on the eastern slopes of the Capitol. There was, however, a shortage of wives for the new settlers. The problem was overcome by inviting the

army, the calendar, and the College of Augurs. Most legends see him as a great benefactor, but one version shows him as a tyrant who had to be killed by the Senate. Traditionally, however, he disappeared from the world in a thick cloud, during a thunderstorm, and became a god. Soon after his death Romulus is supposed to have appeared to one of his followers. Livy records his words:

"Go," he said, "and tell the Romans that by heaven's will my Rome shall be capital of the world. Let them learn to be soldiers. Let them know, and teach their children, that no power on earth can stand against Roman arms." Having spoken these words, he was taken up again into the sky.

Livy, *History* I, 16

Left: *The rivalry: fourteenth-century manuscript painting of Romulus (at right) and Remus counting the vultures—an omen to decide who should rule.*

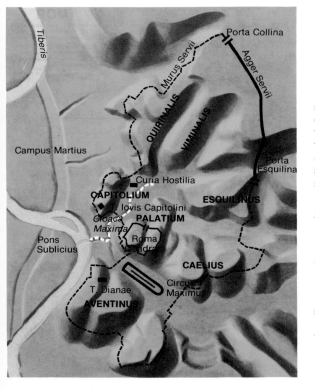

Rome under the monarchy. The map shows the extent of the city by 509 B.C., traditional date for the fall of the last king, and includes major structures: the great sewer (Cloaca Maxima), the first bridge over the Tiber, Temple of Jupiter Capitoline, Temple of Diana, the Comitium and Curia Hostilia (government buildings), and the original Circus Maximus, the stadium that was just a narrow valley between two hill slopes.

neighboring tribes, including the Sabines, to a festival and detaining their young women. In retaliation people from Caenina, Antemnae, and Crustumium attacked but were conquered and subjected to Roman rule. And the Sabines, who had taken over the Capitol, were eventually persuaded to unite with Rome, their king Titus Tatius ruling jointly with Romulus. Further territorial expansion occurred when the right (or west) bank of the Tiber was secured in the face of opposition from the Etruscan towns of Veii and Fidenae. Eventually the city grew to include the Capitol and Aventine hills, which were both fortified.
Romulus is credited with the creation of many Roman institutions including the Senate, the

Romulus kills Remus, provoked by his taunts; engraving by S.D. Mirys. In the background, the fortifications of the Aventine Hill which Romulus had just built: here, according to tradition, the city of Rome was founded.

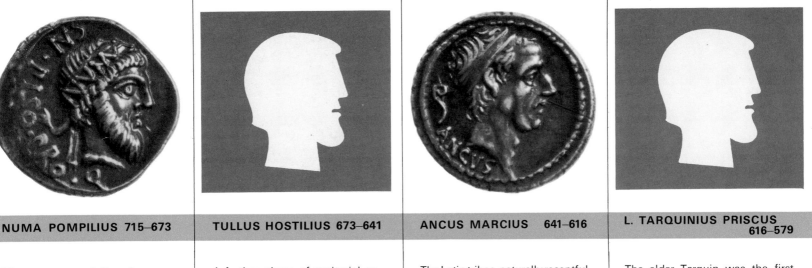

NUMA POMPILIUS 715–673

The successor of Romulus was said to have been a Sabine from the town of Cures. His reign was peaceful and was not one of territorial expansion, but he is believed to have initiated the procedure of dividing newly conquered lands among the citizens. Numerous religious ceremonies are attributed to him as well as an improved method of calculating the seasons.

Once Rome's neighbors had considered her not so much as a city as an armed camp in their midst threatening the general peace; now they came to revere her so profoundly as a community dedicated wholly to worship, that the mere thought of offering her violence seemed to them like sacrilege.

History I, 21

The peace-loving and pious Numa Pompilius, according to legend, received religious and legal enlightenment from his mistress, the water nymph Egeria. This detail

of a nineteenth-century engraving shows Egeria handing the king a scroll of laws as she points towards Rome.

TULLUS HOSTILIUS 673–641

A further phase of territorial expansion took place under Tullus Hostilius. He attacked and conquered Alba Longa—the mother city of Rome—forceably removing the population and settling them on the Caelian Hill—an act which doubled the population of the city. Since the conquest of Alba Longa now placed the sacred Mount Alban under Roman control (it was here that the League of Latin Cities held its meetings), Rome was now in a strong position not only to claim admission to the league but also to seek to dominate it.

Hostilius is also recorded to have fought against the Sabines, ostensibly to protect the interests of Roman traders who were taking part in a fair at the shrine of Feronia.

In his view, Rome had been allowed to lapse into senility, and his one object was to find cause for renewed military adventure.

History I, 23

Rome conquers Alba Longa: three warriors were chosen to represent each side in a partial combat while their armies watched. The last Roman survivor is shown killing the last of the three Albans, in this Renaissance fresco.

ANCUS MARCIUS 641–616

The Latin tribes, naturally resentful at the conquest of Alba Longa, invaded Rome, but Ancus Marcius, who was believed to be a peace-loving king, beat off the attack and followed up his success by conquering a number of Latin towns whose inhabitants were transferred to Rome. To accommodate them the city was increased in size and was further defended. The Fossa Quiritium, a defensive ditch enclosing the Aventine, is attributed to him.

An extension of trade is indicated at this time by two further acts: the construction of a bridge, the Pons Sublicius, across the Tiber and the foundation of the harbor town of Ostia at the Tiber mouth.

The Tiber, according to Livy, was first spanned by bridge during the reign of Ancus. This bronze medallion from the Republican period depicts the Pons Sublicius, the wooden pile bridge he built.

His fame as both soldier and administrator was unsurpassed by any previous occupant of the throne.

History I, 35

Numa had established religious observances in time of peace; Ancus provided war with an equivalent solemn ceremonial of its own.

History I, 32

L. TARQUINIUS PRISCUS 616–579

The elder Tarquin was the first of the Etruscan kings of Rome, but there is no suggestion in the legends of an Etruscan conquest. Tarquin, it was said, entered the city in an oxcart. How he is supposed to have become king is obscure.

He was a powerful leader and under his rule the city prospered. He expanded the city's territory by fighting against the Sabines and by gradually reducing most of the Latin towns to submission. To mark Roman supremacy he began work on a great temple to Jupiter, sited on the Capitol, where all who were ruled by Rome could worship. Other building works included the laying out of the Circus Maximus in the valley between the Palatine and Aventine and the construction of the great system of sewers *(cloacae)* to drain the valleys. The Cloaca Maxima, which still survives, is traditionally believed to date from the time of Tarquinius.

In most ways he was a man of outstanding character and ability; nevertheless...he was something of a schemer.

History I, 35

Coin showing the Temple of Jupiter Capitoline, allegedly begun by the first Tarquin and completed by his son before 509 B.C.

45

SERVIUS TULLIUS 579–534　　L. TARQUINIUS SUPERBUS 534–509

To the second of the Etruscan kings is ascribed the completion of some part of the great program of rebuilding instituted by the elder Tarquin. His principal construction was said to be the so-called Servian Wall, a massive construction five miles long encircling the city and enclosing not only the Capitol, Palatine, Aventine, and the Forum valley but also the spurs of the more northerly hills. On the Aventine he built the temple to Diana with the assistance of the Latin cities —a political move designed no doubt to encourage unity.

Servius is also credited with a thorough constitutional reform which turned Rome into a military state.

The last king of Rome, Tarquin the Proud, gained for himself the reputation of being a ruthless, domineering tyrant. Like his predecessor he was an enthusiastic builder. He enlarged the drainage system and completed the great temple to Jupiter on the Capitol which had been begun by his father. His oppressive treatment of the Latin cities was, however, strongly resented, and even in Rome he found it necessary to maintain his position with an armed bodyguard.

The unpopularity of the ruling family came to a head when Sextus, son of Tarquin, brutally raped a girl called Lucretia. In the uproar which followed two nobles, Brutus and Valerius, led

quin and even managed to capture the Janiculum, a hill on the west of the Tiber. The Tiber bridge was stormed, but Horatius Cocles's heroic defense saved Rome. In this way monarchic rule ceased and the Republic was born.

However lawless and tyrannical Tarquin may have been as monarch in his own country, as a war leader he did fine work. Indeed, his fame as a soldier might have equaled that of his predecessors, had not his degeneracy in other things obscured its luster.

History I, 52

Tarquin the Proud (Superbus) came to power by murdering his father-in-law Servius Tullius. Above: The death of Servius.

The goddess Diana (Artemis in Greek mythology), from a Roman fresco. Servius Tullius dedicated a temple to Diana on the Aventine, copied from the cult of Artemis in Ephesus. Greek historians refer to inscriptions confirming its existence.

a citizen force and drove the family from the city. Tarquin returned with support from Veii and other Etruscan towns but was repelled. Finally Lars Porsenna, prince of the Etruscan city of Clusium, led a massive army against Rome in support of Tar-

Above: Tarquin's wife Tullia, who instigated her father's murder, rides her chariot across Tullius's corpse. Tarquin's violent reign culminated in the rape of Lucretia, which finally cost him his throne and ended Rome's monarchy.

Far right: Present-day view from the ramparts of the Palatine Hill northwest towards St. Peter's Basilica. The Palatine, which reaches a height of some fifty-one meters, contains the earliest Roman monuments and the oldest archaeological traces (see page 40).

THE MEANING
OF THE SEVEN KINGS

The stories of the seven kings derive, for the most part, from the works of the first-century historian Livy. Livy was governed by the desire to provide Rome with a distinguished past. His raw material consisted largely of folktales, often associated with well-established institutions or topographical and architectural features about the city, and a knowledge of Greek history which provided him with a structure and showed him what was proper. How then can we interpret the "history" of the monarchy? Few people would now accept it as accurate fact but,

Mosaic from Trier, Germany, A.D. 200, of a writer. Early Roman historians such as Livy (59 B.C.–A.D. 17) incorporated legend as well as fact into their chronicles.

equally, few would regard it as entirely spurious.

That there was a period of monarchic rule which ended some time about 500–450 B.C. is generally accepted; so too is the belief in an Etruscan domination of the city, which archaeological evidence would suggest began about 600 B.C. or a little after when the first floors of the Forum were laid following the construction of a drainage system. This is in reasonable accord with the traditional date of Tarquin's reign (616–578), which, in legend, represented the beginnings of Etruscan rule.

Of the pre-Etruscan period there is little "history" to be written. The archaeological evidence, as we have

Legends such as the story of the seven kings, or "Horatio at the bridge" *(left)*, reflect the historical fact of Etruscan encroachment on Rome in the late seventh and sixth centuries. In this engraving by S.D. Mirys, Horatio Cocles single-handedly holds off the Etruscan soldiers from Clusium so that the Romans can destroy the bridge over the Tiber and prevent an invasion.

RUSELLAE

TELAMON

VICUS COSANUS

seen, shows that some of the hills of Rome were occupied as early as the ninth century (or even the tenth in some estimates) and that from about 850 until 600 B.C. the communities increased in size and coalesced. The disparate cultural elements that can be recognized gradually merged. A dim memory of such a fusion may perhaps be seen in the story which describes the period of joint rule between Romulus and the Sabine king.

Right: Funerary sandstone bust of a woman, in native style, from sixth-century Clusium. The city was believed to have sheltered Tarquinius when the Romans drove him out and founded the Republic.

Below left: Plan showing the location of the Pons Sublicius, first bridge to span the Tiber, sixth century B.C.

Below: Archaeological traces of the period of the kings can still be found in Rome, such as this archaic stone cistern on the Palatine, from the sixth century B.C.

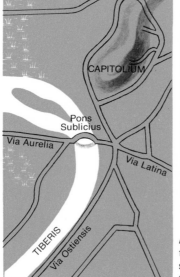

CAPITOLIUM

Pons Sublicius

Via Aurelia

Via Latina

TIBERIS

Via Ostiensis

Etruscan Rome: foundation of the Temple of Jupiter Capitoline, late sixth century, allegedly built by the two Tarquin kings.

Below: Two major Etruscan contributions—the arch and the system of drainage—combine in this segment of the Cloaca Maxima, the great sewer, which survives today.

Above: Tarquinia, strongest of Rome's Etruscan neighbors. View of the necropolis of Castel d'Asso, just outside the city, showing hillside tombs with sculptured façades. Third century B.C.

The four early kings probably represent a mixture of myth, folktales of real heroes, and historical inventiveness designed to provide the great families of Rome with respectable ancestors. There is an orderly arrangement about them that is suspect. Romulus, the warrior, is neatly balanced by Numa, a man of peace, and the attributes of both are duplicated in the next pair of kings, Tullus Hostilius and Ancus Marcius. Ancus was probably inserted into the list to

Opposite, left to right:

Fresco, detail from the Tomb of the Leopards, Tarquinia, Monterozzi necropolis, showing a male dancer bearing a sacrificial bowl.

Mosaic of the port of Ostia, with view of its lighthouse. The port was connected by road with Clusium and Perugia north of Rome.

A late fifth-century head of a youth, called Head of Malavolta, from Veii, an Etruscan town just thirteen miles from Rome.

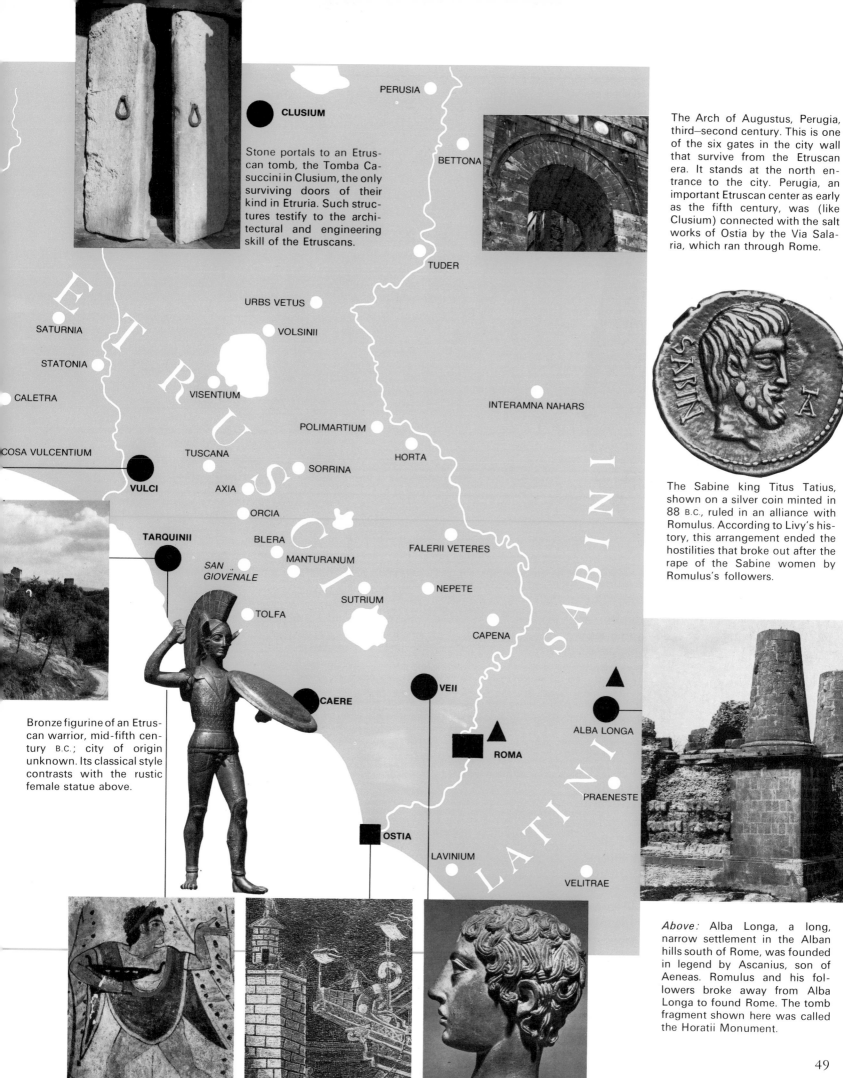

Stone portals to an Etruscan tomb, the Tomba Casuccini in Clusium, the only surviving doors of their kind in Etruria. Such structures testify to the architectural and engineering skill of the Etruscans.

The Arch of Augustus, Perugia, third–second century. This is one of the six gates in the city wall that survive from the Etruscan era. It stands at the north entrance to the city. Perugia, an important Etruscan center as early as the fifth century, was (like Clusium) connected with the salt works of Ostia by the Via Salaria, which ran through Rome.

The Sabine king Titus Tatius, shown on a silver coin minted in 88 B.C., ruled in an alliance with Romulus. According to Livy's history, this arrangement ended the hostilities that broke out after the rape of the Sabine women by Romulus's followers.

Bronze figurine of an Etruscan warrior, mid-fifth century B.C.; city of origin unknown. Its classical style contrasts with the rustic female statue above.

Above: Alba Longa, a long, narrow settlement in the Alban hills south of Rome, was founded in legend by Ascanius, son of Aeneas. Romulus and his followers broke away from Alba Longa to found Rome. The tomb fragment shown here was called the Horatii Monument.

PERUSIA

CLUSIUM

BETTONA

TUDER

URBS VETUS

SATURNIA

VOLSINII

STATONIA

CALETRA

VISENTIUM

INTERAMNA NAHARS

POLIMARTIUM

COSA VULCENTIUM

TUSCANA

SORRINA

HORTA

VULCI

AXIA

ORCIA

TARQUINII

BLERA

FALERII VETERES

SAN GIOVENALE

MANTURANUM

NEPETE

SUTRIUM

TOLFA

CAPENA

VEII

CAERE

ALBA LONGA

ROMA

PRAENESTE

OSTIA

LAVINIUM

VELITRAE

ETRUSCI

SABINI

LATINI

49

provide roots for the prominent Republican family the Marcii, but Hostilius is more likely to be a genuine folk hero, not least since the name of the first Senate house was Curia Hostilia. The early kings then provide a fascinating concoction which, while it reflects many aspects of early Roman society, defies satisfactory analysis.

With the advent of the Etruscan dynasty we are on firmer ground. Archaeological and literary evidence combines to show that the sixth century was a time of rapid expansion for the Etruscans. The extension of their power southward into Campania is well attested. It is hardly surprising therefore that Rome—a major crossing place on the Tiber—should come under their domination. Significantly two of the improvements ascribed to the Etruscan kings—the Tiber bridge and the port of Ostia—were necessary conditions for increased commerce. It was during this period that Rome became a city. The drainage schemes,

defensive circuits, and temple building, together with the constitutional reforms attributed to this period, reflect all the major aspects of urban growth. From the Etruscans Rome learned the principles of architecture—the vaulting of the sewers and the trabeated construction of the temples—while the defensive line chosen at this time to defend the northern approaches was to remain the boundary of this part of the city for several centuries. It was also from the Etruscans that the communal and military organization of Rome derived. In short, the century of Etruscan domination converted a straggling rustic agglomeration into a powerful city, and a loosely organized confederation of communities into a tightly structured military state.

The legendary personification of the Etruscans' rule—the three kings—is not easy to interpret. The Tarquins, however, probably represent the period when the town of Tarquinia controlled Rome, the two kings of this name probably symbolizing the good and bad elements of the period. The story of Servius Tullius, inserted between the divided Tarquins, presents the king very much as the counterpart of a Greek reformer transferring power from the aristocracy to the rising middle class. One opinion has it that he was invented by later Roman historians to provide an acceptable precedent for the domestic reforms demanded by the plebs in the fourth century—but the emperor Claudius, who claimed to have had access to Etruscan sources, equated Servius with Mastarna, a military leader from the Etruscan city of Vulci, who traditionally was in conflict with the Tarquins. One interpretation of this tradition would be to see Servius/Mastarna as a real person who was responsible for establishing the control of Vulci over Rome in place of Tarquinia's rule. Mastarna, whose name means "the general," would have been an appropriate person to reorganize the military structure of Rome.

If, then, Rome came under the sway first of Tarquinia and later of Vulci, we can speculate about whether any other Etruscan town attempted, or managed, to secure the city. In this context the story of Lars Porsenna, prince of Clusium, is interesting. Perhaps the legendary account of his attack on the city (during the reign of the seventh king) represents an attempt by Clusium to gain control. Whether or not he succeeded will have been suppressed by Livy's patriotic approach to history. At any event, Etruscan influence in Rome continued well into the early years of the Republic, as the Etruscan names of many of the early consuls bear witness. The influence of Etruscan culture was far more important in the formative history of Rome than the Roman historians lead us to believe.

PATRICIANS AND PLEBEIANS

Now we trace the history in peace and war of a free nation, governed by annually elected officers of state, and subject not to the caprice of individual men, but to the overriding authority of law.... Brutus, the founder, made the people swear never to allow any man to be king in Rome. He promoted national unity and lessened the friction between the patricians and the plebs.

Livy

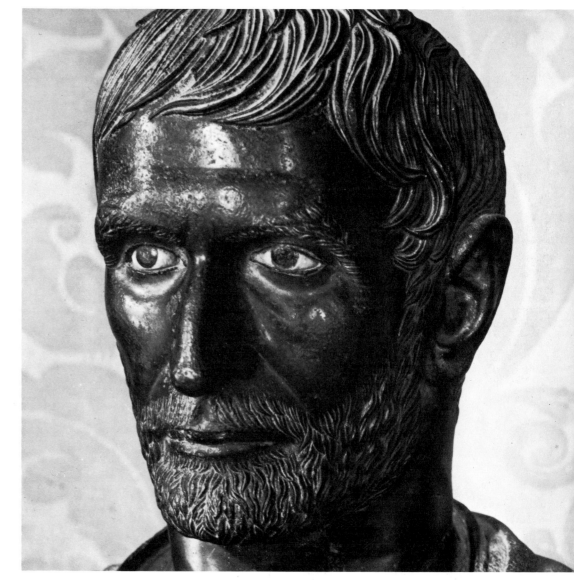

Above: *The patrician ideal. Bronze bust, believed to be of the legendary consul and nobleman Lucius Junius Brutus, who helped found the Republic by ousting the last king of Rome in 509 B.C. Etruscan-Roman workmanship; fourth-third century (possibly a later copy).*

Opposite: *The plebeian force. The new army created by Marius around 100 B.C. drew the unruly populace into a mercenary force that was to change very little over the centuries. This stone relief of a Roman legionary is from Trajan's column; early second century A.D.*

THE REPUBLIC: CHRONOLOGY OF MAJOR EVENTS

509	The traditional date of the foundation of the Republic.
494	The creation of the office of tribune to protect the plebs.
493	Rome joins the Latin League.
480–396	Wars against neighbors—the Volscian War, attacks on Veii and Aequi.
449	Roman law is codified in the Twelve Tables.
390	The Celtic invation of Italy reaches Rome, which is sacked.
343–290	Wars against the Samnites. Rome now dominates central Italy.
275	Rome is now undisputed leader of southern Italy following war with Pyrrhus (282–275).
264–241	The First Punic War against the Carthaginians. Rome becomes a maritime power.
237–219	The Carthaginians conquer Spain and found New Carthage.
218–202	The Second Punic War, during which Hannibal crosses the Alps. Rome triumphant.
200–146	Wars against the Macedonians and in the east, and the destruction of Corinth.
149–146	The Third Punic War and the destruction of Carthage.
133–122	The Gracchus brothers carry out land reforms. Numantia capitulates, and the kingdom of Pergamum is bequeathed to Rome (both in 133).
112–98	The rise of Marius: army reforms.
91–79	The rise of Sulla: his dictatorship.
60	The First Triumvirate: Pompey, Caesar, and Crassus.
58–51	Caesar conquers Gaul.
49–30	The Civil Wars; the Second Triumvirate: Octavian, Antony, and Lepidus.
27	Octavian becomes emperor, assuming the title of Augustus.

ROME AS A REPUBLIC

For nearly five hundred years Rome, with its ever expanding territorial commitment and its rapidly increasing population, was governed as a republic. Inevitably, throughout so long a period there were changes, but the Romans were a conservative people: truly sweeping reforms were avoided whenever possible and change when it had to come was by the careful and controlled modification of the existing system.

In pre-Republican days leadership was in the hands of a "king" who was nominated by the heads of the leading households *(patres)*. He held supreme power *(imperium)* and with it was responsible for ordering the affairs of the state: he oversaw religious worship, led the city in war, dispensed justice, and appointed officials to help him in his duties. At his side was the Senate, a council of heads of leading families appointed for life. Their function was to nominate new kings, who were appointed by the whole assembly of the people, and to advise them when requested. Such a system, elegant in its simplicity, formed the basis of Republican government.

The first significant change to take place was the abolition of kingship and its replacement with two annually elected magistrates called consuls. The consuls were colleagues, and since they could veto each other's actions, decisions had to be taken in concert. Clearly such a system, which henceforth runs throughout Roman history, was designed to counter the abuse of power in the leadership. In practice it effectively increased the influence of the Senate.

So long as the community remained small the senatorial system, whereby the real power of the state was vested in the principal families, could work without discord, but with an increase in population, particularly among the small traders and the urban poor who sold their labor, tensions began to develop. These so-called "plebs," as citizens, were all members of the Assembly, but even so they were exposed to abuse all the time that power was retained by the "patricians."

In the struggle which followed, the plebs began to hold unofficial councils of their own. Negotiations with the patricians were at first abortive, but

Senate

In the early years of the Republic the Senate was a council composed of the heads of the leading Roman households. Once elected they held office for life. Throughout the fifth and fourth centuries their power was eroded as more complex forms of government were instituted. Later the clanlike aristocratic nature of the body became diluted when plebeians gained the right to enter its ranks after having held various magistracies. During the wars of the third century the Senate, virtually alone, ran the country with a high degree of efficiency, but by the second and first centuries its power was eclipsed and the body became a pawn in the power struggle which eventually led to the collapse of the Republic.

Tribunes

This category, which stood outside the regular government system, included various types of officers and magistrates. *Military tribunes* were superior officers appointed by consuls. *Consular tribunes* served at times in place of consuls. *Tribunes of the people* were named by the plebs to defend their rights, beginning in the early fifth century. They increased from two to four to ten officials. These tribunes protected the plebs from arbitrary arrest, suits, bondage and could veto measures taken by the Senate or consuls, except in wartime.

Praetors

The name praetor was first used to describe the office which later came to be called the consul. In 366 B.C. a new post was created—that of *praetor urbanus*—the magistrate who held it being responsible for the administration of justice in Rome: in addition he could hold a military command and could initiate legislation. In the mid-third century a second praetor *(praetor peregrinus)* was appointed to deal with lawsuits involving foreigners, and as Rome's overseas possessions multiplied, the number further increased to four in 227 (to look after Sicily and Sardinia) and six in 197 B.C. (to administer Spain). By the second century the *praetor urbanus* and *praetor peregrinus* were restricted to a judicial role but could proceed to provincial governorships after the magistracy was over.

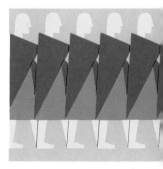

Consuls

The two annually elected chief magistrates,

appointed by the people and ratified by the Senate. Each had the power to veto the other's acts.

Dictators

In times of crisis sole power could be invested

in one man who would be given a fixed term of office and was appointed for a specific purpose.

Censors

The office of censor was instituted in the mid-fourth century B.C., the two censors taking over from the consuls the task

of compiling lists of citizens. They wielded considerable power since they were responsible for taking judicial proceedings against any individual suspected of giving false information about his status or property. They could remove from the roll of *equites* anyone held to be unsuitable or acting illegally. They could also deprive a senator of his rank if he could be shown to have acted against the public morality. The power of the censors was, however, drastically reduced by Sulla (83–80 B.C.) and thereafter declined rapidly.

Aediles

Originally the aediles were two officers elected from among the plebs to assist the tribunes, but when, in 367 B.C., two additional *aediles curales* were appointed from the patricians, the office became a magistracy of the entire body politic open to either order. The functions of the aediles were wide: they were responsible for maintaining the streets of the city and regulating traffic; for overseeing religious affairs; for the upkeep

of public order and the extraction of fines; for water supply, markets, and weights and measures. Later they were required to look after and distribute the corn supply and, until the time of Augustus, to oversee the provision of public games and entertainments.

Quaestors

At first each consul appointed a quaestor, but after the mid-fifth century the quaestors were elected by the Assembly. There were two at first, but the number gradually increased until under Sulla it reached twenty; Caesar doubled it. Quaestors undertook a range of administrative functions principally financial, usually in a supportive role to other magistrates. Although the office was a lowly one, ex-quaestors would normally become senators.

Citizenry

Plebs were the lowest of Rome's classes. At the top stood the *equites* (knights), who dominated the army and later became the prosperous commercial leaders. Citizens participated directly either in the Assembly or in the Council of Plebs.

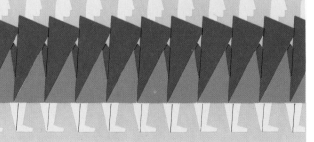

when the plebs threatened to withdraw their labor by leaving Rome and founding a city of their own, a compromise was rapidly reached (494 B.C.). Henceforth the Council of the Plebs could appoint two magistrates of their own called tribunes of the people (later the number was increased to ten) whose function was expressly to protect the interests of the plebs. The next step towards democracy came in 449 when the Council of the Plebs decreed that any resolution they made was binding on the state as a whole. Thus the plebiscite became a powerful means of affecting national policy and the monopoly of the patricians was greatly weakened.

Further reforms followed in the late fourth and early third centuries. The priesthood was now opened to both orders, one consulship was to be held by a plebeian, and, perhaps most important of all, decisions taken by the Council of the Plebs no longer needed to be ratified by the Senate.

It must have seemed to many that the Senate as an institution was doomed to extinction. But this was not to be, for in wartime it could direct affairs of state far more efficiently than cumbersome councils—and since from the middle of the third century Rome was almost constantly at war, the Senate survived, though in a much modified form. Senators were now appointed from among ex-magistrates (i.e., former holders of any political post), and since most magistracies were open to plebs and patricians alike, old class distinctions were no longer relevant to public office. The Senate therefore ceased to be the preserve of the jealous aristocrats appointed on hereditary qualifications alone and emerged as an assembly of men experienced in responsible government.

EARLY REPUBLICAN ROME

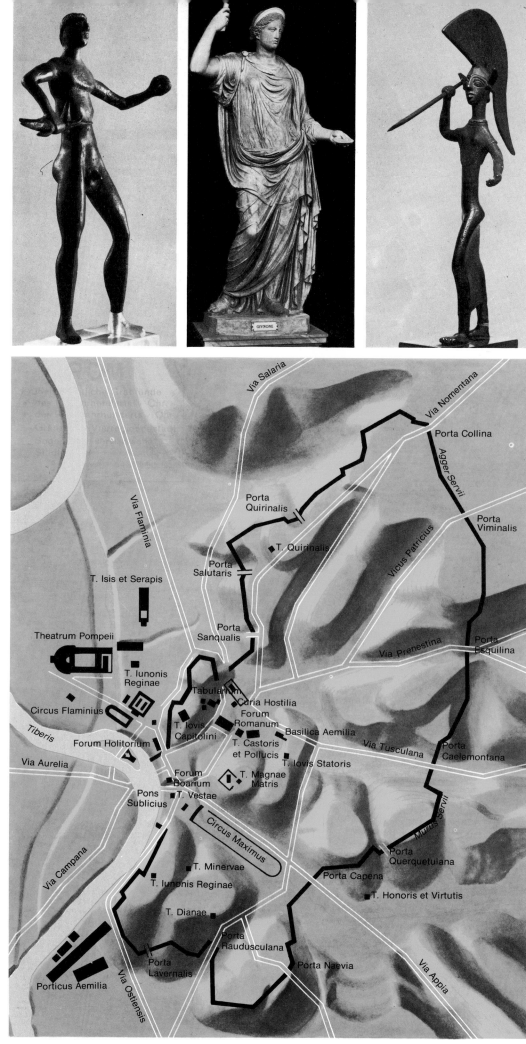

A vivid impression of the early city as it was before its destruction by the Gauls in 390 B.C. is provided by the Greek writer Dionysius. "Some sections of the town," he says, "those standing on hills and sheer cliffs, have been fortified by nature herself and require little garrisoning. Others were protected by the River Tiber, with only one bridge built of timber which is removed in times of war. But one section which is the most vulnerable part of the city, extending from the Esquiline Gate to the Colline Gate, is strengthened artificially." This is a rather different view from the traditional account, which sees the early city enclosed by the so-called Servian Wall, but it is closely borne out by the archaeological evidence which shows that the wall must postdate the Gallic attack. The early artificial defense, to which Dionysius refers, has, however, been discovered in the form of a massive bank and ditch which could date back to the sixth century.

The fifth-century city was then a rather haphazard, ill-contained growth sprawling over the hills and valleys. It was dominated by a large and flamboyant temple, set high on the Capitol, dedicated to the worship of Jupiter, Juno, and Minerva, replacing we are told "many altars of the gods and lesser divinities" which had to be

moved to clear the site. The plan of the temple, erected about 500 B.C., shows it to have been a great three-roomed structure built on a high podium in Etruscan manner. Elsewhere within the city other temples abounded, if the ancient writers are to be believed; temples to Mercury and to Ceres, Liber, and Libera existed on the Aventine while Saturn and Castor and Pollux were worshipped in the Forum Romanum.

The Forum itself was an open area lying in the valley to the east of the Capitol. It was a place to which, as the poet Varro said, people brought both their disputes and articles which they wished to sell. Public meetings were held close by on the slopes of the Capitol in another open area called the Comitium. Behind this, at a higher level, was the old Senate house, the Curia Hostilia. Livy records how along the boundary wall of the Comitium famous statues and monuments were placed including a tomb traditionally thought to be that of Romulus.

Of the other buildings little is known. The Circus Maximus, in the valley between the Palatine and Aventine, was supposed to have been built in the sixth century, though it may have been little more than tiers of wooden seats along the valley slopes.

Rome of the fifth century, with its narrow, steeply winding streets, was

still essentially a city built of timber and terra-cotta. The intricacies of its architectural decoration and the brilliance of its color would have been in staggering, almost barbarous, contrast to the city of Augustus five hundred years later.

ENEMIES
FROM THE NORTH

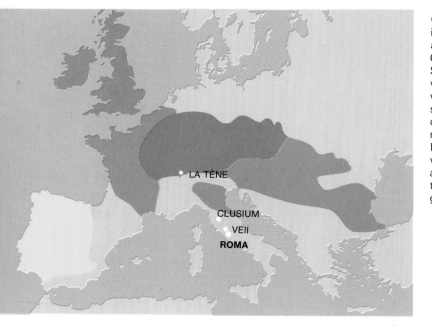

Veii, the closest Etruscan city to Rome (20 kilometers away), was a natural target during Roman expansion in the early fifth century. Veii took ten years to conquer. Shown here are foundations of the Portonaccio sanctuary, devoted to Minerva, where famous statues were found.

Fifth-century Rome was surrounded by enemies. To the north lay the towns of Etruria which until recently had vied with each other to control the city, while in the mountains to the east and south were powerful and dangerous tribes casting covetous eyes on the rich lands of the plains. Meanwhile, in the far north, beyond the Po, warlike Celts from central Europe were slipping through the mountain passes and setting up their homes on the southern flanks of the Alps.

By 493 Rome had established close treaty relationships with neighboring Latin towns and together they began to beat back the hill tribes of Aequi and Volsci from the plains. This was a

In 477 the Roman army failed to defeat Veii at the battle of Cremera, but throughout the next decades Roman infiltration of southern Etruria prepared the way for the final onslaught. In 396 Veii was destroyed; the way now lay open for Rome, using the excellent network of Etruscan roads, to establish its dominion by force or diplomacy over most of the cities of the south Etruscan homeland. At the height of this period of suc-

ter tribe swept down to settle on the fertile lands of the Po where they set up their small scattered farms. As the pressures built up, the land could no longer contain them and in 391 a force of thirty thousand Gauls crossed the Apennines to ravage the south.

"The whole race," said Strabo, "is war mad, high spirited and quick to battle, but otherwise straightforward and not of evil character. . . . When they are stirred up they assemble in their bands for battle quite openly and without forethought." Another firsthand account describes how in battle the two opposing sides would draw up facing each other and then the chariots would drive up and down the enemy ranks, the warriors shouting abuse at their opponents, while behind them the sides of the wagons, parked on the flank, would be beaten to increase the din. War trumpets were also popular. One contemporary writer says that they were "of a particularly barbaric kind. They blow into them and produce a harsh sound which suits the tumult of war." In early Celtic warfare, after the noise of the opening stages had died down, it was customary for the chief warriors to be driven into the field, there to deliver personal challenges accompanied by much boasting. Only after these individual contests were over would the battle commence.

The individual warrior, armed with a sword and spear, protected himself with a wooden or leather shield and with a helmet sometimes made of bronze, with crests in the form of animals or birds adding to his apparent height. Other groups called Gaesatae—apparently extratribal mercenaries—threw off their clothes before the fight and went into battle adorned only with neck torques and armlets of gold. The battle was hysterical and

Celtic expansion and invasion of Rome. The red area on the map is the Celtic homeland.
Soon after 500 B.C. this warlike people began to wander far afield and to settle in the areas indicated in brown on the map. The Celts in northern Italy attacked Rome by way of Clusium and Veii around 390 B.C. In yellow, the Celtiberians, a related group.

testing time for Rome during which she sharpened her diplomatic and organizational skills and emerged as undisputed leader of the Latins.

Not far from Rome, across the Tiber, lay the Etruscan city of Veii—a powerful and long-established town which, in commercial terms if not military, was a constant threat to Rome.

cessful expansion the northern barbarians struck. Already, throughout the fifth century B.C., these Gauls—a Celtic people—had been infiltrating the Po valley spurred on, as Livy believed, by population pressures building up in their central European homeland. By 400 B.C. folk movements began to intensify and tribe af-

Savage Celtic warriors with their battle trumpets are shown on a silver basin from Gunderstrup, Denmark, first century B.C. After sacking Rome, the Celtic invaders stayed on in Italy, where they remained a threat for more than thirty years. Finally, in 349 B.C., the Romans won a decisive victory and the remnants of the Celtic army fled into Apulia. A few years later Gallic raids had ceased altogether, and by 331, treaties were being arranged. Thereafter Rome became the aggressor. The Celts were defeated in several battles during the next century, culminating in the battle of Bologna in 191 B.C., after which vast numbers of Celts were driven back into central Europe.

violent. "They cut off the heads of their enemies slain in battle," says Diodorus, "and tie them to the necks of their horses. They nail these first fruits to their house [and] embalm the heads of distinguished enemies in cedar oil. These they preserve carefully in a chest to display with pride to strangers."

Such was the enemy who now threatened Rome. Their first move was south to besiege the Etruscan city of Clusium. Clusium, now an ally of Rome, appealed for help. Envoys were sent, but a battle broke out during which one of the Roman envoys killed a Celtic chieftain. The Celts immediately demanded his surrender, but the Romans refused, thereby declaring war.

Rome lay 120 kilometers to the south—only four days' march away. The terror which the city must have felt at this time is brilliantly summed up in the speech which Livy ascribed to the consul M. Popillius Laenas in his attempt to rally the citizens. "You are not facing a Latin or Sabine foe who will become your ally when you've beaten him. We have drawn our swords against wild beasts whose blood we must shed or spill our own."

On 18 July at Allia on the left bank of the Tiber the Roman defenses broke, leaving Rome at the mercy of the Gaulish army. The barbarians entered the city and pillaged and burned all of it except the Capitol, which managed to hold out for seven months. Eventually, suffering from diseases and lack of food, the Gauls moved off with their plunder. The Gaulish army for all its ferocity had little staying power for sieges. Even so, it took two centuries for the Gauls to be driven from Italian soil.

THE CITY REBUILT

Opposite: Detail from the funerary monument of the Haterii found in Rome: second century A.D. The crane, powered by slaves, gives a vivid idea of the kind of weight-lifting engines available to the builders of the late Republic and early Empire. Attached to the crane are a number of ropes and pulleys.

The Gaulish attack was a staggering blow for Rome: large areas of the city had been destroyed and its prestige was at a low ebb. But such was the resilience of the community that rebuilding began almost immediately. In 378 work began on the colossal system of defenses, known as the Ser-

Coin of 59 B.C. showing the Basilica Aemilia (in the Roman Forum), a two-storied hall for meetings and business.

vian Wall, which was designed to link the seven hills together in a single unified defensive concept. The wall, all eight kilometers of it, was faced with large blocks of yellow tufa from the quarries near Veii, each block measuring one to two meters in length. The old rampart which protected the Esquiline and Viminal was refaced and its ditch enlarged. No expense was spared to ensure that the city was safe from further attacks.

Rome was evidently rebuilt in haste and, surprisingly perhaps, no attempt was made to impose upon the plan the formality and regularity which were clear for all to see in the neighboring Greek towns of the south. Rome remained a city of steep slopes and narrow, winding streets. Livy records how the Macedonians still denigrated Rome as late as 200 B.C.: "It was not yet made beautiful in either its public or its private quarters."

The Forum Romanum, though partially paved, was still just an ill-ordered open space flanked along its south side by a row of temples and crossed by the Cloaca Maxima—here an open channel. In the fourth century, however, a new dignity was imparted to the area when food sellers were removed to a separate region and the business of the Forum was restricted to banking and money changing.

Where Rome took the lead was in the field of utilitarian architecture like the great subterranean aqueduct, the Aqua Appia, and the famous military road, the Via Appia, both named after the third-century censor Appius Claudius. It was the Via Appia and its extension southwards to Tarentum which helped the Roman armies gain control of southern Italy and brought Rome into contact with the Hellenistic kingdoms of the south.

The Tabularium, built during the Republic (78 B.C.), contains the oldest surviving examples of concrete vaulting. View of the first-floor gallery, which looks out over the Forum. This building on the Capitoline Hill contained the Roman state archives. See page 57 for a view of the exterior.

EXPANSION IN ITALY

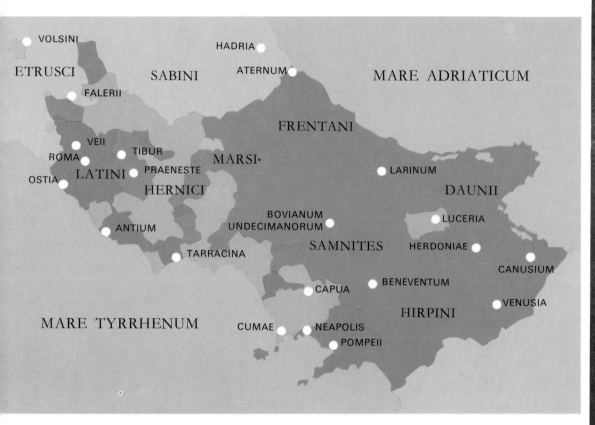

In 340 B.C., Rome's territory (in red on the map) was just one of the many city-states of central Italy, surrounded by the Etruscans and Sabines to the north, the Samnites and other tribes to the south.

Even from the early years the Republic showed a particular genius in dealing with her neighbors. Indeed her influence and power were maintained not so much by military supremacy as by her ability to treat all men, conquered and allies alike, with respect and consideration. Already her Latin allies had been granted certain rights and privileges which approximated to those of Roman citizens and bestowed upon the holder wide protection under Roman law. The conferment of "Latin Rights," or half-franchise, was a privilege eagerly sought by communities coming under Roman sway. Soon an even closer form of relationship was developed to cope with new allies who by tradition were accustomed to self-government. This involved leaving the processes of local government largely intact while conferring upon all free members of the community the privileges of full Roman citizenship including the right to stand for public office. In return the new citizens were required to pay war tax. Cities granted these privileges were called *municipia* (burden-holders).

The importance of urbanization to the stability of a territory was clearly recognized. Where no suitable urban community existed, colonies *(coloniae)* were founded, peopled by landless citizens, who were given sufficient land around their new town to provide them with an attractive livelihood. These *coloniae*, sometimes with full citizenship, sometimes with Latin

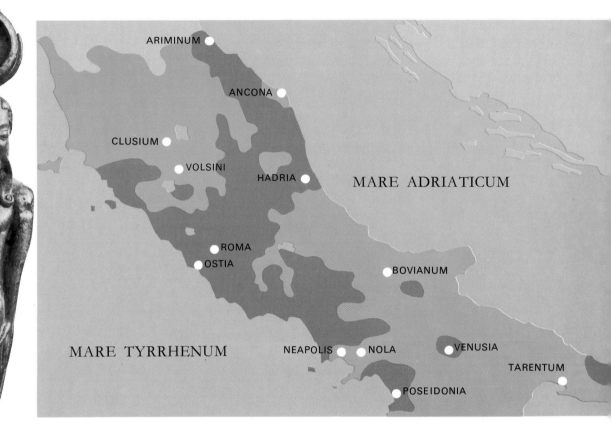

ARIMINUM

ANCONA

CLUSIUM

VOLSINI

HADRIA

MARE ADRIATICUM

ROMA

OSTIA

BOVIANUM

MARE TYRRHENUM

NEAPOLIS

NOLA

VENUSIA

TARENTUM

POSEIDONIA

By 240 B.C. Rome controlled all of central Italy. The shading on the map indicates the two ranks of communities associated with Rome: *municipia* (dark red) or preexisting cities, and *coloniae* (light red), newer towns.

Rights, were a vital tool in the process of Romanizing the more backward areas of the peninsula. They provided the added advantage of siphoning off the growing numbers of urban poor who might otherwise have created serious discontent at home.

Gradually Rome became more and more involved in her neighbors' affairs. In 343 B.C. she was called in to assist the cities of Campania in their struggle against the attacks by Samnites from the hills—an involvement which led to a series of wars lasting until 290. The events of this struggle were complex and the repercussions far-reaching. As a result the old Latin League ceased to exist, the army was reorganized to make it a far more efficient fighting force, and Rome emerged as virtual master of all Italy. In the center lay Roman territory—a small area, no more than a few hundred square miles. Beyond, in Latium, Campania, and, after 268, the Sabine Hill, was an area of land well on the way to being Romanized in which most cities were tied to the center by grants of civic franchise. Beyond this came the less favored states—the Etruscans and the Samnites controlled by *coloniae* scattered liberally among them. All these territories were, by about 240, part of the Roman confederacy. All that remained beyond the control of the Republic were the Gaulish settlers in the Po valley and the Greek cities of the south, together with their barbarian mountain-dwelling neighbors.

63

STRUGGLE FOR THE SEA

Hiero of Syracuse (r. 269–216 B.C.), whose battles against pirates led to the outbreak of the first Roman-Carthaginian war. He assisted Rome during the first two Punic Wars. Portrait from a Greek coin.

In the early years of the Republic Rome had had little need of sea power. Control of the western Mediterranean was divided, somewhat uneasily, between the two great maritime powers, Greece and Carthage. The Greek cities had control of the Tyrrhenian Sea, from eastern Sicily across to the south coast of France, where their colony Massilia (Marseilles) had been established in about 600 B.C., while the Carthaginians commanded the southern part of the west Mediterranean from the Straits of Gibraltar to eastern Sicily and from the coast of North Africa to Sardinia. Rome was content with the status quo. Treaties with Carthage dated back to the sixth century; in 348 B.C. Rome recognized the Carthaginian rights over Africa and Spain in return for the guarantee of her own trade routes with Sicily and the immunity of the Italian coastal ports from raids. Another treaty, of 306 B.C., agreed to limit the number of Roman ships in the southern Mediterranean. So long as the three great powers respected each others' legitimate interests there could be peace.

Temperamentally and culturally the Carthaginians differed considerably from the Romans. They were a Semitic people from the east Mediterranean coast (now Lebanon) who had arrived in North Africa towards the beginning of the first millennium B.C. Their religion, which demanded child sacrifice, was somber and oppressive, while their artistic and literary development, to judge from the surviving evidence, was limited in the extreme. Above all they were a merchant oligarchy totally dependent upon the sea for their trading livelihood.

When the clash came it was centered on Sicily. In 264 B.C. a group of mercenaries from Campania had taken

THE FIRST PUNIC WAR (264–241)

264–263 Rome enters the war. Hiero of Syracuse sides with Rome against the Carthaginians. The next year Agrigentum is besieged. Carthaginians terrorize coast.
New two legions sent south to relieve the town of Messana.

260 Victory at Mylae, near Messana.

258 Corsica captured.

256 Roman victory near Cape Ecnomus.
The Roman consuls Regulus and Manlius head a fleet of over three hundred vessels against equal numbers of Carthaginian ships. Regulus leads army to Africa.

255 Roman army defeated near Carthage. Roman fleet foundered en route to Africa, another wrecked two years later.

254–243 The war in Sicily drags on. Carthaginian fortress at Panormus captured (254); Lilybaeum besieged but Hamilcar Barca successfully leads Carthaginian resistance.

242–241 Roman triumph.
New fleet sent out (242): victory off Aegates Islands (241). Hamilcar forced to negotiate peace terms.

Below right: The cliffs of Eryx (Monte San Giuliano), south coast of Sicily, where Hamilcar had his stronghold.

Below: An Indian elephant manned by two Macedonian warriors on a plate from Capena.

Rome's first naval war was fought for control of Sicily, with brief action in Africa. Rome annexed Corsica and Sardinia.

The coin at right is traditionally taken to represent the Carthaginian general Hamilcar Barca (270?–228 B.C.), father of Hannibal. Coined in Carthage, third century B.C.

Below center: Triumphal column set up by Caius Duilius in the Forum Romanum decorated with the prows of captured Carthaginian ships.

Bottom right: Coin showing a Mamertine pirate, minted by the Mamertines in the third century B.C. Their raids set off the war.

Overleaf: Dramatic meeting, at the climax of the Second Punic War (218–202 B.C.), between the two enemy commanders. The Roman general Scipio, at left, faces Hannibal in a last effort to negotiate peace. "The generals met: they were not only the two greatest soldiers of their time," Livy wrote, "but the equals of any king or commander in the whole history of the world. For a minute mutual admiration struck them dumb, and they looked at each other in silence." Flemish tapestry, Quirinale Palace, Rome.

control of Messana (Messina), which they used as a base for pirate attacks on shipping in the strait between Italy and Sicily. The powerful Greek colony of Syracuse led by Hiero II decided to rid the island of the menace and besieged Messana, whereupon the city sent for help—to Carthage and to Rome! In the inevitable conflict and confusion which followed, Rome gained control of Messana. Hiero at

was to be their first major adventure in naval warfare, but their inexperience meant that still no significant advance could be made. Eventually the Senate took the dramatic decision to send an army of forty thousand men to Africa to defeat the Carthagians at home.

Rome's first overseas expedition failed completely when the Roman army was soundly beaten near modern

Tunis in 255 B.C. and the fleet, sent to rescue the army survivors, foundered. Henceforth the war in Africa was abandoned and efforts were made once more to oust the Carthaginians from Sicily. Deploying a new fleet, the Romans managed to take Panormus (modern Palermo) in 254 and when, four years later, the Carthaginians made an attempt to recapture it, assisted by 120 elephants, they were defeated, losing the elephants to the Romans. The next year, 249 B.C., the Romans once more took the offensive. With a new fleet of two hundred ships they sailed on Drepanum but the fleet was totally destroyed. So the war dragged on through seven more years of undecisive fighting until, with yet another fleet, the Romans eventually won a decisive naval victory. In 241 B.C. a peace treaty was signed. By its terms Carthage agreed to prevent its quinqueremes from entering Roman waters, not to attack Roman allies, to pay a massive indemnity within ten years, and to give up all claim to Sicily.

With Sicily Rome gained its first overseas territory and its first direct contact with the Hellenistic world.

Learning quickly, the Romans developed ships (as seen on this coin) especially equipped to hook onto and capsize enemy vessels.

first sided with the Carthaginians but changed sides after a successful Roman landing, and henceforth the Greeks and Romans together opposed the Carthaginians.

Gradually the Carthaginian territory was whittled away, but the principal towns of eastern Sicily remained in Carthaginian hands since they could be easily supplied by ship. Clearly, to break the stalemate the Romans had to gain control of the sea. To do this they set about building a fleet of 120 quinqueremes using as their model a stranded Carthaginian vessel. This

SCIPIO ET ANNIBAL
SVPERIOVAS
AD INVICEM
CONVENIVNT

CARTHAGE AGAINST ROME

The First Punic War, which lasted a quarter of a century, had stretched Rome to the utmost: colossal expenditure and continuous demands on manpower for fighting and for shipbuilding had severely tested the Roman confederacy, but it had survived. Now in 218 the threat of Carthage began to loom once more.

In many ways Rome was much better prepared. Success in the first war had created a new spirit of self-assurance, the armies had gained valuable experience, command of the seas was assured, and Rome's leadership of the confederacy was now unquestioned. Moreover Italy could provide considerable reserves of manpower. Estimates vary, but on the order of three-quarters of a million men were probably available for service if required.

Hannibal, who led the Carthaginian assault on Rome, came with 30,000 infantry and 9,000 cavalry all trained to the peak of efficiency. His numbers were comparatively small, but he was banking on the support of the Gauls, settled in the Po valley, to swell the ranks. As it turned out the Gauls were enthusiastic, but somewhat uncontrollable, allies. Hannibal also assumed that, once he reached central Italy, many of the towns would go over to his side. In this, his judgment was less than sound.

The story of the Second Punic War may be briefly told. The first stage saw Hannibal's almost unbelievable march from Spain, over the Alps, and deep into Italy. In two years and after four great battles—Ticinus, Trebia, Trasimene, and Cannae—it must have seemed that Rome was finished. But for some reason, perhaps because of lack of support from the Italian

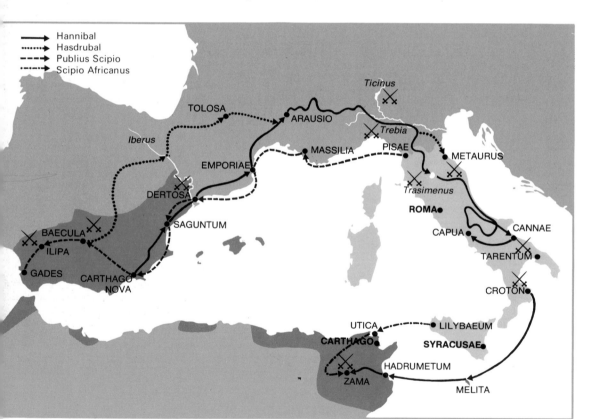

Hannibal
Hasdrubal
Publius Scipio
Scipio Africanus

THE SECOND PUNIC WAR (218–202 B.C.)

218 Hannibal leaves New Carthage for Rome. Battles of Ticinus and Trebia: victories for Carthage.

217 Battle of Trasimene. Roman force annihilated: Hannibal enters Apulia.

216 Battle of Cannae. Latin towns including Capua go over to Hannibal.

212 Syracuse besieged. Marcellus leads Roman armies into city after which the rest of Sicily is soon reduced.

204–202 Scipio lands in Africa. Utica is besieged, and finally at Zama the Carthaginian force is beaten. Hannibal capitulates.

The scientist and mathematician Archimedes lived in Syracuse during the siege of 212. He is credited with having invented machines and devices to discourage the Roman attackers and may well have been involved in the planning of the ingenious defenses of the Euryalus fort which protected the approaches to the city. He died when Marcellus broke through and sacked the city.

towns, Hannibal's overwhelming victories were not followed up; it is almost as though in the moment of success his resolve had begun to falter. Meanwhile the scope of the war had widened. Campaigning in Spain led by Publius Scipio began to go spec-

Opposite: Portrait busts of Hannibal *(far left)* and Scipio. The Roman general Scipio (237–183 B.C.) won the name Africanus in celebration of his victory over Carthage. Hannibal (247–183 B.C.), defeated, later driven into exile, spent the rest of his life fighting Rome on the side of the Syrians. He committed suicide when faced with capture.

Right: Hannibal crossing the Alps. Ice, snow, hostile tribes, food shortages, and accidents (as in this engraving) beset him at every turn. His exact route is still debated.

Below: Hannibal's elephants at the Rhône River. Livy describes the struggles to get them on rafts, to keep from capsizing, and to rescue elephants that fell overboard. French eighteenth-century engraving.

tacularly well for the Romans after initial setbacks, and Sicily, which had been up in arms, was efficiently reduced. In 207 Hasdrubal, marching with reinforcements to meet his brother Hannibal, was defeated and killed. The time was now ripe for a major Roman initiative—the war was to be taken to Carthage. After a year of preparation Scipio landed in Africa in 204 B.C. and took the Carthaginian town of Utica. Further Roman successes followed, and the situation was now so serious that Hannibal with the remnants of his army left for home.

The final act took place at Zama in the Tunisian hills. The two armies met, the Romans strongly supported by cavalry supplied by the Numidian king Massinissa. The result was a decisive victory for Rome.

The conditions imposed on Carthage were humiliating. A vast indemnity had to be paid, the entire fleet (except for ten vessels) was to be destroyed, all overseas territories given up, and no war or treaty was to be made without the permission of Rome. In other words, Carthage was reduced to a position of extreme subservience.

The struggle for survival which Rome had just come through can fairly be said to have changed the direction of Western civilization. It was not so much the defeat of the Carthaginians that mattered, but the effects which victory had on Rome. Gone were the old ideals of the confederacy—Rome was now firmly and fully in charge. Any city which had stepped out of line, like Capua and Tarentum which had gone over to Hannibal, was viciously punished and deprived of all rights. When new territories were annexed, as for example that of the Ligurians in the north, vast populations would be transported at the whim of the state. The war had also increased the power of the ruling class. In times of crisis it was necessary for decisions to be made rapidly by the Senate without recourse to the Assembly; in the aftermath the Senate was reluctant to give up its powers.

In Italy the dislocation of population had been considerable; now, in the resettlement which followed, people flocked to the towns, and in the countryside new estates were carved out for wealthy urban-based landowners. In this way divisions between rich and poor widened and the power of the small ruling oligarchy dramatically increased. The progress towards democracy evident in the fourth century had been halted and reversed. Rome was now set on a course of aggressive imperialism.

THE DESTRUCTION OF CARTHAGE

Scipio Aemilianus (185–129 B.C.), hero of the Third Punic War. A grandson by adoption of Scipio Africanus, he commanded the Roman army against Carthage in 147–146, defeating the Carthaginians and destroying their city. He later served in Spain and captured Numantia for Rome in 133 B.C.

The conditions which Rome had imposed on Carthage, after the Second Punic War, were harsh: an indemnity of crippling proportions, the virtual destruction of its fleet, surrender of all overseas territories, and political constraints which in effect gave the Numidian king Massinissa a considerable degree of protection and allowed him to pursue an aggressive role against Carthage whenever he chose.

It was as the result of increasing Carthaginian alarm at Massinissa's advances that a Roman commission of inquiry was eventually sent to Africa in 153. Cato, who took part, was vividly impressed by the commercial prosperity of the city and, convinced that it had once more become a rival

that Carthage must be destroyed." Others took a different view, some going so far as to argue that Rome needed the constant threat of powerful competitors to encourage the people to maintain vigilance and to prevent moral decline. In the event, Cato's opinion prevailed.

Carthaginians had for some decades been politically divided between those who wished to keep peace with Rome and those who believed that if Carthage were to survive she would have to defend herself. The latter group took control, and in 151 war was declared on Massinissa. It went disastrously for Carthage and although apologies were quickly sent to Rome, a *casus belli* had now been established.

out to command the Roman forces. He decided on a complete blockade of the city, and to effect this, built a mole across the harbor mouth. Although the Carthaginians responded by cutting a new outlet, their plight was now impossible and gradually morale in the besieged city weakened.

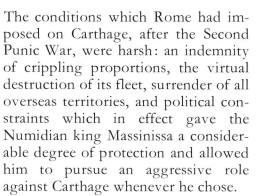

"Carthage must be destroyed." This rallying cry by Cato the Elder *(right)* helped to persuade the Roman Senate to go to war again, but the great orator (234–149 B.C.) did not live long enough to see his wish fulfilled.

Left: Excavated ruins of the acropolis at Carthage, destroyed by the Romans in 146 B.C. After one unsuccessful attempt to establish a Roman colony on the site, Augustus founded the city of Colonia Julia completing the work of Julius Caesar there in 29 B.C. It grew into a thriving Roman metropolis during the Empire.

to Rome, he tried to persuade the Roman Senate to attack. The story is told that on his return he showed the Senate a bunch of African figs, still fresh, as a reminder of the agricultural wealth of Africa and of the fact that Carthage was only three days' journey from Rome. Thereafter all of his speeches to the Senate ended with the words "For the rest, it is my opinion

In 149 Roman armies landed in Africa. The Carthaginian government immediately sued for peace but refused to meet Rome's harsh demands for total surrender. Thus began the final conflict to the death. The subjugation of Carthage was not as easy as Rome had anticipated and discipline in the army was lax, but eventually an able young general, Scipio Aemilianus, was sent

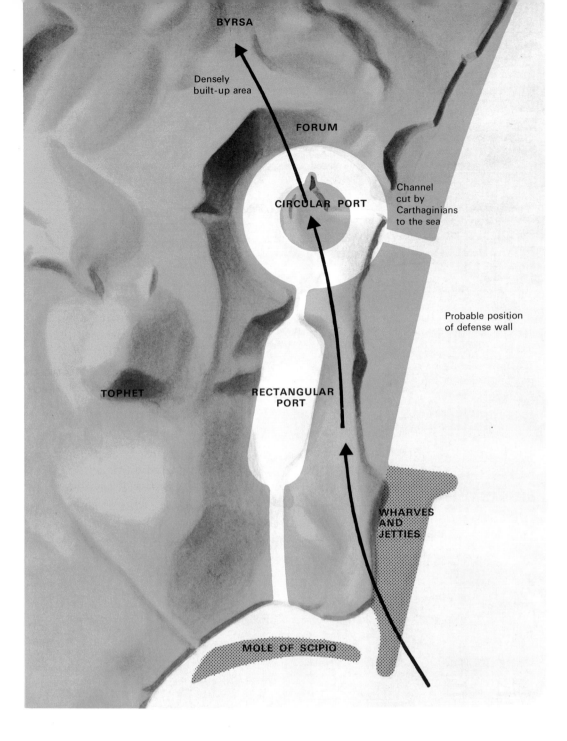

BYRSA

Densely
built-up area

FORUM

CIRCULAR PORT

Channel
cut by
Carthaginians
to the sea

Probable position
of defense wall

TOPHET

RECTANGULAR
PORT

WHARVES
AND
JETTIES

MOLE OF SCIPIO

The Romans' blockade of Carthage, 146 B.C.
Scipio built a mole across the harbor mouth, but
the Carthaginians cut a new channel to link
their circular harbor to the sea. The arrow indicates the probable route of Scipio's attack.

The eyewitness. Polybius (202–120 B.C.), Greek
general and historian, on an Attic gravestone
relief. He was present with Scipio at the razing
of Carthage, as the historian Appian relates.

*Scipio looked over the city which had flourished
for over seven hundred years since its foundation,
which had ruled over such extensive territories,
islands, and seas, and been as rich in arms, fleets,
elephants, and money as the greatest empires,
but which had surpassed them in daring and
high courage, since though deprived of all its
arms and ships it had yet withstood a great
siege and famine for three years, and was now
coming to an end in total destruction; and he
is said to have wept and openly lamented the
fate of his enemy. After meditating a long time
on the fact that not only individuals but cities,
nations, and empires must all inevitably come to
an end, and on the fate of Troy, that once glorious
city, on the fall of the Assyrian, Median, and
Persian empires, and on the more recent
destruction of the brilliant empire of the
Macedonians, deliberately or subconsciously
he quoted the words of Hector from Homer—
"The day shall come when sacred Troy shall
fall, and King Priam and all his warrior
people with him." And when Polybius, who
was with him, asked him what he meant, he
turned and took him by the hand, saying:
"This is a glorious moment, Polybius; and yet
I am seized with fear and foreboding that some
day the same fate will befall my own country."*

Appian, *Libyca* 132

Eventually, in the winter of 147–146
Scipio attacked. The city wall was
breached and amid the flames of the
burning port the Roman troops
reached the inner circular harbor.
Vicious street fighting ensued but on
the seventh day the Byrsa—the citadel
of Carthage—fell and the last of the
defenders perished.

For at least ten days the city burned.
Finally what little remained standing
was leveled and then the last symbolic
act took place: the site was cursed and
a plough drawn across the rubble
scratching a furrow into which salt
was thrown, to signify that Carthage
should forever remain barren.

Below: Photograph of the site today (looking
southward): a suburb of Tunis.

GREECE AND MACEDONIA

Alexander the Great (356–323 B.C.). Bronze statue from Herculaneum. Museo Nazionale, Naples.

Below left: Map of Alexander's conquests, which were divided up into competing states after his death. A century later, Rome began to intervene in the worsening conflicts in the Aegean.

The death of Alexander the Great in 323 marked the beginning of the end for the Hellenistic world. The great empire which he had created in so short a period was divided between

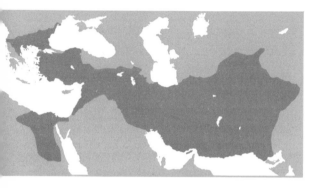

his generals; in the aftermath three became dominant: Antigonus took Macedonia, Greece, and the Aegean; Seleucus inherited Asia Minor, Syria, and the east; and Ptolemy commanded Eygpt. Each founded a dynasty and in this division lay the seeds of political rivalry which was to rack the eastern Mediterranean with intrigue and wars for generations to come. Inevitably Rome was drawn into the conflict.

The first confrontation came in 230 when the Senate authorized intervention against the pirates of the Illyrian coast (now Yugoslavia) who were preying on Roman shipping in the Aegean. The Greek states welcomed the initiative, but the king of Macedonia regarded it as an invasion of his own sphere of interest and reacted accordingly by siding with the pirates. Nine years later Rome had to intervene once more, successfully destroying the pirate stronghold. This blow to Macedonian prestige ensured for Rome a new and powerful enemy who was to become a constant threat throughout the Second Punic War.

By the beginning of the second century B.C. the Macedonian kingdom was

in a state of unrest. The states of the Peloponnesus, most of whom had joined together in a confederacy known as the Achaean League, were growing rebellious; so too were the peoples of Thessaly and the mountain tribes living north of the Gulf of Corinth who had combined to form the Aetolian League. Individually the Greek states were too weak to challenge Macedonian domination, and their confederacies were so divided by internal rivalries that, unaided, they were unlikely ever to be able to make a stand against the Macedonians.

In 202 Philip, king of Macedonia, began to assume control of the Aegean, and Rome, exhausted after the Second Punic War, was somewhat unwillingly drawn in as champion of the Greek states. Why Rome should have intervened is not difficult to see: on the one hand the pro-Greek lobby, led by Scipio, would have considered it their duty to support Greece in its hour of need, while on the other hand fear of Macedonia (particularly after Philip's intervention on the side of Hannibal in the recent war) must have been present in many minds. So in the year 200 a small Roman force landed in Illyria to begin their invasion of Thessaly, where the Macedonian army was in control.

After a series of successful campaigns the Roman commander Flamininus was able to obtain the submission of Philip together with an agreement that he would henceforth confine his political interests to Macedonia. As soon as the boundaries of the Greek states had been redefined to his satis-

faction, Flamininus was able to announce the liberation of Greece, before departing for home with his army in 196.

At this stage, then, Rome showed no inclination to do more than establish peace and get out. But Antiochus, king of Asia (western Turkey), entered the arena by crossing to Thrace in order to claim certain Aegean territories as his own. Once more a Roman force was dispatched, and in 191 at the famous pass of Thermopylae the invader was beaten and the war was driven eastward onto Asian soil. It remained for Rome to deal with those states which had sided

Coin portrait from Attica of Consul Titus Quintus Flamininus (230–174 B.C.), who led the Roman army to defend Thessaly against Macedonia (200–196).

with Antiochus before leaving Greece to its own destiny. But like it or not, Rome was now involved in Greek politics and the petty bickerings between the rival Greek states required the attention of one Roman commission after another.

The situation gradually deteriorated as Macedonian power increased. Finally in 172 war was declared, with

Corinth was destroyed by Rome in 146, the same year as the razing of Carthage. View of the Corinthian isthmus where the ancient city was located.

the inevitable result that Macedonia was conquered. Yet again Rome shrank from taking direct control, preferring to divide Macedonia into four self-governing territories while those Greek states which had provided help to the Macedonians were severely handled. The political solution was at best a temporary expedient and in 149 the Macedonians were in arms again. Rome had no option. The next year the insurrection was put down and Macedonia became a Roman province.

But in spite of political turmoil, it was still the clear intention of Rome to leave Greece to its own devices.

ed off to Rome by shipload. Significantly perhaps, this occurred in 146, the year in which Carthage was razed. Rome's attitudes to Greece had changed dramatically in the half-century following the end of the Second Punic War. To begin with there had been an ambivalence, a respect for all Greece had stood for tempered with a contempt for what she had become. Only reluctantly had Rome become

The Greeks should not go to war with each other at all . . . we ought to be unanimous and on our guard, when we see the bloated armaments and the vast proportions assumed by the war in the west. For it is in every way improbable that the victors will remain contented with the empire of Sicily and Italy. They will move forward: and will extend their forces and their designs farther than we could wish. . . . If once you allow the clouds now gathering in the west to settle upon Greece, I fear exceedingly that the power of making peace or war, and in a word all these games which we are now playing against each other, will be completely knocked out of the hands of us all.

Agelaus's speech, Polybius, Histories V, 104

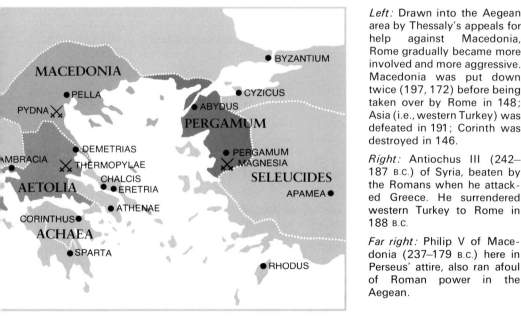

Left: Drawn into the Aegean area by Thessaly's appeals for help against Macedonia, Rome gradually became more involved and more aggressive. Macedonia was put down twice (197, 172) before being taken over by Rome in 148; Asia (i.e., western Turkey) was defeated in 191; Corinth was destroyed in 146.

Right: Antiochus III (242–187 B.C.) of Syria, beaten by the Romans when he attacked Greece. He surrendered western Turkey to Rome in 188 B.C.

Far right: Philip V of Macedonia (237–179 B.C.) here in Perseus' attire, also ran afoul of Roman power in the Aegean.

However, matters came to a head in 147 when a senatorial deputation to Corinth was severely handled by a Greek mob. Rome's patience was finally exhausted. The army was ordered down from Macedonia, and Corinth was besieged and taken. Thereupon its citizens were sold into slavery, its fine buildings were destroyed, and its art treasures were cart-

embroiled in the affairs of Greece and Macedonia. By the middle of the century, however, attitudes had hardened—a new aggressive imperialism was in the air—the Greeks had been an irritant for too long. The sack of Corinth, to many, must have seemed not only thoroughly justified but an essential act in Rome's progress towards world domination.

Sulla made off with the sacred treasures of Greece, sending for the most beautiful and valuable offerings deposited both in Epidaurus and at Olympia. He also wrote to the Amphictyons at Delphi, saying that it would be better to have the treasure of the god brought to him. . . . But the silver jar, the last of the royal gifts still in existence, was too heavy for the baggage animals to carry and the Amphictyons were compelled to cut it into pieces. As they did so they called to mind the names of Titus Flamininus and Manius Acilius and Aemilius Paulus too. One of these had driven Antiochus out of Greece and the others had conquered the kings of Macedonia. Plutarch, Life of Sulla

PERGAMUM

Located in Asia Minor (modern-day Turkey) near the Aegean seacoast, Pergamum was a major artistic center in the third and second centuries B.C. and a model of Hellenistic town planning. The third-century acropolis *(diagram at right)*, a citadel with temples and the royal residence, stood high above the rest of the town and commanded a wide view of the plains below. Excavations began in 1878.

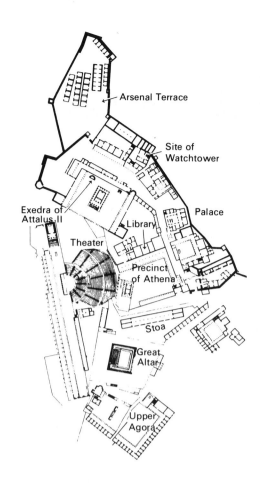

The emergence of the kingdom of Pergamum in Asia Minor, is one of the most astonishing interludes in the history of the Hellenistic world. The story begins in the period of political intrigue which followed the death of Alexander the Great. One of his generals, Lysimachus, had amassed a considerable fortune which he decided to house in the citadel of the market town of Pergamum. When, some years later, Lysimachus died, the treasure was still largely intact, closely guarded by one Philetaeros. Suddenly in possession of unexpected wealth, Philetaeros decided to establish a power base at Pergamum from which to control an expanding kingdom in Asia Minor. By the time of his death in 263 he was, in all but name, king of a considerable territory stretching as far north as the Troad.

He was succeeded by his nephew Eumenes I, the first ruler of a dynasty which was to wield enormous power and influence in Asia for the next 130 years. One of the principal achievements of Pergamum during this period was to stand up against the threat of continued attacks from Gaulish marauders who had crossed to Asia in 279 and who were intent on plundering the wealthy cities of the coastal areas. In 230 Attalus I won a resounding victory against the Gauls and in doing so established Pergamum as the savior of Hellenism in Asia.

It was at this stage that Rome entered the scene. The natural enemy of Pergamum was Macedonia. Thus when Attalus I and Rhodes declared war on Philip V of Macedon, they took care to involve Rome in the struggle on their side with the result, as we have seen, that Macedonian power was severely curtailed—by Rome's effort and to Pergamum's advantage. A little later, when Antiochus attempted to fill the power vacuum, Pergamum persuaded the Greek cities of Asia to appeal for Rome's help on the rather dubious ground that they were all Trojans by origin. Once more Rome's intervention, leading to the defeat of Antiochus, greatly benefited the expansionist policies of Pergamum's kings. Rome also benefited since Pergamum was now a firm ally and could be used as a Roman buffer state against both Macedonia and Syria. Some years later, when Macedonian power was on the increase, Rome once more intervened at the request of Rhodes and Pergamum; and eventually Macedonia was annexed.

The story is a fascinating one in that it shows how, by careful manipulation, Rome could be drawn further and further into the affairs of the east.

The last king, Attalus III, was reputed to be a scholar and scientist though, according to contemporary accounts, somewhat eccentric and cruel. His death in 133 brought a great shock to many—in the terms of his will he bequeathed his kingdom to Rome. Like it or not, the Romans were now committed in Asia Minor. After some initial trouble Pergamum became the province of Asia in 128.

DEMATA. CORONAE. REGVM AVT DVCVM CAPTORVM

REGES CAPTIVICVM FAMILIA FILIIS FILIA BVSQVE SVIS

In 133 B.C., when Attalus III willed Pergamum to Rome, the Romans acquired not only vast territory but also impressive artistic and cultural treasures. Above is the Great Altar of Zeus (180–160 B.C.), with stairs, portico, and at the base the famous frieze of relief sculpture depicting the battle of the gods and giants—one of many Hellenistic masterpieces found on the site. (The altar is near the southern end of the citadel; see town plan opposite.) Pergamum also boasted a library of 200,000 volumes which rivaled the renowned collection at Alexandria. The jealous Alexandrians cut off supplies of papyrus, forcing Pergamum to develop a new writing material, parchment. Pergamum had endowed public building programs in many Greek cities including Delphi and Athens.

Left: Ruins of the theater, third century B.C., carved in the steep western slope of the hill, a marvel of the ancient world.

Below: Triumphal procession in Rome as portrayed by an eighteenth-century artist. During the late Republic and the Empire these celebrations followed each major foreign conquest. At far left, chariots bear the crowns and regalia of vanquished leaders. Walking just ahead of the arch, a captured king and queen, hands bound behind them, followed by their children and servants. At center are wagons bearing spoils. At right, the victor, crowned with laurel.

IS QVI VICTIS INSVLTABAT TRIVMPHANTEM MONEBAT

IMPERATOR TRIVMPHANS

ODORVM

TIBICINES. CITHAROEDI. PHONASSI.

CONFLICT OF IDEALS

If the wars against Carthage in the second half of the third century had brought Rome face to face with Greek civilization for the first time in southern Italy and in Sicily, it was the campaigns of the early second century against the Hellenistic kingdoms of the east that were to have the greatest impact on Roman art, learning, and society. Livy sums up the situation exactly when he says that Rome's enthusiasm for Greek art had been awakened by the statues and paintings plundered from Syracuse, which were brought to Rome in the triumph of Marcellus in 212 B.C.; but elsewhere

have retained some of the simplicity of the earlier years, the Hellenized culture of the eastern kingdoms had changed to suit the pattern of oriental despotism prevalent in these regions. Rome, then, was suddenly being exposed to a wide range of new cultural influences Greek in origin but oriental in their excesses.

In the new age which followed the Second Punic War there were those who gladly embraced Hellenistic culture and those who abhorred it, jealously upholding the traditional Roman virtues—serious-mindedness, piety, and simplicity. Among the lat-

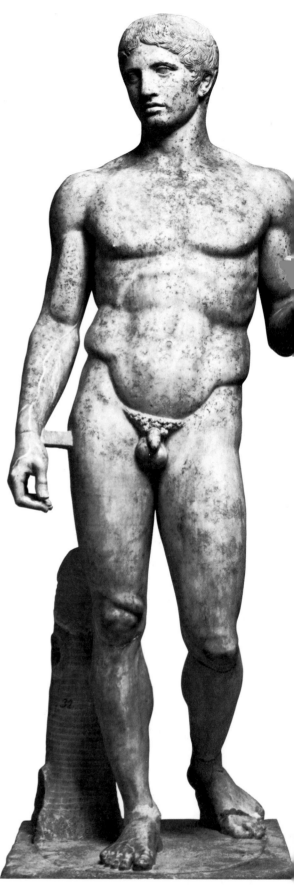

Classical Greek style is shown in the Ionic columns of the so-called Temple of Fortuna Virilis, Rome. This well-preserved building from the second century B.C. was saved from destruction by being used as a Christian church.

Theatrical scenes carved in relief on marble. From Pompeii, first century B.C. This section depicts figures wearing masks from Greek New Comedy. "Traditional morals have been utterly ruined by this imported laxity!" (Tacitus).

he notes that the beginning of a taste for foreign luxury was introduced into the city by the army returning from Asia about 187 B.C. The distinction is interesting in that it reminds us that the Greek tradition had developed significantly since the great days of fifth-century Athens. While the western Greek communities might still

ter Cato the Elder was the most vociferous. Backed by a distinguished career as a soldier (against Hannibal), a civil administrator, and a statesman, he set himself to fight relentlessly against these new and insidious influences which he believed to be undermining all that was good in Rome. The Greeks to him were "a scoundrel

Roman copy of a lost Greek masterpiece. Polycleitus, fifth-century sculptor and theoretician, created the famous *Doryphoros* (spear carrier) in the mid-fifth century. The work was meant to demonstrate the principles of perfect harmony and proportion worked out in Polycleitus's book *The Canon*. Roman sculptors strove to emulate his statues.

and incorrigible race." When the Athenian philosophers Diogenes and Carneades, in Rome on official business, found time to give lectures in the city, Cato ensured that they were removed as soon as possible: their presence was "like a great wind sounding about the city"—great winds were dangerous. No doubt Cato's attitudes owed much to the extremes of his own complex psychological make-up, but he did stand for values which many still upheld. The citizen was subservient to the state. Austerity, self-denial, and service were the ideals, while uncontrolled self-ex-

barbarian alike. Such a man, who flaunted tradition whenever it got in his way, and offered himself to the Roman people as a hero, represented everything that Cato despised and feared. Scipio was the product of the new situation and although he died in exile, outlawed by his old opponent Cato, his was to be the style of the future.

No doubt the growing popularity of Greek culture had much to do with the rise of individualism. When Livius Andronicus, a Greek slave captured at

also provided the model for many early Latin works. Ennius, a native of Brundisium, when composing his epic incorporating the history of the Second Punic War, naturally used the *Iliad* as his model.

Greek theater had a considerable influence on the Roman playwrights of the time. The works of Plautus, for example, owe much to the style of Menander though his plots and characters were clearly designed to appeal to the baser tastes of his Roman audiences. His succesor Terence, who remained closer to the Greek style, failed to attract a popular following.

pression and the cult of the individual would destroy all that was good.

The antithesis of Cato's beliefs was personified by Scipio Africanus—the hero of the Second Punic War—a man of dazzling individuality who gained his spectacular success by the sheer power of his personality. He was able to charm any audience, Roman and

Tarentum, translated Homer's *Odyssey* into Latin, he was presenting his Roman readers with a whole gallery of lively characters, men like Odysseus and Agamemnon, human in their failings and individual in their deeds, whose vitality contrasted dramatically with the dour coldness of the early Roman heroes. Greek literary form

GREECE AND ROME: A SYMBIOSIS

In the aftermath of the wars of the third century B.C., Greek culture in all its manifestations was suddenly thrust before the largely unsuspecting Roman audience. The works of sculptors, philosophers, scientists, dramatists, poets, and historians became widely available, to disturb and to invigorate the hitherto unimaginative Roman population. Every branch of Greek cultural tradition, with the notable exception of experimental science, inspired imitators among the sympathetic while among the more traditionally minded it stirred up often-violent reaction.

Epicurus offered Rome a philosophy freer and more intellectually demanding than anything the Republic had yet experienced, and in the writings of Lucretius, his Roman followers found an interpreter able to provide the philosophy with a mature Roman aspect. Yet the alternative, the Stoic philosophy of Zeno, was far more congenial to those who believed in the old order. Thus a conflict developed: on the one hand the new men—flamboyant, believing in individualism, and ready to welcome Greek culture in all its aspects—on the other the traditionalists like the Catos ardently upholding the old values of simplicity, piety, and serious-mindedness, violently opposed to new and insidious outside influences. To them everything Greek was suspect.

In this polarization of opposites lay the roots of the angry conflict which was to divide the Republic for generations, until men of stature like Cicero emerged to distill the best of both and thus to create a new spirit of enlightenment.

Historians and poets of the Augustan age were able to create their works of genius in a truly Roman idiom.

EPICURUS   340–270 B.C.

Epicurus of Athens gives his name to a school of philosophy, a watered-down version of which gained popularity in late Republican Rome. He believed that all matter was composed of "atoms" which, as they fall through space, swerve and collide and thus come together to form a variety of objects. Because of their swerving path, nothing is rigid; there is no universal law. Since man is composed of atoms, a swerve of the atoms of the mind gives scope for a conscious act of will: thus man has the power of free will. Epicurus also believed that the pursuit of happiness was a desirable human striving, but by happiness he meant the absence of conflict and disturbance, not indulgence. Loosely interpreted, Epicureanism led in Rome to a newfound desire for self-expression and individualism and provided an excuse for excessive behavior. Many saw it as the very antithesis of the traditional Roman principles and virtues.

ZENO   334–262

Zeno of Citium, who lived and taught in Athens, was the founder of the philosophic system known as Stoicism. We have only a few fragments of Zeno's writing; he is known to us primarily through his influence.

The essence of the Stoics' beliefs was that in every human being there is a share of the divine spark—the Logos—which animates the universe. From this followed two principal conclusions: that all men are brothers and that the laws of nature are absolute and applicable to all. Moreover, since man shares divinity, it is his prime duty to strive towards moral perfection.

Stoicism was extremely popular in Rome, for it confirmed the traditional Roman belief in the importance of high moral integrity. In this it appealed particularly to the old aristocratic class, while the view that men were a brotherhood deserving of one set of universal laws seemed to provide a justification for Roman imperialism. Cicero and Cato were firm believers in Stoicism.

EUCLID   Active ca. 300 B.C.

Euclid is believed to have been a teacher of mathematics in Alexandria around 300 B.C. He is best known for his great work the *Elements*, in thirteen books, which has remained in use throughout the world for two thousand years. The work summarized most of the knowledge of geometry of Euclid's time, and by its usefulness and thoroughness eclipsed previous mathematical studies. Euclid's source materials have been lost, and thus it is impossible to know how much of his work was original and how much was merely passed along from prior thinkers.

In the *Elements* we find geometry treated as an abstract system of thought, as opposed to early mathematical work that was oriented entirely around problem-solving. Book I of the *Elements* contains the core of elementary geometry as taught in schools through the centuries—a series of definitions, postulates, common notions (axioms), and propositions (theorems). The cornerstone axiom is "Things that are equal to the same thing are equal to each other." Subsequent sections of the *Elements* enter into algebra, number theory, and other advanced fields.

Euclid wrote additional works, including *Elements of Music, Optics, Data*, and others that have been lost. The Romans apparently studied him in the original Greek until the fourth century A.D. when a Latin translation of the *Elements* appeared.

ARCHIMEDES Ca. 287–212

Both a mathematician and an inventor, Archimedes was born in Syracuse, son of an astronomer, and died in the same city when it was sacked by the Romans under Marcellus. His mathematical works show great originality. For calculating the surface area of a sphere, the area of a parabola, and so on, he developed a method close to modern integral calculus; in the *Sand-Reckoner* he displayed an ability to cope with very large numbers, quite novel in the ancient world; he also developed a whole new field of hydrostatics.

On a more practical level he is credited with creating a screw for raising water and a range of spectacular anti-siege machines used against the Romans. Archimedes has inspired many anecdotes and legends. In his bath, he supposedly cried out "Eureka" when he discovered a method for measuring the purity of gold, based on his studies of the relationship of density to volume. Another famous line—"Give me a place to stand and I will move the earth"—refers to his mastery of the principle of leverage.

CATO THE ELDER 234–149

M. Porcius Cato was brought up on his father's Sabine farm. He fought against Hannibal in Italy and served in Sicily and Africa, becoming praetor of Sardinia in 198. Later in Rome he held the offices of consul and censor. Livy says he was good at everything he turned his hand to, which included farming, writing and the law. Working ceaselessly all his life, he led an austere existence and was scrupulously honest in all his dealings. Though a scholar and a Greek speaker, he fought hard against the influence of Hellenism on Rome, believing that it undermined the moral integrity of the citizen. His ideal was a state based on traditional Roman values in which, through hard work and by exercising high moral principles, a citizen could realize himself.

The trader I consider to be an energetic man, and one bent on making money; but it is a dangerous career and one subject to disaster. On the other hand, it is from the farming class that the bravest men and the sturdiest soldiers come, their calling is most highly respected, their livelihood is most assured and is looked on with the least hostility, and those who are engaged in that pursuit are least inclined to be disaffected.

Hellenism, which placed emphasis on individual freedom and self-expression, was anathema to him. The Epicureans he loathed. His asceticism was extreme almost to the point of perversion.

HIPPARCHUS 190–126

Born in Nicaea in present-day Turkey, Hipparchus spent most of his life studying astronomy in Rhodes. He was a scientist in the true sense of the word— a careful observer and a highly accurate recorder. Believing his data to be too incomplete to allow the formulation of general theories of planetary movements, he contented himself with perfecting means of measuring astronomical phenomena. His observations allowed him to estimate the length of the year as $365 \ 1/4 - 1/300$ days and to construct the first theory of the motion of the sun and the moon based on carefully observed data.

CICERO 106–43

Cicero, Rome's foremost orator, was born in Arpinum and migrated to Rome to begin his career in politics. As a politician he was outstandingly successful, serving in many offices including consul (in 63 B.C.) and proconsul of Cilicia. Although not a member of the old urban aristocracy by birth, he soon became accepted by it. His published works are numerous, in-

Plato's *Republic* (ca. 375 B.C.) was written at the philosopher's Academy in Athens, portrayed in this Roman mosaic (Museo Nazionale, Naples). The work influenced political theorists in both Greece and Rome.

Cicero's *Republic* (54–51 B.C.) combined Greek political theory with Roman pragmatism. The two-column manuscript shown here (fourth century) was covered with another text, in small letters, in the seventh century.

cluding volumes of letters, essays on literary criticism and education, collected speeches delivered in the law courts or in the Senate, political treatises, and several philosophical works. They betray a man never quite at home with the aristocracy, a man whose principles reflect his middle-class upbringing. He believed in all the traditional Roman qualities—service to the state, loyalty to the ideal of the Republic, and high moral behavior—while at the same time he was deeply influenced by Greek culture. In his writings he was able to unify these two strains.
Rome was passing through a century of political chaos: it was Cicero's desire

to create a new order and to provide social stability. To do this he proposed a "united front" composed of men of goodwill which would prevent the extreme behavior of the revolutionaries and would counter the growth of autocratic leadership. His last philosophical work condones the murder of Caesar, and for this Cicero was murdered at the instruction of Antony.

And then if people argue that pain is the supreme evil, I cannot see what role they can assign to that other Cardinal Virtue, fortitude—seeing that this means disregard for pains and troubles. It is true that Epicurus, in his observations concerning pain, frequently displays a respect for fortitude. But such sayings lack significance beside the fundamental question: what place can fortitude logically occupy in a system which identifies good with pleasure and evil with pain?
Cicero, *On Duties* III

POSIDONIUS 135–CA. 50

Posidonius, born in Syrian Apamea, was a scientist, a philosopher, and an historian. Educated in Athens, he spent some years traveling in Africa and the western Mediterranean before settling in Rhodes to teach and study. His scientific work created a new enthusiasm for the understanding of the physical world. Little now survives except in the works of later writers, but in the fifty-

two books of his *Histories* he dealt with the events of the Roman world from 146 to the dictatorship of Sulla, giving particular emphasis to the barbarian peoples, in particular the Celts and the Germans, with whom the Romans came into contact. He believed that since the Roman empire reflected the commonwealth of God, Roman imperialism was justified.

LUCRETIUS 96–53

The poet-philosopher Lucretius is known for his one great book, *The Nature of the Universe*, a brilliant work of missionary zeal in which he presents his view of the detailed workings of the universe in terms of Epicurean philosophy. He develops the theme that all existence is composed of atoms, and thus souls as well as bodies dissolve on death. For Lucretius as for Epicurus the supreme aim of man is happiness—in the sense of freedom from disturbances such as fear and superstition.
In spite of the quality of his poetry, Lucretius was not influential in Rome, not least because his rigorous intellectual Epicureanism was more demanding than that practiced by many of those who professed to follow the teachings of Epicurus.

When human life lay groveling in all men's sight, crushed to the earth under the dead weight of superstition whose grim features loured menacingly upon mortals from the four quarters of the sky, a man of Greece was first to raise mortal eyes in defiance, first to stand erect and brave the challenge. Fables of the gods did not crush him, nor the lightning flash and the growling menace of the sky. Rather they quickened his manhood, so that he, first of all men, longed to smash the constraining locks of nature's doors.
Lucretius, *Nature of the Universe* I

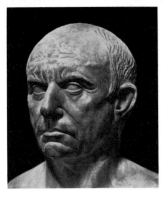

While Caesar stands guard, peace is assured, the peace
No power can break. . . .
All men shall keep good faith with the Julian
Edicts: the Cossack born by the banks of Don,
Wild Thracian, deep blue Danube drinker,
Treacherous Parthian, distant Tartar.

Horace, from *Odes* IV, 15

CATO THE YOUNGER 95–46

Marcus Porcius Cato was the great-grandson of the elder Cato, and like his illustrious ancestor he adhered rigorously to Stoicism and a belief in the old Roman principles: he was the last of the famous diehards. Intimately involved in the political events of his time, he resolutely opposed the democrats though, as tribune, he was forced to placate the mob by increasing the corn dole. Eventually in 52 he compromised his principles to some extent by siding with Pompey. After Pompey's defeat he joined the Pompeians in Africa, where he acted as a moderating force holding the rival factions together. In the aftermath of the battle of Thapsus, a resounding defeat for his cause, he committed suicide at Utica.

VIRGIL 70–19 B.C.

Publius Vergilius Maro, perhaps Rome's greatest poet, was born on a farm near Mantua in Cisalpine Gaul in 70 B.C. After receiving a broadly based education in Rome, he spent most of his life in literary pursuits in Naples. Three of his major works survive: *Eclogues*, a group of gentle pastoral poems; *Georgics*, poems dealing principally with farming matters; and the *Aeneid*, the most famous of all—a brilliant epic poem, inspired by Homer's *Odyssey*, in which he sets out to tell the tale of the journeys of Aeneas from Troy to his eventual arrival in Latium (see pages 26–27). In the *Aeneid*, Virgil was providing Rome with the story of

its legendary beginnings told in a grand epic style to rival the sagas of the early Greeks.

As a firm believer in the greatness of Rome, he saw Augustus as a savior. Augustus became his patron and in 19 B.C. they set out together to travel to Greece, but Virgil became ill and was forced to return to Brundisium, where he died.

HORACE 65–8 B.C.

Horace, a contemporary of Virgil and Livy, came from a very different background—he was the son or grandson of a slave from the provincial city of Venusia in southeast Italy. Through his poetry he was a keen observer of contemporary life, strongly supporting Augustus though in by no means a servile manner. His poetic technique was original and while he was influenced by the earlier Greek poets, he adapted and modified rather than imitated.

LIVY 59 B.C.–A.D. 17

Titus Livius was a provincial. Born in Padua, he retained his local accent throughout his life even though much of it was spent in Rome. Little is known about his life. He appears to have studied philosophy but did not, as was the custom, go to university in Greece. In Rome he remained in close contact

with the events of the day but without holding office, nor does he appear to have been a confidant of Augustus. Indeed Augustus seems to have disapproved of Livy's treatment of recent history.

His great work, which he spent most of his life writing, was the *History of Rome*, covering the period from the foundation of the city to 9 B.C. Of the 142 books of which it was composed, 35 survive.

Livy was both a pessimist and an optimist. He believed that the state of Rome as he found it was the result of moral decline, but in the Principate of Augustus he saw the beginnings of a new Golden Age. For man to aspire to these new heights he must be educated and invigorated by the study of history.

OVID 43 B.C.–A.D. 17

Ovid was born in Sulmo, in Italy, and died at Constanta on the Black Sea after nine years of exile. His principal works include the *Metamorphoses*, a retelling of many myths dealing with changes of form; the *Amores*; and the *Art of Love*. He was a poet whose work reflects the lighter, almost trivial side of Augustan high society: he writes of love, of female susceptibility, and of the mutual joy of men and women in sexual union. In one poem he criticizes the bourgeois morality of Augustus. It was probably for this that he was exiled.

REVOLUTION AND REFORM

Poverty became un urgent problem in the second century B.C. As Rome expanded her territory (taking Carthage and Corinth in 146 B.C., Numantia and Pergamum in 133), unemployed peasants crowded into the city. The corn dole, which Gaius Gracchus instituted to feed them, is illustrated in a mosaic from Ostia *(opposite)*. Grain is carried in sacks to an urn for distribution.

Left: Scales for weighing meat, detail from a relief showing a butcher shop, Ostia.

In 133 Rome was on the brink of revolution. The roots of the social discontent were deeply embedded in the past. Three principal elements may be disentangled: the great increase in the number of urban poor in the city of Rome; conflict between the new and growing middle class and the old aristocratic order; and the resentment felt by the towns of Italy which had not yet been awarded full franchise. The dreadful disruptions of the Second Punic War had done much to exacerbate these problems, for not only had the war greatly encouraged the drift of population to the city and widened the gap between rich and poor, it had forcefully demonstrated to Rome's Italian allies their second-rate position.

In the aftermath of the war new social groupings were beginning to emerge and the old distinction between patricians and plebs was blurring. The fiercely conservative aristocratic oligarchy remained, but a new middle class was emerging composed largely of traders and artisans drawn partly from the ranks of the plebs and partly from among the enfranchised immigrants. The aristocracy regarded commercial pursuits as unsuited to their status; yet the Roman state had grown to such a size that a considerable service element had to develop to maintain the workings of the system. In other words, the rise of the middle class was not only inevitable, it was essential. One of the many causes of the social upheavals of the second century was the striving of this *nouveau riche* for status and power.

The urban poor presented a more immediate problem. As a citizen body this group had rights, which it jealously guarded, and a degree of power that allowed it to influence elections and political decisions. In the hands of the unscrupulous the mob could be manipulated in the interests of personal ambition. More serious still, it was becoming increasingly parasitic on the state. Clearly the mob represented a destructive force of considerable potential.

In 133 B.C. Tiberius Gracchus was elected tribune. He was a man with a solution to Rome's social ills, he knew he was right, and with impulsive obstinacy he was determined to trample down all opposition. While traveling through Etruria, Gracchus had become impressed by the rural depopulation. All that was needed to relieve Rome's problem, he believed, was to resettle the landless mob in the countryside. In theory this was possible, for vast areas of land, annexed in the past, belonged to the state and much of this *ager publicus* was let on annual leases. But inevitably the tenants, many of whom were the large landowners, had over the years established squatters' rights. If, however, the letter of the law was obeyed, and individual holdings of public land were restricted to three hundred acres, there would be plenty for the landless citizens.

In spite of the reasoned nature of the proposals there was considerable opposition to them. Yet Tiberius Gracchus forced them through, setting up a Land Commission and arranging for the freed territory to be divided into twenty-acre plots for the new lessees. Matters came to a head when, in the face of all precedents, he announced that he intended to stand for a second year in office. Street fighting broke out between the factions, culminating in a battle in the Forum in which three hundred people including Gracchus himself were killed.

Even though the Land Commission was allowed to continue to function, and up to eighty thousand people were resettled, opposition hardened. Not only were the aristocracy upset, but so too were the Italian communities who had no rights of appeal against the decisions of the Commissioners. When one faction decided to support the Italians' case by proposing to extend the franchise to include them, the opposition quickly responded by expelling large numbers of Italians from the city. In the ensuing chaos the town of Fregellae rebelled against Rome and was immediately destroyed. Three separate group interests had now crystallized: the Senate, which was opposed to reform of any kind; the urban mob, who demanded land reform but refused to allow the franchise to be extended lest the influx of new citizens should dilute their privileges and their power; and the Italians, who wanted the grant of citizenship to protect their legitimate interests. To placate all three groups was the daunting task which the new democratic leader Gaius Gracchus, brother of Tiberius, took upon himself.

Gaius was elected tribune in 123. To secure his power base over the masses and thus to buy time to push forward his own measures, he took control of the cities' corn supplies and arranged a regular monthly dole for each citizen. While these measures were of

Gaius Gracchus was naturally turbulent and played the rogue voluntarily;
and he far surpassed the other in his gift of language. . . .
All the nobility and the senatorial party, if he had lived longer,
would have been overthrown, but, as it was,
his great power caused him to be hated even by his followers,
and he was overthrown by his own methods.

Dio Cassius, *History* XXV

highly dubious value in the long term, at least one potential source of opposition was now temporarily quieted.

Of far greater substance were his economic programs, designed to encourage trade and thus to gain credit with the Roman bourgeoisie. Communications were greatly improved. Proposals were put forward to create three new colonies, at Capua, Tarentum, and Carthage, each chosen for the great commercial possibilities of its location. To buy himself further support from his middle-class capitalist supporters Gaius Gracchus distributed the lucra-tive tax-collecting contracts in Asia among them. Clearly his intention was to build up the power and prestige of the middle classes, and in doing so to weaken the hold of the aristocracy.

When Gracchus proposed to transfer the jury courts to the middle class, the Senate could no longer have been in doubt that they were to be reduced to insignificance.

The franchise problem he decided to attack with a moderate package of compromise proposals; but opposition mounted, spurred on by senatorial supporters, and gradually the mob swung against Gracchus. When time came for the election, he was not ree-lected. In the political turmoil which followed, violence once more broke out; Gracchus was declared a public enemy, and in 121 B.C., unable to escape, he put an end to his life. In the aftermath three thousand democrats were executed.

The democratic experiment which Gracchus had tried on the Roman people had failed, and once more the Senate emerged shaken but triumphant.

THE RISE OF THE MILITARY DEMAGOGUES

The death of Gaius Gracchus in 121 effectively marked the end of the power of the tribune demagogues. But although the land reforms of the Gracchi were gradually nullified in the following years, attempts by the Senate to curb the powers of the middle class—the *equites*—were of little effect. It was now, in the closing years of the second century, that a new power emerged—the power of the generals.

To understand how this came about it is necessary to examine briefly the career of Gaius Marius. A tough and forceful man, Marius managed to engineer his own appointment to the military command of the Roman forces in Africa who at this time (112–105 B.C.) were waging war against a native chieftain, Jugurtha.

cient property to qualify for service. The result was that instead of recruiting men anxious to return to their farms, Marius was able to attract men with few ties, many already veterans who would be prepared to serve for longer periods in return for the promise of land on retirement. In this way the new army was born. Not only was it a far more effective fighting machine, but it owed unswerving allegiance to its leader since he was the soldiers' guarantee of a comfortable old age. Thus, along with the new army, a new political force, the military demagogue, came into being.

Marius won considerable military successes not only in Africa in 105 but also in 102 and 101 in major battles against the Cimbri and the Teutones, two north European tribes who had

democrats, but in the ensuing violence he found himself forced, by honoring the law, to turn against his supporters. Sickened by the turn of events, he left Rome in the following year for a tour of the east and remained out of the political arena for almost a decade.

Meanwhile the age-old problem of the enfranchisement of the Italians was rapidly coming to a head. Their demand for equal rights finally led to

Before leaving for Africa, Marius took the revolutionary step of raising his fighting force not from among the citizen farmers, which had been the traditional recruiting ground throughout the Republic, but from the poorer urban population, who under the old system would not have owned suffi-

been threatening Italy for some years. He returned to Rome in 100, a national hero, to be elected consul for the sixth time.

Once more the struggle was raging between the Senate and the democrats. Marius by virtue of his upbringing was naturally aligned with the

a war with Rome, which became known as the Social War (90–89 B.C.). It was clear to many that the only satisfactory solution was to compromise. Thus although Rome maintained military superiority, all the free-born inhabitants of Italy south of the Po were at last granted Roman

Oldest surviving copy of Sallust's *History of the Jugurthine War*, the war that changed Rome's army forever. Gaius Marius *(right)* reorganized the army at this time (107–106 B.C.), broadening its base and making it more effective in combat. The Jugurthine War also marks the beginning of Marius's rivalry with Lucius Sulla, another general who raised his own army and issued coins *(far right)*.

Below: The making of a soldier; marble relief from the Altar of Domitius Ahenobarbus (115–100 B.C.). According to one interpretation, the scenes at left follow a young man as he enrolls (far left), takes the oath, dons his uniform, and then attends the sacrifice of animals (center) in honor of Mars.

citizenship, ending one of the major areas of conflict which had bedeviled Roman history for centuries.

Two Roman generals distinguished themselves in the Social War: Marius and his aristocratic rival Sulla who had fought alongside him in Africa. Both men now had considerable followings and both were evidently anticipating lucrative appointments for themselves and their troops in the east. The Senate naturally backed the aristocrat Sulla. The democratic supporters of Marius intervened and Sulla quickly left the city to take the unprecedented step of joining his troops to lead them on Rome. Marius fled and some of his supporters were killed. It was a remarkable event: for the first time in the history of the city a standing army had been used to

Inevitably in his four-year absence there was a democratic backlash. Marius appeared on the scene again and there followed an appalling reign of terror during which virtually all the conservative elements of the Senate were murdered, property was confiscated, and mutilated bodies, we are told, littered the streets. It was at this stage, having finally regained power, that Marius died. Gradually law and order were reestablished: the democrats developed a firm hold on the city and declared Sulla to be an outlaw. As the time for Sulla's return approached, frantic preparations were made.

Eventually in the spring of 83 Sulla landed with his army at Brundisium, and in a series of successful maneuvers and campaigns, culminating in a vicious battle outside the Colline Gate

among his followers. In the end, when the horror was over, Sulla had himself appointed as dictator for an indefinite period and set about dismantling the democratic legislation of the previous century. The power of the Senate was restored, that of the tribunes was drastically curtailed, the corn dole was discontinued, three hundred conservatives were appointed to the Senate, checks were put on the rate of promotion, new courts were set up, and provincial government was completely overhauled. Sulla's constitutional reforms represent a far-reaching piece of reactionary legislation. He had made the Senate supreme once more and provided it with the tools to carry out its job. His task complete, he promptly resigned his dictatorship and retired to his country villa.

back up the political claims of its leader. Sulla, now in complete control, set about strengthening the aristocratic oligarchy by enlarging the Senate with three hundred specially chosen conservative nominees. Having thus secured his position, he set off with his troops to the east.

of Rome, he gained complete mastery. In the following months the city was seized by a plague of violence and political murder the like of which Rome had never before experienced. Thousands of people—Sulla's democratic opponents—were slaughtered and their property was redistributed

In two decades, under Marius and Sulla, Rome had for the first time experienced the power of army-backed demagogues. During this time there had been half a million political murders. This was to be the pattern for the next fifty years, until the end of the Republic.

THE NEW ARMY

Before Marius opened the ranks of the army to all Roman citizens irrespective of property qualifications, it had been essentially a militia system designed for home defense and composed of property-owning citizens called to service for a specified period in the interests of the state. Men between the ages of seventeen and forty-six were liable for call-up. Citizens, particularly those with property, had, it was believed, the duty of defending the homeland against attack. For this reason pay was kept low and was regarded more in terms of expenses than as a living wage. Indeed the cost of food and equipment provided by the state was deducted from it. But there were rewards, not least a share of any booty taken, and for many men professional warfare had its attractions. The others knew that they would be able to return home at the end of the hostilities.

The system had of course grown up for home defense, and so long as campaigns were fought in Italy it was likely to be effective. The Second Punic War brought dramatic changes. Men were now expected to serve for long periods in foreign lands, which

many were reluctant to do. Moreover, after the war the number of eligible citizens had fallen drastically as the migration to the cities swelled the ranks of the urban poor.

For the next century and a half changes were gradually made modifying the system to suit the new situation: in many ways the reforms of Marius were merely the culmination of this process. What Marius now created was a standing army of professional soldiers who were signed on for periods of sixteen to twenty years. But his reforms were more far-reaching. In the old days the legion had

fought in three lines each divided into widely spaced contingents called *maniples*. Now he created a closed fighting unit based on the *cohort*. There were ten cohorts in each legion and each cohort was divided into six *centuries* nominally of one hundred men. The effect of this change was to give the legion a greater degree of solidity and resilience in the face of unstructured barbarian onslaughts. It was also at about this time that the command structure was modified by the creation of a single *legatus* to control each legion. This replaced the far less efficient system in which the six military tribunes belonging to the legion each took command in turn.

The army reforms of Marius were therefore profound. Rome now had a professional army, but this in its turn brought problems since idle troops could be dangerous. The simplest way to keep them active was to execute or encourage wars of defense and conquest. Another spur to conquest was the need for spoils to keep the soldiers satisfied. Thus a deliberate policy of aggressive imperialism developed; it was to dominate the Roman world for three hundred years.

"Caesar withdrew to a hill close at hand and sent out his cavalry to meet the enemy's attack. In the meantime he formed up his four veteran legions in three lines halfway up the hill and posted the two recently levied in Italy on the summit with all the auxiliaries so that the whole of the hillside above him was occupied with troops. The baggage and packs he ordered to be collected in one place, and defense works to be dug around them by the veterans posted in the top line."

Caesar's deployment of his army at Bibracte in 58 B.C. to face the Helvetii (from his *Commentaries on the Gallic War* I, 24). At right, an artist's concept of the scene, from a Swiss engraving (of the late eighteenth century). The artist has placed the two newer legions, the auxiliaries, and baggage wagons at the top left; the veteran legions are shown in three rows in the middle; and Caesar appears in the bottom right-hand corner, on foot, ready to lead the army into battle.

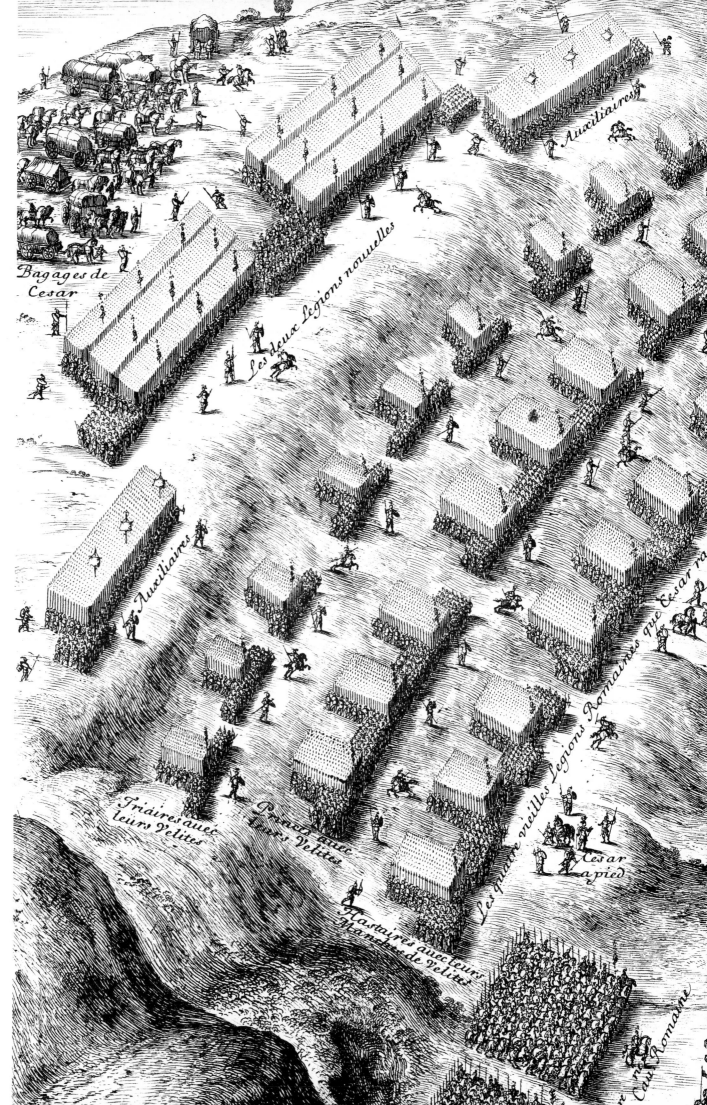

Bagages de Cesar

Auxiliaires

Les deux Legions nouuelles

Auxiliaires

Les quatre vieilles Legions Romaines que Cesar ran...

Triaires auec leurs Velites

Princes auec leurs Velites

Hastaires auec leurs Tranche de Velites

Cesar a pied

...e Gaule Romaine

THE PROBLEMS OF EXPANSION

*In Rome itself there were most alarming revolutionary tendencies—
the result of the unequal distribution of wealth. . . .
Money had accumulated in the hands of people whose families were unknown
and of no account. So only a spark was needed
to set everything on fire and, since the whole state was rotten within itself,
it was in the power of any bold man to overthrow it.*

Plutarch

The creation of an empire and the social and economic changes that resulted from it brought problems which could only be alleviated by further imperial growth—Rome had now passed the point of no return. After the Second Punic War the population of Rome had dramatically increased. The city was like a magnet and people flocked in from the countryside of Italy. One immediate effect was that the state now had to make food available to provide for the urban population who, almost by definition, were no longer food-producers themselves. Grain could, for the most part, be imported from the new provinces, first from Sicily and later in enormous quantities from Africa and Egypt. Much of the other food was produced in Italy, but clearly unless the farming system was reorganized, the vastly increased consumer market could not be satisfied. The traditional yeoman farm-

Signs of the accumulation of private wealth. *Above:* A perfectly preserved hoard of silver coins found in Sicily. *Right:* Pompeian banker and speculator Lucius Caecilius, whose home was filled with tablets recording rent receipts.

er of the old days was concerned to produce sufficient for his own needs. What was needed now was a new system geared to yielding a large surplus. Thus a farming revolution took place.

Estates were greatly increased in size (partly resulting from and partly encouraging the migration from the land), and they were now run by their absentee aristocratic owners for maximum production and profit. The elder Cato, in his book *De Agri Cultura*, gives hardheaded advice to the aristoc-

racy on how to make their estates profitable. They should, he said, concentrate on producing olives, grapes, and vegetables, not grain. An olive grove of 160 acres could be run by thirteen slaves; a vineyard of 60 acres required sixteen slaves. In short the only way to produce at the

Coinage increased with Rome's territorial expansion, as each province received its own money. The examples at right come from diverse points in the empire.

Denarius, 40 B.C.: the lighthouse of Messana, in Sicily.

required levels was by exploiting cheap labor in the form of slaves—of which the wars of defense and of conquest had provided a ready supply. In 176 B.C., for example, when the Romans crushed a revolt in Sardinia, eighty thousand inhabitants were killed or captured. One can be sure that a reasonable percentage reached the slave markets.

As Rome became a slave-consuming society—some might say because of economic necessity—so the temptation must have been to engage in slave-producing exploits. Up to the time of the battle of Zama (202) one could argue a degree of legitimacy about Rome's military activities. After that the profit motive of imperialism was ever present.

In the city the landless urban population was now engaged in various kinds of production and services. So long as the consumer market was being increased—by providing for the war machine, by the need for new buildings and engineering works in

Towards the end of the Republic, Italy relied increasingly on food importation, especially from Africa. In this wall painting from Ostia, a grain ship is being packed for transport to Italy. The large Italian estates were converted from grain production to the more profitable olives, grapes, and vegetables.

the city and its neighborhood, and by satisfying the growing sophistication of the urban population itself—there was enough work to keep the city dwellers employed and quiet. But as soon as population growth outstripped the demand for labor, a crisis would result, such as occurred in the late second century B.C. when the Gracchi attempted to alleviate unrest by providing subsidized food and by the redistribution of land in order to disperse the surplus population.

The growing economic complexity of the Republic required reorganization to facilitate exchange and commerce. used to pay soldiers and to facilitate exchange at home market level, it was also essential in trade with overseas states. The growth of the money supply led inevitably to the emergence of professional bankers, money lenders, and traders who constituted the more wealthy element in the increasingly

Denarius, 56 B.C.: the temple in Eryx, Sicily.

Denarius, 83 B.C.: elephant with bells, north Italy.

Denarius, 80 B.C.: flagon, north Italy.

Denarius, 83 B.C.: eagle and standards, Gaul.

Quinarius, 29 B.C.: victory and palm branch, "Asia Recepta."

Rome's territory by the year 100 B.C. nearly encircled the Mediterranean, and the city's dependence on its empire was by now evident, culturally as well as economically. The presence of a Greek tutor (as below), who was also a slave, became common in wealthy households.

It was as late as 269 B.C. that Rome issued her first regular coinage, which was modeled on the coinage of the south Greek cities with whom it was intended to be used. Thereafter coinage became common. Not only was it powerful middle class. The problems which the late Republic had to face, then, were in essence concerned with the readjustment of society to contain the rapidly expanding economic system.

THE SUCCESSION OF POWER 88–31 B.C.

The first century B.C. saw the rise of military demagogues. Before then military commanders had come forward when the state required them and had retired once their task was over. With Marius all this changed. Personal ambition was now backed by military power and the laws of the Republic could be flouted whenever it was thought to be expedient.

Armies, who now owed their allegiance to their commanders, thought nothing of slaughtering their own people if required to do so. In the ensuing chaos powerful men combined to impose their will upon the state. The First Triumvirate brought Pom-

pey, Caesar, and Crassus together. Antony, Octavian, and Lepidus formed the Second Triumvirate. Gradually Rome slipped into a civil war which was to rage across the Mediterranean world from 49 to 30 B.C. One by one, aspiring leaders were killed off by their competitors until one man—Octavian—remained. As the first emperor, Augustus, he was to reform Rome's constitution totally and unite the Empire once more.

155–86 B.C. MARIUS

Gaius Marius came to power in 107, when he was elected consul and appointed to head the war in Africa. With his thoroughly reorganized army he achieved great success, capturing Jugurtha in 105, and in the next few years led his army against the Cimbri and Teutones, who were threatening Provence and northern Italy; he destroyed them successively in two great battles in 102 (Aix-en-Provence) and 101 (Vercellae). His sixth consulship (100), spent in Rome, required of him a degree of skill and diplomacy which he evidently did not possess.

In the Social War he served with distinction but was retired in 89 and passed over in favor of his rival Sulla when the new command against the king of Pontus was being considered. Furious at the insult, Marius seized power but was driven out by Sulla and was forced to flee to Africa. But as soon as Sulla had left for the east, he returned to initiate a vicious campaign of massacres against all who had opposed him. He died in 86.

Although undoubtedly a soldier of some brilliance, Marius lacked political skill. In resorting to violence when thwarted by political rivals, he set a precedent for the years to come.

138–78 SULLA

Lucius Cornelius Sulla was an aristocrat and a soldier. He served with distinction as a quaestor under Marius in Africa, and it was here that the animosity between the two men began to develop. During the Social War (90–89) he gained significant successes and was elected to be consul in 88, but in the face of violent opposition by Marius, was forced to use his army to provide support—the first time that the army had been used in this way in Rome.

From 87 to 84 he conducted a successful campaign against Mithridates in the east and returned to Italy in 83 to reestablish his position, and that of the aristocratic party, in the face of democratic dominance. To do this it was necessary for him to fight

his way through Italy to the gates of Rome. In the autumn of 83 he entered the city and at once began the systematic extermination of all influential democrats. In 81 he had himself appointed dictator for an indefinite period and immediately set about far-reaching constitutional reforms which firmly reestablished the power of the Senate and the aristocracy. In the next year, his task complete, he retired to obscurity.

Throughout his life he was known to be a man of contradictions and excesses. His callousness in his public life was matched only by overindulgence in his private affairs.

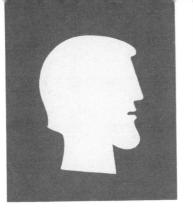

The generals had risen by violence rather than by merit. They needed armies to fight one another rather than the public enemy.

Plutarch

106–48 POMPEY

115–53 CRASSUS

100–44 JULIUS CAESAR

Gnaeus Pompeius was a soldier of considerable ability who had distinguished himself under Sulla's command. A superb organizer and brilliant leader, he was somewhat unimaginative and undecided in his political dealings.

His first major command came in 77 when he was sent to Spain to put down a revolt. After a spell in Rome (serving as consul with Crassus in 70) he was given the unprecedented command of ridding the Mediterranean of pirates (67)—a task he completed with spectacular success in seven weeks, returning to Rome as a hero. The next year he was sent to the east to control Cilicia, Bithynia, and Asia, where he won new territory for Rome. On his return to Italy he disbanded his army and joined with Crassus and Caesar to form the First Triumvirate.

Inactivity and political intrigue in Rome did not suit him, but in the rapidly deteriorating political situation, it was now dangerous to leave. When in 56 he was awarded the governorship of Spain for five years, he chose to rule by proxy from Rome.

From 54 the partnership between Caesar and Pompey began to break down, Pompey becoming a staunch supporter of the senatorial party while Caesar remained an avid democrat. Eventually, to counter Caesar's growing power, a law was passed which would have had the effect of ending his Gallic command in 49. In the armed confrontation which ensued Caesar marched on Rome while Pompey together with his supporters crossed to Greece.

In 48 in the vicinity of Dyrrhachium Caesar blockaded Pompey, whose forces were routed, Pompey himself escaping to Egypt where he was murdered.

Left: *Coin (ca. 75 B.C.) showing Mithridates VI of Pontus, conquered by Sulla.* Right: *Gladiator-slave uprising under Spartacus, 73 B.C., suppressed by Crassus.*

M. Licinius Crassus served under Sulla as a young lieutenant, and during the Sullan purge of the democrats he created the basis of a personal fortune by buying up property at a very cheap rate. When, in 73, a slave revolt terrorized much of southern Italy, Crassus was appointed with six legions to clear the menace. This he did effectively, crucifying six thousand slaves along the Appian Way. Crassus was clever, sharp-witted, and totally unscrupulous —a perfect foil for the well-meaning Pompey with whom he allied himself. In 70 the two men became consuls together, spending their year in office restoring the constitution to its pre-Sullan democratic form. He remained in the political arena in Rome, wielding the power of his

great wealth, and he and Pompey agreed to back Caesar for the consulship, creating a power block which became known as the First Triumvirate (60).

In 54 he went as proconsul to Syria, using this post as a base from which to campaign beyond the Euphrates, no doubt in search of military glory, but in 53 in the aftermath of a disastrous defeat at Carrhae at the hands of the Parthians, he was killed.

Magnetic, generous, determined, ruthless, opportunist, Caesar was a remarkable man, who, born in the chaos of the disintegrating Republic, used his extraordinary powers of leadership to underpin the crumbling edifice and to ease it towards a more stable future. Before his consulship of 59 B.C. Caesar had been well schooled. Narrowly escaping from Sulla's reign of terror, he had sailed to Asia to undertake studies and various minor diplomatic duties and was later appointed as quaestor in Spain, which he found to be an excellent place to test his military abilities. His return to Rome in 60 brought him once more into the political arena where, with Crassus and Pompey, he established the First Triumvirate—a power base from which to launch a number of constitutional reforms. To further his career he needed spectacular military successes to match those of Pompey. Accordingly he cajoled the Senate into giving him command of Cisalpine Gaul (northern Italy) and Gallia Narbonensis (southern Gaul) for a period of five years; here if anywhere would be scope for his military talents. Moreover such a command provided him with the legitimate means of creating a large army and keeping it under his personal control. Caesar's brilliant successes in Gaul, Britain, and Germany will be described later (pp. 180–181); his prestige, broadcast through his own commentaries on the wars, grew to phenomenal proportions. Meanwhile in Rome fear of Caesar was growing and political opposition to his democratic policies hardened, particularly after Pompey was persuaded to support the senatorial cause. As Caesar's period of appointment neared its end, an act was passed which meant that once his command had terminated he would not be eligible for reelection: in March 49 he would be without a post or an army. The strength of the opposition to him was further emphasized when Marcel-

lus, a consul in 51, proposed that Caesar's Gallic command should be terminated within two years; thereafter he would no longer be immune from prosecution. From a safe distance Caesar attempted to negotiate to protect his position, but in 49 the Senate passed a motion which stated that unless he retired at the appropriate time he would be declared a public enemy. The tribunes (Antony and Cassius) immediately vetoed the measure, but the Senate overrode them. This was an unconstitutional act contrary to democratic government, which Caesar could now exploit to give a degree of legitimacy to his own actions.

On 11 January in 49 B.C. he crossed the River Rubicon, and marched with his army into Italy;

The elder Caesar, from a Renaissance relief. Rivals, fearing his growing power, assassinated him in 44 B.C.

at the news, the opposition fled. Caesar was left in sole control of Rome, a position which he rapidly consolidated by appointing his trusted supporters to key positions.

Further afield, however, in Spain, Africa, and the east there was considerable opposition to him. In a single rapid campaign in Spain he gained control of the west, and at the beginning of the next year (48 B.C.) he landed on the coast of Epirus intent on destroying the opposition led by Pompey. In the ensuing battle

93

Pompey escaped to Egypt, and when Caesar followed him there a little later, Pompey's head was presented to him. He left (July 47) to put down troubles in Asia, but by September he was back in Italy dealing with a financial crisis and placating mutinous troops before sailing to Africa (December 47) to destroy more Pompeian forces at Thapsus. Back in Rome in July 46, he was initiating widespread reforms before leaving in December for Spain, where at Munda in March 45 the last of the Pompeian resistance was quashed. It was a remarkable whirlwind of activity which totally destroyed all military opposition. He was now firmly in charge of the entire Roman world.

In Rome, having been awarded dictatorial powers for life, Caesar proceeded with his sweeping reforms. He worked with his accustomed energy and thorough-

ness, but many felt they could now detect the signs of growing megalomania. A conspiracy to rid Rome of the tyrant soon took root, and on 15 March in 44 B.C. Caesar was stabbed to death.

Above: *One of the assassins, Marcus Brutus (85–42 B.C.), on a coin of 42 B.C.*

Cleopatra enters Rome, 46 B.C.: fresco (about 1750) by Tiepolo. The queen was involved first with Caesar, later with Antony.

Marcus Antonius was a supporter of Julius Caesar. In 49 when Caesar marched on Rome and took control, Antony was rewarded by an appointment which assigned to him the defense of Italy. In 44 B.C. it was Antony, now consul, who offered Caesar the crown which he publicly refused. After Caesar's death later in the year, Antony managed to swing the crowd against the conspirators and to take firm control of the situation, securing for himself authority to take over Cisalpine Gaul (northern Italy) where Decimus Brutus commanded a military force. Immediately he was out of Rome, however, senatorial opposition to him hardened, encouraged by Cicero's polemics, and in the ensuing conflict, Antony was beaten. He immediately fled westwards to join Lepidus, governor of Gallia Narbonensis.

This was the situation when Octavian, who had led the opposition against him, proposed that, together with Lepidus, they should form the Second Triumvirate dedicated to "reestablishing the commonwealth." In the rash of political murders which followed, Cicero was killed and a little later at Philippi in Macedonia the last significant opposition, led by Cassius and Brutus, was crushed by the triumvirs (42). Meeting at Brundisium in 40 B.C., Antony and Octavian agreed to a division in their spheres of influence. This allowed Antony to operate in the east, where he soon became entangled with Cleopatra and undertook a series of disastrous campaigns in Armenia (36). Meanwhile Octavian, having established his own base in the west, persuaded the Senate to deprive Antony of his powers as a triumvir. In the struggle Antony and Cleopatra were defeated at the naval battle of Actium (31) and fled to Egypt, where they both committed suicide a year later.

Octavian was eighteen in 44 B.C. when his great-uncle Julius Caesar was murdered, bequeathing to him his name and fortune—an act which was clearly designed to give Octavian the right of succession. Yet it took him fourteen years of scheming and conflict before the ground was cleared of opponents and he could take his place as sole commander of the Empire.

His skills of political manipulation were remarkable even for the age. Throughout he maintained control of the Senate, and realizing his need for support, he soon created a working relationship with Antony, his only serious rival; together they removed the rest of the opposition. After the treaty of Brundisium in 40 B.C. he established himself in the west, gradually consolidating his own position at home. The final act, the removal of Antony, was stage-managed with skill and precision. Octavian was now in sole charge of the Roman world.

Octavian inherited the name Caesar, as this coin shows. Issued in 29–27 B.C., it depicts a triumphal arch with Octavian driving the quadriga of victory.

THE CULMINATION OF THE REPUBLIC

But, I must believe, it was
already written in the book of fate
that this great city of ours
should arise, and the first steps be taken
to the founding of the mightiest
empire the world has known.

Livy

800–350 B.C. The emergence of the city of Rome to a preeminent position complete by ca. 500 B.C. Thereafter expansion in Italy (in league with Latin cities) and wars against Volscians and Etruscans and neighboring hill tribes. The influx of Celts from the north soon after 400 puts a temporary halt to expansion, but the main force of the Celtic attack had wasted by 350.

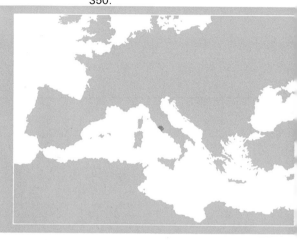

By any standards it is fair to say that the Roman world grew at an astonishing rate under the Republic. More surprisingly still, the vast bulk of the territorial gains were made in little over a century, in the period 241–133 B.C. Clearly the reasons for such an expansion are complex and interwoven.

The character of the Romans themselves was undoubtedly a significant factor; the solid morality of the early years and the self-assured aggression of the later Republic singly and in

man people themselves in the story of expansion, one should not underestimate the other forces which were also at work. Population growth, sometimes at a very rapid rate, was occurring in many areas of the Mediterranean world at this time, forcing communities to expand and to compete for territory. In such a situation the rates of economic and social change cannot have failed to increase, creating a new momentum difficult to reverse. Not surprisingly the conflicts, which led to the acquisition of Rome's

combination played their part. Important, too, were the early stages of development under Etruscan domination which left Rome with both an effective constitution, flexible enough to expand to meet new situations, and a solid military tradition, rooted in the citizen body, which was molded and consolidated for several centuries in the defense of the state. Thus endowed, Rome was able to meet and survive the onslaught of the Gaulish barbarians on the one hand and demands for social reform on the other. Adaptability, improvisation, and a thoroughly pragmatic approach were among the strengths upon which Rome's greatness was based.

While it is correct to stress the importance of the characteristics of the Ro-

Rome's great warrior dynasty, the Scipios, traced their glory to Cornelius Lucius Scipio "Barbatus," hero of the third Samnite war (d. 273 B.C.). His tomb inscription on the Appian Way reads in part: "A strong and wise man . . . he was consul, censor, and aedile, defeated Taurasia and Cisauna in Samnium, and conquered all of Lucaria."

Below: Minerva shield, from the Capitolium.

first overseas territories, took place in the highly populated and urbanized region of Sicily; as a result Rome found herself in charge of the island, knowing that to maintain peace and to safeguard her own commercial concerns her permanent presence was needed. The same logic was used when, a little later, Sardinia and Corsica were annexed.

The next major clash, the Second Punic War, was altogether more serious. Once more commercial reasons were paramount, but the struggle with Hannibal was a fight to the death between two powerful rivals: the western Mediterranean was too small for both. Rome's eventual victory in 202 left her in control of a large new territory in Spain, which varied

350–264 Rome expands south into Campania. This leads to wars with the Samnites (343–341, 327–304, 299–290) and with the Latin allies (340). Much of the south now comes under Roman control. The war against Pyrrhus (282–275) centered on southern Italy adds considerably to Rome's prestige. Many colonies are founded in Italy.

264–218 The first war with Carthage (264–241) leaves Rome in control of southern Italy and Sicily. Sardinia is annexed in 239 and later made a province with Corsica in 227. Corcyra and the adjacent Adriatic coast becomes a Roman protectorate. Meanwhile the Gauls settled in the north of Italy are driven back after battles at Telamon (225) and Mediolanium (222).

218–128 Massive expansion. Second Punic War (218–202) brings the Iberian coast under Rome: the provinces of Hither and Further Spain created in 197. Wars with Macedonia (200–196, 172–167) add territory in the Balkans; Roman presence in Asia Minor is strengthened in 133 when the kingdom of Pergamum is bequeathed. Third Punic War (149–146) adds Africa to the empire.

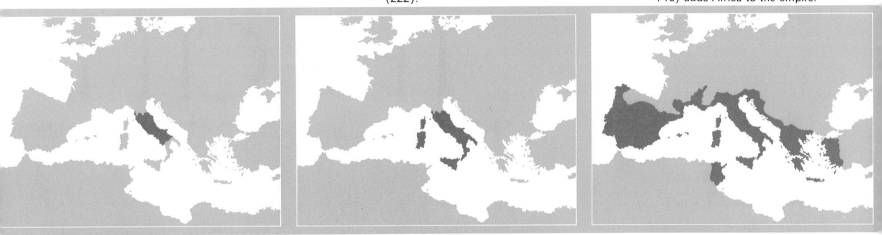

considerably from area to area in level of civilization and degree of subservience to its new conquerors. To quit Spain would have left the country open once more to Carthaginian infiltration. Accordingly in 197 two provinces were created, leaving the cities with autonomous rights. Rome was now committed, but it was not until 133 that the major unruly elements of the barbarian hinterland were finally subdued.

We have discussed elsewhere (p. 69) the effects of the Second Punic War on Roman social and economic development. Attitudes had now hardened and a new aggressive individualism was emerging. More to the point, Rome was now being seen by some of the eastern Mediterranean states as a power which could be used to good effect in the political and military arena. The Greek states' cry for help in 200 and the subsequent clever use which Pergamum made of Rome in her struggle for power with the Macedonians and with Antiochus bear witness to Rome's willingness to be drawn into squabbles which did not directly concern her. Why was she prepared to join these eastern conflicts? Financial gain, no doubt; fear of the growing power of the eastern

demagogues, this was certainly so; but there was another factor—a mixture of pride and a sense of duty. The gods had made Rome powerful; it was necessary therefore for her to respond to reasonable requests for help—it was her destiny.

For a half-century or so Rome found herself drawn into eastern wars but with no discernible desire for territorial gain. By the middle of the second century, however, a noticeable change had taken place. In a fit of ruthless arrogance, born perhaps of success, she destroyed two great and ancient cities, Carthage and Corinth.

As a result of these wars Rome acquired the provinces of Africa, Macedonia, and Achaea. A few years later the gift of the kingdom of Pergamum added another—Asia—and the empire now stretched around all sides of the Mediterranean.

An empire of this magnitude brought with it its own problems. Not least it had to be manned and maintained, which frequently meant that powerful military leaders, heading large armies, were needed to keep the peace in far-flung territories out of easy reach of the Senate. Then in the first century B.C. the provinces took on a new aspect: they became convenient theaters

in which aspiring politico-military leaders like Sulla, Pompey, and Caesar could display their talents to the awe and wonder of an admiring metropolitan populace. It was in Africa, Spain, Macedonia, and the east that the more decisive acts of the late Republican drama were played out. As a result, between 100 B.C. and Caesar's death in 44, Rome's territory almost doubled in extent.

Thus within the space of just over one hundred years (146–44) Rome had become master of an empire. It remained for Augustus, the first emperor, to devise a satisfactory system to govern it.

Next to the Immortals, Augustus most honored the memory of those citizens who had raised the Roman people from small beginnings to their present glory; which was why he restored many public buildings erected by men of this caliber, complete with their original dress, in the twin colonnades of his Forum. Then he proclaimed: "This has been done to make my fellow-citizens insist that both I (while I live), and my successors, shall not fall below the standard set by those great men of old." Suetonius

THE IDEA OF THE CITY

A city's public buildings serve three purposes: defense, religion, and convenience. To ward off hostile attack, we must defend the city with walls, towers, and gates. For the sake of religion, we plan shrines and sacred temples to the immortal gods. For convenience, we arrange public sites for general use—harbors, open spaces, colonnades, theaters, promenades, baths, and all amenities for like purpose. All must be carried out with strength, utility, grace.

Vitruvius

Imperial Rome, with the Circus Maximus and emperors' palaces in the foreground, looking north towards the Colosseum. From a model of the city (1:250) by Italo Gismondi, Museo della Civiltà Romana.

Opposite: The goddess Roma holds the world in her hand: statue, first century A.D., on the Capitol. The coin above shows Roma in a similar pose bearing an effigy of the emperor Antoninus Pius (A.D. 138–161) in her outstretched hand.

To understand the meaning of a city it is necessary to focus not so much on the buildings themselves as upon the functions they performed. A city, above all, provided a range of services for its territory. It was therefore essentially a physical manifestation of the social and economic forces at work in a community; it provided a focus for government and a structure within which all the diverse activities of a society could take place. At an early stage in the integration of a nonurban society, the coming together of dispersed communities was often centered around a common religious ceremony. On such occasions there would have been an opportunity for people to meet and exchange ideas, to establish treaties and agreements, to find wives, and of course to relax, compete, and trade. Once these activities became formalized in architecture, temples, marketplaces, and theaters would emerge.

A successful focal point of this kind would gradually encourage the establishment of a resident population to serve its various activities. Surplus could then be used to support full-time manufacturers and thus a city would be born, developing its own rules and regulations and establishing the rights and privileges of its own residents.

Once small urban communities had begun to develop in this organic manner, the impetus would be difficult to halt until an equilibrium was reached. In Greece it was the city-state, in Etruria a confederation of towns, but in Rome it went much further: Rome became a megalopolis dominating an empire.

In the following pages we take apart the Roman concept of the city and look at each of the elements which made up the whole. A ruined aqueduct or an amphitheater may be fascinating and emotive in their own right, but seen in relation to each other, and more particularly in the context of the community they served, they can be made to live again.

THE ROOTS
OF THE ROMAN CITY

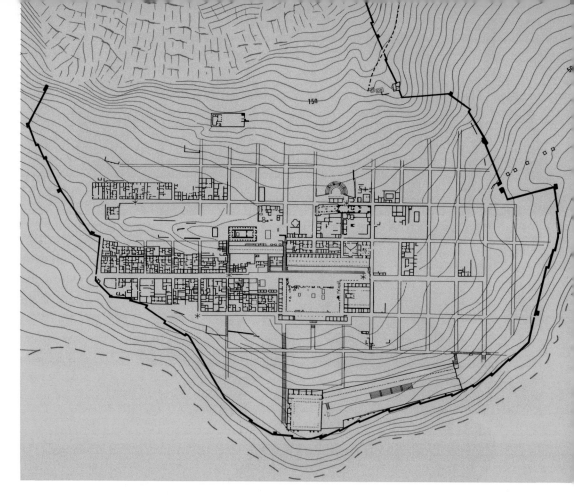

Cities did not appear in the Mediterranean area before the Greeks. Earlier, in the Mycenaean-Minoan world, populations had began to cluster together under the protection of citadels or around palace centers, and while many of the functions of urban life can already be discerned, ordered planning which belies civic organization does not make its appearance until the eighth or seventh century. Then it is among the Greek settlements of western Anatolia (Turkey) that the first true cities can be dimly recognized. Significantly this area is the homeland of the famous architect

The Greek model: Priene, in Anatolia (Turkey), rebuilt around 350 B.C. on a strict rectilinear plan typical of the period and region. The streets become stairways in some places, in order to adhere to the grid pattern despite the hilly terrain. Greek colonies in southern Italy followed this type of plan, while Rome and the Etruscan cities were irregularly laid out, with curved and zigzagging streets.

At left are three sites of Priene, as seen today (*upper row*), and as they originally looked (*lower row*).

Far left: The theater, facing south.

Center: Arched gateway at the eastern entrance to the marketplace or Agora.

Left: The *Bouleuterion*, or council meeting hall, a tiered chamber with 640 seats facing an altar at center. It is located at the northeast corner of the marketplace.

Hippodamus of Miletus who, according to Aristotle, invented the rigorous checkerboard city plan which from the mid-fifth century B.C. was widely adopted in the Greek world. At Miletus Hippodamus laid out the city afresh soon after 466 B.C., and at the request of Pericles he imposed his system on Piraeus. A few years later he sailed with the Athenian colonists to

Thurii in southern Italy where, according to the historian Diodorus, "they divided the city lengthwise by four streets... and breadthwise they divided it by three streets... and since the blocks formed by these streets were filled with dwellings the city had a well-built appearance."

In this way the Hippodamian system was introduced to Italy. In the Greek

south, orderly planning was attempted wherever possible, while in the Etruscan north, a land of more rugged hills, slopes were allowed to control the form of the city and crooked streets became the norm.

While Rome remained a city of winding lanes, it was not backward in seizing upon the ordered Greek model for its colonies. Paestum, the

terracing and retaining walls, for the most part uncommon among early Greek cities, were techniques well known to the Etruscans. From them the Romans learned well, adapting and modifying as they went. But the arch, perhaps the greatest architectural innovation of the classical world, was substantially a Roman development—a development forced on them by the rugged nature of the landscape in which they lived. How else were roads and water supplies for cities to be taken across gorges and steep val-

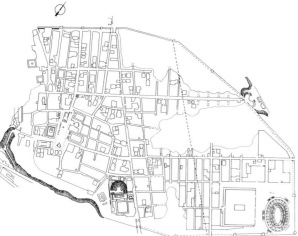

Top: In their new cities the Romans followed a regular plan based on the Greek-Anatolian model. Aerial view of Timgad (present-day Algeria), built around A.D. 100.

Above: Plan of ancient Pompeii. Its haphazard older sections (to the left) contrast with the straight lines of the new suburbs (right).

old Greek town on the Bay of Salerno, was refounded as a Roman colony in 273 B.C., and it is probably to this phase that its regular street plan belongs, sitting rather awkwardly across the alignment of the earlier Greek temples which still dominate the site today. Pompeii fared rather differently. Here the nucleus of the somewhat irregular town was retained

as the urban center while new suburban zones were laid out to the north and east in blocks surveyed with less accuracy than those of Paestum. The impression given is of piecemeal development rather than the imposition of an overall plan.

By the first century B.C. the Greek-style town plan, to some extent modified by Roman military ideas, was being widely adopted, particularly in the foundation of new cities, the *coloniae*. At Carthage, for example, one hundred years after its destruction, and following an abortive attempt by Gracchus to settle veterans there, Caesar founded Colonia Julia—a vast city laid out according to a very strict plan which was imposed without deviation upon a broken, hilly landscape. The regularity of schemes such as this clearly appealed to the Roman sense of order. From the first century onwards almost every new *colonia* to be founded was based on a grid system.

Roman urban architecture and engineering owed much to its Etruscan origins. Large-scale public works such as sewers, storage systems, roads, water, bridge building, and the use of

Military headquarters building in Lambaesis (in present-day Algeria), a late city that developed out of a Roman garrison. The fort was founded between A.D. 123 and 129; it became a town after 161 and was later made capital of the province of Numidia. Many of the Empire's cities developed in the same manner, having been founded as forts.

leys? Once the mathematics of the arch had been mastered, the technique of vaulting using concrete was soon to follow. It was this, perhaps, more than any other invention, that was to transform the face of the city. The way was now open for the creation of such architectural masterpieces as the Pantheon in Rome and later the Hagia Sophia in Istanbul.

THE CENTER OF THE WORLD

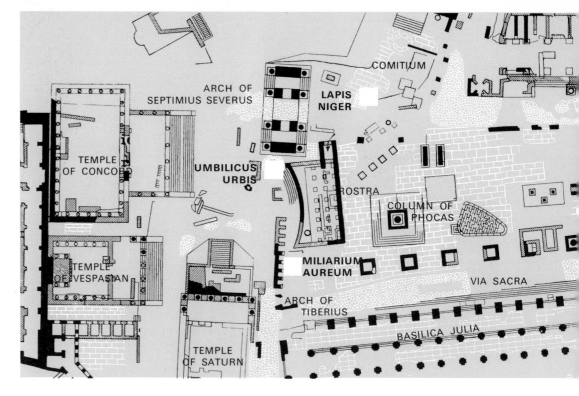

The heart of Rome, in the period of the Empire. This plan shows the center of the Forum Romanum, the city's foremost religious, financial, and governmental center. A more detailed plan of the Forum appears on page 125.

To call Rome the center of the world is no idle exaggeration, for it was here that the power lay and to Rome all contenders for leadership had eventually to come. Sulla and Marius had both used force to possess the city, and Caesar had followed their unconstitutional lead some years later when in danger of being outlawed. Once Caesar controlled Rome, however, there were rumors that he was considering shifting his power base to Alexandria, but nothing came of them. Augustus, for his part, was evidently well content with Rome as the Empire's capital.

By the beginning of the Empire Rome was an ancient settlement: its hills had been in continuous occupation for almost a thousand years. For the more historically minded citizen, every corner of the city must have been redolent with association—the Old Rostra, where stood the column fitted with the beaks of ships captured in Rome's first great naval battle against the Carthaginians in 260 B.C.; the New Rostra, where Antony had Cicero's head and right hand exhibited for all to see; and the statue of Pompey in the hall next to Pompey's Theater, where Caesar's bleeding body had fallen.

Above left: The Umbilicus Romae—the Navel of Rome. The circular brick base, at the back of the Rostra in the Forum Romanum, was built to support a cone-shaped object which symbolized the center of Rome. The idea, Greek in origin, may well have been long established in Rome, but the existing structure was probably built in the early third century A.D.

Above: The Miliarium Aureum—Golden Milestone—was erected close to the southwest corner of the Rostra. It was a marble column, encased in bronze and inscribed in gold letters, erected by Augustus in 20 B.C. when he took over the maintenance of roads throughout the Empire. On it were recorded the distances between Rome and all the major cities of the Empire.

Left: The Lapis Niger—an enigmatic monument on the edge of the Forum Romanum—consists of a pavement of black marble beneath which lay a number of objects including a rectangular block of stone inscribed in early Latin recording ritual law. It probably dates from the late sixth century B.C.

Right: Coin showing the ancient Temple of Jupiter Capitoline, originally erected in the sixth century B.C. and often rebuilt, one of Rome's most important early temples.

Right bottom: Modern artist's view of the Roman Forum looking towards the Capitoline Hill. Right foreground: Arch of Septimius Severus. Center: the temples of Saturn, of Vespasian, and of Concord. At top: the Tabularium.

The site of the city—a matter which calls for the most careful consideration of a founder who wishes to set up a state that will long endure—was chosen by Romulus with almost unbelievable foresight.... With admirable prudence he realized that maritime sites are by no means the most advantageous for cities founded in the hope of permanence and empire, firstly, because cities so placed are exposed not merely to numerous dangers, but also to those that cannot be foreseen.... I believe, Romulus foresaw that this city would provide a visiting place and a home for a world empire: for certainly no city placed in any other part of Italy could more readily have wielded such great authority as Rome.

Cicero, *On the Republic*

One may say that the earlier Romans cared little for the beauty of their city, since they were preoccupied with other, more utilitarian measures. But later generations—and especially those of the modern age and our own times—have by no means fallen short on this score, but have filled the city with many and splendid endowments of their munificence. For example, Pompey, the late Julius Caesar, Augustus, his friends and sons, his wife and sister have surpassed all others in their zeal for building and willingness to meet its expenses....
Again if one should go to the Old Forum, and see one Forum after another ranged beside it, with their basilicas and temples, and then see the Capitol and the great works of art on it, and the Palatine, and the Porticus of Livia, it would be easy to forget the world outside. Such, then, is Rome.

Strabo, *Geography*

From my own home, I turn to the sights of splendid Rome, and in my mind's eye I survey them all. Now I remember the fora, the temples, the theaters covered with marble, the colonnades where the ground has been leveled—now the grass of the Campus Martius and the views over noble gardens, the lakes, the waterway, the Aqua Virgo...

Ovid, *Letters from Pontus*

First settlements, during the Bronze Age, attested by remains of pottery and dwellings.

550–510 B.C. Legendary date for construction of the first Temple of Jupiter Capitoline, under kings Tarquinius Priscus and Tarquinius Superbus.

133 Death of Tiberius Gracchus during rioting on the Capitol.

83 The most important buildings on the Capitol destroyed by fire. Reconstruction until 69. The architect Lucius Cornelius is mentioned in a contemporary written document as one of those responsible for reconstruction.

42 B.C.–A.D. 69 Under Caesar, and especially under Augustus, the Forum is extended and its political significance grows, while religious ceremonies are consistently encouraged by political leaders. Provincial cities copy the basic design of the Forum and Capitol for their own urban centers.

A.D. 69 Following Nero's death, a war of succession, between supporters of Vespasian and Vitellius takes place on the Capitol. Most houses are burned.

80 Restoration under Titus is hardly completed when a new fire reduces the area to rubble.

81 Reconstruction under Domitian. Many ruins survive from this period, especially the Portico of the Consenting Gods and the Temple of Vespasian, on the slope adjoining the Forum.

98–117 Under Trajan the Empire reaches its greatest extension. According to old Roman tradition, foreign gods also receive sanctuaries. The area of the Forum and the Capitol becomes at this time the religious and political hub of the world.

330 Constantinople becomes Christian capital of the Empire, in deliberate opposition to heathen Rome.

410 Goths under Alaric seize and plunder Rome. Capitol partly destroyed.

500 Emperor Theodoric spends a half-year in Rome and has a law passed forbidding the plundering of ruined areas of the Capitol and the Forum.

ca. 700 A Greek community settles in the area of the Forum Boarium (near the Tiber) and becomes the center of the city. Rome is controlled by the Papacy. Nearly all the medieval rulers decorate their palaces and churches with stone fragments from the ancient Forum.

1143 The people, with the help of a group of nobles, seize the Capitol and restore the Senate to power there. Rome becomes a Commune comparable to other Italian cities of the period.

1398 Pope Boniface IX abolishes the Commune and places a defensive dike around the Capitol.

1478 The old market is removed from the Capitol.

1538 The square on the Capitol is adorned with the equestrian statue of Marcus Aurelius, a work created during the Empire and located heretofore in the Lateran Palace. The Capitol remains a political center in name, although the city continues to be ruled by the popes.

1590 Renovation of the Senatorial Palace on the Capitol; completion of work begun earlier under Michelangelo.

1670 The third palace built on the Capitol. The Capitol assumes a primarily cultural significance. Numerous excavations are carried out in the Forum beside it, which stress the Capitol's ancient role.

THE CITY OF AUGUSTUS

When Augustus made his proud and often repeated remark that he found Rome a city of brick and left it a city of marble, he was not exaggerating. His reign coincided with the opening up of the marble quarries at Luna in Tuscany which provided the brilliant white marble so beloved by architects of the Augustan period. The coincidence was fortunate; so too was the fact that he inherited from his predecessor, Julius Caesar, the beginnings of a great program of urban renewal left unfinished on Caesar's death in 44 B.C. Augustus had the leisure of a long and peaceful reign to continue the program and to impose his own energetic mark upon it.

His patronage was prodigious. His own claim to have built or restored eighty-two temples accords well with his pious attempts to introduce a new

from buying all the land he needed for his scheme and in consequence the plan of his building had to be modified to fit the available space. Nonetheless the great open space which he created, dominated by the Temple of Mars Ultor, is a *tour de force* not least because it effectively combines traditionally Roman architectural values with a number of Hellenizing influences, such as the use of caryatids.

morality among the citizens. For the most part Augustus's building was of a conventional kind, no doubt influenced in part by the severe restrictions on space which the growing city had imposed. The Forum of Augustus shows this well. Attached to the side of the Forum of Julius Caesar, the new Imperial Fora lay beyond the old Forum Romanum, but as Suetonius records, Augustus was prevented

Model of the Temple of Mars Ultor, 42–2 B.C., in the Forum of Augustus, and ruins (*above*) of its Corinthian-style columns showing the Hellenistic influence so important during the Augustine period. *Left:* The triple columns that still stand in the Roman Forum. *Right:* Plan of imperial Rome, with identification of the important buildings of Augustus's time.

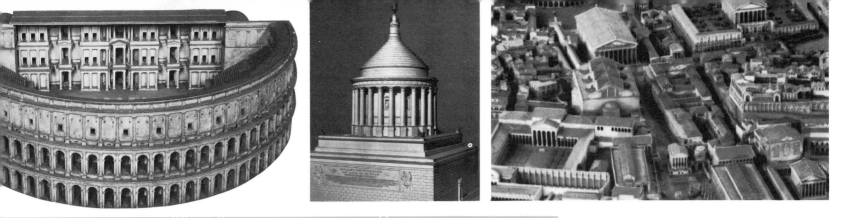

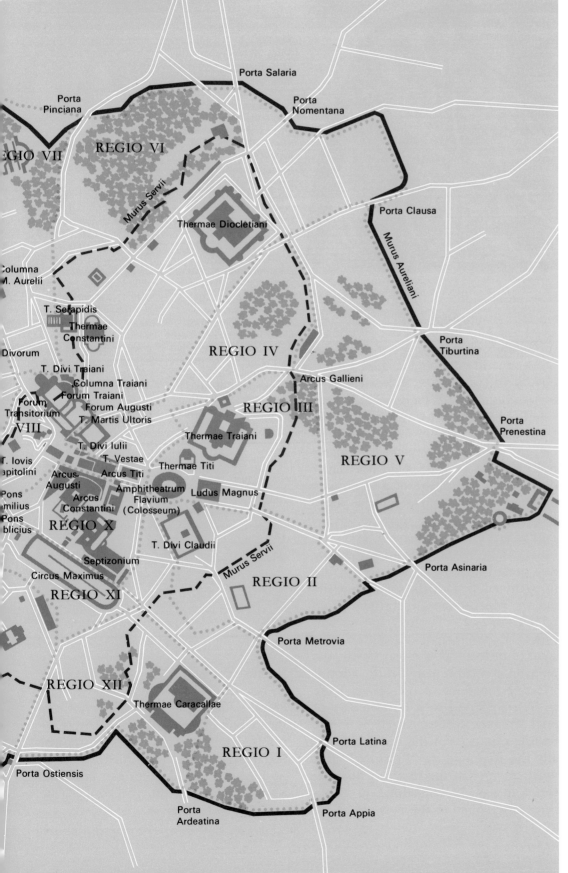

This mixture of styles also recurs in the works sponsored by Augustus's friend Marcus Agrippa. Much of Agrippa's work was utilitarian—new aqueducts were built doubling the city's water supply, the drainage system was greatly improved, and warehouses were built—but in addition he masterminded a new complex of public buildings, put up in the low-lying area of the Campus Martius. These included a bath suite, a basilica, and the first version of the Pantheon, which Pliny tells us was "decorated with caryatids sculpted by the Athenian Diogenes." It is perhaps significant that Agrippa was also responsible for building the odeum (Greek *odeion*) in the Athenian agora—a project which would probably have brought him into contact with Greek craftsmen and ideas.

Not all of the building of the Augustan period incorporated a taste for Hellenism. The Theater of Marcellus, completed in the period 13–11 B.C., was essentially a traditional Republican building in style, but the engineering innovations incorporated in it were a necessary prelude to the great buildings of the later age such as the Colosseum.

The Augustan period in architecture was then a mixture of conservatism and innovation, but an innovation brought about largely by the need to import craftsmen from the east to work the new fashionable marble which was flooding the market. What emerged was solidly Roman, and by its sheer quantity and variety it was to make a strong impression on succeeding generations. But more important still, Roman architecture had now reached a stage of assurance. From this point onward, a truly Roman architectural tradition was to make its mark on the world.

ROME AS AN EMPIRE

In theory the control of the Empire was divided between the Senate and the *princeps* or emperor: it was a power-sharing partnership—a diarchy. In reality the emperor's will predominated.

Senate

The Senate retained a range of responsibilities. They governed certain provinces, appointing their own governors (called *proconsuls*) from the ranks of ex-consuls and ex-praetors, and nominally they controlled Italy. Under Augustus the Senate was given greater powers to legislate, without the need for ratification by the people, and in addition it now took on the functions of a high court, its meetings presided over by the consul, though the emperor could pass judgment if he wished to do so. Taxes from senatorial provinces and from Italy were retained by the Senate to pay for such public works as the maintenance of roads and buildings and for funding religious ceremonies.

Magistrates

Magistrates of various types continued to be elected by the people to undertake specific tasks, with little significant change from Republican times, but *praetors* now took over the state treasury (*aerarium*) from the *questors*. Former magistrates provided a pool of talent from which *proconsuls* could be appointed.

After the battle of Actium in 31 B.C., Augustus (then Octavian) inherited the tattered fragments of the war-torn Republic which for a century had been at the mercy of one military dictator after another, each intent upon securing his own power irrespective of the Roman constitution. Rome was in a state close to anarchy. Yet four years after Actium, in January of 27 B.C., Augustus could go before the Roman Senate and announce that the Republic was to be restored and that henceforth he would renounce all powers with the exception of the consulship to which he had been elected for the year. In Augustus's own words:

After I had put out the flames of civil war and by universal consent had become possessed of the control of affairs, I transferred the state from my own power to the will of the Senate and the people of Rome. For this service I received by decree of the Senate the name of Augustus. Res Gestae XII

He received something more than that, for the Senate immediately bestowed on him the command of the legions and those frontier provinces in which they were based, for an initial period of ten years. A few years later he abandoned the somewhat inconvenient position of consul and instead assumed, again perfectly constitutionally, the grant of tribunician power for life. This gave him immunity in the law and the right to initiate legislation. Thus his power base was legally established. More special privileges were to follow; among them he had the right to commend candidates for election, and he held the chief position in the college of priests, giving him virtual control of the religious life of the state. Strictly speaking, as first citizen *(princeps)*, excelling others only in the authority *(auctoritas)* vested in him, he was seen to be in partnership with the Senate—a situation which some historians have referred to as a "diarchy." In practice, however, the Senate's position was weak: ultimate power lay with the *princeps*, and soon many of the administrative functions of the Senate were to be transferred to a bureaucracy of civil servants, created largely from the middle class to run the state. Nominally the Republic was "restored" but what emerged as the result of this restoration was a totally different structure more suited to the new situation.

Because the Empire was now too large to be run efficiently by the old oligarchical system, a professional civil service was required. Moreover, the Empire's extended frontiers provided too many opportunities for those with politico-military ambitions. For this reason control of the army had to be retained by the *princeps*.

The Emperor

The emperor was, in practice, autonomous. He could impose his will, not only on his own staff but also on the Senate, but most early emperors treated the Senate with respect.

The Council

Augustus created a political council (*consilium*)—a standing committee composed of senators with whom he could discuss matters before they were brought to the Senate.

Fiscal

Augustus was dependent on a large army of freed men to provide the basic substructure upon which his rule was based. They provided among other functions, his secretaries and his accountants (*procuratores fisci*), administering his own personal property (*patrimonium*) as well as the imperial treasury (*fiscus*)

which received the taxes from the imperial provinces and paid for the maintenance of the army, navy, the administration of these provinces, and provided the corn supply for Rome. The emperor issued his own coinage in gold and silver, while the Senate minted in copper.

The civil service became a vital element in the administration, but some emperors, estranged from the other tiers of government, relied too heavily on it.

Officials

To cope with the complex affairs of state now under his personal control, Augustus created a civil service of his own. He recruited personnel from the *equites* (free-born men with a certain property qualification)—a class which included the sons of senators below twenty-five years of age. From this group (*ordo*), jurors were selected and arranged in three panels (*decuriae*). A wide range of posts were open to members of the *ordo*. Most would begin in military service and graduate to civil appointments in senatorial or imperial provinces. The most successful would stand a chance of becoming prefect of the Praetorian Guard—a personal bodyguard established by Augustus in 27 B.C.

Army

The army was under the direct control of the emperor: he paid their salaries, appointed their commanders, and deployed them at will about the imperial provinces. The more important provinces were governed by senators who were known as *legati Augusti pro praetore*; the less important provinces were given to *procurators* drawn from the equestrian order. Two additional consuls could serve as governors if needed.

The Citizenry

Popular assemblies continued to function for a short time under the Empire and in theory every citizen could vote approval or disapproval of new laws. This practice soon became a mere formality and then was dispensed with altogether. Citizens who met certain qualifications of birth and property were eligible to become senators or civil servants.

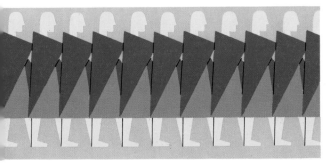

Augustus's reforms of the old Republican system of provincial administration were sweeping. To curb abuses he abolished almost all the rights of the contract tax collectors and replaced them with procurators, whose responsibility it was to collect the taxes on land and property. To ensure a fair system of assessment, he ordered censuses to be carried out in many provinces. But perhaps more significant was the fact that the procurator was answerable directly to the emperor, not to the provincial governor: collusion was therefore impossible. Another improvement was to extend the normal term of office for a governor to three years, thus enabling a degree of continuity to be achieved. In addition governors were now paid a salary, reducing the temptation of extortion.

The Augustan reforms were fundamental both at home and abroad. Stability had been restored and a system established which was to last with little significant modification for three hundred years.

He seduced the army with bonuses, and his cheap food policy was successful bait for civilians. Indeed, he attracted everybody's goodwill by the enjoyable gift of peace. Then he gradually pushed ahead and absorbed the functions of the Senate, the officials, and even the law. Opposition did not exist. War or judicial murder had disposed of all men of spirit. Upper-class survivors found that slavish obedience was the way to succeed, both politically and financially. They had profited from the revolution, and so now they liked the security of the existing arrangement better than the dangerous uncertainties of the old régime.

Tacitus, *Annals* I, 2

THE ARA PACIS

On 4 July in 13 B.C., the emperor Augustus, having just returned from an extended visit to the western provinces, led a procession to the Campus Martius to consecrate the site he had chosen for the Ara Pacis—the Altar of Peace. This act, and indeed the altar itself, which was completed in 9 B.C., was to symbolize the new atmosphere of calm and piety which now prevailed, carefully nurtured and maintained by the emperor himself and by writers and artists of the period. The altar and its surrounding screen wall were extensively decorated with sculpture. The frieze around the outside of the enclosure wall depicts the

The Altar of Peace, contained in a raised square enclosure (approximately 10 by 12 meters), built 13–9 B.C., is shown as reconstructed in this century. It symbolized Augustus's pious and stable reign.

procession of 13 B.C. above a zone of flowers and foliage, while the inside of the wall is covered with traditional bulls' skulls, garlands, and fruit. The altar itself is decorated with a frieze of Vestal Virgins, priests, animals, and the whole panoply of the sacrificial procession.

The emperor Augustus, seen here in the famous statue now in the Louvre. Augustus served as *pontifex maximus*, head of the state religion. This religious office was henceforth assumed by all emperors, and the Latin title was transferred to the Popes.

Two relief scenes from the Ara Pacis:

Left: Terra Mater, the Mother Earth, seated between figures symbolizing water (with swan) and air. The signs of fertile abundance (infants, plants, streams, animals) contribute to the impression of the reign of Augustus as a golden age, a theme also stressed by poets such as Virgil: "The great march of the centuries begins anew. Now the maiden returns, now Saturn is king again, and a new race descends from on high" (*Eclogue* IV).

Below: Relief from the south wall. Procession with Augustus and his family; the emperor is shown dressed as *pontifex maximus*. The outstanding workmanship of these reliefs suggests that Greek sculptors were primarily responsible for the Ara Pacis.

The work was executed with a skill and assurance hardly before seen in Rome. The external frieze is a masterpiece. The emperor and his family are depicted, together with other state dignitaries, in two planes, the principal characters to the fore with the lesser participants all interspersed between them in lower relief, providing a main friezes, while in details such as the bulls' skulls and garlands the hand of Pergamene artists can be detected. Foreign craftsmen such as these would have been necessary to the success of the project, since there must at the time have been few Roman sculptors used to working marble on a monumental scale. Yet in spite of the Mater—the matronly earth mother sitting at ease surrounded by the richness of nature, plump infants, docile animals, and luxurious flowers and fruit.

The Ara Pacis marks a turning point not only in the artistic development of the Empire but in the use of art as a medium for propaganda. No Roman

visual variety and a rhythm that enlivens and excites the eye; the procession vibrates with movement.

The style and execution of the work, quite reminiscent of the Parthenon friezes, strongly suggests that Augustus used Attic sculptors, skilled in marble working, to design and cut the Hellenized style of the work, its spirit is purely Roman. Everything about it is redolent of the Augustan age. Piety and peace are emphasized, as the emperor, shown as a mere mortal among equals, leads the people in their devotions. And as a reminder to the people of their good life we have the Terra looking at the Ara Pacis could have failed to be overwhelmed by a sense of relief at the passing of the horrors of the late Republican age. He would have looked forward to a stable future secure in his belief in the new leadership of the *princeps*.

THE ROMAN PANTHEON

JUPITER AND JUNO

Brother and sister as well as husband and wife, the two principal Roman gods reigned on Mount Olympus. Jupiter was responsible for weather, especially storms; Juno was goddess of marriage and women.

MINERVA   ASCLEPIUS

Minerva: Goddess of war, she alone had access to Jupiter's Thunder Hammer. Like Athena, she also had a peaceful function as goddess of wisdom. Roma was often depicted in the figure of Minerva.

Asclepius: Son of Apollo, god of health and protector of doctors.

JANUS
God of beginnings and origins; two-headed; a war god.

APOLLO
Jupiter's son, god of the sun, light, and beauty.

VICTORIA
Goddess of battle and of struggles with Olympus.

VENUS
Goddess of love and of sea journeys.

SOL
Sun god, who appeared and vanished daily.

GODS OF THE SEA

NEPTUNE
Ruler over all the waters of earth.

AMPHITRITE
Neptune's wife cared for the inhabitants of the sea.

TRITONS
Helped to draw the wagon of the sea god through the waves.

NEREIDS
Sea nymphs who looked after the surface of the sea.

SIRENS
Bird-like women whose singing entranced sailors.

GODS OF THE EARTH

CERES
Goddess of fruitfulness and of the harvest.

BACCHUS
God of wine and of ecstatic liberation.

PRIAPUS
God of gardens and fields, a symbol of fertility.

PAN
Protector of shepherds and of livestock cultivation.

SATYRS
High-spirited figures in Bacchus's retinue.

GODS OF THE UNDERWORLD

PLUTO
The lord of the underworld, shown riding in his chariot accompanied by his wife, Persephone.

PERSEPHONE
Goddess of the underworld, daughter of Ceres.

THE FURIES
Daughters of night and darkness who tormented the dead.

SOMNUS AND MORS

MERCURY

God of riches and trade, protector of merchants. Also messenger of the gods.

MARS

Mars originated in Italy as a god of spring but developed very early as a powerful war god. All spoils of war were consecrated to him as offerings, and no Roman commander would go into battle without first having entered the temple of Mars to pray for the god's protection and blessing.

THE MUSES

These nine feminine figures served as goddesses of the fine arts and patrons of human learning and cultivation. They enlivened dinners of the gods with their singing. All artists and performers depended on them. Polymnia (muse of mime) is shown here.

THE LARES

Lares, as enlightened spirits of departed ancestors, were believed to bless and protect their descendants and the land, and to oversee all the critical moments of family life, birth and death, marriage, long voyages, changes of domicile. Sacrifices were made to them on all festive occasions. An altar devoted to the Lares stood in nearly every home.

DIANA   **MITHRAS**

Diana: Goddess of fertility and of the hunt. She is always shown with her arrows and was considered a helper of her father, Jupiter.

Mithras: A sun god of Persian origin, Mithras was worshipped in Rome during the last centuries of the Empire. He was especially beloved of soldiers, and several soldier-emperors appealed to him to inspire and spur on their troops.

GALATEA

A Nereid, who became famous as the lover of the Cyclops Polyphemus.

ARIADNE

Abandoned by Theseus, she was saved by Bacchus and taken off to Olympus.

NYMPHS

They had the power to make themselves invisible.

FAUNUS

A prophetic god of the countryside.

FLORA

Beautiful goddess of flowers and fruitfulness.

The quality in which the Roman commonwealth is most distinctly superior is in my opinion the nature of their religious convictions. I believe that what maintains the cohesion of the Roman state is the very thing which among other peoples is an object of reproach: I mean superstition.... Since every multitude is fickle, full of lawless desires, unreasoned passion, and violent anger, the multitude must be held in by invisible terrors and suchlike pageantry. For this reason I think, not that the ancients acted rashly and at haphazard in introducing among the people notions concerning the gods and beliefs in the terrors of hell, but that the moderns are most rash and foolish in banishing such beliefs.   Polybius, Histories VI, 56

The gods of sleep and of death, sons of Night.

CERBERUS

The three-headed watchdog of the underworld, who was overcome only by Hercules.

GORGONS

Three hideous, monstrous creatures, which symbolized human terrors.

CHARON

Ferryman of the dead across the River Styx.

CULTS AND RITUALS

The gods were everywhere, in the countryside, in the city, and in the home: to a traditionally minded Roman they watched over all aspects of everyday existence. At home the Lares—the spirits of the land—had their own small shrine, the *Lararium*, usually in the form of a model temple, while the Penates, who kept an eye on household stores and food, were remembered each mealtime with a libation. Vesta too would be honored with a piece of salt cake thrown onto the fire. These homely superstitions,

A Bacchic procession: two satyrs and a maenad; marble relief from the Villa Quintiliana, on the Appian Way.

A longstanding Roman cult, the worship of Vesta (goddess of the hearth and home) was supposedly introduced in the dawn of Rome's history by King Numa, second of the seven legendary monarchs. This statue of Numa comes from the House of the Vestals, in the Forum.

Right: Vestal Virgin, marble statue from the House of the Vestals. Vestal Virgins entered service as children (aged six to ten) and continued for thirty years or more. They looked after the sacred fire and performed other duties.

ensuring the continuance of fire, food, and shelter, were clearly very ancient—a reminder perhaps of one's primitive roots but hardly a manifestation of religious fervor.

Nor, by the end of the Republic, was participation in state religion a more

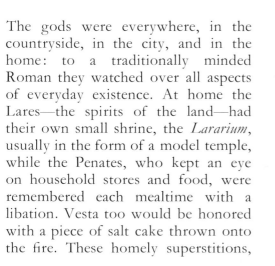

inspiring experience. True, the gods of the city—particularly the Capitoline triad, Jupiter, Juno, and Minerva—were regularly worshipped according to a set calendar by professional priests headed by the *pontifex maximus*; however, these ceremonies had become little more than a symbolic demonstration of the unity of the state and an opportunity for the populace to catch the flavor of their historic past: they were displays of wistful antiquarianism. For the humbler people, however, religious celebrations pro-

something of a religious revival brought about by the introduction of new cults. The influx of foreigners, particularly from the Hellenistic world, and the return of armies from the eastern campaigns in the second and first centuries B.C. brought to

her oriental priests, and housed in the Temple of Victory in response to the Sibylline oracle who required Rome to welcome the goddess if they were to be saved from Hannibal. It was typical of Roman conservatism that citizens were forbidden to take an active part in the more exotic ceremonies associated with her worship; instead, Romanized festivals were organized by a commission who were responsible for public worship.

Foreign cults were not readily accepted. Laws governing religions were

Two maenads, female servants of Bacchus, in their typically frenzied dance around an altar. They wield the thyrsus, a staff with a pine cone.

Left: Emperor Marcus Aurelius, as state high priest (*pontifex maximus*), preparing to sacrifice to the gods.

The most complete available depiction of a religious sacrifice is this altar relief inscribed to C. Manlius (censor from Caere, first century A.D.).

vided a chance to relax and enjoy themselves while their masters could pride themselves on their upholding of traditional moral values.

In the later years of the Republic, in an age of growing materialism and far greater sophistication, there was

Rome a knowledge and appreciation of a surprising range of new deities more full-blooded and more intellectually satisfying than the pallid gods of Rome. One of the first to appear was Cybele, the "Great Mother," who was brought from Asia, together with

quite rigorous, particularly after 186 B.C. when a fit of Bacchic frenzy suddenly spread through Rome, greatly alarming the traditionalists. The worship of Bacchus/Dionysus was banned, but with typical Roman ambivalence; if a citizen felt particularly moved to worship the god, a magistrate could grant him permission to do so, so long as no more than five people assembled together.

After the initial horror occasioned by the apparent excesses of the eastern cults, they began to grow in popularity among certain sectors of the community. The old official polytheism had little to offer by way of comfort or intellectual stimulus, but the eastern mystery religions were both reassuring and demanding. They offered an explanation of the world, a code of rules for personal behavior, and an afterlife in which men could believe. By the second century A.D., foreign cults were spreading rapidly throughout the city. Claudius, in the first century A.D., had already Romanized the liturgy of Cybele and Attis, and a little later Domitian was responsible for the rebuilding in sumptuous style of the Temple of Isis which had been destroyed by fire, and it was also around this time that the earliest shrine to Mithras was established in Rome.

Most mystery religions were demanding of their initiates. The worship of the Persian god Mithras, popular among traders and soldiers, required the convert to work his way through seven grades of membership before being fully admitted, the *rites de passage* forcing him to submit to ordeals of exposure to severe heat and cold. In Gaul initiates to the cult of Cybele had to undergo the rite of *taurobolium* which entailed their descending into a pit covered by a grating upon which a bull was then sacrificed. The bull's blood, gushing down into the pit, soaked the body of the willing applicant, who bathed in it and drank it. Experiences of this kind, frequently accompanied by vows of secrecy, must have bound the convert to his faith.

The popularity of the mystery religions in the Roman world is not difficult to understand. They offered a sense of group unity in an ever expanding world and a taste of the afterlife. Each had something different to give—Isis provided a calm for meditation, Aesculapius a reassurance for the ailing, Mithras a philosophy for the intellectually able.

Christianity was a comparative newcomer to the Roman scene. There were some who regarded it as yet another mystery religion, and indeed there were many superficial resemblances, but there were also striking differences. The Alexandrians who worshipped both Sarapis and Jesus would not have been regarded as unreasonable by the priests of Sarapis, but to the early apostles such a combination would have been anathema. Christ required exclusive devotion: nothing, not even obedience to the state, could be allowed to compromise the Christian faith. It is small wonder that the early emperors dealt harshly with the Christians.

Bronze sculpture, from Rome, of a hand adorned with religious symbols to ward off the evil eye.

Mithras slaying the sacrificial bull, surrounded by signs of the zodiac. Marble relief, Sidon, Asia Minor, A.D. 400. Mithras was the Persian god of light and guardian against evil. The cults of Mithras and of Isis (from Egypt) became popular in Rome under the Empire.

Opposite: The worship of Isis. This wall painting from Herculaneum evokes a ceremony taking place in the tree-lined courtyard in front of the Temple of Isis. In the doorway of the temple, at top, a priest holding a golden vessel looks down upon the ceremony below where a priest is conducting the worshippers with a wand while another fans the flames of the altar fire. A flute player is seated at right.

TEMPLES

Doors of the Temple of Janus, in the Roman Forum, which were supposedly closed only in peacetime. Coin of Nero, A.D. 64–66.

Below: The colossal Temple of "Bacchus" at Baalbek, Lebanon, built in the late second century, with details of the richly engraved capitals and entablature.

"The design of a temple," said the Roman architect Vitruvius, "depends on symmetry...for without symmetry and proportion there can be no principles in the design of any temple." These words, an eloquent distillation of the very essence of the temple, were as true for Greece as for Rome. Yet by the time that Vitruvius was writing, in the first century B.C., Roman temple architecture had developed its own rules. Instead of standing on a low platform, as was the Greek style, the Roman temple was perched high on a podium fronted by steep steps; instead of a gently ordered surrounding colonnade, emphasis was given to the front elevation, often made more striking by a deep-set porch. While a Greek temple sat in harmony with its entire surroundings, a Roman temple was there to dominate, much as the old Graeco-Etruscan temple on the Capitol, rebuilt many times, had dominated Rome for hundreds of years.

Just as each god had a distinctive quality, so had each temple:

Left: The Temple of Jupiter, Juno, and Minerva at Dougga in northern Tunisia, built A.D. 166–167.

Below: Doric columns of the Temple of Venus and Rome, at the east end of the Roman Forum. Second century A.D.

The temples of Minerva, Mars, and Hercules will be Doric since the virile strength of these gods makes daintiness entirely inappropriate to their houses. In temples to Venus, Flora, Proserpine, Spring-Water, and the Nymphs, the Corinthian order will be found to have peculiar significance because these are delicate divinities and so its rather slender outlines, its flowers, leaves, and ornamental volutes will lend propriety where it is due. The construction of temples of the Ionic order to Juno, Diana, and Bacchus, and other gods of that kind, will be in keeping with the middle

position which they hold: for the building of such will be an appropriate combination of the severity of the Doric and the delicacy of the Corinthian.　　　*On Architecture* I, ii, 5

The temple itself was principally intended to house the cult figures and to provide an inner sanctum for the priests. The assembled worshippers would therefore remain outside in the open in a courtyard which usually contained the main sacrificial altar. These courtyards were frequently surrounded with colonnades to provide protection from the extremes of weather. Pliny, writing to his architect about the rebuilding on his estate of a

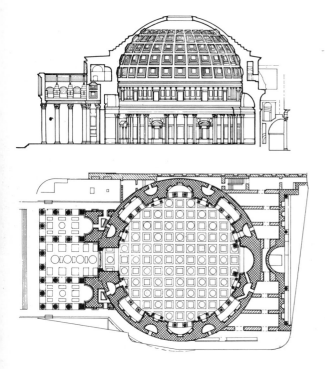

rural temple dedicated to Ceres, gives a charming insight into these matters:

The temple needs enlarging and improving for it is certainly very old and too small considering how crowded it is on its special anniversary when great crowds gather there from the whole district.... There is no shelter nearby from rain or sun, so I think it

will be an act of generosity and piety alike to build as fine a temple as I can and add porticoes—the temple for the goddess, the porticoes for the public.　　*Letters* IX, 39

Though most temples followed the same general rules of planning, they varied considerably in size, from the modest rural structure of the type described by Pliny to enormous grandiose schemes like the so-called Temple of Bacchus at Baalbek (Lebanon) completed by Caracalla and measuring ninety meters long and nearly forty meters wide. Plans too varied, from the conventional rectangular form to circular structures and even those with octagonal and triangular plans. But no variation in size or plan could have prepared the visitor to Rome for the staggering originality of the Pantheon, built by Hadrian in the early second century. Here we see the beginning of an architectural revolution. No longer was the exterior composition of significance as it was with the Greek temple, but all emphasis was now on the breathtaking interior. Architecture had been turned inside out.

The Pantheon, built between A.D. 118 and 128 to replace an earlier temple, can justifiably be regarded as one of the great architectural masterpieces of the world. It is composed of two elements, a traditional porch attached somewhat inelegantly to a domed rotunda, simple in its geometry but staggering in its impact. The rotunda consists of a circular drum, half the height of its diameter, crowned by a hemispherical dome, the maximum height of the dome above the floor being therefore exactly the same as the diameter of the building at floor level. The only light for the interior floods in through a single central oculus to illuminate the richly decorated walls and coffered dome. The structural engineering involved in so elaborate a building was ingenious. The entire structure stood on a foundation which consisted of a ring beam of

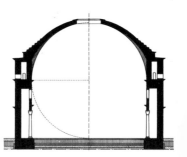

concrete four and a half meters deep and more than ten meters wide, made of dense basalt set in mortar. Upon this stood the drum walls, six meters thick, lightened by cavities which not only provided visual relief but also facilitated the drying of the mortar. The dome itself was a brilliant achievement constructed in concrete decreasing to less than two meters in thickness and made as light as possible towards the center by using an aggregate of pumice. This aggregate material was carefully graded at each level of the building to ensure that the actual turning moment of the structure remained constant—which shows an exceptional awareness of structural mechanics on the part of the architect.

THE POLITICAL ARENA

Cato's description of the orator as "a good man skilled in speaking" gives the impression of rustic simplicity to a profession which was in fact both rigorous in its training and contrived in its performance. Teachers of rhetoric worked according to a system. Every speech was divided into six parts each of which consisted of a

number of elements that could be polished, adapted, and combined. Students would be led through a series of exercises designed to familiarize them with the approved structure and to teach them how to modify accepted formulas to suit individual cases. After much practice the would-be orator was turned loose on the public to deliver his first harangue. It might be in the form of a general debate *(suasoria)* or a defense or indictment *(controversia)* based on an imaginary situation created within an historical framework. Seneca gives a good example of one set topic:

Popilius, accused of parricide, was defended by Cicero and acquitted. Later, Cicero, proscribed by Antony, was slain by Popilius. Sustain an accusation against Popilius on the grounds of evil morals.

Controversiae VII, 2

Such exercises, often ludicrous in their basic suppositions, provided the young men with amusing, if irrelevant, material upon which to sharpen their wits. The more absurd the invented situation and the more inconceivable the difficulties to be overcome, the more the particular exercise was relished—at least by the instructors.

The irrelevancy of much of the training given by the teachers of rhetoric was bewailed by more than one thoughtful writer. Tacitus summed up the feelings of many when he said of the exercises set:

The tyrannicides, the plague cures, the incests of mothers which are so grandiloquently discussed in the schools bear no relation to the forum, and all this bombast hurls defiance at the truth.   *Dialogus 35*

Yet it was through schools of rhetoric that the great speakers of Rome were to pass. Rigorous training did not necessarily dull the minds of the more able.

A man trained in public speaking would have many opportunities to use his powers, principally in the law courts and in the Senate. From the time of Cicero Romans developed a particular taste for litigation, to such an extent that the courts overflowed: by the late first century Suetonius seriously wondered whether there were sufficient advocates to cope. Even as early as 2 B.C. Augustus had to allow the forum he had built to be used, and by the second century courts were being held in at least ten different locations in the center of Rome, daily for criminal cases and on 230 days a year for civil prosecutions.

Opposite: Ruins of the Rostra, or speakers' platform, in the Roman Forum (24 by 12 meters, 2 meters high).
Typical gestures of the orator are illustrated in the figures on these two pages. Emperors are among the persons portrayed in this posture, as shown in the coins of Hadrian (*far left*) and Caligula (*far right*). They are both presented on raised platforms with the right arm extended. The statues (*left to right*) represent M. Nonius Balbus of Herculaneum; the emperor Titus; Julius Caesar; an unidentified orator (largest figure) from Sanguineto, first century B.C.; and L. Mammius Maximus.

Pliny did not think much of the speeches he heard. "I am ashamed to describe the speeches of today," he writes, "the mincing accents in which they are delivered and the puerile applause they receive" (*Letters* II, 14). But in another letter to a friend, he describes with indulgent delight a recent speech of his own delivered before the Centumviral Court:

It is long but I feel sure it will be as popular as a short one, for the interest is kept up by the lively arrangement of the abundant material, the frequent use of short anecdotes, and the variety of the oratorial style. Much of it is in the grand manner and full of fire, but there are long sections in a plainer style where I was obliged to introduce calculations into the midst of my impassioned and lofty arguments.... I gave full play to my feelings of wrath and indignation, and steered by course through this vastly important case with the wind full in my favor.   Letters VI, 33

Pliny's speech was heard in the moderately comfortable Basilica Julia. The

Senate, on the other hand, met in more cramped circumstances in the Curia, which at best could seat only three hundred, one third of those eligible to attend. Sessions began at dawn and ended at nightfall, but senators were allowed to move at will and come and go as they pleased. With the coming of the Empire the nature of

the Senate's business changed. During the Republic most of the great events had been debated here and decisions made, but Augustus and his successors changed all this: daily business became more mundane and the Senate's function as a High Court began to take up more of its time. On one such occasion, when the Senate, presided over by Trajan, was hearing the case against a proconsul, Pliny spoke for five hours nonstop while Trajan suggested, more than once, that he should spare his voice and lungs. Pliny regarded this as a sign of the emperor's concern for his health— but one wonders.

Overleaf: Rare in the Roman world, the forum of Jerash, in present-day Jordan, is oval rather than rectangular in layout. The second-century A.D. structure served a commercial function, as opposed to the political and religious nature of the Forum Romanum.

THE FORUM

Many primitive societies moving towards urbanization set aside specific locations where they could meet together, trade, and enact common laws. In Athens such an area became known as the agora, in Rome it was called the forum: both were essentially open spaces for the assembly of the populace. The Roman Forum lay in the valley between the Capitol and the Palatine. Halls, courtyards, temples, and triumphal monuments abounded. By Caesar's time the original site—the Forum Romanum—was so crammed with structures that a new area immediately adjacent to it began to be colonized. It was here that Caesar, Augustus, Nerva, and Trajan created a grandiose scheme of buildings which became known as the Imperial Fora.

The forum was the heart of Rome. It was here that the commercial activities of the Empire centered, where the most sacred rituals of the state were performed, where the Senate and the Assembly met, and where the law courts were situated—it was, in short, the center of the world. Banquets, funerals, triumphs, moving orations, and bloody massacres were all enacted here. But it was above all a place of the people, senators and beggars alike. The playwright Plautus described the scene in the second century B.C.:

I'll show you where to find all sorts of men, good or bad or honest men or rascals. Whoever wants someone to swear through thick and thin—I'll send him to the law courts. Your prodigal rich husband you must look for at the exchange. There too you'll find stale harlots ready for any bargain.... Above the lake [are] malevolent and foul-mouthed fellows such as boldly deal and slander without cause. At the old shops are those who lend out money or borrow it on usury.... In Tuscan street are those who sell themselves....   Curculio 467–482

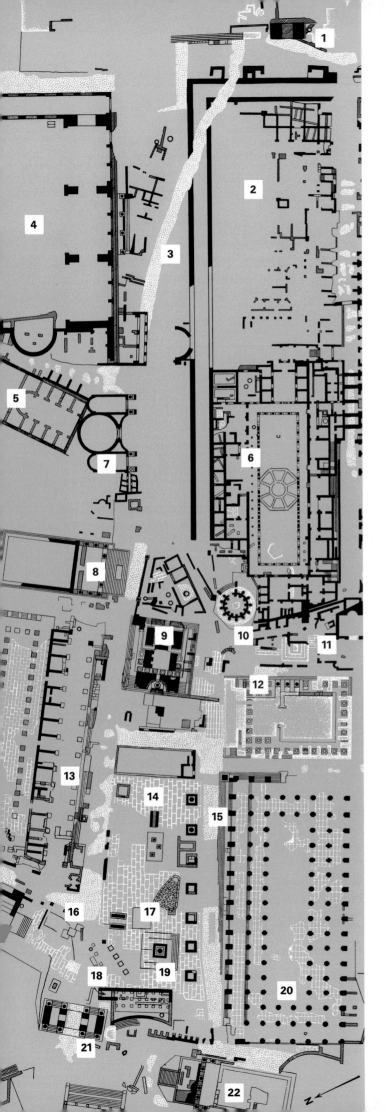

1 ARCH OF TITUS: Fine example of a monumental arch built to commemorate the emperor's victory over the Jews and his destruction of Jerusalem in A.D. 70.

2 PORTICUS MARGARITARIA: Possibly the Vestibule of the Golden House of Nero built on the neighboring Palatine.

3 VIA SACRA: Ancient street which ran through the Forum area—possibly taking its name from the religious processions here.

4 BASILICA NOVA OF MAXENTIUS: Great basilica hall begun by Maxentius (306–312) and completed by Constantine (312–337): the climax of Roman building in the Forum.

5 LIBRARY OF THE FORUM OF PEACE: The great new Forum to which the library was attached was built by Vespasian following his victory over the Jews.

6 HOUSE OF THE VESTALS: The virgins who watched over and served the shrine of Vesta lived here in a large courtyard house, the present structure representing a second-century A.D. reconstruction. (The coin below portrays this building.)

7 TEMPLE OF ROMULUS: Circular shrine probably dedicated to Romulus, the deified son of the emperor Maxentius, early in the fourth century A.D.

8 TEMPLE OF ANTONINUS AND FAUSTINA: Well-preserved temple erected by the emperor Antoninus to his deified wife Faustina. When Antoninus died twenty years later, the Senate decreed that the temple should be rededicated to include both.

9 TEMPLE OF CAESAR: Erected to the deified Caesar on the spot where his body was cremated in 44 B.C.

10 TEMPLE OF VESTA: The most sacred building in Rome, traditionally attributed to the reign of the legendary king Numa Pompilius (715–672 B.C.). It was here that the sacred fire was tended.

11 SPRING OF JUTURNA: It was here that two young warriors (Castor and Pollux) were said to have watered their horses after the battle of Lake Regillus. Modified during imperial times.

12 TEMPLE OF CASTOR AND POLLUX: Traditionally built 484 B.C. to commemorate the battle of Lake Regillus. Reconstructed many times, extensively by Delmaticus (117 B.C.) and finally by Tiberius. It is probably to this phase that the surviving structure belongs.

13 BASILICA AEMILIA: Constructed in 179 B.C., reconstructed a hundred years later, and extensively rebuilt by the founder's family (55–34 B.C.) and restored after a fire by Augustus in 14 B.C. The basilica was the main business center of the city.

14 STATUES OF DOMITIAN AND CONSTANTINE: Equestrian statues erected in the late first and fourth centuries.

15 FORUM: The ancient heart of Rome was laid out as a paved open space ca. 575 B.C. Under the Republic it was the center of Rome's trading activity, but the new Imperial Fora to the north provided extended facilities, taking pressure off the old precinct.

16 COMITIUM: The building in which the Comitia, or assemblies of the people, met. Elections to the tribunate were held here together with certain kinds of trials.

17 LACUS CURTIUS: A well-like hole cut in the ground to commemorate the immolation of Marcus Curtius. According to legend, a crevasse opened up in the ground at this spot, in the fourth century B.C.. The oracle announced that a sacrifice was necessary to save Rome, whereupon M. Curtius rode his horse into the breach, causing it to close.

18 ROSTRA: The new rostra was built by Caesar. It was a speaker's platform retained for ceremonies such as funeral orations.

19 COLUMN OF PHOCAS: The last monument to be erected in the Forum (602–610) by Smaragdus, the Byzantine governor of Italy, in honor of the emperor Phocas.

20 BASILICA JULIA: Erected by Caesar and restored and enlarged by Augustus. It accommodated the law courts, particularly the Centumviri who dealt with civil cases.

21 ARCH OF SEPTIMIUS SEVERUS: Erected in A.D. 203 to celebrate the victories of the emperor and his sons over the Parthians and their allies in Assyria and Mesopotamia.

22 TEMPLE OF SATURN: One of the most sacred locations in the Forum, reputed to be the spot where Hercules himself dedicated an altar. Traditionally, temple building began in the seventh century B.C. and many reconstructions ensued. The present surviving portico dates from the fourth century A.D.

Top: Great forum of Leptis Magna, in Libya, built by Septimius Severus (r. 193–211) in grandiose style to beautify the city of his birth. In scale and plan it resembled the Imperial Fora of Rome and was quite out of proportion for a city of the size of Leptis.

The forum of Pompeii. The Capitolium (Temple to Jupiter, Juno, and Minerva) lay at one end; the main civic buildings, at the other, with the basilica close by. Other temples and specialized markets flanked the other sides. Vesuvius is shown in the background.

The forum was an essential attribute for all Roman towns no matter where or how they developed. Under the Republic fora tended to be irregular in layout and frequently unenclosed, but later a new formality developed and quite often we find the open space regularized and contained within colonnades.

Often associated with the forum was an aisled hall known as a basilica, which developed essentially as the roofing over the area where public assemblies habitually met. The earliest basilica to be built in Rome—the Basilica Porcia—was erected by Cato in about 184 B.C. A little later the larger and more famous Basilica Aemilia was added. Thereafter basilical halls were commonly built in direct association with fora.

In the provinces plans varied, but whenever a regular street grid was laid down, either afresh as in the case of planted colonies or to tidy up a preexisting urban development, it is not uncommon to find a whole *insula* reserved for the forum and its associated structures. In Gallic towns colonnaded fora were frequently laid out immediately adjacent to the precinct of the town's major temple, the two being on the same axis so that the temple could be viewed from the forum. Modifications of this scheme sometimes combined the two, the forum now serving also as the temple precinct.

In Britain a different arrangement was adopted. Here it was more usual for the forum to be surrounded on three sides by colonnades, with the fourth side occupied by a basilica planned so as to enclose the square completely. This kind of plan closely resembles the arrangement of the headquarters buildings *(principia)* found in Roman forts.

PLANS OF FIVE PROVINCIAL FORA:

Forum of Cosa (Italy): one of the earliest known in Italy. The open piazza was lined along the north side by a basilica, two temples, and the comitium (circular meeting hall).

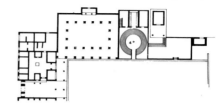

The ancient forum of Leptis Magna (Libya) in its Augustan form. The forum is quadrangular, with the basilica at the east end, three temples at the west.

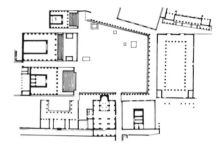

Forum of Zadar (Yugoslavia): colonnaded square, aisleless basilica on the south side. A street isolates the free-standing temple.

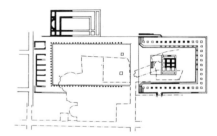

Forum of Timgad (Algeria) laid out by military architects in A.D. 100. The basilica lies to the east of the rectangular forum.

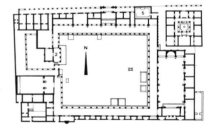

New forum of Leptis Magna, built by Septimius Severus, dominated by a temple to the emperor's family. Basilica across full width.

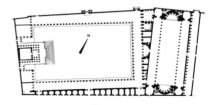

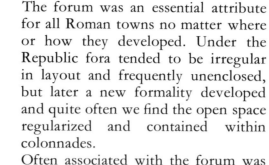

Right: Libyco-Punic Mausoleum erected to the memory of Ateban, a Numidian who died in the late second century B.C. It bore a bilingual inscription in the local Numidian script and in Punic.

Bottom: Temple of Caelestis, the heavenly Juno, also in Dougga. Built by a wealthy local citizen, ca. A.D. 222.

The town of Dougga (Tunisia) is a typical native hill town which rose to importance under the Numidian king Massinissa and was later absorbed into the Roman province of Africa. It reached its peak of prosperity in the late second and early third centuries A.D. The winding streets reflect its unplanned native origins.

1 Capitolium—a temple, in a fine state of preservation, dedicated in A.D. 166 to the three ancient Roman deities, Jupiter, Juno, and Minerva and to emperors Marcus Aurelius and Lucius Verus.

2 Marketplace—dominated by the temple and flanked on the east and west sides by arcades, each with ten shops.

3 The square of the winds. An open, paved area built in the second century A.D., inscribed with a compass indicating the names of twelve winds.

4 Forum—small paved precinct surrounded on three sides by colonnades erected in the late second century. Mutilated by a fort built in the Byzantine period.

5 The Licinian baths. An elaborate suite of public baths built in the third century A.D. during the reign of Gallienus.

6 The "house of El Acheb"—a building of uncertain use put up in A.D. 165. It may have been a specialized market, perhaps for butchers.

7 Theater—a finely preserved structure set into the hill slope. Built in A.D. 188 by a local citizen, it looks out across the Numidian landscape.

WATER

Stone fountain head in Herculaneum, from one of the city's public fountains.

In the early days of Rome the city's need for water was met quite adequately from the local springs and from wells. But as the population rose and the consumption of water per head increased, particularly as bathing became more common, a more adequate permanent supply of water had to be assured.

Appius Claudius was the first to build an aqueduct, in 312 B.C., though this work, like that of its successor constructed by Anio Vertus in 272, was largely a subterranean channel. The first overground structure, the Aqua Marcia, was erected by Quintus Mar-

cius Rex between 144 and 140 to bring water from the River Anio into the center of the city. For the first time the water channel, capped with large stone slabs and lined with a hard mortar containing pounded brick, was carried high above the ground on arches, initiating a tradition which was to spread throughout the Roman world.

By the first century B.C. the dynamics involved in transporting water were well understood. The architect Vitruvius explains that three methods could be used: masonry channels, leaden pipes, or ceramic pipes. He was not much in favor of lead piping: "lead is found to be harmful for the reason that white lead is derived from it, and this is said to be hurtful to the human system." He goes on to describe the general pallor and ill health of plumbers and concludes that water ought not to be conducted in lead pipes. Ceramic pipes had the advantage of being both safe and comparatively

Built	Length	Daily Yield	Aqueduct
2 B.C.	33.3 km	16,228 m³	ALSIETINA
A.D. 109	57.0	118,127	TRAJANA

The Aqua Trajana aqueduct served the area west of the Tiber and also the Baths of Trajan. It crossed the Janiculum hill, to the west of Rome. The Aqua Alsietina served the Naumachia palace, west of the Tiber.

Left: Three-chambered water distribution tank at Pompeii. Sited close to the city wall, it received water from an aqueduct, separated the water into three compartments, and distributed it to the public fountains, baths, and private homes.

When [the water pipe] has reached the city, build a reservoir with a distribution tank in three compartments connected with the reservoir to receive the water, and let the reservoir have three pipes, one for each of the connecting tanks, so that when the water runs over from the tanks at the ends, it may run into the one between them.

From this central tank pipes will be laid to all the basins as fountains; from the second tank to baths so that they may yield an annual income to the state; and from the third, to private houses, so that water for public use will not run short.

Vitruvius, *On Architecture* VIII, vi, 1–2

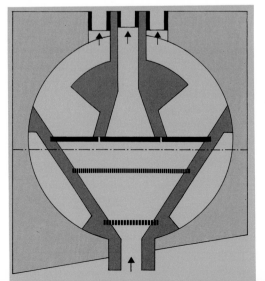

cheap. To withstand pressure, the pipes were made two inches thick, and tongued at one end and socketed at the other to effect an overlapped joint. The binding material recommended by Vitruvius was quicklime mixed with oil, and to ensure an absolutely watertight seal he suggested that ash should be put into the pipes before the water was let in so that if there was a leak the ash would work into it to seal it up.

Aqueduct	Built	Length	Daily Yield
VIRGO	19 B.C.	21.2 km	103,916 m³

By the second century A.D., Rome was being served by ten principal aqueducts, as indicated on the map below.

Below right: Ruins of the Aqua Claudia (built A.D. 38–52), best preserved of the aqueducts in the countryside outside Rome. Within the city, the Aqua Claudia split into two branches, as indicated on the map.

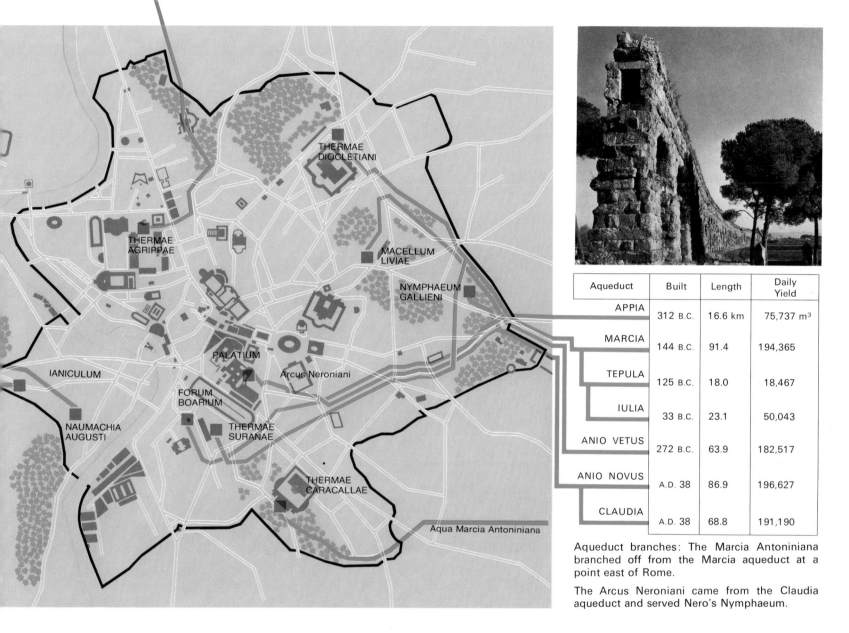

THERMAE DIOCLETIANI

THERMAE AGRIPPAE

MACELLUM LIVIAE

NYMPHAEUM GALLIENI

IANICULUM

PALATIUM

Arcus Neroniani

FORUM BOARIUM

NAUMACHIA AUGUSTI

THERMAE SURANAE

THERMAE CARACALLAE

Aqua Marcia Antoniniana

Aqueduct	Built	Length	Daily Yield
APPIA	312 B.C.	16.6 km	75,737 m³
MARCIA	144 B.C.	91.4	194,365
TEPULA	125 B.C.	18.0	18,467
IULIA	33 B.C.	23.1	50,043
ANIO VETUS	272 B.C.	63.9	182,517
ANIO NOVUS	A.D. 38	86.9	196,627
CLAUDIA	A.D. 38	68.8	191,190

Aqueduct branches: The Marcia Antoniniana branched off from the Marcia aqueduct at a point east of Rome.

The Arcus Neroniani came from the Claudia aqueduct and served Nero's Nymphaeum.

If, however, masonry conduits were adopted, the gradient had to be very carefully controlled (not less than an inch in every hundred feet, Vitruvius suggested) and it was necessary to seal the top of the culvert to prevent the sun from causing undue evaporation. A further precaution which became regular practice was to make the channel large enough for a man to be able to walk along it to carry out repairs or to clean out the silt.

Culverts could be taken across country almost on the level on arches or in subterranean channels, but if pipes were used they would normally have been made to follow up-and-down contours of valleys. This would produce problems, but in order to prevent undue pressure from building up and bursting the junctions, Vitruvius recommended the construction of venters in the valley bottoms. These were elongated masonry structures fit-

ted with baffles to cushion the velocity of the water and to slow down the rate at which it rose up the opposite slope. Vitruvius leaves us with the firm impression that hydraulic engineering had already been perfected by the end of the Republican period.

When, during the reign of Trajan, Frontinus described the aqueducts of Rome, he could list no less than eight, bringing the city more than 222 million gallons of water a day.

AQUEDUCTS

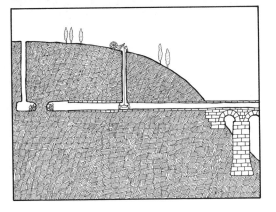

Aqueducts had not only to cross rivers and valleys, but also to pass at times through hillsides. This drawing indicates the Romans' tunneling method: At intervals of some twenty meters, vertical shafts were dug into the hill to the appropriate depth. From the bottom of the shafts, workers dug tunnels in both directions.

The Roman world was strung with aqueducts supplying the major cities, but none can match the grandeur of the aqueduct which served Roman Carthage. Nearly eighty kilometers long, it wove its way across the countryside from the mountain of Zaghouan to the great battery of cisterns which supplied the city.

A legend records how a Roman soldier fell in love with a proud Berber princess who displayed a notable lack of interest in him. When pressed to accept his offer of marriage, she refused saying she would not marry him until the waters of Zaghouan flowed to Carthage. Undaunted, the Roman accepted the challenge by building the vast aqueduct, only to find on finishing it that the incredulous and despairing lady had committed suicide. The tale vividly illustrates the wonder with which subsequent generations regarded this great feat of determined engineering.

The spring, at the foot of Zaghouan even today, produces seventeen million cubic meters of water a day, and in the Roman period the quantity is thought to have been almost double.

Near Izmir, Turkey, stands one of the Romans' impressive examples of aqueducts that bridged deep valleys. Others are found in Constantine in North Africa; Mérida, Segovia, and Tarragona in Spain; and the Pont du Gard in France (pages 134–135). To finance their aqueducts, Romans at first used profits from military conquests or depended on private philanthropy; under the Empire, public funds were budgeted for water supply. Most of the water brought into a city was for public fountains and baths; few homes had water facilities.

At the source Hadrian built an oval basin, designed to collect the water, adorned with elegant colonnades and a shrine to the nymphs who resided there. It was from here that the aqueduct began its journey to Carthage. The aqueduct was vital to the life of the city, particularly after Antoninus Pius built there one of the largest suites of public baths in the Empire.

Above: The aqueduct of Los Milagros, Mérida, Spain, which served the Roman city of Augusta Emerita (capital of the province of Lusitania) from a reservoir five kilometers away.

Satellite photograph of the coast of Tunisia, with a tracing of the zigzagging 80-kilometer course of the Carthage aqueduct. Water was carried from the mountains of Zaghouan (at bottom of picture) all the way to the Mediterranean coast, to serve Carthage and its vicinity, with a population of about 300,000 at its peak. Built by the Romans in the second century A.D., the aqueduct was restored by Septimius Severus in 203. It was cut by the Vandal invaders of North Africa in 409, reconstructed by Count Belisarius in 534, only to be finally destroyed by the Arabs in 698. Considerable vestiges remain, as can be seen below, and on the next page.

Below: Hadrian's shrine at the spring of Zaghouan, source for the Carthage aqueduct. In the Tunisian plains today (bottom), ruins of the Zaghouan-Carthage aqueduct seem to have become part of the natural landscape.

Left: The aqueduct casts its shadow. Carthage, rebuilt as a Roman colony long after the Punic Wars, became a thriving city; its Antonine Baths (ca. A.D. 160), the largest outside Rome, were fed by this aqueduct.

Overleaf: Pages 132–133: The aqueduct of Carthage at its grandest, running across the plain of northern Tunisia from the mountains of Zaghouan to the city of Carthage.

Pages 134–135: The Pont du Gard, built in 19 B.C. across the ravine of Bornègre for the 50-kilometer aqueduct which served the city of Nîmes. The bridge, 370 meters long and 48 meters high, includes foot passages and an arched roadway (on the first tier) added in 1747.

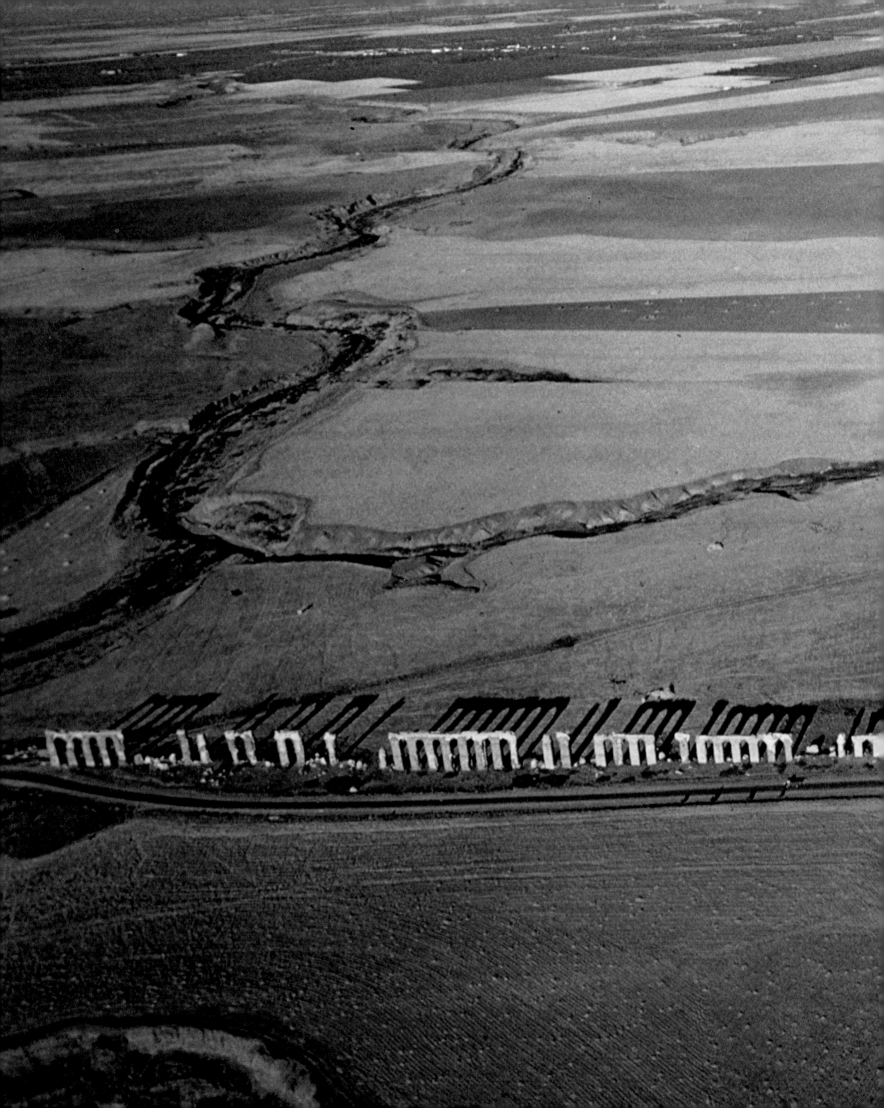

THE BATHS

Roman public baths were at first small-scale buildings, like the examples from Pompeii, Ostia, and Herculaneum shown here. The Forum baths at Pompeii (ca. 80 B.C.), among the oldest surviving bathing establishments, are small and simply laid out *(see plan, below right)*. In the vaulted warm room or *tepidarium* of the men's baths *(below)*, hot air circulated through vents, heating the floor and walls, and bathers would sponge themselves with water from the marble basin.

I have lodgings right over a bathing establishment. So picture to yourself the assortment of sounds, which are strong enough to make me hate my very powers of hearing! When your strenuous gentleman, for example, is exercising himself by flourishing leaden weights; when he is working hard, or else pretends to be working hard, I can hear him grunt; and whenever he releases his imprisoned breath, I can hear him panting in wheezy and high-pitched tones. Or perhaps I notice some lazy fellow, content with a cheap rubdown, and hear the crack of the pummeling hand on his shoulder, varying in sound according as the hand is laid on flat or hollow. Then, perhaps, a professional comes along, shouting out the score; that is the finishing touch. Add to this the arresting of an occasional roisterer or pickpocket, the racket of the man who always likes to hear his own voice in the bathroom, or the enthusiast who plunges into the swimming tank with unconscionable noise and splashing. Besides all those whose voices, if nothing else, are good, imagine the hair-plucker with his penetrating, shrill voice— for purposes of advertisement—continually giving it vent and never holding his tongue except when he is plucking the armpits and making his victim yell instead. Then the cake-seller with his varied cries, the sausageman, the confectioner, and all the vendors of food hawking their wares, each with his own distinctive intonation.

Seneca, *Letters* LVI

The floor plan of the Pompeii Forum baths shows bathing at its simplest: an undressing room, with circular cold room adjoining, followed by a tepid room and a hot room. The men's baths are in the center, behind a row of shops (left); women's baths, lower right.

Mosaic floor from the *frigidarium* (cold bath) of the Neptune baths at Ostia. The sea god is drawn by four spirited sea horses. Late second century A.D.

Below left: Narrow courtyard of the "suburban" baths at Herculaneum lighted from above.

Below right: Main baths of Herculaneum: women's undressing room, vaulted, with shelves to hold clothing; the floor mosaic shows various sea creatures.

in Rome no less than 170 were counted when Agrippa took a census in 33 B.C.; by the fourth century they were to approach a thousand. The two early bath suites of Pompeii, the Stabian baths, built in the second century B.C., and the Forum baths, put up when the colony was established in 80 B.C., give a clear idea of the essential elements of bathing establishments free from all the architectural elaborations which were to follow under the Empire. There were three principal rooms arranged in sequence: the undressing room *(apodyterium)*, the warm room *(tepidarium)*, and the hot room *(caldarium)*. These were the essentials, but other facilities might include cold plunge baths *(frigidaria)*, and intensely hot rooms *(laconica)* to promote profuse sweating. Vitruvius describes how the temperatures of these specialized hot baths could be carefully regulated by raising or lowering a bronze disk set in an aperture in the domed roof.

In early times the heat source was usually a charcoal brazier, but from the beginning of the first century B.C. a new system came widely into use. Air, heated by means of an external furnace, was drawn into a space beneath the floor and up through vents in the walls. Such a system had considerable advantages: it kept the air of the room free from dirt and dust, it allowed a greater and more sustained heat to be produced, and moreover, a single source could be used to heat more than one room, providing a graded range of temperatures. It is hardly surprising that the hot air system spread rapidly.

Rome was well endowed with bathing establishments. Agrippa, a friend of Augustus, built the first suite of truly public (i.e., free) baths in Rome. Nero erected a suite in the Campus Martius; Titus, building near the Colosseum,

Seneca's evocation of throbbing life in a suite of urban baths captures brilliantly the atmosphere which must have prevailed in virtually every town in the Roman Empire. The baths were the social center of the city—a place of relaxation and recreation, a place to sit and read and talk. Most Romans would visit the baths once a day, usually in late afternoon or early evening, though some may have bathed more frequently. Bathing was an essential part of life. "Baths, wine, and women corrupt our bodies," a Roman wrote, "but these things make life itself."

Private houses with small suites of ill-lit baths were known in the third century B.C., but public baths did not become common until the first century:

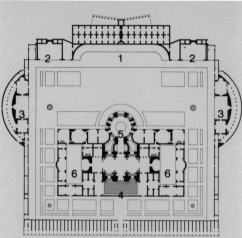

followed him; and Trajan built several in different parts of the city. Among the best-known of Rome's *thermae* are the so-called Baths of Caracalla founded by Septimius Severus in 206 and completed by Alexander Severus between 222 and 235, covering in all an area of some twenty-seven acres. Nearly a century later Diocletian was to build an establishment which approached thirty-two acres in extent. The last great series of baths were erected a few years later on the Quirinal by Constantine. These vast establishments, cavernous in their interior space, luxurious in their detail, still retained the basic elements of bathing, of the kind found in even the most modest provincial suites like those at Pompeii; but their ancillary facilities were greatly extended. Shops, gardens, walks, gymnasiums, exercise courts, and libraries were all included. In fact, the great imperial baths were essentially self-contained leisure centers. The development of this concept owes a great deal to Greek influence. While the baths themselves were a traditional Roman feature, the addition of colonnaded courtyards *(palaestrae)* to provide facilities for exercise and athletics was a distinctively Greek contribution. Vitruvius says as much. He goes on to advise: "In these colonnades, construct spacious recesses with seats in them where philosophers, rhetoricians, and others who delight in learning may sit and converse." He mentions running tracks, covered walks, and suggests how the plan can be arranged so that the strollers do not get in the way of those who have oiled themselves and are taking exercise. Exercise usually preceded bathing. If not already undressed, the bather would undress in the *apodyterium* before proceeding to one of the small very hot dry rooms attached to the *caldarium*.

In Rome, bathing establishments became increasingly grandiose under the Empire. This plan of the Thermae Antoninianae of Caracalla, dedicated in A.D. 216, shows the enormous enclosing wall (350 meters long on each side), with its stadium (1) and libraries (2, 3); within the walls, courtyards surround the symmetrical central building with its large cold bath (4), circular hot bath (5), and exercise courts (6).

Top: Caracalla (r. 211–217); Capitoline Museum.

He would sweat profusely for a while (as in a modern sauna bath) in one of these small rooms before moving into the *caldarium* with its hot, damp atmosphere. This was where the cleansing took place—where the body could be oiled and then scraped clean with a *strigil* (a tool made of metal or ivory). Next the bather would go to the *tepidarium* to cool gradually before taking a final dip in the plunge pool of the *frigidarium*. Although there were of course variations in the routine, this was the procedure recommended by the elder Pliny.

During the first century A.D. the practice of mixed bathing seems to have become widespread. Inevitably promiscuity led to scandal, and Hadrian was forced to decree that the practice be prohibited. There were already many small baths *(balneae)* about the city, some of which were reserved exclusively for females; but at the main *thermae* Hadrian's decree meant either that extensive alterations had to be undertaken to duplicate facilities or that different hours had to be arranged. This latter course was more normally adopted, females being admitted from ten o'clock until one, males from one until closing time, at about six or seven.

Largest of all the baths, the Baths of Diocletian in the center of Rome survive partially today. Portions of the structure have been converted into churches; other parts house the important Terme Museum. Photographs of the museum *(left and right)* give an idea of the cavernous proportions of the interior of the main building, which was originally 250 by 180 meters in area (the entire complex, with walls and courtyards, measured 380 by 370 meters); the baths could accommodate 3,000 persons at a time. Like the Baths of Caracalla, this structure had a symmetrical floor plan in which many of the bathing facilities were duplicated. The baths were erected nearly a century after the Baths of Caracalla, between A.D. 298 and 306. Many buildings were razed to make room for this bathing establishment, which contained facilities for every kind of leisure activity, including gymnastics, reading, lectures, shopping, strolling.

COMMERCE

Nowhere better than in Rome is it possible to appreciate the complexity and the intensity of Roman trade. More than 150 different corporations can be recognized, ranging from the sellers of melons *(peponarii)* to the ballast-loaders *(saburrarii)*, from fishwives *(piscatrices)* to pastry cooks *(siliginarii)*, all following their different trades and professions in and along the crowded streets and squares of the city. The noise was intolerable and the busy confusion of commerce was everywhere to be seen, with the traders and tinkers spreading out their wares over the public sidewalks. So serious was the congestion that the emperor Domitian felt it necessary to pass an edict forbidding traders from using the streets to display their goods. Martial wrote,

No column is now surrounded with chained flagons . . . nor does the dirty cookshop

monopolize the public way. Barber, tavern keeper, cook, and butcher stay within their own thresholds. Now Rome exists, which so recently was one vast shop.

Epigrams VII, 61

The organization of any single aspect of trade was now complex and would be practiced at a variety of levels. The food supply industry naturally dominated the scene. Wine, for example, produced in the countryside or imported from abroad, would be controlled by the wholesale shippers *(magnarii)* who might employ a range of transporters, including wagoners *(catabolenses)* or boatmen *(lenuncularii)*, to carry the product to the market where it would be bought by the tavern keepers *(thermopolae)* for sale to customers. But a tavern keeper might also deal directly with a traveling *vinarius*, who functioned as a middle-

Free grain distribution became the foundation of Rome's economic life during the late Republic and under the Empire. The grain supply, reorganized by Augustus, soon reached 150,000 tons a year; some grain was sold to bakers, and the rest was handed out free to resident citizens, both rich and poor. This coin (24–20 B.C.) showing six ears of wheat commemorates Augustus's institutionalization of the dole.

Right: Scenes from the marketplace:

Greengrocer behind his stand, surrounded by produce which he points out to passersby. Shop sign, relief, Ostia.

A Roman knife seller, detail of a relief, first century A.D. Vatican Museum, Rome.

Butcher wielding a meat cleaver. At right, other cuts of meat hang from hooks. From Ostia Museum.

Gallic shoemaker (with hammer), Reims. Wooden shoes and sandals were a specialty of the province of Gaul.

Left: Shepherd tending his sheep, along with goats (at top) and cattle; sarcophagus relief from Domitilla Catacombs, near Rome, third century B.C. In this earlier period, the city was fed and supplied by farms in its immediate vicinity. Producers of crops and livestock came to town themselves to sell directly to city consumers. Under the Empire, with the growth of land holdings and of Rome's population, food supply and distribution depended more on middlemen who came between producer and consumer.

Right: Bustling activity in a Roman shop. At center, a woman sells fruit to a slave, while at left the merchant helps a customer select a fowl from the supply hanging on the rack. Animals are on sale at far right: two monkeys are chained to the counter, and rabbits peer out of cages at bottom. Shopping facilities were everywhere in ancient Rome—in the large covered markets, in the innumerable small shops lining the narrow streets, and even, for a time, outside on the pavement itself. Many shops were operated by slaves or freedmen, who slept on the premises.

man buying up wine from the country markets and farms and bringing it in his own carts to his city retailers. Similarly, vegetable dealers *(olitores)* might well sell the products of their own market gardens direct to the public, while other retailers like fruiterers *(fructuarii)* would be dependent on suppliers. At another level were those who converted the raw material into consumer delicacies. Grain would be brought to the city for milling before the pastry cooks and the bakers could produce their specialities.

The Roman city was in reality a massive manufacturing center. Raw materials of all kinds would pour in to be distributed among the small establishments for conversion into a wide range of commodities—wood for the cabinet-makers *(citrarii)*, gold for the jewelers *(aurifices)*, hides for the boot makers *(caligarii)*—all of whom would work in their shops, usually in full view of their customers, and display their finished products on the open counter. The fresh smells of spices and of baking would merge with those of stale wine from the taverns or ammonia from the fulling works as one passed by.

A POMPEIAN STREET

Stone sign over a Pompeian tavern: four phalluses, and a dice cup (center). These symbols refer to the establishment's varied amenities: prostitution upstairs, gambling below.

Below left: A loaf of bread carbonized during the eruption of Vesuvius.

Below: Bakery in Pompeii. The large mill stones in the foreground were probably worked by two men. Bread, made on the premises, was fired in the oven seen at the rear.

After the clamor and bustle of Rome, Pompeii must have appeared a tranquil, almost rural, place, even though it was a center of trade and commerce serving a modest resident population of twenty thousand or so, as well as those living in the hinterland around. In the rich countryside, olive oil, wine, cereals, and wool were produced in abundance to be transported to the town for sale

Far left: Tavern scene in Pompeii. The two players throwing dice on a gaming board. One says, "I'm out"; the other replies, "That's a two, not a three."

Carpenter, seated, working with a hammer and chisel. Detail from a wall painting in the Casa dei Vettii, Pompeii, of Daedulus's presentation of a wooden bull to Pasiphaë.

Below: The bar of a streetcorner tavern, Herculaneum. The containers set within the counter were well insulated by the masonry to keep the food hot.

and consumption. In the part so far excavated, twenty taverns and well over a hundred wine bars have been found, as well as forty bakeries and a number of fulling works; together they reflect something of the high degree of commercialization which was overtaking the town at its moment of destruction.

"Gain is joy" and "Welcome gain," scratched on the walls, fairly sum up the commercial attitude of the citizens. By A.D. 79 Pompeii was a town dominated by its *nouveaux riches*—men like Lucius Caecilius Jucundus, a property speculator and banker whose father, a freedman, had founded a profitable family business. It was in his house that a collection of wooden tablets were found recording a wide range of business transactions, including receipts for loans and for rents, particularly those

relating to agricultural and manufacturing properties. Another family, the Vettii (whose house with its garish and vulgar wall paintings is well known to modern visitors), built up their fortune from the wine produced on their various farms. Even the old-established aristocratic families now frequently engaged in profitable wine production.

Originally most of the trading activity would have taken place in and around the forum, but as the town spread, shops sprang up in the front rooms of many of the private houses, quite often representing the mercantile interests of the house owner or his clients. A street like the Via dell'Abbondanza soon became lined with shop fronts and street corner taverns, between which were elegant front doors leading to secluded residences tucked away behind the noisy commercial façade. Elsewhere in the town, once fashionable residential areas declined as manufacturers took over derelict houses to set up their mills and bakeries, or their fulling works. When Vesuvius struck, Pompeii was essentially a town locked in a gradual progression towards widespread industrialization.

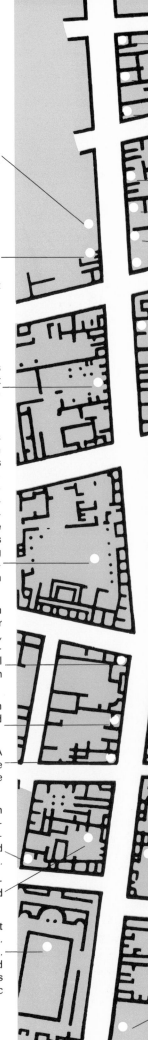
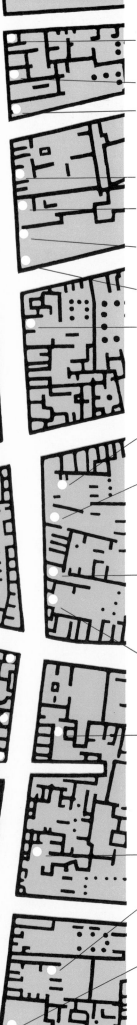

The Via dell'Abbondanza runs northeast from the forum (at bottom). This segment is about a half-kilometer long.

Taverna, a small shop or stall, usually only a few meters wide and fully open at the front. The street is lined with many shops of this kind.

Cloth factory and shop of M. Vecilius Verecundus. Its painted sign showed workers processing cloth in water tanks heated by a wood fire. The sign also bore an election slogan: "The feltworkers support V. Firmus for aedile."

House of Epidius Rufus, a big elaborately painted town house which contained reliefs of gods and maenads. This house is raised slightly above street level, reached by steps on either side of the entry.

The Stabian baths. Approximately 40 by 60 meters in area, they are larger than the Pompeii Forum baths (see page 136). The building enclosed a large central exercise court or *palaestra* complete with outdoor swimming pool. The floor of the *tepidarium* has been destroyed, revealing hollow-brick pillars underneath that conveyed warm air for heating.

Corner house, intersection with Via del Lupanar (Street of the Brothel), which led to one of Pompeii's many houses of ill repute decorated with erotic frescoes.

House of a banker, in which were discovered moneybags and receipts.

Kitchen of the house. A wall painting portrays the sacrifice of a pig to the lares or household gods.

Bedroom of the Dirne, in the so-called House of Ganymede. It contains a fresco of a curious quadruped whose legs are phalluses.

House of Ganymede, cupbearer of the gods, named for the fresco found here.

Building of Eumachía, part of the Forum of Pompeii. The cloth fullers' guild hall. Here, at the southwest end of the street, large stones were placed to keep traffic out of the forum.

House of Sacerdos Amandus, with fresco of Icarus's fall.

Shop, open to the street.

House of Corinthus: paintings of gods and landscapes.

House of C. Cuspius Pansae. In the vestibule, mosaic floor of a dog on a chain, a favorite motif.

Homeric House—mosaics of themes from the Greek epics.

Large shop complex of Fullonica Stephani (a cloth fuller).

Elaborately painted shop.

Kanachosapoll House. Late examples of wall decorations showing theater scenes, masks, landscapes.

Row of narrow shops *(tavernae)* often with tiny mezzanine dwellings or *perculae* upstairs. At the rear, with entrance from a side street, the House of the Guitarist, a palatial town house.

Domus Cornelia, another richly decorated home.

House of Mescinius Gelo. All these houses followed the typical Pompeian arrangement, with rooms placed around series of interior courtyards exposed to the sky. The outside walls were windowless. The kitchen of this house is adorned with pictures of lares and of food.

House called Domus Postumiorum. Among many artworks found here are figures of minor deities, and a Judgment of Paris.

Wall paintings of Mercury and of the goddess Fortuna adorn this shop.

House of a doctor, with many wall paintings (Venus and Adonis, nymphs, banquet scenes, animals). At the very back was the *triclinium* or dining room. Shops line the front, and an alleyway alongside leads to a house behind.

Two additional houses, richly decorated with mythological paintings.

At this corner, where the street begins, stands the Comitium, a meeting hall for the local council. The building, as in many cities, was part of the forum.

On August 24 and 25 in A.D. 79, the wealthy cities of Pompeii and Herculaneum, near Naples, were buried, by the eruption of Mount Vesuvius, in a thick layer of ash and mud. Excavations, beginning in 1748, have unearthed the vanished cities. One of Pompeii's major commercial thoroughfares, the Via dell'Abbondanza or Street of Plenty, is shown in the photograph below, looking northeast from the forum. At left, a diagram of the first few blocks of the street.

We saw the sea sucked away and apparently forced back by the earthquake: at any rate it receded from the shore so that quantities of sea creatures were left stranded on dry sand. On the landward side a fearful black cloud was rent by forked and quivering bursts of flame, and parted to reveal great tongues of fire.... Ashes were already falling, not as yet very thickly. I looked round: a dense black cloud was coming up behind us, spreading over the earth like a flood. "Let us leave the road while we can still see," I said, "or we shall be knocked down and trampled underfoot in the dark by the crowd behind." We had scarcely sat down to rest when darkness fell....

A gleam of light returned, but we took this to be a warning of the approaching flames rather than daylight. However, the flames remained some distance off; then darkness came on once more and ashes began to fall again, this time in heavy showers. We rose from time to time and shook them off, otherwise we should have been buried and crushed beneath their weight.... At last the darkness thinned and dispersed into smoke or cloud; then there was genuine daylight, and the sun actually shone out, but yellowish as it is during an eclipse. We were terrified to see everything changed, buried deep in ashes like snowdrifts.

Pliny the Younger, eyewitness account of the eruption of Vesuvius, A.D. 79.

OSTIA

Ostia, Rome's first colony, founded in the mid-fourth century, was strategically located at the mouth of the Tiber, fifteen miles downriver from the city. Thus, it could protect the river approaches from pirate attack and serve as a base where the cargoes from seagoing vessels could be transferred to the lighter river craft. The importance of the site to Rome's expanding economy was considerable: by the second century, settlement had spread well beyond the confines of the original fort, down towards the old coastline and along the main road to Rome, eventually to be enclosed by a new defensive wall built by Sulla in the early first century B.C.

The town was, above all, a thriving commercial port. Nowhere is this better represented than in the building known as the Square of the Corporations which lies between the theater and the old course of the River Tiber. The square, a large open courtyard containing a temple possibly dedicated to the goddess Ceres, was surrounded by colonnades; behind them lay sixty-one small rooms of more or less equal size, which served as the offices for merchants and guilds each of whom signified his business in the mosaic-work of his threshold. The range of crafts and occupations is fascinating—caulkers and rope makers reflect the shipfitting industry, corn measurers (*mensones frumentarii*) and weighers (*sacomarii*) remind us of the importance of official standards of measurement, while the furriers and timber merchants give some idea of the range of imports. Most of the offices were, however, devoted to the corporations of fitters (*navicularii*), each proclaiming his port of origin—Sabratha and Hippo on the North African coast, Alexandria in Egypt, Arles and Narbonne in Gaul, Porto Torres and Cagliari in Sardinia, and many others. The Square of the Corporations is a vivid visual reminder of Rome's far-flung commercial contacts.

Cleary such a volume of overseas trade could not have been carried out without adequate port facilities. Originally the habor lay at Ostia itself, but the silting of the river mouth began to cause problems. Claudius therefore decided, against expert advice, to build a new harbor to the north, joined to the Tiber by canals. Suetonius reports:

Modern plan reconstruction of Ostia in the second century A.D. The original town is at the right, beside the winding Tiber; at left, linked by canal to the river, are the manmade ports built under Claudius (r. A.D. 41–54) and Trajan (98–117).

Opposite below: Mosaic from Ostia. The man transfers a wine amphora from a seagoing ship to a river boat.

Opposite bottom: Mosaic threshold from a shipping office in the Square of the Corporations, Ostia. The name below the ships identifies the port with which the office traded.

Coin, issued under Nero in A.D. 64–66, showing bird's-eye view of the port of Ostia as rebuilt by Claudius. Ships are in the harbor, which is surrounded by colonnaded warehouses. Neptune appears at bottom.

Center: Gravestone carving (second–third century A.D.) of a Roman ship of the Mosell, loaded with wine barrels. Rheinisches Landesmuseum, Trier.

Bottom: Ostia Antica as it appears today; excavation began in the early nineteenth century.

At Ostia, Claudius threw out curved breakwaters on either side of the harbor and built a deep-water mole by its entrance. For the base of this mole he used the ship in which Caligula had transported a great obelisk from Heliopolis; it was first sunk, then secured with piles, and finally crowned with a very tall lighthouse . . . that guided ships into the harbor at night by the beams of a lamp. Lives of the Caesars

The new harbor was not, however, particularly effective, and in A.D. 62 two hundred corn ships taking shelter inside were destroyed in a fierce storm. Some years later Trajan embarked on a new scheme which involved the excavation of a hexagonal basin, suitable for mooring in excess of three hundred

ships, surrounded by extensive areas of warehousing. The new establishment, Portus Ostiae, developed into a small harbor town, but Ostia remained the principal commercial center until the fourth century. It then became known as Portus Romae, reflecting the direct links which had developed between port and city.

Warehousing facilities around the ports covered vast areas, well in excess of ten hectares (twenty-five acres) by Hadrian's time. The storage sheds (*horrea*) were mostly used for grain or for general purposes, but some were designed to hold specialized commodities like the *horrea candelaria* for candles and tallow and the *horrea piperatoria* near the city forum where spices and pepper were stored. Some were privately owned, but others, particularly those used for storing Rome's grain supply, were imperial property. The colossal storage capacity both at the harbor towns themselves and along the wharves of Rome, is a clear reminder of the level of daily consumption in the capital.

145

WINE

Among the most widely traded commodities in the Roman world were wine and oil. At Ostia both were imported in sealed ceramic containers (*amphorae*) which would then have been transferred from the ocean-going ships to river barges for the last leg of their journey up the Tiber to the storehouses of Rome.

Ostia has so far yielded evidence of four warehouses where liquids were stored in large *amphorae* set in the

the volume must have been considerable.

One of the principal vine-growing areas in Italy was Campania where, according to Pliny the Elder, vintage wine of some quality was produced, particularly on the slopes of Vesuvius. The countryside hereabouts was peppered with specialized farming establishments like the farm (Villa Rustica) at Boscoreale where all the fittings relating to the production of olive

little doubt that production was carefully controlled and highly specialized. It would also be profitable, as Cato makes clear when he writes: "Those who are prepared to combine diligence with scientific knowledge get a return *per iugerum* that will enable them to win hands down against those who hang on to their hay and their pot herbs."

Although Italy was well able to produce much of its own needs in late Republican times and into the early Empire, by the second century A.D. not only had the population increased considerably but production had drastically declined, so much so that the restrictive laws which forbade the cultivation of vines and olives in North Africa (and thus protected the Italian estate owners) were repealed. It was at this time that the volume of foreign imports, Greek, African, and Spanish, began to increase dramatically. The situation had changed significantly since the first century B.C. and the early first century A.D. when Italian agriculture was sufficiently buoyant for shiploads of wine to be sent to far-flung parts like Britain for trading with the then-unconquered barbarians.

Grapes were pressed the simplest way, although the workers in this relief are using large rods to assist their feet.

Below: Three colorless glass wine decanters, found in Pompeii but probably imported.

ground to keep the contents cool. Each vessel could contain about a thousand liters, and in one establishment more than two hundred such containers were found. This gives some idea of the quantities kept back for the use of the local community. How much passed upriver it is difficult to assess, but

oil and wine have been found. An establishment of this kind had a storage capacity of more than a hundred thousand liters and would no doubt have served the nearby market of Pompeii.

The attention given to vine growing in Roman books on agriculture leaves

Wine production was an important part of Rome's economy, just as wine consumption figured prominently in Roman daily life. This Pompeian relief, showing two slaves transporting a full wine amphora, was a sign for either a wine shop or a wine merchants' corporation.

Opposite top: Gravestone of a wine dealer named Sebern. The crudely chiseled wine barrel at left identifies his trade, and the symbol at center marks him as a Christian. Rome, Lateran Museum.

Below: Trouble in a Pompeian tavern. Two drunken dice players disagree about the score, and a fight appears to be imminent. The inscription on the painting says that they should settle the argument outside.

TRAJAN'S MARKETS

In A.D. 100–112, to the north of the Forum Romanum, Emperor Trajan *(right)* built his own forum and a vast five-story market with 150 shops.

Below left: Interior of the main hall, located uphill on the fourth level (in the northwest corner).

Center: In the sketch, the cobblestoned Via Biberatica climbs the slope dividing the Market's two main sections.

Trajan returned from his Dacian wars, loaded down with spoils and determined to make his mark upon the city of Rome. He chose for one of his ambitious architectural projects a steeply contoured stretch of land between the Quirinal and the Capitoline hills immediately adjacent to the Forum of Augustus. There he created a masterpiece of civic architecture—a vast complex of forum, basilica, libraries, and markets. It was here that his famous column was to stand, depicting scenes from his recent battles, its height (thirty-

predecessor. Grand though these buildings were and fine in their detailing, they were traditional in both form and construction. Yet to the northeast of the forum, tucked away in the rather constricted, steeply sloping area against the Quirinal, lay a complex of brilliant originality—Trajan's Markets. The Markets, constructed on three different levels, were a commercial quarter comprising about 150 shops and offices, together with a market hall. The architecture was functional in the extreme. The entire structure, built of brick-

The five stories of the market complex were concerned mainly with the sale of foodstuffs. Though the exact arrangements are still far from clear, it is likely that the ground-floor shops, at forum level, were devoted to the sale of fruit and flowers. At the first floor, storage space was provided for oil and wine which would have been sold in shops fronting onto a loggia.

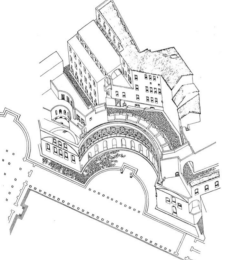

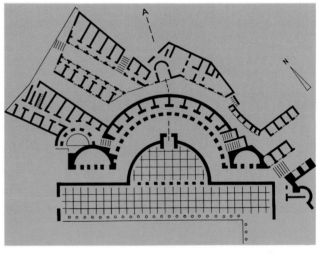

Plan of the Markets, a beehive of shops.

Below: Middle level (Via Biberatica) looking east, showing the main doors of spice shops.

eight meters) representing the depth of soil and rock quarried away to make level space for the elegant public squares and colonnades.

The overall plan was simple: a huge colonnaded forum occupied three-fifths of the area. It was conventional in every respect except that its fourth side, usually occupied by a temple, was closed by a great basilica—the Basilica Ulpia. Beyond this, visually isolated from the rest of the complex, lay a smaller courtyard with the column in the center flanked on either side by libraries. Further on again the original plan is lost, but it was here that Hadrian constructed a temple to his deified

faced concrete, was composed of a series of modules, each a single square or rectangular room with vaulted roof and wide door opening, giving a maximum degree of flexibility both in the arrangement of the overall plan and in the use to which the individual shop was put. Here in austere utilitarian architecture, molded into the curve of the land, using modern building techniques and eschewing the desire for grandiose façades and lines of vision, the architect was taking a major step towards the "new architecture" of the later Empire, which placed major emphasis on massive dimensions and cavernous interiors.

Below: The façade of the Markets, a great hemicircle which faced Trajan's Forum; the building's five levels climb the slope of the Quirinale. This complex structure exemplifies the Empire's new style in utilitarian architecture on a large scale. Primarily used for the sale of foodstuffs, the Markets also contained a center for the distribution of free food.

Overleaf: The market in the North African town of Leptis Magna, rebuilt by Septimius Severus (r. 193–211). The large paved precinct contained two *tholoi* (circular structures) enclosed by octagonal colonnades. The arched windows in the *tholos* were provided with broad sills upon which the traders could display their merchandise.

Above this, on the second and third floors, was the pepper and spice market, the memory of which is enshrined in the medieval name for the Roman street which winds up the hill between the stalls—the Via Biberatica (from *pipera* meaning spice). On the next floor, the fourth, was the hall where public distributions of food and money were made and where the offices of those

in charge of public assistance were situated. Finally, on the fifth floor, was the first market served by two aqueducts, one with fresh water and the other salt water, to keep the goods fresh for the table.

Trajan's Markets were revolutionary not only in their architecture but in their functional conception. Indeed it might be said that they foreshadowed

in many ways the modern shopping center. Trajan's overall scheme, which entailed dividing the grand from the prosaic, was the culmination of a development which had begun in the last century of the Republic. What was entirely novel was the way in which totally different architectural modes were developed to suit the separated functions.

ENTERTAINMENT

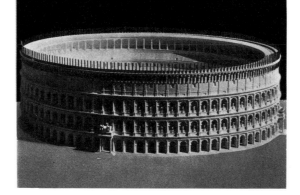

The passion of the Roman populace for entertainment was enormous. During the reign of Claudius 93 days each year were expressly devoted to games and spectacles provided at the public expense; by the end of the second century the number had risen to 135! Contemporary writers were in no doubt how this should be interpreted:

Now that no one buys our votes, the public has long since cast off its cares; the people that once bestowed commands, consulships, legions, and all else now meddles no more

The message is clear enough—to control the Roman mob, colossal sums of private and public money had to be spent to keep them in amused idleness. Any emperor who failed to comply with convention and to outshine the generosity and inventiveness of his predecessors would leave himself open to dangerous criticism. But it was more than that. Shows and spectacles were usually attended by the emperor and his court: he watched with rapt attention, shared with the masses their excitement, and consulted with them over who should live and who should

Left: The emperor Theodosius I and his family in the royal box overlooking the circus at Constantinople. The relief forms the base for an Egyptian obelisk erected on the *spina* of the circus.

Right: Gladiators in combat. The left-hand pair represent a lightly clad *retiarius* (or net-fighter), wounded in the leg, competing against a *secutores* armed with rectangular shield and a short sword. On his left leg he wears a greave, while his right arm is protected by leather bands. The center pair are heavily armed. The individual with two leg greaves and small square shield is a "Thracian" who would normally fight with a curved sword *(sica)*. His opponent is a "Samnite" distinguished by his crested helmet, long shield, and greave on the left leg only. Standing next to them are a similar pair—a triumphant "Thracian," this time with circular shield and lance, and a wounded "Samnite" disputing with his trainer.

and longs eagerly for just two things—bread and circuses.   Juvenal, *Satires* X, 77–81

The Roman people is absorbed by two things above all else, its food supplies and shows. His wisdom [Trajan's] never failed to pay attention to the star performers of the theater, the circus of the arena, for he well knew that the excellence of a government is shown no less in its care for the amusements of the people than in serious matters and that although the distribution of grain and money may satisfy the individual, spectacles are necessary for the contentment of the masses.   Fronto, *Principles of History*

die. These occasions provided the moments when the common mob could feel a oneness with their rulers, when *princeps* and people alike were intimately bound up in the same group emotions, and were moved as one body by the events they were together witnessing.

When the actor Pylades, chided by Augustus for his exhibitionism, said, "It is in *your* interest, Caesar, that the people should keep their thoughts on us," he was expressing only half the truth. Performances certainly provided the masses with the necessary distrac-

Left: Modern model reconstruction of the Colosseum in Rome, and a coin commemorating the completion in A.D. 80 of this amphitheater which it took twenty years to build. Shown here filled with spectators, the Colosseum had a seating capacity of fifty thousand.

Right: Boxers and athletes shown on a mosaic which originally adorned the Baths of Caracalla in Rome. The man at the far right wears boxing gloves weighted with metal and held in place with leather arm straps.

Three mosaics from Leptis Magna in North Africa depicting gladiatorial combat. Musicians played an essential part in these popular shows. The ensemble depicted in the scene at left includes a trumpet *(tuba)* player, a performer on the hydraulic organ, and two seated figures each playing the horn *(cornu)*. Musical interludes amused the audience during intervals, but instruments also announced, and probably accompanied, the contests. The trumpet would herald the beginning of a fight while the horns might be used to increase the excitement of the spectacle. The mosaic shows that the contest has reached a crucial stage, the victor being constrained by his trainer.

Ad bestias: the horrors of the amphitheater. A man, possibly a Garamantian captive, bound to a stake, is wheeled out into the arena to be savaged by a leopard. Elsewhere other more fortunate performers amuse the audience. A spear man stands by as two hunting dogs chase and maul a stag and a goat. Nearby a man is engaged in a bare-handed fight with a wild boar.

Animals were important to amphitheater spectacles, because they acted both as executioner (as the leopard shown here) and as victim. Rome imported animals from all over the Empire and beyond—including leopards from the Near East, tigers from India, wild bulls from the north, and many other beasts from Africa, the main source. To celebrate the grand opening of the Colosseum, gladiators fought the beasts for 100 days, reportedly killing 9,000 animals.

tions, but they also provided a vehicle for communal experience.

Two ancient traditions lay behind the pattern of Roman amusements: Etruscan funerary games and Greek theater. Both were modified and debased in order to satisfy the increasingly sadistic demands of the Roman populace. There emerged three different types of performance: chariot races in the circus, gladiatorial events in the amphitheater, and scripted performances in the theater and odeum. In each case the buildings were carefully structured to suit the different functions.

Circuses, which were designed specifically for races, consisted simply of a

Chariots would be drawn normally by four horses *(quadrigae)*, though teams of two *(bigae)* or three *(trigae)* were not uncommon, and occasionally teams of six or more were to be seen. Racing was big business. It was, moreover, thoroughly organized. Those whose responsibility it was to arrange the spectacle would negotiate to pay a suitable fee to each of the four main parties *(factiones)*, who in return would provide at least one team for each race, and there might be anything up to twenty-four races a day. The cost would have been considerable, for each *factio* had to maintain its own stables, buying, training, and caring for the

Rome idolized her star chariot racers and their horses as well. The mosaic at left lists the names of the four horses shown; it comes from Spain, where many horses were bred for Roman racing.

Right: A *quadriga* (four-horse chariot) on a terracotta Roman relief, British Museum.

These races were lively social occasions. To vary the entertainment, chariot events were interspersed with horse racing, the jockeys often displaying considerable bravery and skill in their acrobatics designed to amuse and excite the public. The day might be further enlivened by gifts showered on the spectators by the organizers.

long flat track flanked by tiers of seats arranged either along sloping valley sides or upon masonry substructures, whatever the local topography demanded. They could range from the very simplest rural location to colossal man-made structures like the Circus Maximus at Rome with a seating capacity of more than a quarter of a million spectators.

horses. It had to pay for the training and upkeep of its riders and cover the costs of providing all ancillary workers such as grooms, saddlers, and veterinary surgeons. The four *factiones* were distinguished by their colors, the whites, greens, blues, and reds, and the rivalry between them and their supporters often assumed the proportions of a political conflict.

Far left: Coin of A.D. 104–111 representing Rome's Circus Maximus, the most elaborate chariot-racing stadium of the time, with a seating capacity of more than 200,000. The coin shows its obelisks, colonnades, and statues of *quadrigae* above arches at each end.

Emperor Domitian (A.D. 81–96) erected a much plainer *circus*, shown *(center left)* in a modern reconstruction, with the Pantheon in the top left corner a few houses away. Today the oblong Piazza Navona occupies the site *(left)*, retaining the original shape of the site.

ANNIAE
ARESCVSA

T.337.

THEATER

Although theaters continued to be built and rebuilt throughout the Roman Empire, creative theater in the Greek sense was already dead. Plautus and Terence represent not the beginnings of a new Roman approach to drama and comedy, but the end of the Greek-inspired tradition. Admittedly plays

The Theater of Pompey, in a model reconstruction. Built in 55 B.C., this was Rome's first theater made of stone. Its vast dimensions set the style for the future.

Right: Terra-cotta statue of an actor wearing the mask of tragic youth. From Pompeii.

Below: Characters rehearse for a Greek satyr play. The bald seated figure is the chorus master; before him two actors dance to the music of a pipe. Mosaic from Pompeii.

Right: Spectator's view of the stage, theater of Leptis Magna in North Africa. Built in A.D. 1–2, and later renovated.

continued to be written, but they were now intended for reading aloud to small audiences rather than for acting in the vast and thoroughly unsuitable Roman theaters. Indeed it was the very size of these structures that forced the evolution of a new dramatic form. Roman productions early disposed of the tradition which required the mem-

bers of the chorus to remain in the orchestra and instead brought them up on to the stage with the actors, at the same time gradually cutting down the dialogue until there emerged a new form of drama in which the action, accompanied by a minimum of words, was enlivened at intervals by short bursts of lyrics *(cantica)*. These *cantica*

became the preserve of soloists who soon emerged as the stars and the prima donnas of the theater, skilled not only in singing but in dancing and mime as well. But another change was in progress—the divorce between the voice and the action. By the second century this was complete: the chorus was left to sing the *cantica*

AMPHITHEATERS

accompanied by musicians while the actor mimed the action. In this way the pantomime was perfected; opera had transformed itself into ballet.

Changes in dramatic form brought with them physical changes in the theater itself. The backdrop (scaena) grew in size and elaboration, while the stage, now the chief location for the action, was extended out into the orchestra. The elegant simplicity of the Greek theater was totally swamped by the Roman desire to monumentalize. Of the plays themselves there is little to be said. They usually fell into one of two categories: formal tragedies often based on mythology, or general entertainment of the coarser, more brutal kind involving incest, rape, torture, and murder. Political topics were sometimes treated, but inevitably, under the Empire, they bowed in their interpretation to conform with the official state line: criticism of government was unheard of.

In many ways mime offered a new freedom to theatrical form. Old conventions such as masks and standardized dress were dispensed with, and there was now ample scope for improvisation. At its best, mime could be highly creative, but in reality the need of the theater to compete with the arena for its audience meant that the newfound realism turned more and more towards the sexual and sadistic. Actresses were allowed to undress, and acts of violence were often real. The ultimate depths were reached under Domitian when a criminal, substituted for an actor, held his hand in the fire while another was publicly crucified on the stage. The culmination of another play, *The Death of Hercules*, came when the hero was actually burned to death in front of the audience. Perversion had plumbed the depths.

The idea of the amphitheater—an oval arena enclosed on all sides by tiers of seats—probably originated in Campania. Indeed one of the earliest known examples was built at Pompeii early in the first century B.C. The introduction of the idea to Rome is credited to Curio the Younger, who in 53 B.C., to gain the favor of the mob, arranged to put on a series of shows. To accommodate them he built two timber theaters back to back, arranged on swivels so that, after the separate performances had taken place, the theaters could be swung on their axes to face each other and thus to enclose a single arena for the games which followed. The novel event excited the spectators, but Rome's earliest stone amphitheater was not erected until 29 B.C.

The amphitheater was strictly a place where human sacrifice was carried out for the amusement and titillation of the populace. Gladiatorial contests date back to the Etruscan period when contests, leading to death, would often accompany the funeral ceremony of a chieftain. The earliest recorded example of such games in Rome took place in 264 B.C. at the funeral of a nobleman at which three pairs of gladiators fought each other. Clearly these early examples represent a primitive ritual in which the gods, placated by the sacrifice of one or more humans, were thus put in a good humor to receive the dead chieftain. Since slaves were expendable, it was they who were made to fight. By the first century B.C. these contests had lost all of their ritual significance and had become merely spectacles for the increasingly sadistic masses. In Julius Caesar's time a single program of games (manus) involved 320 pairs of gladiators. Under later emperors not only did the numbers increase, but the length of the games was

The brutalizing effect of the arena on Roman society is not hard to estimate, nor is it difficult to rationalize; but what is beyond comprehension is why so many men of culture failed to condemn it. Pliny and Cicero made excuses, others ignored it. Only a few, like Seneca, were prepared to give vent to their disgust.

I've happened to drop in upon the midday entertainment of the arena in hope of some milder diversions, a spice of comedy, a touch of the relief in which men's eyes may find rest after a glut of human blood. No, no: far from it. All the previous fighting was mere softness of heart. Away with such bagatelles: now for butchery pure and simple! The combatants have nothing to protect them: their bodies are utterly open to every blow: never a thrust but finds its mark. Most people prefer this kind of thing to all other matches, whether part of the program or by special request. Naturally so. The sword is not checked by helmet or shield. What good is armor? What good is swordsmanship? All these things only put off death a little. In the morning men are matched with lions and bears, at noon with their spectators. These pit butcher actual against butcher prospectively and reserve the winner for another bloody bout: death is the fighters' only exit. "But this, that, or the other fellow has committed highway robbery!" Well? "And murder!" As a murderer, then, he deserves what he's getting: what's your *crime, unlucky creature, that you should watch it? "Kill! Flog! Burn! Why does he jib at cold steel? Why boggle at killing? Why die so squeamishly?" The lash forces them on to the sword. "Let them have at each other in the nude—get in at the bare chest!" There's an interval in the display. "Cut a few throats meanwhile to keep things going!" Come now, can't you people see even this much—that bad examples recoil on those who set them?*

Seneca, *Moral Epistles* VII, 2

pointed to ensure an adequate supply of trained manpower for the arena.

To provide the spectators with some variety, animal shows *(venationes)* would be staged, ranging from circus-like displays of well-trained beasts performing tricks, to simulated hunts and mass slaughter. The carnage could reach unbelievable proportions. During the inauguration of the Colosseum in A.D. 80, five thousand animals were

The Roman Colosseum, view of the underground passages and chambers that were covered by the arena. This basement contained cages for the wild animals and mechanisms to transport them rapidly into the arena. Here too, lay an intricate water system which allowed the arena to be flooded to convert it into a *naumachia* for sea battles.

greatly extended. One program organized by Trajan lasted 117 days and involved nearly 5,000 pairs of fighters. In all, it is estimated that in the brief period 106–114 A.D. some 23,000 individuals fought for their lives to entertain the citizens, at least half of them prisoners from the Dacian wars.

Gladiators were slaves or dropouts under the control of contractors *(lanistae)* whose profession it was to have available for hire a suitable troup

whenever the local magistrates required one. The *lanistae* ran the training schools in which their gladiators practiced and the barracks where they were housed. The men were trained to fight in one of several modes—as Thracians with dagger and small round shield, as Samnites with sword and shield, as *murmillones* with helmets, or as *retiarii* with net and trident. In Rome, with its colossal consumption of gladiators, special officials *(procuratores)* were ap-

killed in a single day! To vary the diet and add piquancy, animals could be set against each other or against defenseless prisoners condemned to death *ad bestias*. It was in this manner that many Christians, male and female alike, were to die. The craving for novelty was insatiable. And when the day was done, the bodies removed, and the sand raked, the mob would return home to look forward to the excitements of the next morning.

Masked actors in a comedy, believed to represent a drunken youth (at left) supported by his slave who must help him stagger home. Marble relief, Museo Nazionale, Naples, early first century A.D.

THE THEATER

The Roman theater derived from the Greek, which itself, in origin, was nothing more than a circular dance floor (orchestra) partially surrounded by seats for spectators (auditorium). In the Greek theater much of the action took place in the orchestra in front of a permanent backdrop (skene) behind which lay the changing room. It

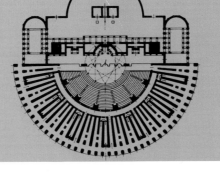

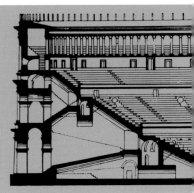

was in the orchestra that the chorus would remain while the actors performed on a narrow stage in front of the skene. Gradually, as the significance of the chorus declined, the stage became wider and higher to accommodate the action. The Roman architect Vitruvius, writing in the first century B.C., distinguishes two types of performers—the scenici who were on the stage and the thy-

THE ODEUM

The odeum (Greek odeion) was essentially a small permanently roofed theater set aside for musical performances and recitations. One odeum was built in Rome but is now lost. Perhaps the best known is the small theater or odeum at Pompeii, which was built ca. 80–75 B.C. immediately adjacent to the large theater. It

was tiny in comparison, with a seating capacity of between 1,000 and 1,500, but was wholly suitable for intimate performances. Another famous structure of this type, the Odeum of Agrippa, was built in the agora at Athens during the reign of Augustus to provide accommodation for about 1,000 spectators. The hall was roofed in a single span of 25 meters. The entire building, shown

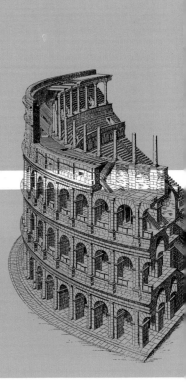

THE AMPHITHEATER

The amphitheater was simply an oval arena completely surrounded by tiers of seats. The first permanent amphitheater in Rome was built in 29 B.C., but the idea was already well established in the south in Campania. By the second century A.D. few towns of importance in the western provinces and North Africa were without

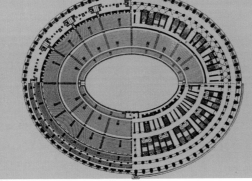

them. Most famous of all is the Colosseum in Rome, begun by Vespasian and finished by Titus in A.D. 80. (Left: Floor plan of the Colosseum. Right: Isometric section.) It had a capacity of 50,000. Entrance was obtained through 80 arched openings (76 were available to the public), which led into a wide corridor surrounding the building from which stairways led to the various sec-

THE CIRCUS

The circus consisted of a long race track flanked by tiers of seats (cavea), as shown in the plan of the Circus of Gaius and Nero (right), A.D. 40–60. The track was divided lengthwise by a longitudinal bank or wall (spina) with terminal markers (metae) at each end. This spina became progressively more elaborate.

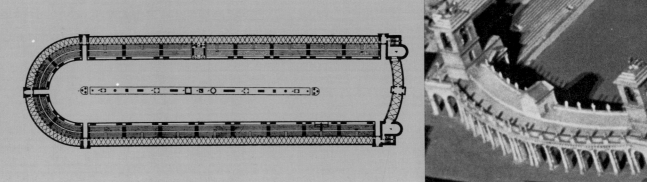

Roman relief floor plan showing the auditorium of the Theater of Marcellus, which was completed by Augustus in 13 B.C. The Theater of Marcellus is also depicted, directly below, in the three illustrations to the left: floor plan, elevation sketch, and a model reconstruction showing the stage and part of the façade.

Overleaf: The Colosseum in Rome, built by Vespasian on the site of the lake near Nero's Golden House.

Pages 164–165: Amphitheater of El Djem, the Roman town of Thysdrus, in Tunisia. Probably built by the proconsul Gordianus, A.D. 230–238, the amphitheater is the largest in Africa.

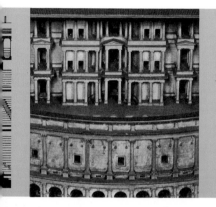

melici who remained in the orchestra. The latter were not the same as the Greek chorus; they were more like musical contestants. For Vitruvius the distinction is an important one and is emphasized by the height of the stage which he advises to be in the order of three to four meters.

In the Roman theater the stage is backed by the *scaenae frons* several stories high in order,

according to Vitruvius, to improve the acoustics. Above, a timber roof projected outwards to cover the full extent of the stage. The *scaenae frons* was usually an elaborately decorated architectural façade designed to represent a palace and provided with a number of doors through which the actors could enter.

Left: Theater of Dougga, ruins of the *scaenae frons*.

in floor plan *(far left)* was surrounded by colonnades.

The Odeum of Domitian in Rome, constructed between A.D. 81 and 96, was unusual in form and scale. Built on a semicircular plan, as shown in the model reconstruction *(left)* it reportedly could accommodate some 10,000 persons. The building stood near the Theater of Pompey in Rome. Only one pillar has survived.

Odeum of Gorthys, Crete *(left)*, which the Romans erected in 67 B.C. over an original Greek building. It was covered with a permanent roof. Gorthys became the Roman headquarters on Crete. The modern arcades at rear protect the wall that contains a famous law inscription which dates from 500 B.C. and which had been built into the odeum.

tions of the *cavea* (rows of seats). Encircling corridors were provided at each level. Thus the entire structure could have been emptied in minutes.

Shown at left are two examples from outside Rome. In the fresco, the amphitheater of Pompeii, begun in 70 B.C. The well-preserved first-century A.D. amphitheater of Pola, in present-day Yugoslavia, appears in the photograph.

In the Circus Maximus, the most famous of all circuses *(model at left)*, the *spina* contained the eggs representing the seven laps which charioteers had to make. After each lap, an egg was removed. Agrippa added seven bronze dolphins which could be reversed with each lap. Augustus added an Egyptian obelisk to the *spina*; Claudius gilded the *metae* and rebuilt the

stables in marble. The wooden seats of the Circus Maximus were partially replaced in stone, and the track was gradually enlarged until it reached its final enormous proportions, 200 meters wide by 600 meters long, with a seating capacity of over 200,000.

The hippodrome at Aphrodisias in Asia Minor *(right)* presents a far more simple scheme, with seats built on hill slopes.

THE RICH AND THE POOR

Luxurious self-indulgence of a wealthy young man, shown reclining with a half-nude courtesan. He drinks from a rhyton while the woman signals to a servant. The table in the foreground holds materials for the mixing of drinks. Wall painting from Herculaneum.

Below: The famous *Aldobrandini Wedding*, fresco of the late first century B.C. from a house on the Esquiline. The bride is seated on the nuptial bed; women at either side prepare the rites.

Roman society was rigorously stratified both in law and in wealth. By the second century B.C., citizens were legally divided into two categories: the *honestiones* and the *humiliores*. To the first category belonged the upper classes, senators, knights, magistrates, soldiers, and veterans. They were in a protected position in the eyes of the law, and even if they were found guilty of some offense their punishments would be lenient and in no way designed to degrade them. The *humiliores*, on the other hand, could be punished without restraint with torture, death, or servitude. If this was how lowly Roman citizens could be treated, then lesser classes—noncitizens and slaves—could expect no mercy. Slaves were property, and as such were

> In their dress,
> their table, their houses,
> and their furniture, the favorites
> of fortune united every
> refinement of convenience, of elegance,
> and of splendor, whatever could
> soothe their pride or gratify
> their sensuality. Such refinements...
> have been severely arraigned
> by the moralists.
>
> Gibbon

performing functions ranging from cook to teacher. Although five hundred was a respectable number for a wealthy man, Pliny the Elder records one individual who owned more than four thousand and it is estimated that the emperor had five times that number. For some, particularly those working on the farms, life could be very hard. Cato in his advice to farmers made it perfectly clear that good slave management was essential to keep up their level of production, much as one would feed and tend an animal. "Being also of the opinion that the greater cause of misbehavior in slaves was their sexual passions, he arranged for the males to consort with the females—at a fixed price." And when a slave was too old to work, like an

without significant rights. They were employed in colossal numbers. In the first century A.D., between a quarter and a third of Rome's population were in slavery. Little wonder that when it was proposed to make them wear distinctive dress, the idea was turned down on the grounds that it would be too dangerous to let them see how numerous they were. The average

wealthy family might own five hundred or so (this was about the number that Pliny the Younger possessed), and anyone who couldn't muster eight was of very little account. A man's slaves would be divided into two groups, one for his country estates and one for his town house; the latter would be divided again between the outdoor and indoor staff, the indoor slaves

animal he would be sold off. Others, such as Seneca, were more humane:

Please reflect that the man you call your slave was born of the same seed, has the same good sky above him, breathes air you do, lives as you do, dies as you do.... Treat your slave with kindness, with courtesy too; let him share your conversation, your deliberations, and your company. Moral Epistles XLVII

The life of the poor offers a stark contrast: Slaves are forced into exhausting manual work in the great tread-wheel which operates a builder's crane. Detail from the funerary monument of the Haterii, Rome: second century A.D. The poor occupied tenement blocks. Those built at Ostia *(below)* were comfortable compared with the unsafe garrets of Rome.

An educated slave from an enlightened household would have been much better off than a high percentage of the urban poor.

The gulf between rich and poor had reached frightening proportions by the early Empire: between one-third and a half of the city's population lived on state assistance. In Trajan's time (98–117), taking into account slaves and noncitizens, only about twelve percent of the residents could have supported themselves without state aid.

Relative standards of living are difficult to gauge with any accuracy, but a modest middle-class existence could have been maintained on 20,000 sesterces a year. This approximated to the lowest level of a centurion's pay and also to the income on an invested

capital of 400,000 sesterces, which was regarded as the minimum wealth assessment for a member of the Equestrian Order. To be admitted to the Senatorial Order, one would have had to have around two and a half times that sum. There was a world of difference between the *petit bourgeois* with his fortune of 400,000 sesterces and a man like Pliny the Younger, a successful advo-

cate and administrator, with 20 million—and even then Pliny believed himself to be rather poorly off. While the urban poor lived in cramped apartment blocks and rickety timber garrets, grossly overcrowded and constantly at the mercy of fires and epidemics, the rich might have had several spacious

residences. Vitruvius demanded that the house be designed to suit the status of the occupant:

Men of rank must have lofty entrance courts in regal style and most spacious atriums and peristyles, with plantations and walks of some extent in them appropriate to their dignity. They need also libraries, picture galleries, and basilicas.

On Architecture VI, v, 2

The grand architect-designed house must have been something of a contrast to the crumbling tenements which the exploited poor inhabited, "a city propped up for the most part by slats: for that is how the landlord patches up the crack in the old wall, bidding the inmates sleep at ease under

168

the ruin that hangs above their heads" (Juvenal III, 190–196).

As Vitruvius makes explicit, high-rise tenements were a response to a rapidly growing population. If properly planned and constructed, like the apartment blocks at Ostia, with their units of five or six rooms linked by a wide corridor, they would have provided ample and congenial living space for the family. "The accommodation within the city walls being thus multiplied as a result of many floors high in the air," writes Vitruvius, "the Roman people easily find excellent places in which to live" (II, viii, 17). This may well have been so, but the prospects of increasing the number of rents which could be extracted from every plot encouraged landlords to erect unsafe structures and to pack in as many people as possible. There was also a tendency for landlords to evict tenants from older properties so that they could redevelop in tall apartment style. Crassus greatly

Above left: In this detail of a mural from the Villa dei Misteri, a woman watches religious rites.

Below: Pompeii's largest atrium (measuring 17 by 12 meters), House of the Silver Wedding, with a skylight and a basin to collect rainwater.

increased his fortune by buying up fire-damaged properties and rebuilding in this way. Inevitably, whenever there is pressure on housing arising from a rapid increase in population, the poor are likely to fall victim to the speculator. Contrast the cramped tenements of the poor with the palaces erected for the emperors. Admittedly the house of Augustus on the Palatine was comparatively modest, but his successors were not so restrained. Tacitus claims that Tiberius built no less than twelve villas on Capri, the island which had, incidentally, been acquired by Augustus for his summer residence some years before. But what most shocked the world was the vast establishment built in Rome by Nero, between A.D. 64 and 68 following the disastrous fire which swept through the city. In the very heart of Rome he created a huge country palace sprawling over the Palatine, Caelian, and Esquiline set in an artificial landscape complete with

The houses of wealthy Romans often included a peristyle—a colonnaded garden sometimes with a pool. These courtyards, with access from many rooms, gave the house an effect of spaciousness. The rear wall in this peristyle bears a painting of a garden.

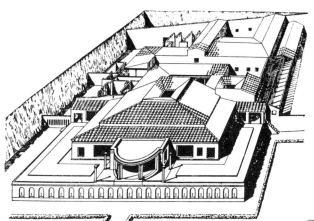

A luxurious suburban house filled with brilliant wall paintings, the Villa dei Misteri *(far left)* is located just outside Pompeii's western gate. The murals illustrate an initiation rite possibly associated with the worship of Dionysus.

Left: Artist's sketch of the villa showing enclosed courtyards and a bowed terrace-room with a view of the sea.

Right: Spaciousness, or the illusion of spaciousness, was an important characteristic of Roman architecture. This wall painting in a small room of the Villa dei Misteri uses perspective to create a three-dimensional effect.

Below: Cavernous domed octagonal hall in Nero's Golden House (Domus Aurea), built in A.D. 64–68, one of the most spectacular buildings ever planned for Rome.

ornamental lake (where the Colosseum now stands). Here, said Nero, he could begin to live as a human being. Suetonius was more sarcastic. "All Rome is transformed into a villa! Romans flee to Veii, if only the villa does not also spread itself to Veii" (Suetonius, *Nero* XXXIX). Critics might be aghast at the almost manic scale of the scheme, requiring 350 acres or so to be cleared in the city center, and at the dangerous arrogance of an emperor who could erect a colossal gilt bronze statue of himself forty meters high, but they had to admit that Nero's "Golden House" was a masterpiece of architectural ingenuity. It set new standards for the future and established a style which the wealthy would wish to emulate.

HADRIAN'S VILLA

The villa was built on a site previously owned by the emperor's family, twenty kilometers from Rome. Begun in A.D. 126, it was probably still undergoing final amendments when the emperor died twelve years later. Hadrian apparently planned the villa as an Empire in miniature, a mirror image of the outside world for his own private possession and enjoyment.

Below: A model reconstruction and labeled plan of the villa, which extended nearly a thousand meters along its north-south axis.

Perhaps the most ambitious expression of contrived architectural landscape is to be seen in Hadrian's great villa built at Tivoli, fifteen miles from Rome—a vast agglomeration of loosely linked elements strewn across the gently rolling countryside. It intimately reflects the aspirations and loves of its creator—original in its architecture, elegant in its spaciousness, and nostalgic in its backward-looking antiquarianism. Some parts are named after corners of Athens which the emperor knew and admired—the Poikile, the Prytaneum, and the Academy—others after elements of mythical landscapes like the Styx and the Elysian Fields. All of it was designed to remind the aging emperor of the culture and the beauty of the Graeco-Roman heritage. Yet in spite of this, the architecture was totally modern. Concepts incipient in Nero's Golden House were here developed and worked out to their logical conclusions. At the Piazza d'Oro, one of the many separate palaces in the complex, the entrance vestibule with its pumpkin-like dome stands for all to see, no longer hidden within confining walls, while across the great courtyard is the main hall, the entire roof of which is carried on only eight piers interwoven with graceful curving colonnades. It is an architecture of lightness, rooted in tradition but looking forward to the great creations of volume and space which were soon to follow.

The villa was almost finished in A.D. 134 when Hadrian returned at long last from his travels: he was to die four years later at Baiae in July 138. Four winters (for the villa was almost certainly a winter palace) were but little time for the man to enjoy his creation which had been so long in the making.

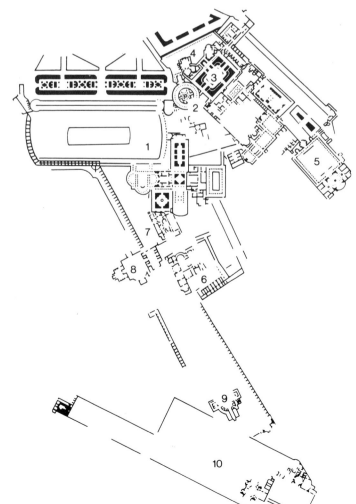

1 Belvedere plaza, a rectangular walled garden built around a large pond, for private strolls.

2 "Teatro Marittimo" or island villa, a circular house surrounded by a moat behind outer walls. Hadrian's favorite retreat.

3 Peristyle, a courtyard beside the library.

4 Belvedere tower; connected to the island villa by a hidden stairway and corridor.

5 "Piazza d'Oro," a large house built around a peristyle; its octangular vestibule was imitated in a church which Borromini built in Rome in 1642–1660.

6 Large baths. The spacious bathing facilities show that the estate could accommodate impressive numbers of guests.

7 Small baths.

8 Vestibule, the main entrance into the establishment.

9 The Canopus valley, named after an arm of the Nile—an example of the villa's nostalgic landscaping and architecture.

10 "Academy," an area patterned and named after the Academy in Athens.

Below: Aerial photograph of the villa site today, with the Belvedere plaza (number 1 on the plan) and its reflecting pool at center. At right, the circular island villa (or Teatro Marittimo, number 2). Another of the villa's courtyards with rectangular pool is seen in the foreground. Neither these ruins nor the model at left, can give an accurate idea of the richly colored, decorated buildings as they originally looked, with their murals, mosaics, and Hellenistic statuary. Artists and architects were imported from Greece.

Little is known of the later history of the palace, but it is clear from busts of the later emperors found in the excavations that occupation continued into the mid-third century and it is known that Queen Zenobia of Palmyra was confined to the villa in A.D. 273.

The site has been actively explored and exploited since the late fifteenth century, many of its art treasures being dispersed throughout the museums of the world. Serious scientific excavation began in 1870.

Overleaf: The contrast of wealth and poverty:

Page 172: The courtyard of the House of Neptune and Amphitrite, Herculaneum. The house has no garden but its small enclosed yard is beautifully decorated with wall mosaics. The end wall has been turned into a *nymphaeum* (fountain) with spectacular glittering mosaics.

Page 173: Marble relief showing a typical Italian walled, hill-town tightly packed with tall, narrow buildings. From Lake Fucino. First century A.D.

EXPANSION OF THE EMPIRE

What corner of the earth had escaped the Romans, unless heat or cold made it of no value to them? From every side fortune had passed to them, and God... now abode in Italy. It was an immutable and unchallenged law among beasts and men alike, that all must submit to the stronger, and that power belonged to those supreme in arms. That was why their ancestors in soul and body had submitted to Rome... had they not known that God was on the Roman side?

Josephus, The Jewish War

The reliefs on Trajan's Column in Rome (A.D. 113) give a vivid image of Rome's wars against the barbarians. In the detail above, we see Roman cavalry pursuing bearded Dacian noblemen, including the chieftain Decebalus, through a forest. In the next scene Decebalus, caught by the troops, commits suicide.

Right: *The hub of power. Rome and the major Roman roads, from the Tabula Peutingeriana, a medieval copy of the famous map of the entire Empire created in A.D. 365. To see the whole map, see pages 216f. Austrian National Library, Vienna.*

Via Flaminia
Via Cornelia
Via Aurelia
A Portuensis
Via Nomentana
Via Tiburtina
Via Prenestina
Via Tusculana
Via Latina
Via Appia
Via Ostiensis

Overleaf: A cavalry parade depicted on the base of the column of Antoninus Pius (r. 138–161). The horsemen gallop around two groups of infantry men each with their standards. ▶

58–51 B.C.	Caesar's wars against the Gauls. Expedition across the Rhine and to southeast Britain. Gaul becomes a province.
17 B.C.– A.D. 16	Campaigns along the Rhine and Danube and beyond. Tiberius annexes Raetia (15 B.C.); Silius annexes Noricum (15); Pannonia annexed (12); Moesia (11). Drusus campaigns against the Germans beyond the Rhine (12–9). Further campaigns led by Tiberius following Drusus's death in 9 B.C. A.D. 9: Varus and legions wiped out by Germans in Black Forest. Germanicus in Germany A.D. 14–16.
A.D. 43–84	Conquest of Britain. Aulus Plautius lands in Kent, A.D. 43. The revolt of Boudicca, 60–61. Campaigns in the north culminating in the Roman victory at Mons Graupius in the north of Scotland.
47–84	Further campaigns against the Germans. Corbulo against the Frisii and Chausi (47); Vespasian in the Black Forest (73); Domitian against the Chatti (83–84).
66–70	The Jewish rebellion.
85–89	Dacians north of the Danube make trouble in the Roman province of Moesia to the south.
101–106	Trajan's campaigns against the Dacians led by Decebalus. Dacia annexed.
113–117	Trajan in the east. Invades and annexes Armenia (113). In northern Mesopotamia (114). Moves to the Tigris and occupies Ctesiphon (115), moves to Persian Gulf and Babylon (116). Northern Mesopotamia and Assyria made provinces but abandoned by Hadrian (117).
117–137	Hadrian as emperor: tours the frontiers consolidating frontier works and administrative structures. He regards the period of expansion as at an end.

ROME AGAINST THE BARBARIANS

After rapid conquests during the Republic, Rome faced fiercer enemies in the hinterlands. *Above:* Two Germanic captives.

Statue of Lord Sanatruq of Parthia (Mesopotamia), late second century A.D. The relief shows Romans with eastern prisoners.

Until Caesar's time the Roman army had not had a great deal of experience fighting barbarian people. The Celtiberians of Spain and the tribes of the more westerly regions of Iberia had, admittedly, put up a spirited resistance and had caused Rome to expend much effort in conquering them, but elsewhere direct and aggressive contact with barbarians had been slight. Massinissa and his Numidians in North Africa had been Roman allies, while relations with distant Armenia were more diplomatic in nature, at least un-

the Hellenistic towns of the east. The conquest of cities and city-states was comparatively easy, for the cities themselves provided a natural focus for attack. Once the city had been taken, the victor controlled the social and economic power base of its whole region. Barbarians, on the other hand, particu-

a change towards an urban-centered state system; consequently Caesar's compaigns could be rapid and effective in these areas. It was in the socially backward north and west, Belgica and Armorica, that he met with his more serious difficulties, and his campaigns into the wilder regions of Britain and

Left: The Roman world under the Republic. In 100 B.C. Rome controlled little more than Italy and the northern coast of the Mediterranean. Wars against Carthage in the west and campaigns in the Aegean area had brought Rome her overseas territories. Closer to home, the Romans had displaced the Celts from northern Italy and managed to control the Gallic and Illyrian coastlines. In the last century of the Republic, under Marius, Sulla, Caesar, Pompey, and Octavian, further territory was won, but not stabilized.

Right: Map of the Roman Empire at its height. By A.D. 117, when Trajan died, the Empire had grown to its fullest extent. The whole of the Mediterranean seaboard now was ruled by Rome. While the Mediterranean became more thoroughly Romanized, the legions pushed on in the west, the north, and the east, during a century and a half of steady expansion. Major campaigns against barbarian peoples were led by Caesar in Gaul, by Tiberius in Germany and the Danube, by Trajan in Dacia (Rumania), Armenia, and Parthia. Trajan's feverish conquests were short-lived, however; his successor, Hadrian, gave up the easternmost provinces and concentrated on stabilization of the existing frontiers rather than further expansion.

til Antony's nearly disastrous attempts at conquest. For the most part, then, Rome had faced civilized or semi-civilized foes whose economies and governments were based on urban systems—the Carthaginian towns of Africa and Iberia, the Hellenized coastal strip of Spain and southern France, the world of Macedonia and Greece, and

larly those with dispersed settlement patterns, were far more difficult to subdue. This was a lesson Rome was to learn many times during the next two centuries.

In many ways the pattern of conquest reflects this point very well. Much of central and southern Gaul had, by Caesar's time, recently undergone

Germany were far from successful. When, almost a century later, the conquest of Britain began in earnest, it was the same story: those parts of the southeast which had by this time developed an urban economy were easily overrun, while Wales and the north, posed serious difficulties of conquest and government for decades.

A Dacian prisoner (*left*). From Mesopotamia, two second-century statues (*above*) representing King Uthal and Princess Washfari.

Relief from Trajan's victory monument (Trophaeum Trajanum) in Dacia showing prisoners led in chains by a Roman soldier. Adamklissi, Rumania.

Central and eastern Europe presented similar problems. Urbanized areas north of the Alps and south of the Danube, were soon absorbed and became the provinces of Noricum, Raetia, Pannonia, and Moesia; but beyond the Rhine, in barbarian Germany, the Roman armies faced insup-

raid the province of Moesia to the south. Trajan's successes against Dacia which followed, were in no small measure due to their now centralized urban economy. Significantly, Trajan made no attempt to subdue the semi-nomadic peoples of Sarmatian stock who were situated on either side of his

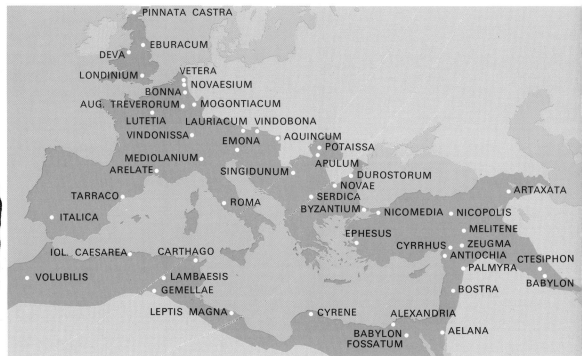

erable problems and it was left to Claudius to abandon the more adventurous entreprises and withdraw to the Rhine frontier.

Within the next half-century or so, the Dacians in Transylvania (now Rumania) had made rapid social and economic advances—so much so that they felt strong enough (in A.D. 85–89) to

Dacian conquests. Instead he turned his attention to the east where the old cities of the Tigris and Euphrates valleys offered easier prey. Thus by the time Hadrian had come to the throne (A.D. 117), only the wilder barbarian regions remained beyond the frontiers. In his wisdom Hadrian decided to leave them unmolested.

THE SUBJUGATION OF THE GAULS

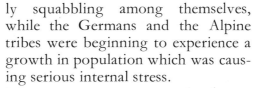

Gaul is divided into three parts,
inhabited respectively by the Belgae,
the Aquitani, and the people
who call themselves Celts, whom we call
Gauls. All three have
different languages, customs, and laws.

Caesar, *De Bello Gallico*

Beyond the Mediterranean coastal strip, the Roman Province, lay Gallia Comata—the land of the shaggy-haired Gauls. Further north again, in the vicinity of the Rhine and beyond, were the warlike Germans, groups of whom, the Cimbri and the Teutones, had already, in the late second century

ly squabbling among themselves, while the Germans and the Alpine tribes were beginning to experience a growth in population which was causing serious internal stress.

In 59 B.C. matters came to a head: two tribes in northeast Gaul, the Aedui and Sequani, were locked in political con-

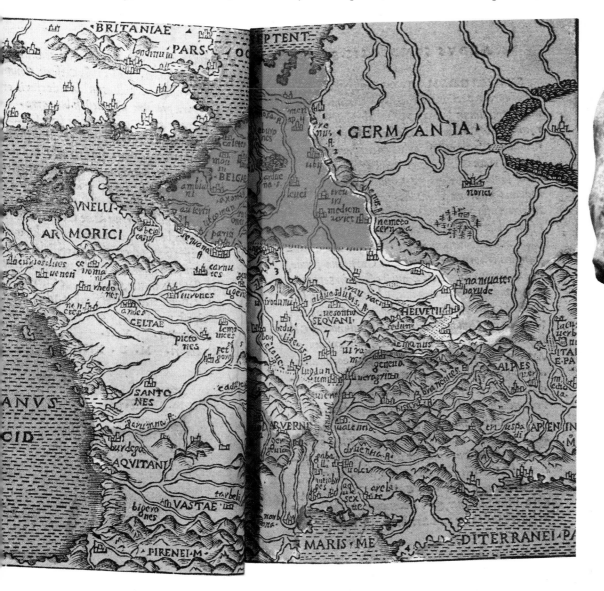

B.C., thrust south through Gaul and into Spain and north Italy, causing near-panic in Rome. The situation had further deteriorated by Caesar's time. The Gaulish tribes were now constant-

flict. The Sequani sought the support of a neighboring German tribe—the Suebi led by Ariovistus—while the Aedui appealed to Rome, their ally, for help. To make matters worse, it was at

Caesar, Pompey (*above*), and Marc Antony divided the Roman world up in 59 B.C.

Julius Caesar (100–44 B.C.) gained fame throughout the Roman world for his daring exploits in Gaul. This statue is a copy of the only surviving full-length portrait of Caesar: the marble original is in the Senatorial Palace, Rome.

De Bello Gallico, The Gallic Wars—or "Gaius Julius Caesar's Notes on His Achievements" as the work was originally called—consisted of eight books, the first seven of which were written or dictated by Caesar himself; the eighth was written shortly after Caesar's death by his secretary and friend Aulus Hirtius. It is not known when the books were composed. Some scholars think that each was written in the autumn after the completion of each season's campaigns, but more likely the seven were written together after the defeat of Vercingetorix in 52 B.C. The books were a blatant piece of propaganda designed to display Caesar's exploits in the best possible light. Achievements were highlighted, failures played down.

Left: Sixteenth-century map of Gaul, an illustration to an edition of *De Bello Gallico* published in France in 1513. Bibliothèque Nationale, Paris.

To make an example of the Veneti,
in order to teach
the natives to be more careful . . .
he had all their chief men
executed and the rest
of the population sold as slaves.

Caesar, *De Bello Gallico*

lized, he said, that Gaul would either have to be taken over by Rome or it would become German. For a man of Caesar's ambition it was a most attractive situation.

Caesar's first campaign was incisive. He marched first to Geneva to prevent the Helvetii from crossing the Rhône, and then chased them through the territory of the Sequani, where they were beaten and the remnants forced to return home. Next we find him in Alsace campaigning successfully against Ariovistus and, to maintain his initiative, stationing a military detachment in the territory of the Sequani.

As he assessed the new situation, it must have been clear to Caesar that the Belgae of northern Gaul were the next tribes to be conquered: they were fierce fighters and lay close to the frontier with the Germans. Once they could be subdued and the channel coast reached, the rest of Gaul to the south, could be easily secured. Thus in a series of brilliant but hard-fought campaigns in 58–57 B.C., the Belgic tribes were picked off; those who put

Caesar fought battles throughout Gaul between 58 B.C. when he marched on Geneva, and the final siege of Uxellodunum in 51. The map indicates the three principal divisions of Gaul: the region of the Belgae to the north; the Aquitani, southwest; and the Celts or Galli in the center. At the far west, the Veneti. Along the Mediterranean lay the Province, territory already controlled by Rome.

The next year (57–56 B.C.), however, rebellion flared up among the Veneti of Armorica. Caesar's immediate response showed a brilliant grasp of the situation: Labienus was sent into Belgic territory to keep it quiet, Crassus to Aquitania, and Sabinus to Normandy. Having thus isolated and surrounded the rebels, Caesar himself moved in and systematically destroyed the resistance in a single campaign culminating in a great sea battle at Quiberon. To make an example of the rebels and "to teach the natives to be more careful in

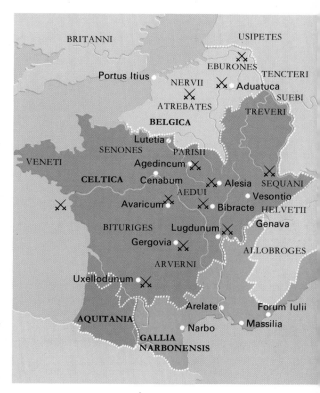

future . . . he had all their councilors executed and the rest of the population sold as slaves." No one could now be in doubt of what opposition to Rome meant.

Supremely confident with his spectacular successes, Caesar now turned his attention to the mysterious island of Britain, where he campaigned in 55 and again in 54 B.C.

precisely this moment that the Helvetii, who lived in the west of Switzerland, decided that their homeland was too small for their growing population and that they must move westward into Gaul—a migration which would have taken them through Roman territory and threatened Roman allies.

For Caesar the situation was clear-cut. Surveying the political scene, he rea-

up the most serious resistance being viciously treated. Of the Nervii, Caesar could proudly boast that he "brought [their] name and nation almost to utter destruction"—an example of callous genocide. After Crassus had been sent to receive the submission of the tribes of Normandy and Brittany, Caesar could record his famous words *"omnis Gallia pacata"*—all Gaul is at peace.

THE GAULS IN REVOLT

The boar was a symbol used by the Celts to ward off danger. It often appears on helmet crests or in shield decorations. This bronze statue of a boar is from Neuvy-en-Sullias, France.

Below: Noble Gallic warrior, life-sized Gallo-Roman stone statue from Vachères in southern France.

Right: Head of a Gaul, on a coin issued in Rome in 48 B.C., to commemorate Caesar's conquests.

elements together in the territory of the Carnutes. The revolt began with the massacre of the Roman officials at Cenabum. Caesar was quick to respond, but the rebels' scorched-earth policy was highly effective. Eventually, however, after Vercingetorix had taken shelter at Gergovia, the Roman army attacked, only to be repelled with staggering losses. Heartened by the turn of events, Rome's old allies, the Aedui, now went over to the rebels and took control of Caesar's main supply base at Noviodunum. The situation looked very serious for Rome.

Caesar had been caught unprepared, but such was his military genius that within a matter of weeks he had recovered the initiative and had driven Vercingetorix to take refuge in a hilltop stronghold at Alesia. Here Caesar bottled him up with a massive complex of siege works: an inner ring of ramparts and ditches nine miles long to keep the rebels in, with an outer line thirteen miles in length carefully designed to protect his own troops from surprise attack from without. This outer defense made use of the surrounding hills as vantage points where many of the eight camps and twenty-three redoubts were sited. With his preparations complete, Caesar could afford to sit down to wait, confident that Vercingetorix and his eighty thousand followers cooped up in the town, would be unable to survive the rigors of the siege for long.

Vercingetorix must have been counting desperately on a relieving force arriving in time. Rumor had no doubt reached him of the enormous army of a quarter of a million troops which Commius had been gathering from all parts of Gaul.

It is not difficult to imagine the feverish excitement that the approach of this force must have aroused in Ale-

At Alesia in 52 B.C., Caesar trapped the rebellious Gauls led by Vercingetorix and besieged them, eventually forcing their surrender. Artist's sketch of the site showing Caesar's double encirclement.

sia—but Caesar was well prepared. The ensuing battle was ferocious: several times the outcome was held in delicate balance, but eventually the relieving force was outmaneuvered and put to flight, not without appalling carnage. Seeing this from the hilltop, Vercingetorix realized that all was lost. The next day the rebels surrendered, Vercingetorix being taken off to Rome to languish in jail for six years before being strangled as part of Caesar's triumphant celebrations.

The revolt of the Veneti was the first of a series of uprisings that Caesar had to face. Two years later the Belgae were up in arms, but the rebellion was once more quickly contained and stamped out.

The final test came in 52 B.C. This time central Gaul, previously quiet and substantially pro-Roman in its political leanings, was the scene of the uprising. The revolt was led by an Arvernian, Vercingetorix, who, taking advantage of Caesar's absence, gathered dissident

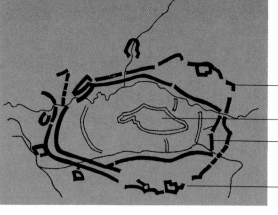

The siege works of Alesia, shown in outline at left, can still be traced on the gound.

Outer siege works, 20 kilometers long, built by Caesar to protect his forces from external attack.

The hilltop fortified by Vercingetorix.

Caesar's siege works, 14 kilometers long, designed to keep the Gauls inside.

Camps placed at intervals on high points to watch for enemy troop movements. The Gauls were awaiting reinforcements from outside.

Above: Reconstruction model of Roman war machinery for breaching walls. Rome, Mostra Augustea.

Left: Caesar's siege works at Alesia, a model from the Musée des Antiquités Nationales, St.-Germain-en-Laye, France. Descriptions and model are based on Caesar's accurate accounts.

Palisaded rampart four meters high, reinforced with a battlemented breastwork, and large forked branches projecting horizontally. Towers were placed along the entire circuit. Ditches fronted the rampart.

Branches and tree trunks stripped and sharpened, were fixed in long trenches 1.5 meters deep, with their lower ends bound together. There were five rows in each trench, all interlaced.

Circular pits one meter deep, each with a stake embedded in the bottom (called "lilies"), sharpened and projecting upwards. The holes, camouflaged with brushwood, were arranged in eight rows three feet apart. In front was a zone of projecting iron spikes.

183

THE GERMAN EXPEDITIONS

"Germania Mourning": coin issued in Rome under Domitian, A.D. 88–89, after the suppression of an uprising in Upper Germany. The figure, seated on a shield, supports her head with her left hand. Beneath her, a broken spear.

After wide conquests of German territory between 12 B.C. and A.D. 16, the Romans retreated to the Rhine and abandoned the rest of Germany. The map shows the most important campaigns in the area, with dates and leaders of each.

In 55 B.C., during a comparative lull in his Gallic war, Caesar took the opportunity to bridge the Rhine somewhere in the vicinity of Bonn and to campaign for eighteen days to the north of the river in the territory of the Sicambri. It was partly as a show of strength—a warning to the Germans of Rome's power and presence—and partly to satisfy his own curiosity and to gain prestige that Caesar undertook the crossing. At this stage there can have been little intention to make any permanent conquests.

The first signs of trouble came in 17 B.C. when a horde of German tribes including the Sugambri and Tencteri crossed the Rhine and badly mauled a Roman legion, carrying off its standards. It was a warning, but Augustus was not yet prepared to take the initiative since there was still much to be done south of the Rhine-Danube line in subduing recalcitrant tribes and organizing the vast newly conquered territories into the provinces of Raetia, Noricum, Pannonia, and Moesia. However, by 12 B.C., when this task had been completed, Augustus was ready for a major forward thrust. The reasons for this are complex. Fear of the Germans was certainly one, but another factor of some importance was that by about this time many of the world's trouble spots had been subdued and Augustus was faced with the unenviable task of finding suitable occupations for approximately fifteen legions which had become available. The conquest of Germany provided an acceptable new theater of warfare.

In 12 B.C. the forward advance began, led by Drusus; and for each year until 8 B.C. the army fought its way across the north European plains, thrusting into the heartland of Germany by land along the River Lippe, or by sea to the mouths of the rivers Ems and Weser

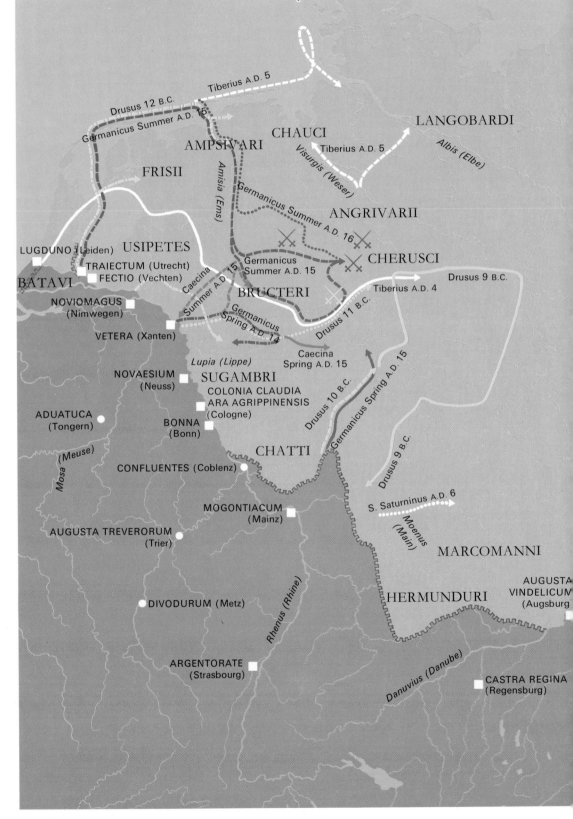

Drusus, who led armies in Germany from 12 to 8 B.C. National Museum, Naples.

Center right: Tiberius, active beyond the Rhine between 8 B.C. and A.D. 5. National Museum, Naples.

Far right: Germanicus campaigned in Germany, A.D. 14–16, coin portrait, A.D. 41–54.

Below: A popular imperial theme—Roman legionaries with two Germanic prisoners. From the Arch of Constantine, A.D. 315.

and thence south by river transport. During this time the coastal Frisians were won over and the Sugambri, Usipetes, Chatti, Marcomanni, and Cherusci were met and partly subdued. By 9 B.C. Drusus had reached the Elbe, but on the way back he died. In the next year Tiberius took over command, but his involvement was slight and for a while Augustus was content to let matters rest.

In A.D. 4 the advance, once more under Tiberius, began again in earnest. The Weser was reached and the tribes of the northwest, the Bructeri and Cherusci, surrendered. The next year, using both sea and land approaches, the Romans reached the Elbe once more. All that was now needed was to subdue the Marcomanni before the Elbe-Danube axis could be finally established as the springboard for yet further advances. But at this precise moment everything went wrong: a revolt of frightening proportions broke out in Pannonia and Dalmatia, and to assuage public fears Tiberius had quickly to extricate himself from Germany to spend the next three years putting down the rebels. By A.D. 9 the Roman army was once more active in Germany, organizing the territory in such a way as to form an incipient province. But twenty years of Roman aggression had begun to harden the German opposition, which now focused around the personality of Arminius, a young chieftain of the Cherusci. Matters finally came to a head in the autumn of A.D. 9 when a large Roman army of three legions, led by Publius Quintilius Varus, a man of little recognizable military ability, was making its way back to winter quarters through the Teutonberg Forest. Arminius struck, and in the resulting confusion virtually the entire Roman force was massacred. It was a staggering blow

for Rome, and a shock from which Augustus never fully recovered. The Rhine was very rapidly strengthened, bringing the total force to eight legions, but apart from the coastal strip virtually the whole of Germany north of the river, was abandoned. Augustus had been over-ambitious. It was one thing to conquer the settled urban, or proto-urban communities of Gaul and the Alpine fringes, but quite another to attempt to subdue a vast territory peopled only by scattered communities who could move and regroup with ease in the forests and marshes which they knew so well. Rome had learned its lesson. The Augustan vision of an ever expanding empire could not be realized, and in spite of three years of further campaigning by Germanicus (A.D. 14–16), Germany was left to itself, the Rhine forming the natural frontier between the two states.

Although the campaigns of Germanicus were of little lasting effect, he was able to visit the battleground where Varus had perished. The accounts of the grim scene which he and his men brought home cannot have failed to have chilled the hearts of those who heard them.

The scene lived up to its horrible associations. Varus's extensive first camp, with its broad extent and headquarters marked out, testified to the whole army's labors. Then a half-ruined breastwork and shallow ditch showed where the last pathetic remnant had gathered. On the open ground were whitening bones, scattered where men had fled, heaped up where they had stood and fought back. Fragments of spears and of horses' limbs lay there—also human heads, fastened to tree trunks. In groves nearby were the outlandish altars at which the Germans had massacred the Roman colonels and senior company commanders.

THE EASTERN PROBLEM

"The traitor of Jerusalem." Portrait of Josephus Flavius, a leader of Jewish resistance in A.D. 66, who went over to the Roman side and wrote an important history of the wars.

Below: The Temple of Jerusalem, which the Romans destroyed in A.D. 70. Detail from a modern reconstruction.

Rome's treatment of the Jews showed a heavy-handed ineptitude which so clearly reflected their uncertainty in the face of ideas and ideals alien to their own traditions. Judea and its politics presented a most difficult subject for a Roman to understand. It retained the opulence and excesses of a decaying Hellenistic kingdom whose leaders could be oriental in their cruelty, but behind this lay a stern religious fanaticism. To add to these complexities, the religious leadership was in deep disarray, with violent divisions

Agrippa I, in control. The experiment misfired, however, when Agrippa began to show signs of delusions of grandeur, eventually proclaiming himself to be a god, but before the situation became too difficult for Rome, he died. Not wishing to face the problem again, Claudius took the easy way out by assuming direct control of the country, governing it through a series of Roman procurators.

From A.D. 44 to 66 the situation in Judea gradually deteriorated. Strife between the ethnic factions, Jews,

to be put down by a Roman cohort, an act which led to widespread rebellion, spurred on by an extremist faction, the Zealots.

So serious was the situation that Vespasian, one of Nero's most able generals, was sent out in A.D. 66 to command the three available legions. He moved first to the region of Galilea, where the Jewish resistance was led by a moderate Pharisee named Josephus. Josephus and his followers held out as long as possible against the Romans, finally retiring to the hilltop defense of Jotapata. Eventually the Roman army prevailed, and all but two of the defenders were either slaughtered or committed suicide. Josephus, one of the survivors, thereupon changed sides and joined Vespasian. Later he was to write an extensive account of the Jewish Wars full of vivid firsthand detail.

By 68 the Romans were firmly in control of the situation, and the siege of Jerusalem had begun. In the next year Hebron was occupied, but with the Roman armies poised for success, Nero died, and Vespasian was proclaimed emperor by his supporters. He departed immediately, leaving the Jewish command in the able hands of his son Titus. The end was now near and Titus, determined for rapid and spectacular success, pushed on relentlessly. In 70 Jerusalem fell amid terrible scenes of carnage, and one by one the other strongholds were picked off, the last to fall, in 73, being Masada.

Rome's revenge was harsh. The Temple was destroyed and its treasures carted off to Rome, and Jerusalem was reduced to a heap of ruins. It was claimed that a million people had died in the rebellion; in addition vast numbers of survivors were shipped to Rome to die in the arena. As a result the Jewish nation was virtually obliterated and Judea became a province.

springing up between the different sects and power blocks. In the early years of the Empire, Rome's attitude seems to have been to steer well clear of trouble. Various experiments were tried, but Claudius decided that the most appropriate solution was to reconstitute the old Judean kingdom of Herod. This he did in A.D. 41 by placing one of Herod's descendants,

Greeks, and Samaritans; class struggles between the lowly Jews and their high priests; and sharp religious differences between the various cults were made worse by the emergence of one messiah after another. The country was in turmoil. Matters came to a head in 66 when the procurator, Gessius Florus, confiscated money from the temple treasury. The ensuing riot had

Coin, "Judea Mourning," a female figure with hands bound behind her, seated beneath a palm tree. Rome, A.D. 69–70.

Below: Romans carry a Jewish menorah, the seven-branched candelabra, in triumph through Rome—one of the spoils of the Roman devastation of Jerusalem. Relief from the Arch of Titus (A.D. 81), Rome.

THE ARMY OF THE SECOND CENTURY

The emperor was in charge of the entire army. Each legion was commanded by a *legatus* supported by six military tribunes, young aristocrats who would serve two or three years in the army as a stage in their senatorial careers.

By the early second century the army had reached its peak of efficiency. The reorganization under Marius and the long, hard experience gained, first in the civil wars of the late Republic and later, during the German, Dacian, and eastern campaigns, had had a considerable effect. The army was now geared both for action in the field and for prolonged frontier duties.

There were now between twenty-five and thirty-five legions, based almost entirely along the frontiers, supported by a very much larger number of specialized auxiliary detachments. Each legion was a totally self-contained unit which included not only the actual fighting men, but every kind of administrator necessary for the efficient running of the force, from the *legatus* who was in overall control, down to the arrow makers and the wound dressers.

The *auxilia* under Augustus became an integral part of the army. Their function was to provide specialist support for the legions and to take the brunt of any attack. The *auxilia* consisted of three basic types of unit—infantry, cavalry, and mounted infantry—which could be organized in units of five hundred (*quingenaria*) or one thousand (*miliaria*). The infantry were divided into cohorts some of which could be mounted (*equitatae*), while the cavalry units (*alae*) were usually composed of sixteen troops (*turmae*) each under a commander (*decurio*). The value of the *auxilia* lay in the varied and specialist nature of the troops. Sarmatians were skilled archers and horse riders; Thracians provided cavalry spearmen; while troops raised among the Moors would be ideal for desert warfare in the east. The *auxilia*, then, provided the army with a flexibility which would otherwise have been lacking among the legions.

Below: Roman legionary in full dress. Reliefs like this work of the second century A.D. provide details of how the soldiers were dressed and are particularly important for archaeologists in showing how individual items of equipment, found in excavations, were used. The soldier's cuirass is made of overlapping metal bands. British Museum.

LEGION (1 legion = 6,000 men)

In addition to its 5,300 active fighting men the legion included a detachment of 120 mounted despatch riders and specialists such as clerks *(librarii)*, the standard bearer *(aquilifer)*, the master builder *(architectus)*, the surveyor *(mensor)*, the water engineer *(hydraularius)*, the catapult maker *(ballistarius)*, and the various medical orderlies *(medici)*.

Below: A Roman cavalry officer in a charge against barbarians. Detail from the great battle sarcophagus of Hortilianus, Terme Museum, Rome.

The battering ram in action. A heavy bulk of timber, capped with a metal head styled like a ram's head is swung constantly against the defenders' wall to smash a hole in it.

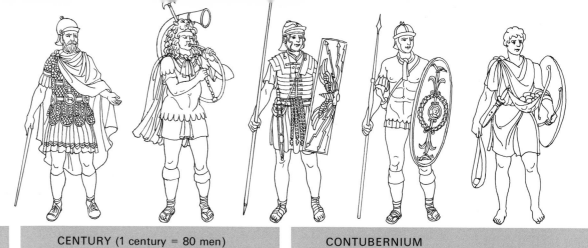

Each legion had a senior professional officer, the *praefectus castrorum (right)*, who oversaw general organization and training. Below him were the specialists like the *cornicines* (horn blowers), the centurions, the legionaries, and any auxiliary troops *(far right)* attached to the legion for special fighting duties.

COHORTS (1 cohort = 480 men)

Each legion was composed of ten cohorts and each cohort, except for the first, was made up of three pairs of centuries (a grouping reflecting the old Republican organisation in maniples; (see pages 88–89)). Thus a normal cohort would have been some 480 men strong. The first cohort was twice the normal size because it included all the specialists and clerks of the headquarters staff.

CENTURY (1 century = 80 men)

The century, as its name implies, was originally a unit of one hundred men, but by the time of the Empire, its fighting strength had been reduced to eighty. It was the smallest administrative unit in the army and was commanded by a *centurion*. Centurions were graded according to status. The senior centurions served with the first cohort.

CONTUBERNIUM
(1 contubernium = 8 men)

Each century was composed of ten *contubernia* (tent parties), the smallest group who, on the march, would share a tent. It normally consisted of eight men. In established forts the *contubernium* would occupy one pair of rooms in the barrack block where they would sleep and store their gear. They would cook and eat together.

Below: The *testudo* or tortoise was a device used to protect the attacking force from missiles as it rushed towards the scaling ladders. Detail from a French engraving of the seventeenth century.

The *aquilifer* (standard bearer), second in command to the centurion, carried the legion's sacred silver eagle. Detail, Trajan's Column.

Troops transported in boats. The great frontier rivers of the Rhine and the Danube were policed by permanent flotillas which could be used to move troops quickly. Detail from a relief, Egizio Museum, Vatican.

Ground plan of the fort at Gelligaer, Wales, built early in the second century to house a *cohors quingenaria peditata*, 500 men plus their baggage animals. The annex contains the regimental baths.

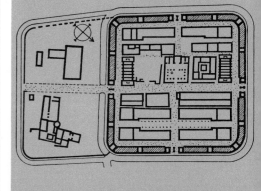

One of the *cornicines* who were attached to every legion. They transmitted messages to the standard bearers. At sacrifices the sound of the horn kept evil spirits away. Detail from Hortilianus sarcophagus.

The emperor Trajan addresses his troops, including the standard bearers, during his Dacian campaigns. Detail from Trajan's Column, A.D. 113. Like Caesar in Gaul, Trajan personally commanded campaigns in Dacia in A.D. 101–106.

Aerial view of the fort of Chester, England, which sits astride Hadrians wall. The excavated buildings include the headquarters and commandant's house (left) and barracks (right).

TRAJAN: THE DANUBE AND BEYOND

Trajan, who ruled from A.D. 98 to 117, extended the Empire to its greatest dimensions (see map, page 179) by his conquests in the north and east. In A.D. 115, the year he reached the Persian Gulf, he issued this commemorative coin of a triumphant procession.

Below left: Marble bust of Trajan in the year A.D. 108, his tenth-anniversary jubilee, at the age of fifty-five. His oak-leaf crown is part of the special regalia for the occasion.

Trajan came to power in A.D. 98 at the age of forty-five, well versed in the problems of both military and civil leadership, having previously commanded troops in Spain and the Rhineland. He must have been well aware of Rome's two great problem areas: the Danube frontier, now constantly threatened by the growing power of the Dacians to the north led by Decebalus, and the amorphous and ill-defined eastern frontier, beyond which lay the empire of the Parthians.

Almost immediately on assuming power he determined to deal with

Decebalus. Having first secured the defences of Pannonia, he thrust north into Transylvania, thus instigating the Dacian wars which were to occupy much of his time in the period 101–106 (pp. 192–193). The results were spectacular—a new province was annexed, thousands of slaves were taken, and sufficient booty was acquired to finance a series of ambitious building programs in Rome and elsewhere, at Ostia and Ancona. With the cessation

of hostilities the emperor settled down in the capital to seven years of sound, but largely unimaginative, government.

By A.D. 113, however, he was becoming restless. Fortunately the eastern problem now offered him the opportunity he wanted. A slight irregularity had arisen over the succession of rulers in Armenia: technically an agreement had been broken and therefore the emperor could legitimately act. Without wasting time in diplomacy, he immediately declared war and in a single campaign had subdued what little resistance there was, annexing Armenia as a province.

His appetite now whetted, he decided to conquer Parthia—a vast expanse of territory stretching from the borders of Syria to the Persian Gulf. It was an ambitious program verging on the foolhardy, but his first campaign, in 114, was entirely successful. He had marched across northern Mesopotamia to Nisibis not far from the Tigris and had received the submission of the local rulers. The next year, with the aid of a specially constructed river flotilla, the army moved down the Tigris to the Parthian capital of Ctesiphon, which soon fell before the Roman onslaught. The emperor could thus continue down to the Persian Gulf, where it is said that, like Alexander the Great, he had visions of conquering India. The next year (116), he had, however, moved east to the valley of the Euphrates and there occupied Babylon.

The whole campaign had been too rapid and the conquered territories were too vast for thorough consolidation, but even so, the emperor proceeded with great haste to organize the captured lands into two new Roman provinces: Mesopotamia and Assyria. Possibly, had he lived to follow up his successes, the land might

have become stabilized under Roman control. The problem is debatable, but Trajan died on his way back to Rome in 117. His successor, Hadrian, had no illusions. In his opinion the Empire was grossly overstretched. All three eastern provinces, Armenia, Mesopotamia, and Assyria, were therefore immediately abandoned.

Trajan's Column, erected in A.D. 113 in the Forum Ulpia in Rome to commemorate the emperor's Dacian campaigns, is a masterpiece of historical art. The column stands 30 meters high, and in a single continuous spiral 200 meters in length, it illustrates scenes from the wars. In all, some 2,500 figures are depicted, arranged to provide a continuous narrative. Originally they were picked out in color and enlivened at intervals with attached bronze spears.

Trajan's victories over Dacia are celebrated in the "Great Trajanic Frieze" (*right and at bottom*). Here the emperor rides at the head of his army against the bearded, long-haired Dacians. Trajan's portrait was later altered to make him resemble Constantine.

Trajan's campaigns showed considerable daring. The heart of the Dacian empire was remote and well-protected: it meant the deep penetration of hostile mountainous territory leaving the flanks of the advance largely unprotected. Dacia was surrounded on three sides by Sarmatians. The thrust east was even more impressive. From his base in Syria the emperor led his armies across hundreds of miles of semi-desert into Mesopotamia, greatly over-extending his lines of communication.

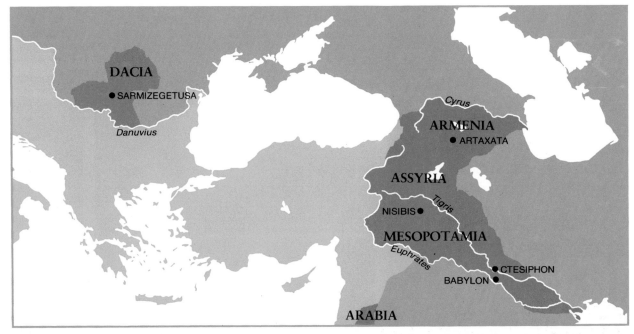

Emperor Trajan is crowned by Victory while his cavalry continue to trample the barbarian Dacians. Panel from the Great Trajanic Frieze. This frieze is believed to have been created for the Temple of the Deified Trajan, which his successor, Hadrian, erected near the famous column. The relief was incorporated in the triumphal arch constructed by Constantine in A.D. 312, and the face of Trajan in each panel was altered so that Constantine was the hero of the work. The Trajanic frieze is more constrained in style and more crowded than the reliefs of the column, but is nonetheless magnificiently energetic.

THE DACIAN CAMPAIGNS

Trajan's Dacian campaigns were fought in the mountains of Transylvania (modern Rumania). The Romans penetrated the defensive cordon of hilltop forts and captured and destroyed the Dacian capital, Sarmizegetusa.

Details of Trajan's Column are shown on these pages. *Below, left to right:* Roman troops building a fort of turf and timber; Trajan addressing the troops; close combat fighting.

The Dacians, who occupied the territory which lay to the north of the lower Danube, had for some while been a potential threat to Rome. During the reign of Domitian, around 85, matters finally came to a head when hordes from the north swept down on the province of Moesia killing the Roman governor. Although the situation was eventually restored, a quite substantial Roman force had been annihilated in the process. Clearly the Dacians, aspiring to statehood under the powerful

army crossed the Danube on a pontoon bridge and thrust deep into Transylvania. The first significant confrontation took place in a thunderstorm at Tapae. The result was indecisive, and after further skirmishes Trajan withdrew south to spend the winter at Drobetae. At this stage his campaign can hardly have been regarded as a success, but the army had gained valuable experience fighting under extremely difficult mountainous conditions and Decebalus had had time to gauge the

native capitals. Decebalus must now have seen that the war was lost. The terms agreed were comparatively moderate. The Dacians were to concede an area of western Dacia (the Banat) and to totally evacuate it, while at their capital, Sarmizegetusae, they were to dismantle the defenses and to receive a permanent Roman garrison. Trajan, well satisfied, returned to Rome in triumph to assume the title Dacicus. Decebalus now bided his time. His losses cannot have been very great,

leadership of Decebalus, were likely to remain a problem so long as they lay beyond the effective control of Rome. It was partly for this reason, and partly no doubt for military glory, made more attractive by the prospect of acquiring the vast quantities of gold and silver, that Trajan decided on invasion. In 101, having made all the necessary preparations, the emperor and his

power of his enemy. It must have been a demoralizing time for the Dacians. The next year Trajan decided to approach the Dacian stronghold by a different route. From Drobetae he crossed onto the plain of Wallacia, thence along the River Aluta to the Red Tower pass. So near was success that he refused to see envoys, and instead pushed on to storm one of the

and in a comparatively short time he had regained his strength and re-established his leadership. In 105 he began deliberately to neglect the conditions of the surrender, welcoming Roman deserters to his camp, rebuilding his arms supply, and raiding his neighbors. Finally, in an act of outright defiance he captured the local Roman commander and held him for ransom,

The famous bridge across the Danube is illustrated in this Trajanic coin and in the relief from Trajan's Column *(below, center)*. In form, it consisted of stone piers supporting a cradle-work of timber which took a planked roadway. The bridge, the longest permanent bridge in the ancient world, was built by the famous Greek architect Apollodorus of Damascus. It is described with enthusiasm by the contemporary historian Cassius Dio.

Below left: Dacian chieftains are shown surrendering, in another detail from Trajan's Column.

Below right: Soldiers pile pack horses or mules with booty captured from the Dacians, mostly silver tableware.

demanding the return of the Banat territories. The Dacian armies then poured into the province of Moesia and caused widespread panic until Trajan was able to arrive and restore order. The Dacians had demonstrated their resilience—there was therefore no other choice but outright annexation. Accordingly Trajan prepared himself for a major forward advance in 106. When the campaigning season began, his two Roman forces marched deep into Dacia making straight for

comparative ease with which Rome could conquer an urbanized community. The Dacians had by this stage acquired a degree of civilization: buildings and defenses were sophisticated; writing, in Greek and Latin, was practiced; the religious and social organization of the state was advanced; and a money economy had already developed parallel with a high degree of centralized production. Trajan merely took over much of the existing structure and imposed a pattern of Roman-

the great Dacian stronghold at Sarmizegetusae. The town was besieged and when it soon became apparent that all was lost, many of the noble Dacians took poison. Decebalus himself escaped but was hotly pursued and finally committed suicide. With all opposition destroyed, Trajan was therefore left in undisputed control.

Here was one more example of the

ization upon it. To make his task simpler, vast numbers of the native population were uprooted and moved, ten thousand of them to die in the arena, many more to be settled in provinces south of the Danube. In their place settlers were brought in from outside in great numbers. Thus, in a brief period of five years, Trajan had destroyed Dacian civilization.

THE SUCCESSION OF POWER
31 B.C.–A.D. 161

When in 27 B.C. the Senate conferred on Octavian the title of Augustus, and insisted that he should retain proconsular power for an initial period of ten years, it was, unwittingly, setting its seal on a pattern of government which was to last for centuries.

The long reign of Augustus became increasingly dominated by problems of succession. Without sons of his own, he had to fall back on the more obscure side-roots of his family tree; but he was constantly thwarted in his plans by the successive deaths of those he had thought most suitable. Eventually he had to resort to the choice of his unfavored stepson, Tiberius, as heir. Although descent was therefore not direct, he had established the right of his dynasty—the Julio-Claudians—to rule. In all, five members of the family were to control Rome for nearly a century.

The death of Nero in A.D. 68, without an heir, marked the end of the dynasty, but the concept of hereditary rights persisted. Out of the chaos of the Year of the Four Emperors, Vespasian emerged triumphant to found a new dynasty, the Flavians, who were to hold power for twenty-eight years until the assassination of Domitian in A.D. 96. This time, however, the Senate was prepared with their own nominee, Nerva, a man chosen, partly at least, because he had no son to succeed him. In this choice the Senate seems to have been deliberately setting out to break the concept of dynastic rule.

It was Nerva who established the new tradition of appointing a successor on merit. Trajan, the man selected, seems to have followed suit, and thus a new pattern was established which lasted for the rest of the century.

31 B.C.–A.D. 14 AUGUSTUS

It is difficult to over-estimate the importance of Augustus to the survival of Roman civilization. He began to take power at the time when the Republic was rapidly disintegrating, and through sheer political skill, emerged triumphant over all his rivals to assume the reins of government. Once in power he proceeded with caution to totally reorganize the administrative system, ostensibly restoring the Republic but in practice gradually assuming more power himself.

ed parents of three or more children with tax exemptions. This was typical of the Augustan period—petty bureaucracy was beginning to govern all aspects of life. Even in literature and the arts the vitality of the earlier periods was disappearing under the restrained proprieties imposed by the emperors. When the exuberant and irreverent poetry of Ovid offended the emperor's vision of public morality—the poet was exiled for life. Nonetheless, more conventional but no less able men

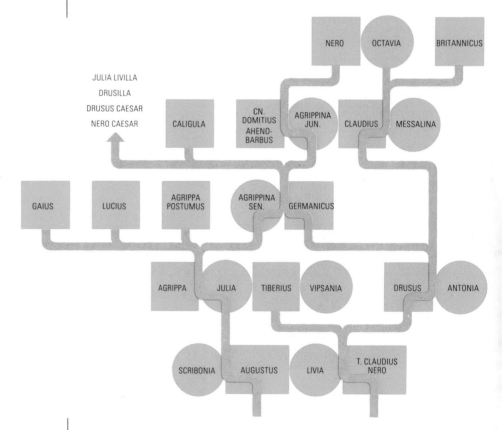

Under Augustus a new morality was introduced. Among his many measures was a law *(Lex Julia)* designed to increase the birth rate. Under this law bachelors were forbidden to receive legacies and married men without children were forced to pay back a considerable part of any inheritance as duty. A later law reward-

like Virgil, Horace, and Livy found the new atmosphere congenial for their work.

Most people benefited from the *Pax Romana*, citizens and provincials alike. Indeed Augustus was the first Roman leader to take a positive and creative interest in the welfare of the provinces, having spent much of his time be-

| A.D. 14–37 TIBERIUS | A.D. 37–41 CALIGULA | 41–54 CLAUDIUS |

tween 27 and 19 B.C. traveling in the west and in Greece and Asia Minor.

The problem of choosing his immediate successor weighed heavily on his mind. Eventually he decided that his daughter Julia should marry his stepson Tiberius; an arrangement which annoyed Tiberius, not least because he was already happily married, and led to a period of coolness between the emperor and his son-in-law. Eventually, however, in A.D. 13, Augustus adopted Tiberius.

Tiberius, son of Augustus's third wife, Livia, by a previous marriage, had served with distinction in the European frontier zone. With Drusus he was responsible for annexing the province of Raetia in 15 B.C. and later, in 12 B.C., he annexed Pannonia. After Drusus's death in 9 B.C., Tiberius was given command of the German campaigns. Three years later, having been made to marry the emperor's daughter (who subsequently proved unfaithful), he resigned his commission and withdrew to Rhodes, where he remained until once more accepting the German command in A.D. 4. Thus by the time of his appointment as emperor in A.D. 14, he had gained wide military experience but had become disenchanted with power politics.

As emperor he seems to have been genuinely concerned to maintain a partnership with the Senate whom he treated with a studied respect. However, some of the Senate's actions, particularly in trying cases of high treason, were thought by his critics to have been influenced directly by the emperor in order to remove his personal enemies and opposition. After the death of his popular and dashing nephew Germanicus (a death for which some considered Tiberius to be responsible), his popularity waned and he became increasingly recalcitrant and cruel. Surrounded by ambitious and powerful females, including his own mother Livia, and Agrippina, the widow of Germanicus, and constantly in fear of intrigue against himself, he finally quitted Rome for the peace and pleasure of the island of Capri, leaving control in the hands of Sejanus, his prefect of the Praetorian Guards.

Tiberius's last years were spent in paranoid cruelty enlivened, so the rumors suggested, by a life of extreme debauchery on Capri.

Augustus, in one of his last portraits, is shown in his priestly garments as pontifex maximus. *First decade* A.D. *Marble statue, Corinth Museum.*

The brief reign of Gaius (or Caligula as he was nicknamed) was an interlude of no significance. In spite of a reasonable start, offering an amnesty to political exiles, he soon appears to have been overcome by his sense of unlimited power. It is indeed possible, as some believed, that a sudden illness left his reason impaired. Many stories are told of him. Believing himself to be a god, he had statues of the gods imported from Greece and ordered their heads to be replaced by representations

Agrippina, Caligula's mother, on a coin isued A.D. 41–54. She was one of the foremost women of antiquity. A granddaughter of Augustus, she married the general Germanicus.

of himself, and it is said that he threatened to place his own statue in the Holy of Holies in Jerusalem. Even allowing for exaggeration by hostile writers, his actions seem extreme.

Foreign policy was almost nonexistent. It would appear that he intended to campaign in Germany and in Britain, but his actions were either deranged or symbolic. At any event his preparation came to nothing, and from the coast of the English Channel his army returned having been ordered to collect sea shells.

After five years of abused power, he was murdered by officers of the Praetorian Guard.

Claudius came to power in A.D. 41, unexpectedly proclaimed by the army. He was unprepared for the part but grew to be a competent ruler.

The principal development of his largely uneventful reign was the growing importance of the bureaucracy run almost entirely by freedmen. Claudius was also concerned to extend the franchise and to Romanize the provinces, for example: by founding *coloniae* in remote frontier zones such as Britain (Colchester) and Ger-

The Castra Praetoria, guards' caserne where Claudius was named emperor. Coin A.D. 44–45.

many (Cologne). His decision to promote Gauls to the Senate met with ridicule and opposition but was part of a sound policy for integrating the disparate parts of the Empire.

The conquest of Britain, which began in A.D. 43, was his only significant program of territorial expansion. There were minor expeditions among the coastal Germans (the Frisii and Chausi), and elsewhere, marginal territories and protectorates, including Mauretania, Lycia, and Thrace, were formally absorbed into the Empire.

At home he was at the mercy of powerful scheming women. His first wife, Messalina, was forced to suicide, but his second wife Agrippina, outlived him, having, it was rumored, poisoned his dish of mushrooms.

Nero was carefully groomed for emperorship by his mother, Agrippina, some years before the death of Claudius, his stepfather. During the early years of his reign he was under the influence and close guidance of his teacher Seneca aided by Burrus, the prefect of the Praetorian Guards. This period was one of moderation and of competent administration, but as the emperor came of age and assumed full control, a more wayward form of government began to prevail. In 61 the death of Burrus and the retirement of Seneca marked the end of the period of restraint. It was in this year that the emperor's mother was murdered, probably at her son's instigation.

Gradually Nero's vices gained the upper hand: he no longer tried to laugh them off, or hide, or deny them, but turned quite brazen. His feasts now lasted from noon till midnight .... Not satisfied with seducing freeborn boys and married women, Nero raped the Vestal Virgin Rubria.
Suetonius

External events centered largely on the conquest of Armenia, where between 57 and 60 Corbulo achieved considerable successes, but his successor lost the initiative and a compromise solution was then negotiated giving Rome nominal control. Elsewhere rebellions broke out. In Britain in A.D. 60 Queen Boudicca led a large native army against the Roman occupation, but the following year the rebels were defeated. In 66 a far more serious rebellion erupted in Judea which was to last for some years.
The last years of Nero's reign were characterized by his growing unpopularity. The great fire of Rome (A.D. 64) was blamed on him. Whether or not the accusation was correct, the fact that he built a vast urban villa for himself in the center of the city cannot have failed to alienate public

opinion still further. In 68 an uprising in Gaul and discontent among the Praetorian Guard drove Nero to suicide.

Nero and his mother, Agrippina the Younger, on a coin of A.D. 54. She was murdered in 61, probably at Nero's direction.

Nero died at the age of thirty-two, on the anniversary of Octavia's murder. In the widespread general rejoicing, citizens ran through the streets wearing caps of liberty, as though they were freed slaves. But a few faithful friends used to lay spring and summer flowers on his grave for some years and had statues made of him.

Suetonius: Twelve Caesars

St. Paul was executed in Rome in about A.D. 67 during the reign of Nero. Relief of St. Paul, Church of St. Trophime, Arles.

Nero died in June 68; by October, Galba, a seventy-three-year-old aristocrat, governor of Spain, was in command of Rome. He was, as Tacitus said, "by common consent well fitted to rule . . . until he tried." A strict disciplinarian, faced with economic chaos, he immediately made himself unpopular with all sections of the community by a series of stern measures and by refusing to bow to the will of the Praetorian Guards. The dangerous and complex situation was ineptly handled. Meanwhile, a new contender came forward for the throne—Otho. In January 69 the Praetorians, now backing Otho, murdered Galba.

The Praetorian Guards, shown in a relief of the early second century A.D., were a major force in Roman politics. They murdered Galba in A.D. 69, only three months after his succession.

Otho had incurred Nero's disfavor and had been sent, in virtual exile, to be governor of Lusitania (Portugal). In 68 he returned to Rome and gained the support of the Praetorians. At their instigation he was proclaimed emperor in January 69. Otho evidently had a reputation for loose living, but on assuming power he seems to have risen to the occasion. As Tacitus puts it, he "did not sink into a lethargic mood of hedonism and idleness. Amusements were postponed, indulgence disguised, and his whole behavior was adjusted to the high standards expected of a ruler."
Meanwhile the armies of Upper and Lower Germany had decided to support a candidate of their

own, Aulus Vitellius. Accordingly they marched south towards Rome but only got as far as the Po valley, where they were met by Otho's army. In the ensuing engagement (April, 69) the Vitellian supporters prevailed and Otho, abandoning the struggle, committed suicide.

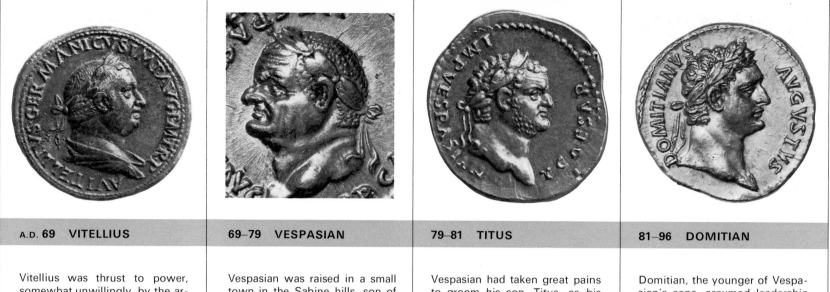

| A.D. 69 VITELLIUS | 69–79 VESPASIAN | 79–81 TITUS | 81–96 DOMITIAN |

Vitellius was thrust to power, somewhat unwillingly, by the army. After their victory in northern Italy in April 69, the new emperor and his troops marched on Rome, plundering cities as they went. Once in Rome the victorious army behaved irresponsibly, and (says Tacitus) "ruined their physique by idleness and their morals by indulgence." Concerning Vitellius's rule, Tacitus was even more scathing: "At such a court no one sought distinction by honesty or hard work."

Meanwhile it was now the turn of the army in the east to put forward a candidate of their own. The man they chose was Flavius Vespasianus, who at this stage was commanding the army in-

Detail of a fifteenth-century tapestry showing Vespasian getting ready for his march against Judea.

volved in the Jewish war. As the eastern armies made their way to Rome, the army of the Danube decided to add their support and in a rapid campaign reached Rome first. In the ensuing carnage Vitellius was killed together with most of his supporters. In October 70, when the situation had calmed, the new emperor arrived in Rome.

Vespasian was raised in a small town in the Sabine hills, son of a tax collector. During his early military career he saw distin-

Temple of Vesta, a circular, four-columned structure, shown in considerable detail in this coin issued by Vespasian in 73.

guished service in Britain at the time of the Claudian conquest, and later in Judea, where he commanded the Roman army. By the time of his elevation to the throne, at the age of sixty-one, he had gained a lifetime of experience both as a military man and as a provincial organizer.

The only serious disruption during his term of office came in the year 69 when the German tribes led by Civilis rebelled, encouraging the Gauls to join them. By the next year however, partly by diplomacy, partly by a show of arms, the revolt was squashed. His rule was strict, hard-working, and soundly balanced. Abroad, frontiers in Germany and the east were strengthened and the troops redeployed in the interests of economy and security, while at home, the system was reorganized to ensure that men of ability rose to prominent positions irrespective of social status. In his relations to the Senate, however, he made it clear that the emperor was now firmly in control.

His rule brought a new political stability to the Empire, while strong fiscal measures re-established the economic balance.

Vespasian had taken great pains to groom his son, Titus, as his successor, making it clear to the world at large that the Flavian dynasty were the legitimate rulers of Rome. The succession therefore passed off without incident. During his brief and largely uneventful reign Titus established a reputation for generosity, even extravagance. When a fire ravaged part of Rome, he is said to have sold some of the furniture of his palace to provide aid for the victims, and in A.D. 79 when Vesuvius erupted, destroying the towns of Pompeii and Herculaneum, the emperor personally made generous donations to the relief fund.

He died after only two years' reign at the age of forty-one.

On Mount Vesuvius broad sheets of fire and leaping flames blazed at several points, their bright glare emphasized by the darkness of night... On the landward side a fearful black cloud was rent by forked and quivering bursts of flame and parted to reveal great tongues of fire, like flashes of lightning magnified in size... ashes were already falling, not as yet very thickly . . . you could hear the shrieks of women, the wailing of infants and the shouting of men.   Pliny writing to Tacitus.

In A.D. 79, during Titus's reign, Vesuvius erupted, destroying Pompeii and Herculaneum.

Domitian, the younger of Vespasian's sons, assumed leadership immediately after the death of Titus. He was not well prepared for the task, having been kept without significant responsibility by his father and brother, but in military matters his judgment was sound and his choice of commanders sensible.

The northern frontier now began to pose serious problems. In 83–84 the emperor personally undertook expeditions against the

"Mourning Germania": coin issued by Domitian in 88–89 after suppression of a rebellion in Lower Germany.

Chatti, but in 85 a war with the Dacians broke out requiring the concentration of military activity in the Danube region, and there followed, in 92, an invasion of Pannonia by a Germanic tribe, the Marcomanni. In addition to these external threats, there was also a rebellion on the Rhine.

At home Domitian's increasingly dictatorial attitude was causing resentment in many quarters. Persecution of Christians and Jews and of groups of intellectuals, became frequent, reflecting the emperor's growing insecurity; while his announcement of his own deification caused fears of even more autocratic actions. Eventually, fearing for her life, his wife Domitia arranged for him to be stabbed to death, an act which greatly pleased the Senate.

96-98 NERVA

98-117 TRAJAN

117–138 HADRIAN

The short reign of Nerva provided a much needed breathing space after the trauma of Domitian's last years. Nerva, a gentle aristocrat, was selected by a small inner clique of Senators before Domitian's assassination. He was thus

Temple of Minerva, in the Forum of Nerva.

Right: *Portrait of Trajan and his wife, Plotina.*

Far right: *Trajan's Column.*

thoroughly acceptable to the Senate, and it is hardly surprising to find that he treated it with respect and consideration.

His three years in office were spent counteracting the worst of Domitian's abuses: free speech was reintroduced, those who had unjustly suffered under his predecessor were restored, and new financial measures adopted to repair the perilous state of the economy. His only significant confrontation was with the Praetorian Guard, who took it into their own hands to punish Domitian's assassin.

Four months before he died Nerva, who was without a son, wrote to Trajan, then serving on the Rhine, informing him that he proposed to adopt him. In this way not only was the succession assured, but the emperor had established the principle that the head of state was to be chosen on merit.

Marcus Ulpius Trajanus was born in Spain, near Seville, son of a onetime governor. He had commanded a legion in Spain and afterwards had been promoted to the command of the Rhine army, when at the age of forty-four, he was elevated to the Principate.

A military man at heart, much of his life was spent in campaigns. He even delayed his return to Rome for some while after he was made emperor, in order to reorganize the defences of the Pannonian frontier. The Dacian Wars occupied much time and energy only to be followed, after an interval, by the eastern campaigns which lasted from 113 until his death.

In Rome, between 106 and 113, he did much to encourage the economic prosperity of Italy. The harbors at Ostia and Ancona were greatly improved and new roads were built to facilitate the internal transport of farm produce and other goods. And in order to revitalize the rapidly decaying agricultural scene in Italy, which was suffering from lack of man-

power and capital, he forbade emigration and forcefully encouraged senators to invest in Italian estates. He took delight in embellishing the city with fine public buildings, the most famous complex of which were his vast forum and basilica with its neighboring libraries and markets.

His long reign marked a period of stability and growing prosperity.

Hadrian came to power at the moment when many must have realized that Trajan had over-

Exotic sculpture adorns the Conopus valley, part of Hadrian's Villa near Rome. This spot was decorated in an Egyptian motif.

stretched his hand. The eastern commitment was colossal and therein lay the prospect of long and costly wars. To Hadrian the course of action was clear—he must abandon Trajan's eastern annexations. This was immediately carried through but not without trouble, from a small clique of Trajan's now out of work generals. The potential revolt was, however, effectively squashed by prompt Senate action.

His achievements were many, but perhaps the most significant of all was his firm demonstration of the unity of the Empire: Rome itself was simply one element in the whole, and all men were susceptible to one system of government—the old Stoic ideal of the universal law *(jus gentium)*. His belief in the importance of the provinces was shown by the fact that out of the twenty-one years of his reign, at least thirteen were spent beyond the boundaries of Italy (see pages 200–201).

So eager was he for travel that he wished to see
with his own eyes everything which he had read
about the places of the earth.

Vita Hadriani

Hadrian's remarkable capacity for travel is easy to understand in a man of such wide artistic and academic interests, and a man whose tidy mind required him to see for himself firsthand the problems of the Empire which he was responsible for administering. He traveled without fuss, lived simply, and lingered where the mood took him. In his wake he left new cities, great public buildings, and an assurance in the hearts of the provincials that the emperor belonged to them.

His policy at home was to systematize the structure of government. Service to the state was now divided into two mainstreams —military and civil—and for the first time it became no longer necessary for a man to have served in the army before he could obtain office in the civil administration. The civil service was also thoroughly overhauled and the freedmen, who had been so dominant under Claudius, were removed from power, with the result that that body now became the preserve of the equestrian class. Inevitably the civil service staff grew in numbers but the overall result of the reorganization was to increase efficiency.

Two other major improvements were made. In 129 Salvius Julianus codified the many and various edicts into a single scheme of law which immediately became the basis of all legal decisions throughout the Empire, while the hitherto informal Council of State was now established with executive powers to make a wide range of civil decisions in the absence of the emperor. One final, and very necessary, innovation, was a scheme designed to ensure peaceful succession. The emperor had no children of his own. He therefore selected Lucius Ceionius Commodus Verus as a successor and formalized his choice by adopting him. Verus, however, died before Hadrian and alternative arrangements had quickly to be made. Hadrian now adopted a respected senator, Titus Aurelius Antoninus, and required him in turn to adopt two sons, Lucius Verus (son of the deceased Commodus) and Marcus Aurelius (Antoninus's own nephew). In this way Hadrian not only ensured the peaceful transition of power at his own death, but laid the basis of the succession for the rest of the century. Hadrian was an unusual man—a man of immense energy and organizing ability who, in spite of the enormous power which he wielded, was able to retain a sense of proportion and balance to the end of his life. Perhaps this was in part due to his wide ranging interests; an inveterate traveler and lover of Greek culture, he demonstrated an informed interest in architecture, science, literature, and art. He painted, helped design buildings, wrote poetry, and sang. More than any of his predecessors he could claim to be a gentleman in the Greek mold.

The reign of Antoninus marks a turning point: up to the time of Hadrian, the Empire had been expanding and secure. Admittedly there had been minor frontier problems, but each was firmly dealt with. Now all this was to begin to change. The emperor himself, a Senator in his middle age and without military pretentions, was prepared to sit back and leave the Empire to run itself. Minor campaigns were fought in the north of Britain and along the Rhine/Danube frontier, but the emperor took little personal interest. Elsewhere, however, particularly in the east, pressures were beginning to build up. There were troubles in Dacia; the Alani, a semi-nomadic people, were raiding Armenia; and Vologeses, king of Parthia, was threatening to declare war. From the safety of Rome these problems must have seemed minor and distant, but they were a foretaste of what was to come.

The reign of Antoninus, peaceful though it must have seemed, was a lull before the storm.

Columns of the Temple of Antoninus and Faustina, Rome, built in 142 and dedicated to the emperor's deified wife, Faustina. She died in 141. The couple's daughter, also called Faustina, became the wife of Emperor Marcus Aurelius.

Trophy—armor and banner symbolizing victory. A relief from the cella (or interior chamber) of the Temple of Hadrian, often called the Temple of Neptune. Now in the Palazzo dei Conservatori, Rome.

Top: *Hadrian married Sabina, the grand-niece of his predecessor, Trajan. Museum of Ostia.*

The feminine figure in this high relief symbolized the Danube province of Dacia. Like the eastern provinces, Dacia was conquered by Trajan but proved difficult to hold because of attacks from neighboring tribes. Hadrian wanted to abandon Dacia just as he had given up Trajan's territory in the east, but finally retained it. Palazzo dei Conservatori, Rome.

HADRIAN: THE CONSOLIDATION OF THE EMPIRE

Hadrian's reign, A.D. 117–138, marks a halfway point in Roman history: expansion had ended, and the beginning of the decline was not far off. The emperor, shown in a bust from the Terme Museum in Rome, spent more than a decade touring the Empire and stabilized its borders.

Below: Reliefs of the time of Hadrian later incorporated by Constantine in his triumphal arch. At left the emperor is shown hunting wild boar; at right he attends a sacrifice to Apollo.

Hadrian's first great journey in 121–125 took him the length and breadth of the Empire. He made first for Gaul to visit its principal cities and thence, via Lugdunum and Augusta Treverorum, he reached Germany to begin a systematic tour of inspection of the frontier region. The full length, from Noricum and Raetia to the Rhine mouth, was examined, necessary works put in hand, towns like Forum Hadriani were founded, and a series of new dispositions made. By the spring of 122, his task complete, he crossed

dria which needed his personal intervention, but by the time he had reached Massilia the problem had blown over and he spent his time visiting the cities of Provence. During the summer of 122 he moved south to Spain, though he did not visit his birthplace of Italica, preferring to

to Antioch, then went overland to the Euphrates where by discussion and diplomacy he was able to avert the crisis.

Once in the east he made a virtue of necessity, traveling extensively in Asia Minor, visiting Troy, the great cities of Pergamum and Ephesus, Rhodes and thence to Thrace, and along the Danube into Pannonia. Having thus virtually circumnavigated the northern and eastern frontiers, he turned south through Macedonia to arrive at his beloved Athens in the autumn of 124.

to Britain where a little before there had been trouble among the northern tribes. Having assessed the situation, he put in hand the creation of a great new frontier system, which though later modified, still bears his name. Shortly after he crossed back to Gaul. It was probably at this stage that he heard that there was trouble in Alexan-

spend the winter at Tarraco. In Spain, news of the Moorish rebellion reached him, but he appears to have left the problem to his generals. The next spring, however, he heard that the Parthians were preparing for war. This was far more serious and required his personal attention. Leaving Spain, he sailed the length of the Mediterranean

Here he was to reside for six months visiting famous sites, instituting new building projects and taking an active part in the cultural and artistic life of the city. Sparta, Corinth, and Delphi received him. Finally, in the summer of 125, after an absence of almost five years, he decided to return to Rome. The next year, however, he was with

the army in Africa visiting the frontier defenses and reviewing the troops. The trip was only a brief one, but late in 128 he set out from Rome on another prolonged journey through the east. The winter was once again spent in Athens. In spring he crossed to Ephesus and thence through Asia Minor to Syria and Cappadocia, returning to Antioch for the winter. The next year saw him in Palmyra, at Jerusalem, where he refounded the city as a Roman colony (thereby incurring the wrath of the Jewish extremists), and

Map of Hadrian's principal journeys between the years 121 and 131. A tireless traveler, the emperor visited most of the Roman world. The imperial presence was a great boost to provincial morale.

thence to Egypt. In Alexandria he spent a while in academic discussion at the museum before sailing down the Nile to Thebes, passing his time in sightseeing, founding cities, and hunting in the desert. From Alexandria he set out once more for Syria and thereafter appears to have visited the towns along the southern shores of the Black Sea. He was probably back in Athens in the autumn of 131, when news of a revolt in Jerusalem reached him. Immediately he sailed for Antioch to assess the situation firsthand and to make the necessary military appointments, returning finally to Rome in the spring of 134.

Even briefly to chronicle the emperor's journeys cannot fail to impress one of the tireless energy he must have possessed. Driven on by curiosity and sense of duty, he was to spend about thirteen years away from Rome. The last four years of his life, spent partly in his great country villa at Tivoli, must have been rich in memories for the now ailing traveler.

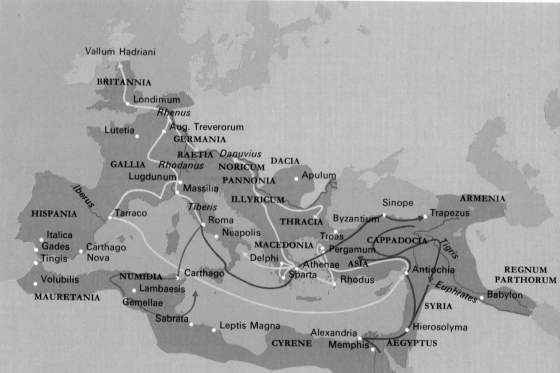

EAST Palmyra in the Syrian desert controlled the trade routes with the east. As trade intensified under the early Empire, it became rich and powerful. During the troubled times of the late third century, when the eastern provinces were being attacked by the Persians, Palmyra, under Queen Zenobia, acted as a buffer against Persian advance and maintained independence of Rome for a brief period. *(Pages 208–209)*

LIFE IN THE PROVINCES

Now indeed it is possible for Hellene or non-Hellene, with or without his property, to travel wherever he will, easily....it suffices to be a Roman citizen, or rather to be one of those united under your hegemony. Homer said, "Earth common to all," and you have made it come true. You have measured and recorded the land of the entire civilized world; you have spanned the rivers...and hewn highways through the mountains... you have accustomed all areas to a settled and orderly way of life.

Aelius Aristides

By the second century A.D., Rome and her Empire were closely bound together. The city had become increasingly dependent on food imports from Spain, North Africa, and Egypt. The marble relief above depicts the busy harbor of Ostia (Rome's seaport) in about the year 200. Distant parts of the Empire became thoroughly Romanized. In the third century North Africa began to lead the Roman world in artistic and architectural development. The theater at Leptis Magna in Libya (right) exemplifies the wealth of the North African cities.

Under Rome's power, the diverse lands of the Mediterranean and the east were given a veneer of uniformity. At the same time, they remained individually quite different in terms of geography, climate, natural resources, and culture. In each region, Rome had to deal with different conditions and react to different problems. To obtain some idea of the variety and complexity of the Roman Empire, it is necessary to see what made each area unique; what role it played in the complex mosaic of the Roman world.

The chief regions of the Empire, which this section treats in turn, are as follows:

AFRICA

The provinces of Mauretania, Numidia, Africa Proconsularis, and Cyrenaica.

EGYPT

The lands of the Nile.

IBERIA

The provinces of Tarraconensis, Lusitania, and Baetica.

GAUL AND BRITAIN

Narbonensis, Lugdunensis, Belgica, and Britannia.

GERMANY AND THE DANUBE

The frontier provinces of Germania, Raetia, Noricum, Pannonia, Moesia, and Dacia.

THE GREEK LANDS

Macedonia, Thrace, and Achaea.

ASIA MINOR

Asia, Bithynia and Pontus, Galatia, Lycia and Pamphylia, Cilicia, Cappadocia.

THE EAST

Judea, Arabia, Syria, Mesopotamia, Armenia.

The long peace of the second century lasting throughout the reign of Hadrian and Antoninus Pius (117–161) was a golden age. The provinces were secure and peaceful. Cities, many of them newly founded, flourished and all parts of the Empire were locked together in a complex network of trading relationships linked by well-maintained roads and bustling ports.

This was the view expressed by many writers of the time, including Aelius Aristides, a philosopher from Asia Minor who wrote praises of Rome in the middle of the second century (see page 210).

The Romanization of the provinces could also be considered in another light. When Tacitus wrote that emperors could be made elsewhere than in Rome, he was voicing the realization that it was in the provinces, rather than Rome, that the strength and vitality of the Empire now lay. The center was fast becoming hollow. Italy was underproductive and parasitic: only with the support of provincial wealth could it continue to maintain its leadership and dominance.

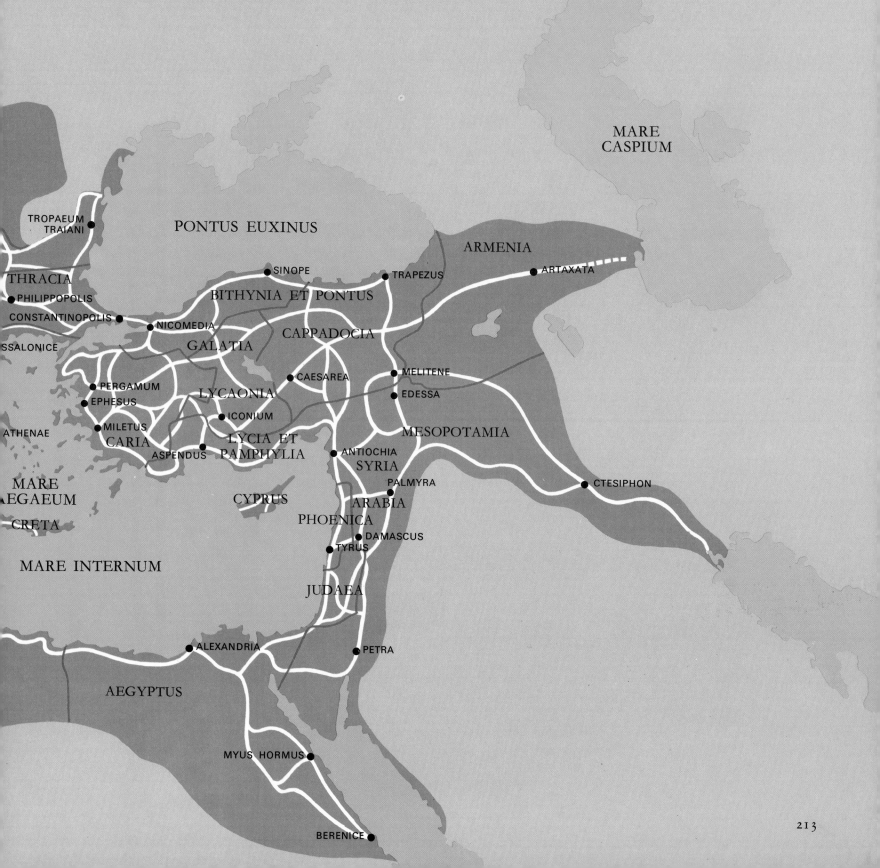

Provincials and Romans hail
the improvement of the arts...the increasing
splendor of the cities, the beautiful
face of the country, cultivated
and adorned like an immense garden;
and the long festival of peace.

Pliny (quoted by Gibbon)

Rome's cultural impact on her diverse, often underdeveloped provinces is vividly shown by the works of art unearthed far and wide. From present-day Switzerland (eastern Gaul and Upper Germany) come these two impressive examples of Roman art: a three-horned steer head from Martigny *(below)*, Musée de Valère in Sion; and a bust of Marcus Aurelius *(right)* from Avenches, Roman Aventicum. Both owe much to native styles.

ROAD MAP OF THE EMPIRE
(Tabula Peutingeriana)

*... up to the known limits
of the earth.*

Miller

Britannia with standard and plaque. The map names five cities in England; all subsequent maps give modern names in England. The first segment of the Tabula, showing central and northern England, Ireland, Iceland, and Spain, is missing.

The Tabula Peutingeriana is a medieval copy of a late classical map of the Roman Empire. The scroll *(rotulus)* is today broken down into 11 parchment pages. In all, it is 6.75 m long and 34 cm wide. In his will of 1508, the famous humanist Konrad Celtes left the manuscript to the Augsburg town clerk Konrad Peutinger, whose name first appeared in the title at the beginning of the seventeenth century. The map maker did not wish to make a true map: the Tabula has neither projection nor scale. Hence the frequent criticisms that late Roman maps are confused, barbaric, and inelegant. As the distances shown between places were quite arbitrary, depending on how much space the map maker had

It is not possible to specify with certainty the time of publication of the map (our copy of which dates back to the twelfth century) but it is believed to have originated around A.D. 365. The Roman cosmographer and philosopher Castorius has been suggested as the possible author.

In producing the map, the author undoubtedly started from Rome, where the roads departed in 12 directions. North, south, east, and west, did not, however, exist for him, only right and left. For the traveler, for whom the map is of course intended, these directions were sufficient to enable him to recognize his destination and to calculate distance. Each time he reached a crossroads he had to choose between left and right, and the map gave him this information.

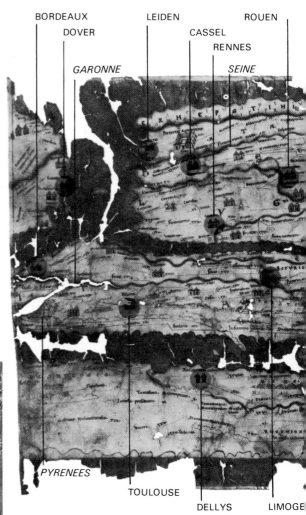

BORDEAUX • DOVER • GARONNE • LEIDEN • CASSEL • RENNES • ROUEN • SEINE • PYRENEES • TOULOUSE • DELLYS • LIMOGE

at his disposal, the greatest value of the map lies in the figures along the routes which give more precise information. A large number of cities, 555 in all, are shown in separate drawings, the vignettes. The vignettes do not reflect the importance, size, or political condition of the places illustrated, but, true to the map's purpose as a travel guide, are concerned with the sights and the lodgings available. It was thus comparable with the "Guides Michelin" of today.

Above: The illustration shows two families on a journey being led by an Amor. In front of the second cart a child is learning to walk with the help of wheels.

WESTERN EUROPE

NORTH SEA • RHINE • MAAS

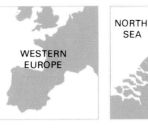

Left: Loading a grain ship.

Right: Terra-cotta disk, a personification of Africa. The province of Africa, the granary of the Roman Empire, is bordered along the whole of its southern length by the Atlas Mountains.

Milestone at Tongern. Roman milestones were usually round stone posts 1½ to 2½ m high and 40 to 50 cm in diameter, with an inscription to the emperor, and the distances to the main towns, here expressed in leagues.

The Celtic horse goddess Epona played an important role among the gods that the Romans received in their Pantheon. The goddess of stable boys and carters, this northern deity influenced the south and she was worshipped throughout the Mediterranean.

The wooded hills (silva) of the Vosges and the Black Forest are illustrated by tree sketches. The artist drew southern species only.

AMIENS CHARTRES   TROYES   COLOGNE METZ   AVENCHES
BOURGES NIJMEGEN XANTEN BONN TRIER   MAINZ
PARIS   TONGERN   MOSEL   STRASBOURG RHINE
                                        MONTGENÊVRE

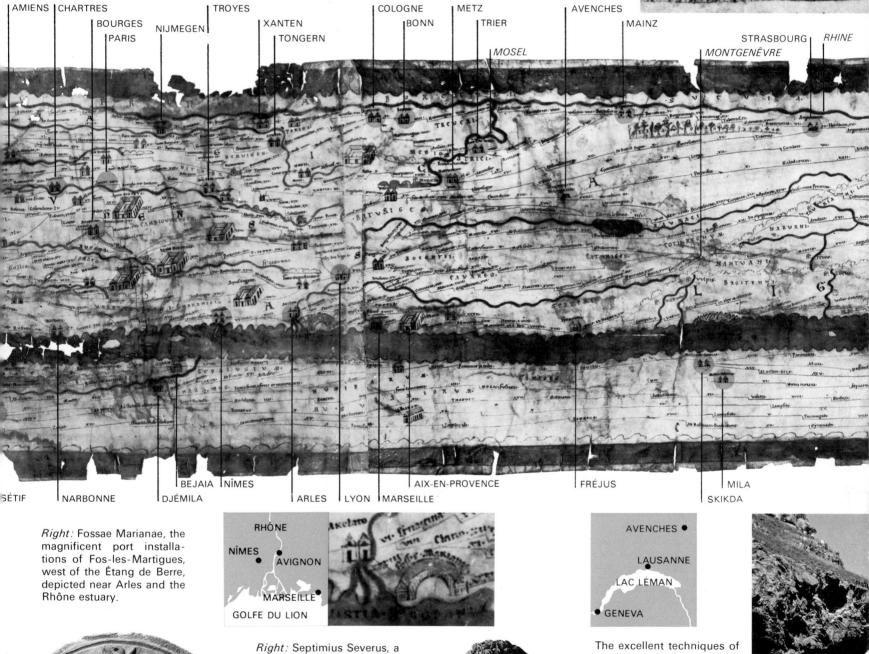

SÉTIF NARBONNE   BEJAIA NÎMES   AIX-EN-PROVENCE   FRÉJUS   MILA
          DJÉMILA   ARLES LYON MARSEILLE   SKIKDA

Right: Fossae Marianae, the magnificent port installations of Fos-les-Martigues, west of the Étang de Berre, depicted near Arles and the Rhône estuary.

RHÔNE
NÎMES
AVIGNON
MARSEILLE
GOLFE DU LION

AVENCHES
LAUSANNE
LAC LÉMAN
GENEVA

Right: Septimius Severus, a descendant of Phoenician settlers who married a Syrian princess, did not feel that he had many obligations to Roman tradition. The first emperor from the province of Africa, his main aim was to use all means to safeguard the throne for himself and his descendants.

The excellent techniques of the Roman engineers made possible, and indeed guaranteed, a water supply for the more than 600 Roman towns in Africa. The illustration on the right shows the aqueduct at Constantine.

Left: To set eternal Rome above all other cities the author placed the goddess Roma at the point from which all the main roads of Italy radiate. The author of the Tabula undoubtedly started with the representation of Italy, whose long shape lent itself to a drawing in the form of strips.

Palace of Diocletian in Split (about A.D. 300). Reconstruction drawing.

Collapse of the Temple of Jupiter, Pompeii, in the earthquake of A.D. 62.

TIVOLI PESCARA VASTO SPLIT TROIA STREMSKA MITROVICA POMPEI BELGRADE

PALESTRINA OSIJEK OPATOVAC SOLIN CANOSA TARANTO

TROGIR

APPENNINI

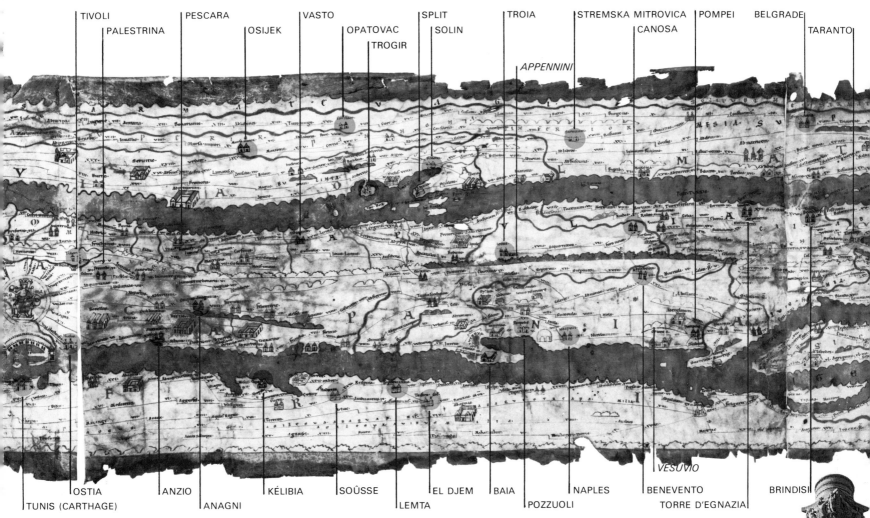

OSTIA ANZIO KÉLIBIA SOÛSSE EL DJEM BAIA NAPLES BENEVENTO BRINDISI

TUNIS (CARTHAGE) ANAGNI LEMTA POZZUOLI TORRE D'EGNAZIA

VESUVIO

Pozzuoli, once a flourishing commercial city with a busy harbor protected by a sea wall. To the right of this was the Crypta Neapolitana, the road tunnel between Naples and Pozzuoli. The large round arch with the two entrances indicates the grotto of the Posilippo. The tunnel was 710 m long and illuminated by candles. Nearby were Virgil's grave and the villa of Cicero.

NAPLES

GOLFO DI NAPOLI

Via Appia in Brindisi. The censor Appius Claudius began its construction in 312 B.C. The column marking the end of the road stretched across the Pontine plain and linked Rome with Capua. It was later extended to Taranto and Brindisi.

Ravenna and Aquileia were of great importance as bases for the Roman Adriatic fleet and as ports for shipping to the east. In addition, Aquileia was a trade center serving all the Danube countries.

The site of St. Peter's Cathedral was once a track for chariot races. Constantine built the old "ad Sanctum Petrum" basilica on its northern side. The floor of the basilica is still preserved in the crypt of the cathedral.

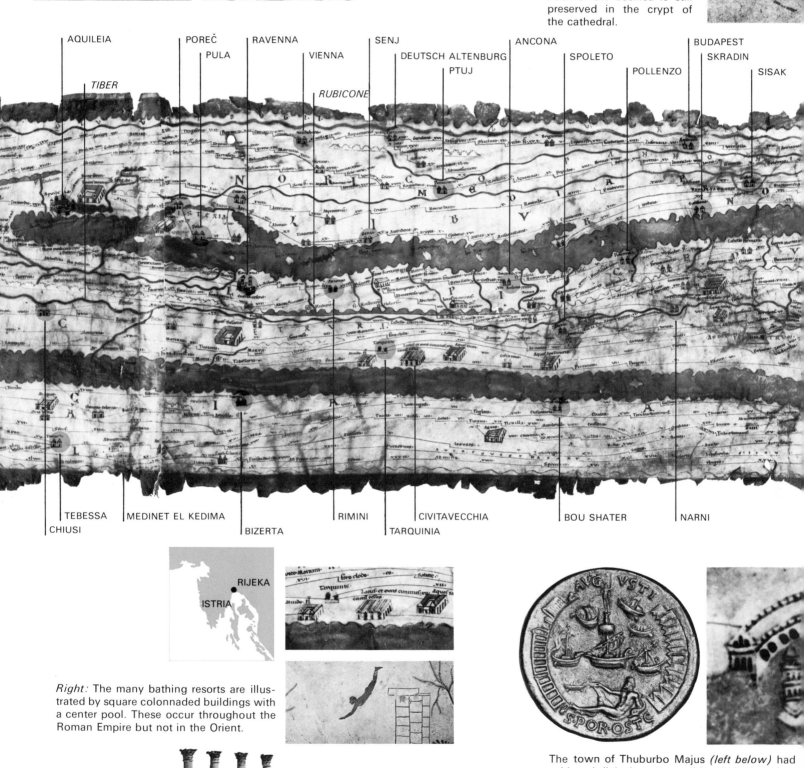

AQUILEIA   POREČ   RAVENNA   SENJ   ANCONA   BUDAPEST
            PULA   VIENNA   DEUTSCH ALTENBURG   SPOLETO   SKRADIN
TIBER   *RUBICONE*   PTUJ   POLLENZO   SISAK

TEBESSA   MEDINET EL KEDIMA   RIMINI   CIVITAVECCHIA   BOU SHATER   NARNI
CHIUSI   BIZERTA   TARQUINIA

ISTRIA   RIJEKA

Right: The many bathing resorts are illustrated by square colonnaded buildings with a center pool. These occur throughout the Roman Empire but not in the Orient.

The town of Thuburbo Majus *(left below)* had achieved all the honors possible within the urban hierarchy. (These rural centers played an important part in Roman life.)

Above: The port of Ostia. The outer harbor basin was extended by Claudius in A.D. 42 and after his death opened by Nero. A large and virtually unmaneuverable ship, built by Caligula, was filled with stones and cement then sunk, to form the foundations of the lighthouse.

Barbarian attacks on the legions guarding the Rhine-Danube frontier constantly forced emperor Marcus Aurelius to take military countermeasures. For this reason, the emperor spent a large part of his time in the threatened border provinces.

Drawing of the Upper Germanic border *(limes)* with a watchtower. The right bank of the Rhine and the left bank of the Danube are almost completely missing. If there had been any hope of retaining or regaining these areas, the Roman cosmographer would certainly not have omitted the right bank of the Rhine, but when the Tabula was produced, the great barbarian migration had already commenced.

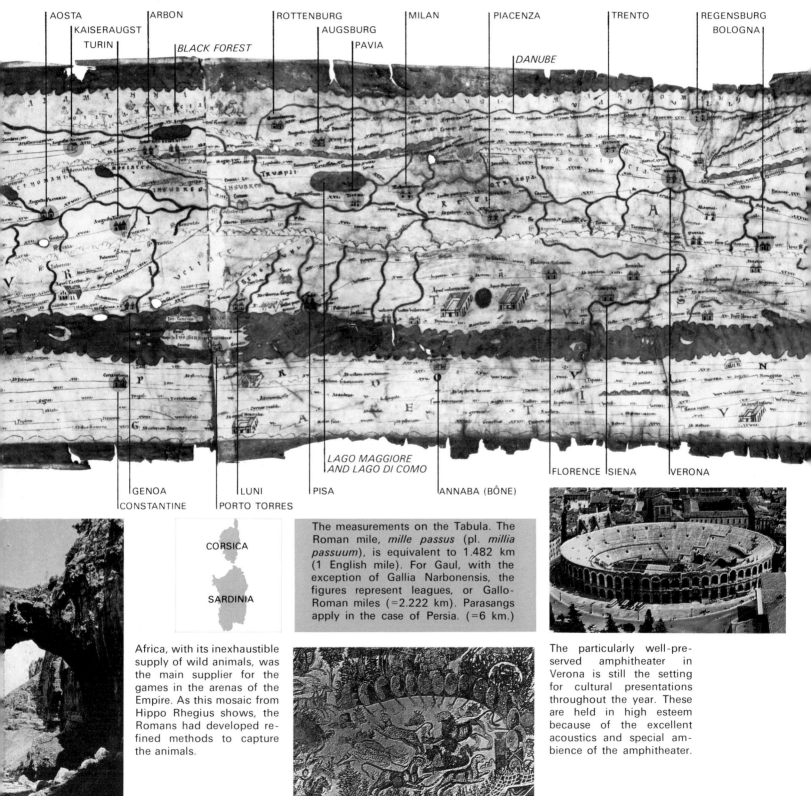

AOSTA
KAISERAUGST
TURIN
ARBON
BLACK FOREST
ROTTENBURG
AUGSBURG
PAVIA
MILAN
PIACENZA
DANUBE
TRENTO
REGENSBURG
BOLOGNA

GENOA
CONSTANTINE
LUNI
PORTO TORRES
PISA
LAGO MAGGIORE AND LAGO DI COMO
ANNABA (BÔNE)
FLORENCE SIENA
VERONA

CORSICA

SARDINIA

The measurements on the Tabula. The Roman mile, *mille passus* (pl. *millia passuum*), is equivalent to 1.482 km (1 English mile). For Gaul, with the exception of Gallia Narbonensis, the figures represent leagues, or Gallo-Roman miles (=2.222 km). Parasangs apply in the case of Persia. (=6 km.)

Africa, with its inexhaustible supply of wild animals, was the main supplier for the games in the arenas of the Empire. As this mosaic from Hippo Rhegius shows, the Romans had developed refined methods to capture the animals.

The particularly well-preserved amphitheater in Verona is still the setting for cultural presentations throughout the year. These are held in high esteem because of the excellent acoustics and special ambience of the amphitheater.

Diana of Ephesus (the most important city of Asia Minor) was widely worshipped. The cult of Diana derived from that of a primeval fertility goddess. Paul's attempt to suppress it, temporarily cost him his freedom.

Philippus Arabus was from Chohba in Hauran. This favorite of the Syrian princesses was the only Arab to attain imperial office. As soon as he entered office, he signed a peace treaty with the Persians, which was unfavorable to Rome.

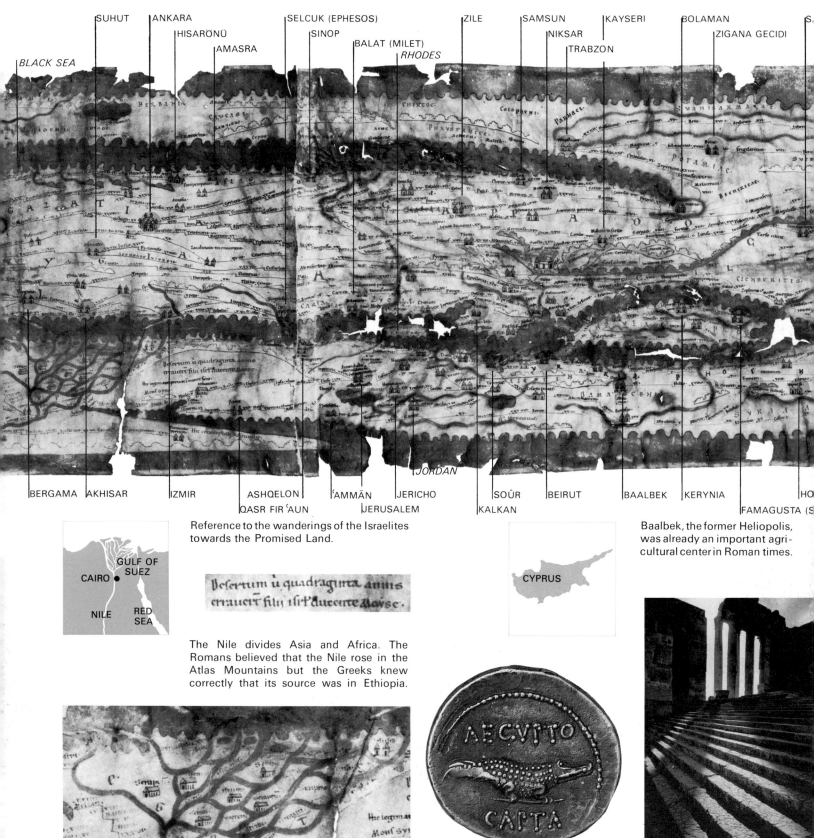

SUHUT ANKARA HISARÖNÜ AMASRA SELCUK (EPHESOS) SINOP BALAT (MILET) RHODES ZILE SAMSUN NIKSAR TRABZON KAYSERI BOLAMAN ZIGANA GECIDI S

BLACK SEA

BERGAMA AKHISAR IZMIR ASHQELON QASR FIR 'AUN 'AMMĀN JERUSALEM JERICHO JORDAN SOÛR KALKAN BEIRUT BAALBEK KERYNIA FAMAGUSTA (S HO

Reference to the wanderings of the Israelites towards the Promised Land.

GULF OF SUEZ
CAIRO
NILE RED SEA

Baalbek, the former Heliopolis, was already an important agricultural center in Roman times.

CYPRUS

Deſertum u quadraginta annis errauerūt filij iſrl'aucente Moyse.

The Nile divides Asia and Africa. The Romans believed that the Nile rose in the Atlas Mountains but the Greeks knew correctly that its source was in Ethiopia.

AEGVPTO CAPTA

In A.D. 330 Constantine declared Constantinople the new Imperial Residence. The deity of the city points to a column which could be identified as the so-called burnt column which Constantine built as a symbol of his new city.

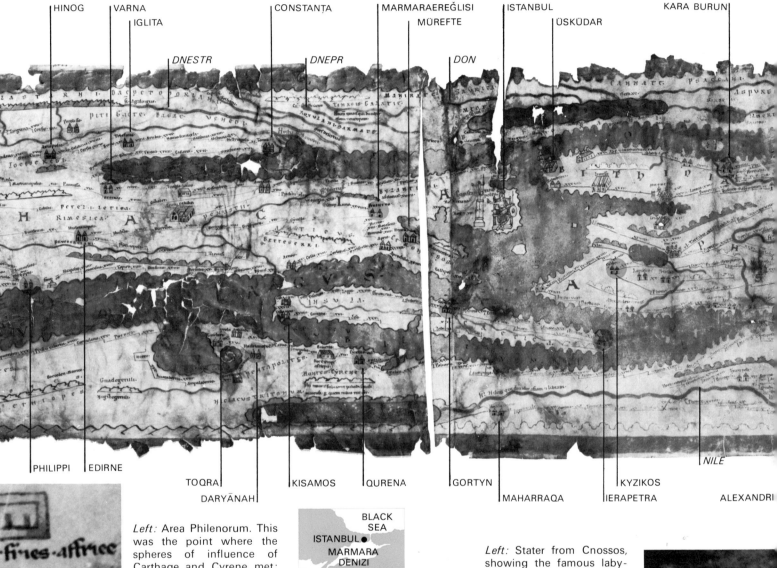

HINOG   VARNA   CONSTANȚA   MARMARAEREĞLISI   ISTANBUL   KARA BURUN
IGLITA   MÜREFTE   ÜSKÜDAR

DNESTR   *DNEPR*   *DON*

PHILIPPI   EDIRNE

TOQRA   KISAMOS   QURENA   GORTYN   KYZIKOS
DARYĀNAH   MAHARRAQA   IERAPETRA   ALEXANDRI

NILE

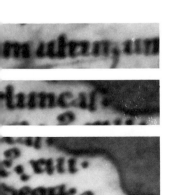

Left: Area Philenorum. This was the point where the spheres of influence of Carthage and Cyrene met; later, the dividing line between the Latin west and the Byzantine east. The name of the altar refers to the tale of two hero brothers, who, while marching from Carthage, allowed themselves to be buried alive in order to mark the boundary. Typical informative inscriptions from the Tabula: "Ad capsum ultimum": At the last mail coach. "Ad speluncam": Inn by the grotto. "Scina Locus Judeorum Augusti": A colony of Jews were settled here by Augustus.

BLACK SEA
ISTANBUL ●
MARMARA DENIZI
TURKEY

Left: Stater from Cnossos, showing the famous labyrinth on the island of Crete, around 350 B.C.
Right: The lighthouse near Chrysopolis (Uesküdar), and Jovisurius ("the bringer of fair winds") at the entrance of the Black Sea to the Bosphorus.
On the map another lighthouse is drawn near Alexandria, whose name and vignette are missing. This antique marvel was not built on land but on the island of Pharos. The tower, about 120 m high, was destroyed in 1326 by an earthquake.

Soldiers of the Roman border army in full armor.

Hadrian, an extremely knowledgeable historian and an admirer of Greek culture, traveled to Athens several times. He took the higher orders in Eleusis and was given the honorary name of Olympios.

Right: The Tanais (Don) divides Europe and Asia.

KOSTOLAC   VLORË   DONJI MILANOVAC   OHRID   SOFIYA   PLOVDIV

JUPA   LARISSA   BITOLA   ALBA IULIA   SILIST   CLUJ

GRADISTE   *DANUBE*

AEGEAN SEA   SALONICA

SICILY   SABRATA   TARABULUS   HOMS   OLYMPIA   CORINTH   ATHENS

SIRACUSA   MESSINA   IGOUMENITSA?   PATRAS   EPIDAVROS

PALERMO

SICILY

GOLFO DI TARANTO

REGGIO CALABRIA

THESSALY

ATHENS

PELOPPONESUS

Few Roman markets had a more intimate atmosphere than that of Leptis Magna *(below).* In the time of the emperor Septimius Severus, native of Leptis, the market was partially rebuilt. The Temple of Venus in Eryx, Sicily *(below left),* surrounded by walls with gate and towers.

The largest and richest of the city vignettes shows Antiochia, the capital of Syria. Comparable to Constantinople and Alexandria in terms of wealth, beauty, and size, it was temporarily the residence of the emperors. It was here that followers of the new faith were first called Christians.

Under Trajan, the Roman Empire was extended to the edge of the Caspian Sea and to the Persian Gulf. Nevertheless, even he was unable to conquer the Parthians decisively. As one of his first official actions, his successor Hadrian surrendered the eastern areas.

A magnificent colonnade leads the traveler to the holy district of the commercial center of Gerasa.

Right: "Area fines Romanorum": Border between the Roman and the Parthian empires. "Fines exercitus Syriaticae et commercium barbarorum." These limits can only refer to the field campaigns of Aurelian in the year A.D. 272, as a result of which the Palmyrenic Empire of the empress Zenobia was destroyed.

Bottom right: The sudden invasion of the Persians under Shapur occurred in A.D. 259. The emperor Valerian, in order to encourage the beseiged towns of Edessa and Karrhai, took part personally in their defense and was taken prisoner. The news of his capture greatly shocked the Romans. Rome was no longer regarded as unassailable.

Arce fines romanorum·
fines exercituf Syriatice
et conmerciuum Barbaroſ

The Romans were already aware of the distant areas of the Alexandrian empire. The trade centers on the Indian subcontinent, in Ceylon, and even in China (the Silk Route) are impressive proof of Rome's worldwide commercial interests.

"Usque quo Alexander?" "How much further, Alexander?" A message from the Oracle persuaded Alexander to turn back when his army refused to follow him.

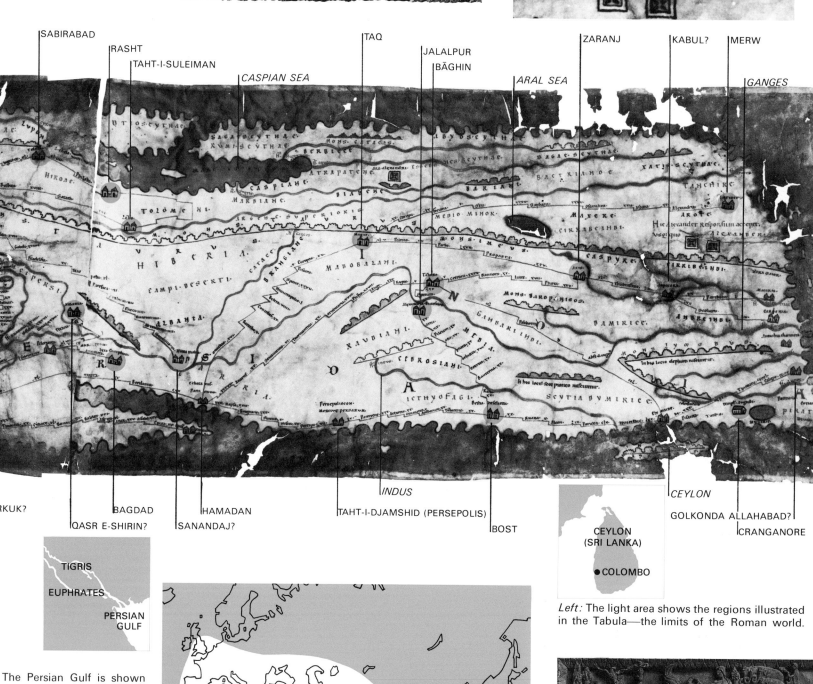

SABIRABAD
RASHT
TAHT-I-SULEIMAN
CASPIAN SEA
TAQ
JALALPUR
BĀGHIN
ARAL SEA
ZARANJ
KABUL?
MERW
GANGES

KIRKUK?
QASR E-SHIRIN?
BAGDAD
SANANDAJ?
HAMADAN
INDUS
TAHT-I-DJAMSHID (PERSEPOLIS)
BOST
CEYLON
GOLKONDA ALLAHABAD?
CRANGANORE

CEYLON
(SRI LANKA)

● COLOMBO

Left: The light area shows the regions illustrated in the Tabula—the limits of the Roman world.

TIGRIS
EUPHRATES
PERSIAN GULF

The Persian Gulf is shown twice. The first drawing refers to Pliny's idea that the Gulf had the shape of a human head, with the neck forming the straits; the second drawing reflects the Roman view that the Persian Gulf was directly to the south of the Caspian Sea.

AFRICA

The city of Djemila, on the fertile Algerian coast, developed as the province of Africa grew in wealth. Founded in the late first century A.D. along the main highway, it grew steadily as a trading town until about 400. View of the "new" town square (early third century): Arch of Caracalla, and the Severan temple (at right).

Between the Mediterranean and the Sahara lay the provinces of North Africa: Mauretania, Numidia, Africa Proconsularis, and Cyrenaica. The landscape varied from the high mountains of the Atlas, to the fertile plains of Tunisia, and from the rich fruit-growing coastal zone to the inland desert fringes. Africa had no great mineral wealth and little industry but it was crucial to Rome, providing the food to satisfy her citizens and the wild beasts to amuse them in the arena. The three cities of Tripolitania, Leptis Magna, Oea, and Sabratha, on the fringe of the Mediterranean world, provided access to the African interior. Beyond them, to the south, lay the rocky wastes of the Fezzan gradually giving way to the Sahara. The region was occupied by various tribes among whom the Garamantes were dominant. Late in the first century A.D. or early in the second, two Roman military expeditions passed southwards through Garamantian territory to the land of the "Aethiopians," and possibly to Lake Chad. No doubt the expeditions were designed to explore the sources of such luxury commodities as ivory, precious stones, rare woods, gold dust, ostrich feathers, and slaves which the Garamantian middlemen were supplying to the coastal towns.

146 B.C. The Roman conquest begins. Carthage destroyed in 146 B.C. The province of Africa Proconsularis is founded and the surrounding areas are divided among native kings. An attempt by Gracchus to found a colony at Carthage fails (123–122).

112–105 Jugurthine War. The native King Jugurtha defies Rome and is beaten. The ports of Tripolitania are taken over.

46 Caesar in Africa. Battles against King Juba of Numidia. Numidia annexed.

33 B.C.–A.D. 40 Mauretania. After death of friendly client King Bocchus (33 B.C.), Rome assumes some responsibility for Mauretania. Juba II takes over as client king under Augustus (25 B.C.); succeeded by son, Ptolemy (A.D. 23). Ptolemy murdered by Caligula and Mauretania annexed in A.D. 40.

17–24 Revolt of Tacfarinas. Local uprising eventually subdued after serious initial setbacks.

238 Gordian I proclaimed emperor. Gordian was proconsul of Africa at the time.

429 Vandals attack Africa. Occupy Carthage in 439.

533 Africa restored. Vandals beaten by Count Belisarius, Africa once more part of the Roman world.

641 The Arab advance begins 641–642 in Egypt, 642 Cyrenaica, 643 Tripoli. In 647–708, Maghreb taken. Carthage captured finally in 698.

North Africa, particularly the Maghreb (modern Tunisia, Algeria, and Morocco), was immensely productive under Roman rule, a richness amply demonstrated by the six hundred cities which flourished throughout the length and breadth of the country. Its wealth was based entirely upon agricultural production focused, in the early years, on the fertile wheat-growing lands of Tunisia, well watered by the River Medjerda and its tributaries. This region had been extensively farmed and

no doubt, well managed, by the Carthaginians. Indeed the only Carthaginian book known to us, is a textbook on agriculture written by Mago and referred to by several Roman writers. The quotations we have imply that a balanced mixed farming was practiced over much of the area and that some of the coastal regions, particularly the Cap Bon peninsula, specialized in fruit growing and market gardening.

With the Roman conquest in 146 B.C. and the successive territorial expansion which followed, more and more land came to belong officially to the Roman state; but in reality most of it was parceled up and let to Roman tenants, or remained in the hands of those already farming it, in return for an annual tribute—the *annona*. At first the farms

must have been of fairly even size, but gradually increasing numbers were bought up by the wealthy and merged into larger estates. By Nero's time the elder Pliny could make the no doubt exaggerated generalization, that half of Africa was owned by six men.

Plowing and sowing, in realistic detail from third-century mosaics now in the Cherchel Museum (Algeria). Africa's agricultural wealth became proverbial in Roman times. By A.D. 100

The fertility of Africa was legendary. Pliny reported that a yield of 150-fold was not uncommon for wheat and that even higher figures were known. Wheat was the major product. In Caesar's time Africa (essentially the Carthaginian territory) produced fifty

Rome had become dependent on grain shipped from Africa as tax payment in kind. Wheat was the principal crop, but by the second century wine and oil exports became important as well.

227

Wheat as a sacred symbol. In this African stele, a priestess of Ceres (goddess of fertility), standing between two torches, holds a wand in one hand, and an ear of wheat in the other. The figure shows that North African religion had adopted Greek goddesses from Eleusis. This cult remained important under Roman rule. First-century A.D. relief, Bardo Museum, Tunis, from a roadside shrine.

Right: The four seasons on an African country estate, fourth-century mosaic. At top left, in winter, the seated lady of the manor receives animals and produce from tenant farmers. Top right, a shepherd with his flock in summertime. At bottom, in springtime, the lady, beside her maid, is offered fish and flowers (left); and the master receives grapes and a live hare (right) in the autumn. The middle row shows hunting scenes and the manor house.

thousand tons annually. A hundred years later, after Numidia and Tripolitania had been added, the annual output was ten times as great. As much as half a million tons of grain was taken as *annona* to Rome every year, supplying two-thirds of Rome's needs, the other third coming from Egypt. It is hardly surprising therefore, that Rome was intent on keeping the African estates in grain production. When Sallust was governing Africa Nova in 46 B.C., he could write, "The soil produces good crops of grain and good pasture but is unsuitable for the cultivation of trees." This latter point was manifestly false, but his statement nevertheless must reflect the dominance of grainfields in the agricultural landscape.

In the early Empire it was in theory, illegal to cultivate olive trees and vines in North Africa, a law enacted presumably to safeguard Rome's grain supplies and at the same time to protect the interests of the wine and oil producers of Italy. But by Trajan's time (r. 98–117) the Italian economy had so stagnated that it could no longer supply its own needs, and the policy was reversed: the state now gave active encouragement

to African farmers to produce wine and oil. An inscription from Aïn El Djemala provides an insight into the problems. It records a request from the local peasants who ask the procurator to "grant us those fields which are swampy and wooded, that we may plant them with olive groves and vines in accordance with the Lex Manciana on the terms applying to the neighboring Saltus Neronianus. —" The procurator replied that "since [the Emperor Hadrian] has ordered all parts of land which are suitable for olives or vines, as well

as for grain, to be cultivated; therefore by the grace of his foresight the right is given to all to enter upon even those parts of the said land which are included in the surveyed units...and which are not exploited by the lessors." In other words, the economic situation was now such that every available acre had to be brought into active production.

The right to farm land also took with it the obligation to pay taxes in kind. An altar from Henchir Mettich in northern Tunisia, raised in the early second century, gives a precise account of the dues which a peasant cultivator was expected to pay: "one-third of the wheat from the threshing floor, one-third of the barley from the threshing floor, one-fourth of the beans from the threshing floor, one-third of the wine from the vat, one-third of the oil from the press, one sextarius of honey from each hive." Even so, there was plenty left over to feed the family and to make a profit.

The farming economy of Africa was therefore subject to pressures from Rome: it was also influenced by internal changes of which two were of con-

A farmhand picking fruit, detail from a mosaic in the Bardo Museum, Tunis. In another scene *(right)* a worker tends the grape vines in wintertime; from a mosaic floor, early third century A.D.

"The Great Hunt": In this detail from a floor mosaic (A.D. 325–350) in the Sicilian villa Piazza Armerina, three men steer an ox-drawn cart used as a cage for tigers and lions.

Wild animals were important to Africa's economy: from Libya, beasts captured inland were shipped to Rome for slaughter or combat in the arena.

Triumphal procession in honor of the foremost citizen of Roman Africa. Septimius Severus, born in Leptis Magna, on the coast of Libya, was emperor of Rome from 193 to 211. He erected this arch of triumph in his hometown in 203–204, employing Hellenistic craftsmen from Asia Minor for its reliefs. Septimius is standing in the chariot with his sons Caracalla and Geta.

Africa's great prosperity is reflected in the hundreds of Roman cities that flourished there. Many were new—planned and built entirely under the Romans—like Timgad (Algeria), where this meticulous official inscription can still be read. The town began as a garrison.

El Djem (Thysdrus), in Tunisia, boasted a remarkable amphitheater, the largest in Africa, built in the early third century. The city prospered as a center of olive oil production. Interior view of the amphitheater.

Below: Djemila, or Cuicul, in Algeria, founded in the late first century A.D., grew into a city of some 10,000 and gradually spread out along its north-south axis. This aerial photograph (looking eastward) shows the three main divisions of the town. At left, the neatly laid-out military settlement,

siderable significance. The first was that the population had risen considerably since the conquest: at first by immigration and later by an increase in the birth rate. Second, the old grain lands, which had been intensively cultivated for centuries, must by now have been showing signs of exhaustion. Both factors combined to encourage an expansion in the area of land cultivated. The Aïn El Djemala inscription, mentioned above, refers to attempts to intensify the agriculture in areas already farmed; but elsewhere around the fringes of the fertile grain-growing

lands, new, hitherto barren, land was being broken for the first time. The famous Christian convert Tertullian, writing in the second century A.D., records that "smiling estates have replaced the most famous deserts, cultivated fields have conquered the forests, flocks of sheep have put wild beasts to flight—certain proof," he adds, "of the increase of mankind."

One of the most dramatic changes of which he must have been aware was the spread of olive growing. Olives could flourish in poor land, totally unsuitable for cereals, so long as the trees were

with its square forum. In the center, the Severan Square with its temple to the family of Septimius Severus, and the Arch of Caracalla. At right, the fourth- and fifth-century Christian quarter.

Decorated arcades from the Severan forum in Leptis Magna, the birthplace of Septimius Severus. The emperor encouraged elaborate architectural development of the town. It became important for its exports of wine, oil, slaves, and animals.

"Roma," scratched on a wall in the Christian basilica in Bône, Tunisia: a graffito that may have been a soldier's expression of homesickness.

Below: The triumphal arch theater, and forum of Timgad stand out clearly from the rectilinear street pattern. Founded A.D. 100

as a settlement for Roman army veterans.

Dougga, in contrast, grew out of an earlier Libyan and Carthaginian city, and represents a fusion of diverse cultures. The hilly town center is shown here, with the Temple of Jupiter, Juno, and Minerva.

Below left: In the rugged Atlas Mountains of Algeria, the Roman aqueduct of Constantine still winds its way along the wall of a natural fissure.

Below: Temple of Caelistis (A.D. 222), Dougga. Sheep are seen grazing at right.

planted far enough apart and irrigation systems were introduced. In this way vast tracts of new territory were brought under cultivation, from the Aures mountains of Algeria across to the east coasts of Tunisia and around the Gulf of Syrte to Tripolitania and Cyrenaica.

For the landowner, life could be very pleasant. Villas were comfortable. There was entertainment to be had in hunting expeditions, and the towns provided more sophisticated kinds of amusements. For the poor, life was hard and oppression, sometimes illegal oppression, was not infrequent; but there were opportunities for those ready to work, and the system was such that in a lifetime a man could greatly increase his wealth and status. Perhaps the most celebrated case was that of a harvester from the town of Mactar in Tunisia whose tombstone, erected in the third century, charmingly records his life history:

I was born of poor parents; my father had neither an income nor his own house. From the day of my birth I always cultivated my field; neither my land nor I ever had any rest.... When the harvestgangs arrived to hire themselves out in the countryside round Cirta, capital of Numidia, or in the plains of the mountain of Jupiter, I was the first to harvest my field. Then, leaving my neighborhood, for twelve years I reaped the harvest for another man, under a fiery sun; for eleven years I was chief of a harvest gang and scythed the corn in the fields of Numidia. Thanks to my labors, and being content with very little, I finally became master of a house and a property: today I live at ease. I have even achieved honors: I was called on to sit in the Senate of my city, and, though once a modest peasant, I became censor. I have watched my children and grandchildren grow up round me; my life has been occupied, peaceful, and honored by all.

EGYPT

Egypt held a fascination for the more educated Roman. The country was remote, isolated by desert barriers, but with a rich and distinctive culture of its own based upon three thousand years of development. Under the Ptolemies, economic and political decay had set in and by the time that Egypt was drawn into the Roman political arena in the second half of the first century B.C., the country was in a state of near collapse. The Roman interlude provided only a temporary respite.

Crocodile with the inscription "Aegypto capta," on a denar issued by Augustus in 28 B.C., three years after his defeat of Antony and Cleopatra at Actium.

Soon after Rome assumed control of Egypt in 27 B.C., a Greek traveler, Strabo, made an extensive tour of the new province in the entourage of the prefect. His account, full of enthusiasm for the strangeness of the land, gives a brilliant insight into the curious, inbred nature of native culture which he contrasts vividly with the cosmopolitan society of Alexandria. In Alexandria he was particularly impressed by the great double harbor

surrounded by vast warehouses. It was a "city intersected by streets used by horses and chariots," well endowed with public precincts and palaces. In the museum there resided men of learning whose property was held in common and who were in the charge of a priest appointed by the emperor. It was here, a century and a half later, that Hadrian was to stay and hold discussions with the scholars during his travels in the east.

332 B.C.   Alexander enters Egypt. The beginning of the period of Macedonian rule. After Alexander's death one of his generals, Ptolemaios, is proclaimed king. The Ptolemies rule until the death of Cleopatra.

48   Caesar in Egypt. Pompey flees to Egypt but is murdered. Caesar follows and, intrigued by Cleopatra, helps to establish her in sole control of the country after extensive fighting in Alexandria.

41–27   The last stages of the Civil War. Antony sets up his base in Alexandria. The Senate declares war. Octavian in Egypt: death of Cleopatra (30). In 27, Egypt comes under the control of Augustus.

38–41   Jewish troubles in Alexandria. Conflict between Greeks and Jews, quietened by the intervention of Claudius.

66–117   Jewish troubles again. Ended by harsh repression under Trajan.

199–201   Visit of Septimius Severus: establishment of city councils at Alexandria and in the metropoleis.

269–271   Palmyra invades Egypt and occupies it for a year.

Two cultures. Beside the pink-granite sphinx at Alexandria rises the so-called Pillar of Pompey, erected around A.D. 300 on the spot where the Roman general Pompey is supposedly buried. On the same site stand scattered ruins of a temple to Serapis. Pompey was killed in Egypt in 48 B.C. during the war with Julius Caesar.

Alexandria, according to Strabo, was bursting with prosperity born of its far-flung trading contacts, for its position allowed it to serve as a port-of-trade between the Mediterranean world on the one hand, and Ethiopia and India on the other; while the productive nature of its own hinterland, the Nile valley, ensured a constant supply of grain for the Mediterranean markets. As one might expect of an international port of this kind, excesses were everywhere evident—"on boats [there was] flute-playing and dancing without restraint, with the utmost lewdness."

Further upriver Strabo came to the site of Cairo (Babylon) where, in his time, the three Roman legions were stationed on a ridge overlooking the Nile. To provide the troops with water, 150 prisoners were engaged on a gigantic

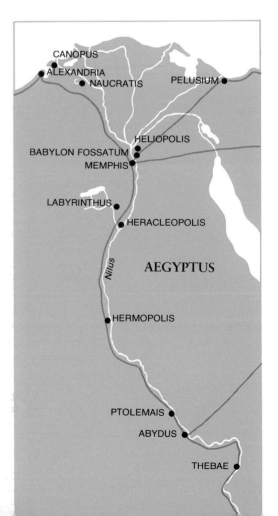

Following in Caesar's footsteps, Mark Antony, shown with an ivy wreath on a coin of 39 B.C. *(far left)*, became enamored of Cleopatra. The couple were defeated by Octavian, Antony's former ally, and committed suicide in Egypt in 30 B.C. Contrasting views of Cleopatra are offered on an Egyptian bas-relief *(center)* and on a Roman coin of 32–31 B.C., with jewels adorning her hair.

treadmill. On the other side of the river lay the city of Memphis and the Pyramids. Here he visited the sacred bull of Apis and stopped to wonder at the sphinx. It was:

a place so sandy that the dunes are piled up by the winds. As a result some of the sphinxes I saw were buried up to the head, and others were only half-visible.

And so his journey continued. Further upriver he came to Arsinoe, once called Crocodilopolis, where the priests kept a sacred crocodile: "It is called Souchos, and is fed on grain and bits of meat and wine, which are always offered to it by the visiting foreigners." The account of the rest of his tour continues with every curiosity described in loving detail: the temple of Isis at Philae, the groaning statue of Memnon, and the city of Thebes, reduced to a mere collection of villages after a Persian attack centuries before.

The impressions gained from visiting the relics of the once-great civilization cannot have failed to astonish Strabo. He was seeing a civilization in decay, which had only recently come under

Roman control, and was not unimpressed by the attempts of the new administrators—"to the best of their ability they have, I might say, set most things right."

Egypt was an extremely difficult province to govern for two principal reasons. The very nature of the country, the long narrow strip of extremely fertile land protected by virtually impenetrable desert, meant that any man who could control it was in an unassailably strong position; but more significant perhaps was the nature of the Egyptian mentality. Used as they were to thousands of years of isolation and

repression, the population had become inbred and superstitious. They had owed their allegiance to the great temples and to the godlike pharaoh. Now, although the power of the priests was much reduced and efforts were made to replace pharaoh-worship with the ideal of Rome, there was always a danger that the excitable population would be drawn to regard an individual Roman as a god. This indeed happened in A.D. 19 when Germanicus was visiting the province. Admittedly it could be said that he encouraged the population by ordering the granaries of Alexandria to be opened to avert a famine, but it

Above: A sign of continuity, the Temple of Hathor at Dendera in Upper (southern) Egypt was begun 233 in the first century B.C. by the Ptolemy kings and was completed under the Roman emperors. View of the open facade, with ornately carved columns and screen walls. Inside, the walls contain reliefs of Roman emperors presenting offerings. The goddess Hathor, sometimes portrayed as a cow or as a woman with horns, had many important attributes in Egyptian mythology and was sometimes confused with Isis.

The bull was important in Egypt as a god of fertility called Apis, a name derived from Hapi, a Nile divinity. A live bull was kept in Memphis and mourned upon its death. Bronze statue, British Museum.

An imaginative conception of the flooding of the Nile. In this floor mosaic from the sanctuary in Praeneste (modern Palestrina), near Rome, the Nile waters have trapped man and beast. The animals convey the exotic Roman notion of Egypt. City towers stand isolated by the water, amid richly varied vegetation and elaborate river craft. Created in the first century B.C.

was necessary for him to issue an edict to prevent the Egyptians from worshipping him in their enthusiasm to personify the power who controlled them.

By actually being in Egypt, Germanicus was disobeying the strict letter of the law; for Augustus had ruled that no man of senatorial rank was allowed to enter the province: indeed it was governed by an *eques* on behalf of Rome. In creating this exception to normal Roman policy, Augustus was in fact making a shrewd assessment both of the Egyptian mentality and of the military significance of the province, no doubt mindful of the way in which Mark Antony had used the country as a refuge during the Civil War.

The *eques*, based in Alexandria, governed the whole province, which was split into three districts under *epistrategoi* who in turn were responsible for smaller territories (*nomes*) controlled by *strategoi*.

Roman policy towards the country was based on three principles: to prevent Egypt being used as a power base, to keep the population subservient, and to extract the maximum amount possible from the land. The only difference from Ptolemaic rule was that instead of the productive surplus being plowed back into the country, Rome exported it for her own use. Although Roman technological improvements, particularly in irrigation, increased productivity, it was only a matter of time before the province became depleted and an irreversible decline set in, causing widespread misery among the rural population.

Unlike most other parts of the Roman Empire, in Egypt urban growth was discouraged. There were, in fact, only three major towns—Alexandria, Ptolemais, and Naucratis—and even Alexandria seems to have been kept without a town council. Elsewhere, each *nomes*

was governed from an urban or semi-urban center called a *metropoleis* where a small body of upper-class citizens provided a pool of manpower from which officials could be drawn, albeit somewhat reluctantly as the recession deepened and duties became more onerous.

Alexandria, with its volatile cosmopolitan population, was a constant problem. Polybius (ca. 100 B.C.) had distinguished different groups among its population. There were the natives, sharp-witted and amenable to urban living, mercenaries, who were insubordinate and rebellious, and the Alexandrians of Greek stock who were "not distinctly inclined to civic life...." A large Jewish population added to the turbulence. In A.D. 38 serious conflict between Greeks and Jews broke out, and following the Jewish revolt of A.D. 66 in Judaea, there were further troubles in Alexandria leading to the death of fifty thousand people. Racial conflicts continued between the different ethnic groups until the early second century when, as the historian Appian succinctly puts it, "Trajan destroyed the Jewish race in Egypt." Thereafter a new faction, the Christians, emerged to add fuel to the fire of ethnic and religious tension. Yet in spite of all this, Alexandria remained one of the great cultural centers of the Roman world, producing philosophers like Philo and Origen—men of considerable intellectual standing.

For the small farmers working in the Nile valley, all this must have seemed remote and irrelevant. Battling against the odds to pay the taxes, forced into ruinous public service, and unable to maintain an adequate labor force, many of them simply abandoned their estates and responsibilities. For them Rome must have seemed a far more demanding master than the pharaohs.

IBERIA

By the time of Augustus the whole of Iberia had come under Roman domination. It was a diverse country: the Mediterranean coastal region had developed its own distinctive culture long before Roman domination. With outlets to the Mediterranean markets through a fringe of Greek and Carthaginian colonies, the inhabitants flourished. Under the Romans a thoroughly urban organization emerged based on the rich mineral wealth of the area and upon the exportation of grain, wine, and oil. Further inland the level of cultural achievement varied: the Lusitanians of the west lived a spartan existence but were excellent horsemen and made good fighters in the auxiliary armies; while in the extreme northwest were the Cantabrians, a wild and intractable people so barbarian that, according to Strabo, they grew their hair long like women, and drank no wine.

237–219 B.C. The Carthaginian army under Hamilcar moves into Spain, causing panic among the Greek traders at Massilia, who in 226 appeal to Rome for help.

218–202 Romans campaign in Spain against the Carthaginians. The first Roman colony in Spain is founded by Scipio at *Italica*.

197 Spain divided into two provinces—Hither and Further Spain. Rebellions among the Turdentani quelled by Cato the Elder; trouble with the Lusitanians.

154–133 Revolt of Lusitanians and Celtiberians culminating in the destruction of Numantia, the Celtiberian capital (133).

104–93 Cimbri enter Spain (104): Further unrest.

83–73 Spain used as a theater of war by the various rival factions supporting Marius and Sulla.

61–59 Julius Caesar, governor of Further Spain, campaigns in the west between the Tagus and Douro rivers.

49–45 The Civil War reaches Spain. Pompeian party destroyed by Caesar at the battle of Munda (45).

26–19 Augustus campaigns in northwest Spain (26–25). Further action against the Cantabrians lasts until 19. Iberia redivided into three provinces. Lusitania, Baetica, and Tarraconensis.

ca. 168 Moors from North Africa raid Baetica.

409 Vandals, Alans, and Suebi cross the Pyrenees into Spain.

Iberia was enormously rich in natural products of all kinds, but perhaps most famous of all were its metals. "Nearly the whole of Spain," said Pliny, "abounds in mines of lead, iron, copper, silver and gold...while in Baetica there is cinnabar."

The exploitation of Iberia's mineral wealth had begun long before the appearance of Rome; indeed, one of the prime reasons for Carthaginian territorial expansion into the peninsula was to gain control of the metal trade, so important was it in Mediterranean commerce. In Hannibal's time a single mine shaft in Cartagena was producing 300 pounds of silver a day, and 40,000 workers were said to be employed in one region alone. Cato's victories in 194 B.C. allowed him to carry off colossal quantities of gold and silver. It was events such as this that impressed upon the Roman mind the value of Iberia. The campaigns of Caesar and later Augustus in the northwest must, in part at least, have been motivated by the desire to gain control of the mines of the area.

Under Roman law mineral wealth usually belonged to the state, although private owners are recorded: mines were worked either directly by the procurators or, more usually in the later periods, were leased out on fixed con-

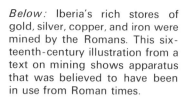

Rome's two Spanish-born emperors. Hadrian *(right)* and his uncle Trajan *(far right)* were both natives of Italica, near Seville. The town flourished during their reigns. At Alcantara, Trajan also built the Empire's highest bridge.

Below: Saguntum, on the Mediterranean coast, was Rome's ally and her first foothold in Spain. Hannibal's attack on the town helped precipitate war with Rome in 218–202 B.C. View of the hillside theater and castle.

Below: Iberia's rich stores of gold, silver, copper, and iron were mined by the Romans. This sixteenth-century illustration from a text on mining shows apparatus that was believed to have been in use from Roman times.

tracts at high rents to individual entrepreneurs, many of whom were from Italy. Regulations controlling the working of the mines were strict. Two inscriptions on bronze, found in the mine at Vipasca, near Aljustrel in Portugal, provide a fascinating insight into the strictly regulated nature of mining in the second century A.D. The mine

Celt-Iberian warrior, with shield and characteristic headgear, and wearing no armor. Relief from Osuna, first century B.C. Strong Celtic resistance and the savage, hilly terrain made Iberia difficult to conquer. Stability finally came under Augustus's rule.

shafts were worked by individual lessees or partnerships, who had to make a considerable down payment to the government before they could begin to smelt the ore. If, for any reason, work stopped, the mine would revert to the state. The extraction of the ore and its smelting could take place only during daylight hours, and harsh penalties were imposed on anyone caught stealing. Safety was carefully considered, with conditions set out for the proper timbering and draining of the shafts and galleries.

The second inscription laid down provisions for the services and amenities in the mining area. The procurators licensed a number of artisans to practice their trades—bath-house keepers, barbers, fullers, auctioneers, and shoemakers—all of whom were subject to controls and regulations. The contractors given the bath-house concession were, for example, charged to provide a constant supply of hot water, to open at different times for men and women, and to make sure that the establishment was kept clean and in good repair.

Of the metals which Spain could provide, gold was the most sought after; it was found in most areas of the peninsula, particularly in the northwest along the River Sil, in Lusitania, in the Tagus valley, and in Baetica in the region around Corduba. Silver was equally widespread, Spanish silver, according to Tacitus, being of the finest quality. In Lusitania the Aljustrel mines produced both silver and copper, but elsewhere the metal was usually found with lead from which it was separated by the process of cupellation. The lead itself had a considerable commercial value and was extensively exported, particularly to Rome in the form of lead pigs (ingots). At one smelting works at Orihuela, in Valencia, more than fifty pigs were found ready for trans-ship-

ment. Spanish-stamped lead pigs have been recorded in Pompeii and Rome and as far afield as Switzerland, Germany, and Africa.

Tin and copper were also extensively exploited. Tin was found in the northwest and the west, while the best copper came from the large mining area centered on Corduba. An even larger establishment was found at Hispalis, where the present Rio Tinto mines continue to exploit the same lodes. One estimate gives the extent of the principal Roman galleries as in excess of seven kilometers.

Finally, Spanish iron was held in high repute. Of Spanish swords Justin could say, "nor was any weapon held in esteem by them which had not been dipped either in Bilbilis or the Chalybs." It was probably at Bilbilis and Toletum, where extensive traces of ironworking have been found, that most of the swords used by the Spanish auxiliaries were manufactured.

It is abundantly clear from the archaeological evidence and from literary sources that the technology of mining engineering had been brought to a point of high perfection by the Romans. Recent surveys of Roman mining installations, still surviving in parts of northwest Spain, have discovered dramatic traces of complex waterworks, storage tanks, and dams, while the writings of the elder Pliny provide a detailed account of the actual working methods against which the physical remains must be assessed. He goes on to explain how vein gold can be extracted by open cast workings or mine shafts. Then comes the crushing or washing processes, followed by smelting and refining. His description of deep mining conjures up terrifying pictures:

By the light of lamps long galleries are excavated into the mountain. The lamps measure the shifts, and the men may not see daylight for months on end.... The miners carry the ore out on their shoulders, each man forming part of a human chain working in

Right: The famous aqueduct at Segovia (Spain), first century A.D., is still in working order. Water is piped from a spring 15 kilometers away, to a water tower, thence to the aqueduct. Eight hundred meters (one-half mile) long, it is composed of 128 arches, of which the highest is 30 meters above ground level. The aqueduct runs through the center of the town.

the dark, only those at the end seeing the daylight. Another form of mining involved the running [of] aqueducts mile after mile along mountain ridges to wash away mining debris.... The incline must be steep to produce a surge, consequently high-level sources are required. Gorges and crevasses are bridged by viaducts. Elsewhere protruding rocks are cut away.... The washing process is ruined if the water is full of silt.... To avoid this the water is made to flow over gravel or pebbles. On the ridge above the minehead, reservoirs are built... The sluices are knocked open so that the violent down rush is sufficient to sweep away rock debris.

Pliny, *Natural History* XXXIII, 67–75

The expenditure of manpower on these great projects was considerable, but the return in terms of wealth, for the province and for the Empire, must have far outweighed it—at least until the middle of the second century, after which a decline set in. Many mines must have become exhausted after four centuries of intensive exploitation. By the fourth century only occasional reference is made to the countries' mineral wealth; the emphasis had now passed to the export of agricultural products.

GAUL AND BRITAIN

Conquerors of Gaul and Britain, Julius Caesar and the emperor Claudius (who reigned A.D. 41–54). For Caesar's Gallic exploits, see pages 180–183. Under Claudius, southeast Britain was controlled by A.D. 47, and the first *colonia*, at Colchester (Camulodunum), was founded in the year 49.

Gaul and Britain together comprised the larger part of the Celtic world. Under Roman domination the natives were quick to learn and eager to embrace the Roman ideal. As Tacitus so cynically puts it,

In place of distaste for the Latin language came a passion to command it. In the same way our national dress came into favor and the toga was everywhere to be seen. And so the Britons were gradually led on to the amenities that make vice agreeable—arcades, baths, and sumptuous banquets. They spoke of such novelties as "civilization," when really they were only a feature of enslavement.
Agricola 21

Yet in spite of an enthusiasm for Roman culture, native nationalism occasionally erupted—particularly in the turbulent 60s of the first century A.D. Thereafter the provinces settled down to a period of peace and prosperity.

196–180 B.C. The conquest of Cisalpine Gaul. The defeat of the Celts in the Po valley and the conquest of Liguria.

125–118 The acquisition of new Gaulish territories. Campaigns against the Allobroges and Arverni (125), creation of Gallia Narbonensis (122).

58–51 Caesar conquers Gaul. Campaigns in Britain, 55 and 54.

27–24 Augustus tours the western provinces.

A.D. 43–85 The conquest of Britain. The conquest begins under Claudius, and culminates with the victory of Agricola at Mons Graupius in northern Scotland.

60–61 The revolt of Queen Boudicca in eastern Britain.

68 The revolt of Vindex in Gaul.

69–70 The revolt of Civilis begins among the Batavi.

122 Hadrian's wall begun as the northern frontier of Britain.

196–212 Albinus, governor of Britain, makes a bid for the throne (196) and depletes northern frontier. Barbarian attacks follow. Septimius Severus campaigns against the Caledonians in the far north, his settlement completed by Caracalla.

Most provinces experienced upheavals in varying degrees before settling down quietly to Roman rule: natives were often unwilling to accept foreign domination, the Roman tax system seemed onerous and difficult to understand and not infrequently, Roman officials were guilty of extortion and maladministration. Inevitably there was unrest leading sometimes to open revolt. Nowhere can these problems be more clearly seen than in Gaul and Britain, where the fury of the insurgents was directed against the newly established towns.

Yet, devastating and brutal though these revolts could be, so strong was the grip of the army, and such was the attraction of Roman culture, that stability was repeatedly re-established and the threads of urban life were once more gathered up. Gaul and Britain, then, will serve here to demonstrate the stresses and strains evident at one time or another in most newly founded provinces. Within three years of the invasion of Britain in A.D. 43, the urbanized area in the southeast had been conquered and the armies were poised ready for further advance across the more difficult

Ten days, 365 kilometers: a journey through Gaul in the year 333. An anonymous pilgrim traveled from Bordeaux (Burdigala) to Jerusalem in that year, and recorded all his stops.

Below, a reconstruction of one stretch of his trip, between Valence and Turin. From *Itinerarium Hierosolymitanum (Burdigalense)*.

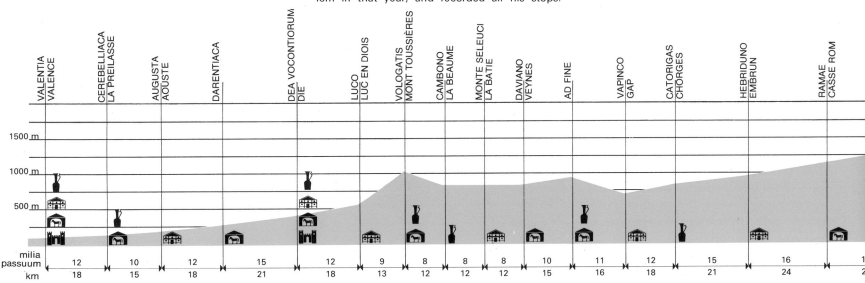

	VALENTIA VALENCE	CEREBELLIACA LA PREILASSE	AUGUSTA AOÜSTE	DARENTIACA	DEA VOCONTIORUM DIE	LUCO LUC EN DIOIS	VOLOGATIS MONT TOUSSIÈRES	CAMBONO LA BEAUME	MONTE SELEUCI LA BATIE	DAVIANO VEYNES	AD FINE	VAPINCO GAP	CATORIGAS CHORGES	HEBRIDUNO EMBRUN	RAMAE CASSE ROM
milia passuum		12	10	12	15	12	9	8	8	8	10	11	12	15	16	1
km		18	15	18	21	18	13	12	12	12	15	16	18	21	24	2

Hadrian's Wall, a defensive line consisting of a stone and turf wall and associated military works, running the width of Britain. It was built under Hadrian's orders following troubles with the natives.

Far right: Excellent roads, such as this one in Yorkshire, connected the Roman garrisons.

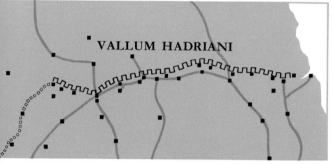

VALLUM HADRIANI

The 130-kilometer course of Hadrian's Wall, and the network of forts and roads surrounding it. Another wall was erected farther north twenty years later.

Right: The horned god Cernunnos, wearing a Celtic neck torque and holding a club, is shown seated between the Roman Apollo and Mercury, in a relief from Reims.

🏰 Major settlement, city

🐎 Change of horses

🏠 Inn

🍶 Rest stop

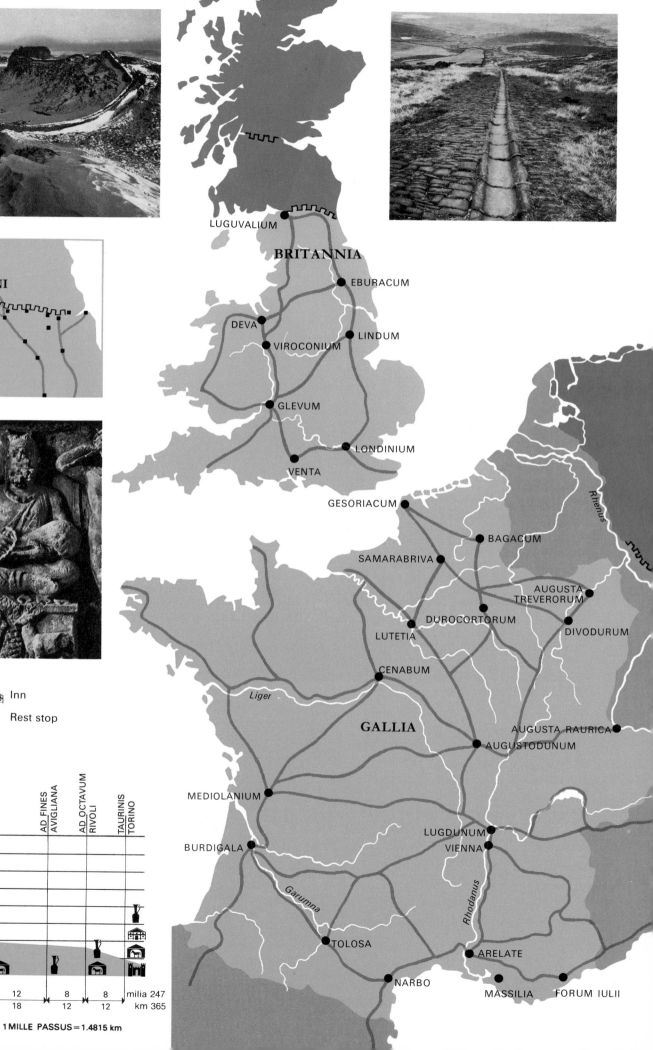

LUGUVALIUM

BRITANNIA

EBURACUM

DEVA

VIROCONIUM

LINDUM

GLEVUM

LONDINIUM

VENTA

GESORIACUM

BAGACUM

SAMARABRIVA

AUGUSTA TREVERORUM

DUROCORTORUM

DIVODURUM

LUTETIA

CENABUM

Liger

Rhenus

GALLIA

AUGUSTA RAURICA

AUGUSTODUNUM

MEDIOLANIUM

LUGDUNUM

VIENNA

BURDIGALA

Garumna

Rhodanus

TOLOSA

ARELATE

NARBO

MASSILIA

FORUM IULII

IN ALPE COTTIA MONT GENÈVRE	GESDAONE CESANNE	AD MARTE OULX	SECUSSIONE SUSA	AD DUODECIMUM BORGONE	AD FINES AVIGLIANA	AD OCTAVUM RIVOLI	TAURINIS TORINO	
10	8	15	12	12	8	8		milia 247
15	12	21	18	18	12	12		km 365

1 MILLE PASSUS = 1.4815 km

terrain of the west and the north. In the wake of the advance a colony for veterans had been established close to the site of the old native capital of Camulodunum (now Colchester) in Essex. Inevitably there was conflict between the natives and the settlers. "The veterans," said Tacitus, "were a special object of their hatred. These men, recently settled,...had been turning them out of their homes, taking away their lands, and calling them prisoners and slaves. The soldiers did nothing to check the insolence of the veterans." Moreover, a Temple of Claudius had been established which had to be maintained out of native wealth. The presence of the alien community together with new systems of taxation cannot have failed to have caused great irritation. Matters, however, were not to come to a head until A.D. 60.

In 59 Prasutagus, the king of the Iceni, a tribe occupying parts of East Anglia, died, in his will leaving his estates divided between the emperor and his two daughters. Tacitus writes:

His hope had been that with such subservience the kingdom and his own property would remain inviolate, but it fell out far otherwise. Both were plundered as though they were the spoils of war, the kingdom by centurions, the royal household by the procurator's slaves. The first outrage was the flogging of his wife Boudicca and the rape of his daughters: then the Icenian nobles were deprived of their ancestral estates as though the Romans had been presented with the whole country and the king's relatives were treated as though they were household slaves. These outrages and fear of worse...moved the Iceni to arms.

Thus, crass mishandling of a delicate situation by the Roman authorities, together with simmering discontent with the new rule, sparked off a rebellion of horrifying violence. The tribes

Roman celebration of the Celtic conquests was everywhere in evidence, in monuments, sculpture, and coins. "Britannia" *(below)*, in cape, armor, and boots, seated on a stone, is holding a shield and the imperial standard; on a sesterce of A.D. 143–144. The second coin, issued in 48 B.C., shows Gallic battle equipment, two crossed trumpets and an oval and a round shield.

Stone relief of chained Celtic captives, from the east side of the triumphal arch of Carpentoracte (now Carpentras) in southern France, early first century A.D. The figure at left is dressed in a tunic; the other prisoner wears an animal skin. The arch, originally the gateway to the town, was later used as the portal to a Romanesque church and now stands in the inner courtyard of the Palais de Justice in Carpentras. Many towns in Roman Gaul had similar arches commemorating the conquest of the country.

The natives of Gaul kept their local gods along with the imported Roman divinities. At right are three figures of Gallic gods dating from Roman times: the boar god, a combined human and animal figure wearing the Celtic neck torque; the goddess Epona *(center)* on horseback, holding a crown (from Alesia); and a relief *(far right)* of the war god Esus.

of the southeast rose up: London, Colchester, and Verulamium were destroyed and their inhabitants, seventy thousand of them, were massacred.

The Ninth Legion was routed and retired in disarray while the procurator fled to Gaul. "The Britons had no thought of taking prisoners or selling them as slaves...but only of slaughter, the gibbet, fire and the cross."

Eventually, after the main body of the Roman army (which at the time the rebellion broke out was campaigning in North Wales) had had time to regroup and march to the scene of the rebellion, the rebels were drawn into direct confrontation. In his famous narrative, Tacitus vividly describes the pre-battle preparations. Boudicca and her daughters drove among the rebel ranks in her chariot, stirring up the emotion of the troops. She came among them as an ordinary woman fighting for her lost freedom, her bruised body, and the outraged virginity of her daughters. Roman greed no longer spared their bodies, old people were killed—but the gods would grant vengeance. Without

victory there could be only servitude. In the ensuing battle the rebels at first rallied, then faltered and were consumed:

The Romans did not spare the women, and the bodies of baggage animals, pierced with spears, were added to the piles of corpses: it was a glorious victory equal to those of the good old days: some estimate as many as 80,000 British dead: there were only 400 Romans killed.

In the aftermath Boudicca committed suicide, and there began a period of vi-

cious reprisals against the natives which were eventually halted only by removing the governor and replacing him with a more moderate man.

A few years later a rebellion of a different kind was to break out in Gaul. Already, in A.D. 21, there had been an uprising among the Treveri and the Aedui against taxation and the activities of an oppressive procurator, but the events of A.D. 68 were inspired by more complex motives. In this year the governor of Lugudunensis, Gaius Julius Vindex, a Gaul enjoying Roman citizenship, called together an assembly of Gallic chiefs to discuss the misdeeds of Nero. Nero, he said, had despoiled the whole world; it was their duty to rise up against him. The ensuing conflict, known to ancient writers as the *Bellum Gallicum*, brought together the Arverni, Aedui, and Sequani in common cause against the emperor. It was they who persuaded Galba, legate in Hispania Tarraconensis, to make a bid for power (page 196) but opposition among the German legions led to the annihilation of Vindex and his force.

Right: Praying figure, on a sarcophagus from Arles during the early Christian era.

Payment of the rent. In this relief from the Rhineland, a tax collector in the foreground counts out a heap of coins on the table, while bearded figures of tenant farmers stand at rear.

A Gallic horse trader is shown dressed in the customary farmer's hooded cloak. At rear, another man brandishes a whip over the two horses. Archaeological Museum, Dijon.

The Celtic Dis Pater, father of the gods: the head is influenced by Roman statues of Jupiter, while the clothing and posture are entirely Gallic. Similar combinations appear in the reliefs *(above right)*: Venus and Mars, from Paris; Celtic Rosmerta with horn of plenty, beside a Gallicized Mercury, from Glanum in Provence.

The events, not clearly analyzed by the classical sources, are full of fascination. Although Vindex was at pains to present his actions as motivated solely by the interests of Rome, Tacitus was of the opinion that behind it all lay the old specter of Gallic nationalism. As events turned out, ancient tribal rivalries between the Gaulish supporters of

Vindex and the Treveri, together with the more Germanic tribes to the north, were to play a significant part in the political intrigues following the death of Nero.

For a while Vitellius, supported by the Rhine legions, held power. The first sign of Gaulish opposition came when the Boii, living in the region of Nevers, rose to support one Mariccus, who claimed to have been sent by the gods to liberate the Gauls. The revolt was easily squashed and Mariccus executed, but the events symbolized the unrest which was now polarizing among the Gauls.

Meanwhile on the Rhine an uprising among the German tribes was being engineered by Julius Civilis, a Batavian who had served as an officer in the Roman army. In the winter of 69, Civilis, Julius Tutor of the Treveri, and Julius Sabinus of the Lingones, joined forces

The physical types and the hair styles shown in these bronze heads are believed to be typical of the Celtic-Helvetian population. The female head, from Thun (near Bern), represents the goddess Rosmerta. The young man, who represents an eastern Gaul, was created by a Roman artist (as the copper eyes testify). Both from the Historical Museum, Bern.

A cloth salesman displays goods to a customer. Gravestone relief, Trier Museum. At center top, bundles of fabric are shown on the shelf.

Ornate gravestone of a wealthy Gallic couple.

Wine transport: a river barge bearing two casks is being towed. Pottery containers are shown above. Cabrières d'Aygues, France.

Among the earliest surviving structures in France are the beehive-shaped dwellings thought by some to date back to the pre-Celtic period. They were sometimes inhabited again long afterwards, during migrations, or in time of war or other disasters. This example, from Vaucluse (southern France), measures 4 meters across the base and 3.5 meters in height.

Below: In constructing an elaborate public bathing facility at Aquae Sulis (modern Bath) in southern England, the Romans took advantage of natural warm springs found in the area. The buildings date back to the first century.

Below left: Model reconstruction of the important Roman garrison at Vindonissa, in eastern Gaul (now Switzerland) near the Empire's Germanic border defenses. Many provincial towns started as military bases.

to proclaim the *Imperium Galliarum*— the Empire of the Gauls. Several other tribes in Gallia Belgica, including the Nervii and Tungri, were now won over, but no general agreement could be reached among the many Gaulish tribes and factions. Eventually a traditional Gaulish council, the *Concilium Galliarum*, was summoned to meet in Reims. Here the problem was carefully debated—should the Gauls choose peace or liberty? The vote went in favor of peace. The Treveri, however, persisted in their opposition to Rome, under the leadership of Civilis, but in 70 Vespasian sent a new force led by Petillius

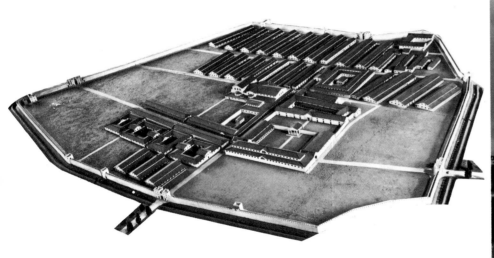

Cerialis to destroy the uprising—a task which was successfully completed in a comparatively short time.

Thus the last manifestations of nationalism succumbed to the will of Rome. The story with all its political complexities gives a very clear demonstration of the old independent spirit of the Celts and of their traditional inability to act in concert. Moreover it underlines the hostilities which still remained between the Gauls of the center and the more Germanic tribes of the north—a point which Cerialis was at pains to emphasize.

At the entrance to many provincial towns, the Romans built municipal arches *(above right)* to commemorate the founding of the city and the exploits of the veterans settling there. Glanum, now St. Rémy de Provence *(right)*, has one of the early Gallo-Roman arches, dating to Augustan times. Beside it stands the funeral monument to Augustus's grandsons Caius and Lucius Caesar, built in the early years of the first century A.D. and still very well preserved. Glanum was destroyed by Germanic invaders in the third century A.D.

Theater at Orange (Arausio), the best-preserved in the Roman world. It was built in the first century A.D., on a hillside site that gave the rows of seats a natural support. (The theater of Arles, with the same dimensions, was free-standing, as were many other Roman theaters.) The *scaenae frons* shown here is particularly well preserved; it is the only Roman theater that still contains its imperial statue: above the stage, with one arm raised, the statue of Augustus (3.55 meters tall).

"Campanian Idyll in the Rhineland," one of very few well-preserved Gallic wall paintings. It shows the Romans' ability to make themselves feel at home in the remotest corners of their empire. At major stations they built luxurious hotels (as in the model below).

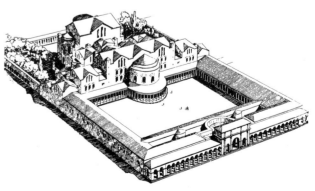

Below: Trier, or Augusta Treverorum, was named capital of Rome's German province in A.D. 293. Earlier, Trier was considered part of northeastern Gaul (Belgica). The drawing below is a reconstruction of the town's Imperial Baths.

The Temple of Rome and Augustus (16 B.C.), Nîmes, known as the "Maison Carrée" *(far left).* *Left:* House at Vaison-la-Romaine.

247

GERMANY AND THE DANUBE PROVINCES

By the time of Claudius it had become clear that the Rhine-Danube line formed a convenient and easily defendable northern frontier for the Empire. Although minor modifications and advances were made, and the territory of Dacia added for a brief period (a century and a half), the two great rivers were to form the northern boundary of the urbanized Roman world for many decades.

The frontier provinces developed a distinctive quality of their own. The armies were ever present, based in their legionary fortresses and forts, but many of these establishments, which commanded important river crossings, benefited from the trade which passed by them. Settlers and merchants were drawn to the vicinity, and vicus settlements (villages outside the forts) developed into towns and cities acquiring administrative functions. In addition *coloniae* were founded in the lee of the frontier line to provide a reserve of veteran troops and to serve as foci for urban growth. Many modern towns, such as Trier, Cologne, Mainz, Bonn, Budapest, owe their origins to this period.

By the third century A.D. the frontier zone had developed a sophisticated culture of its own, but during the troubled times of the third and fourth centuries the barbarians from the north caused widespread devastation.

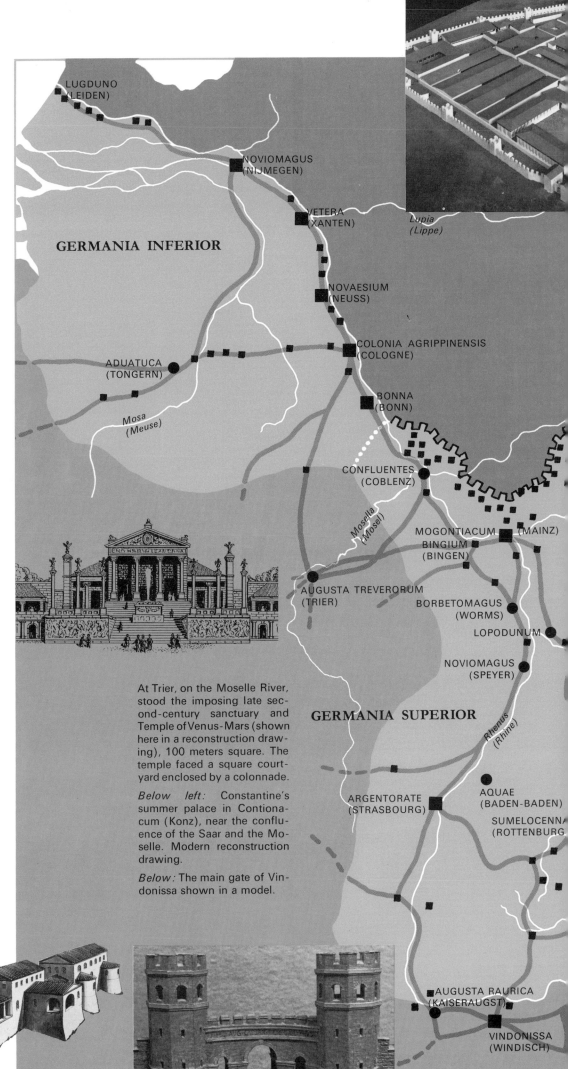

LUGDUNO (LEIDEN)

NOVIOMAGUS (NIJMEGEN)

VETERA (XANTEN)

Lupia (Lippe)

GERMANIA INFERIOR

NOVAESIUM (NEUSS)

COLONIA AGRIPPINENSIS (COLOGNE)

ADUATUCA (TONGERN)

BONNA (BONN)

Mosa (Meuse)

CONFLUENTES (COBLENZ)

Mosella (Mosel)

MOGONTIACUM (MAINZ)

BINGIUM (BINGEN)

AUGUSTA TREVERORUM (TRIER)

BORBETOMAGUS (WORMS)

LOPODUNUM

NOVIOMAGUS (SPEYER)

GERMANIA SUPERIOR

Rhenus (Rhine)

ARGENTORATE (STRASBOURG)

AQUAE (BADEN-BADEN)

SUMELOCENNA (ROTTENBURG)

AUGUSTA RAURICA (KAISERAUGST)

VINDONISSA (WINDISCH)

At Trier, on the Moselle River, stood the imposing late second-century sanctuary and Temple of Venus-Mars (shown here in a reconstruction drawing), 100 meters square. The temple faced a square courtyard enclosed by a colonnade.

Below left: Constantine's summer palace in Contionacum (Konz), near the confluence of the Saar and the Moselle. Modern reconstruction drawing.

Below: The main gate of Vindonissa shown in a model.

Model of the Roman fortress of the 10th Legion Gemina at Nijmegen, with buildings in stone (ca. A.D. 85–104). Rijksmuseum G. M. Kam, Nijmegen, Holland. This was an important fort on the Roman defensive line *(limes)* along the Rhine and Danube that was fortified originally in the first century A.D.

Saalburg (near Frankfurt), a third-century fort, was in large part reconstructed between 1898 and 1907. Headquarters building (at center) and the granary (lower right).

The Porta Praetoria, at Regensburg (Castra Regina), and its adjoining tower are incorporated into a modern building.

Left: Germany was not all garrisons: country villas, as everywhere in the Empire, were frequent. Reconstruction drawing.

Below: The *limes*, 550 kilometers of border defenses, ran from the North Sea to the Danube. It was only a wooden palisade in Hadrian's time (117–138); stone towers were built thereafter, and in the third century a ditch and actual stone wall were added. At left, the *limes* as it looked in the second century; at right, the final phase of construction (third century).

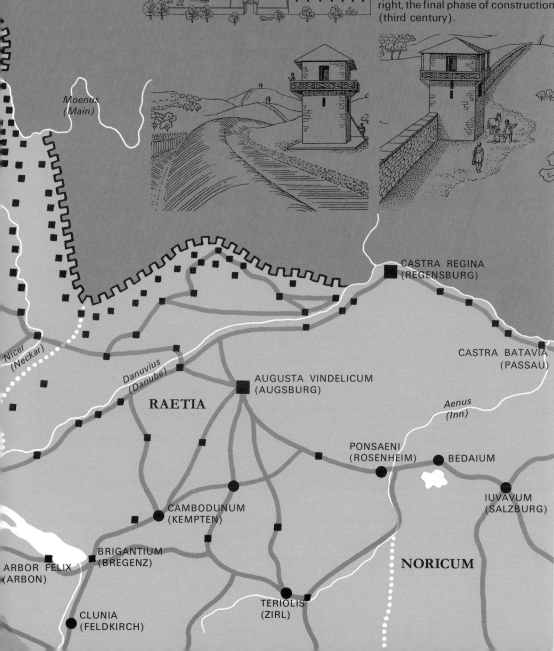

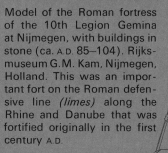

Moenus (Main)

Nicer (Neckar)

Danuvius (Danube)

CASTRA REGINA (REGENSBURG)

CASTRA BATAVIA (PASSAU)

AUGUSTA VINDELICUM (AUGSBURG)

RAETIA

Aenus (Inn)

PONSAENI (ROSENHEIM)

BEDAIUM

IUVAVUM (SALZBURG)

CAMBODUNUM (KEMPTEN)

BRIGANTIUM (BREGENZ)

ARBOR FELIX (ARBON)

NORICUM

TERIOLIS (ZIRL)

CLUNIA (FELDKIRCH)

55 B.C.   Caesar crosses the Rhine.

27–12   Advance to the Danube. Provinces of Noricum and Raetia founded 15 B.C.; Pannonia in 12.

12–6   The conquest of Germany begins. Campaigns between the Rhine and the Elbe led first by Drusus (until 9 B.C.) and later by Tiberius.

A.D. 4–9   Campaigns in Germany. Tiberius moves against the Marcomanni, A.D. 4, but revolt in Pannonia (6–9) deflects advance. Roman army destroyed by Arminius in the Teutonberg Forest (A.D. 9).

14–17   Germanicus in Germany. Further campaigns successful but largely ineffective. Frontier zone divided into Upper and Lower Germany (17).

46–47   Consolidation of the Rhine-Danube frontier. Campaigns against Frisii and Chauci, but Claudius decides on the Rhine as a frontier line. The provinces of Moesia and Thrace are created.

74   Annexation of Black Forest district. Vespasian advances across the re-entrant between the Rhine and the Danube to create a more effective frontier line.

83–89   Domitian's campaigns. Further consolidation of Rhine-Danube re-entrant: campaigns against the Chatti. Moesia overrun by Dacians (85), but the situation is restored.

101–106   Trajan's campaigns. The Dacian wars leading to the creation of the province of Dacia.

TRIER (AUGUSTA TREVERORUM)

Trier lies on the Moselle, a tributary of the Rhine at a point where major routes cross the river. In the pre-Roman period the site proved attractive to settlers, and a sanctuary developed on the banks of a tributary stream called the Altbach. But it was the Roman military presence here, under Augustus, that focused attention on the potential of the location. The civilian settlement

249

Trier, amid the vineyards of the Moselle valley, began a new period of growth and prosperity late in the third century. Diocletian named it the capital of the German province in 293. The plan shows the regular grid of its streets and the outline of its defensive wall. At far right can be seen the dotted oval outline of the circus and the circular amphitheater (20,000 capacity).

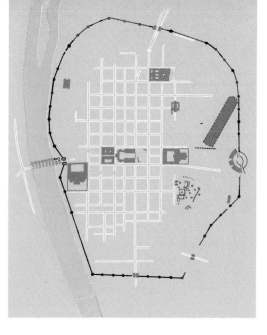

Right: The Porta Nigra, or north gate, of Trier, the best preserved of the Empire's city gateways. The structure, thirty meters high, was designed with defensive purposes in mind: absence of windows on the ground floor, rounded towers affording the widest possible view, an inner gateway for extra security.

which grew up nearby was given the name Augusta. Under Claudius it was formally rededicated as a *colonia*, the *Colonia Augusta Treverorum*, and it is to this period that the nucleus of the street grid, together with the early bridge, belongs.

Trier soon became an important administrative center. By the first century A.D. it had become the residence of the *procurator* (imperial officer) who was responsible for the financial organization of the provinces of Gallia Belgica and Germania Inferior and Superior; and in the third century it was adopted as an imperial residence favored by many of the emperors until the late fourth century. The city continued to flourish as an economic, administrative, and religious center until its destruction by the Franks in the early fifth century.

COLOGNE (COLONIA CLAUDIA ARA AGRIPPINENSIUM)

Cologne was a frontier town par excellence, situated on the left bank of the Rhine facing across what was soon to become dangerous enemy territory. The origins of the community probably date back to 38 B.C. when members of a friendly Germanic tribe, the Ubii, were settled in the area, by Agrippa. The formal layout of the town with its rigorous street grid took place in about 12 B.C. The legionary force was at first based nearby, but the legion was withdrawn by A.D. 30, although the headquarters of the Rhine flotilla remained upstream at Alteburg.

The title of *Colonia Claudia Ara Agrippinensium* was conferred upon the colony in A.D. 50 in honor of the wife of the emperor who was born here, and for two hundred years the city flourished, serving as the administrative center for the province of Germania

Inferior. In the late third century, when external Germanic pressures began to impose themselves upon the area, the walls were put into good defensive order and Cologne became an imperial headquarters. A little later, under Constantine, the Rhine bridge was rebuilt and a strongly defended bridgehead was constructed at Deutz to protect the crossing. Thus strengthened, Cologne prepared itself to face the barbarian onslaught of the later fourth and fifth centuries.

CARNUNTUM

Unlike Cologne and Trier, which soon lost their military significance and developed into purely urban settlements, Carnuntum, on the Danube to the east of Vienna, remained a legionary base throughout the Roman period, the urban settlement growing up some two kilometers away.

The fortress was reconstructed soon after A.D. 14 in timber, to be replaced in stone after about 73. From the time

The so-called Basilica in Trier, erected in A.D. 310 as the throne-room of Constantine's palace. The largest surviving Roman building after the Pantheon in Rome, the Basilica is 70 meters long, 30 meters high.

Cologne, the earliest Roman city in Germany, was made a *colonia* in 50 B.C. Directly east of the city, across the Rhine, was a defensive fort, shown in a model *(above)*, the Festung Divitia (now Deutz). The fort had a capacity of 900 sol-

diers. It was built in the late Roman period. The northwest tower of Cologne's city wall *(above)* is still standing. The prosperous city had important ceramics and glass industries.

Marcus Aurelius *(right)* died in March 180 in Vindobona (Vienna), having spent years in the troubled Rhine-Danube border area, where his presence served only to delay, but not to halt, the invaders. Septimius Severus *(far right)*, general and governor of Upper Pannonia, was named emperor at Carnuntum in 193 on the insistence of his troops. The fourth-century Heidentor *(below)*, a two-way monumental arch, still dominates Carnuntum.

of Augustus it remained the provincial capital of Pannonia and later, when the province was reorganized, of Pannonia Superior. A very extensive civilian settlement (*Canabae*) existed outside the fortress extending for some distance along the road leading from the south gate. The principal civilian town, however, lay to the west. A *municipium* under Hadrian, Carnuntum was elevated in status to a *colonia* by Septimius Severus, no doubt in memory of the fact that it was here, in 193, that his accession to the throne was initially proclaimed. It was here also, in a palace complex identified in excavation, that Marcus Aurelius and his wife set up court during the Marcomannic wars and where the philosopher-emperor wrote the third book of *Meditations*.

The civilian settlement flourished by virtue of its position commanding major trade routes: east and west via the Danube, north along the Morava to the edge of the north European plains, and south, skirting the Alpine fringes, to the head of the Adriatic. It was along this route that quantities of amber from the shores of the Baltic passed south, to satisfy the Mediterranean market. Also the locational factors which ensured the supremacy of Carnuntum as a trading center determined that it should remain of prime military significance throughout the Roman period.

AQUINCUM

Further east, once more on the left bank of the Danube, lies the complex of settlements which taken together make up Aquincum, the predecessor of Buda, the western half of Budapest, now capital of Hungary. The control of this important river crossing began in the pre-Roman Iron Age with the establishment of a strongly defended hilltop enclosure on Gellért hill, serving as a focal point for a large native settlement which spread out before it on the lower slopes.

As Roman interests in the second half of the first century A.D., extended further and further north across what is now Hungary, the Danube came to be used as a frontier line. It was in this initial period of expansion that a fort for an auxiliary detachment was established a few miles upstream from the native settlement; but as the Dacians to the east became more of a threat to the peace of the Roman world, the frontier defenses were strengthened and at Aquincum the auxiliary base was re-

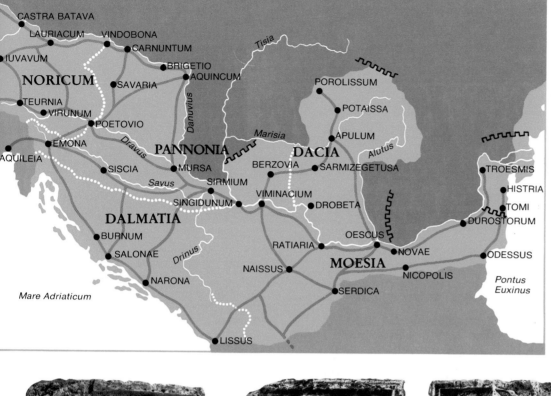

The monument of Adamclisi was erected in Lower Moesia under Trajan. Its unusual shape makes it one of the Empire's most interesting victory trophies. The metopes (rectangular reliefs) depict events and scenes from the battles between Romans and Dacians. Shown below are four of the metopes from the monument, and (bottom) a reconstruction of the whole structure made in 1903 by Adolf Furtwängler.

site the fortress, for the imperial legate: the first man to occupy the post was Hadrian. Some years later, after Hadrian had become emperor, the settlement was upgraded to the status of *municipium*, and at the beginning of the third century Septimius Severus was to confer upon the community the title of *colonia*.

Like Carnuntum, the community grew rich by virtue of its commanding position with regard to trade routes. On the very fringe of the Empire all commerce

placed by a permanent legionary fortress.

By the second century most of the native population appears to have moved away from its old site to the area around the fortress where a new settlement, a *canabae*, began to develop. It was here, augmented by foreign traders, veterans, and other settlers attracted to the markets provided by the fortress, that an urban settlement gradually took shape with its own market center and comfortable well-appointed houses. Further upstream there developed a new urban complex—the civilian town of Aquincum. A great boost to urban development came during the reign of Trajan when, as a result of the Dacian wars, the province of Pannonia was

split into two and Aquincum became the capital of Lower Pannonia. It was at this time that a palace was built on the Danube island of Hajógyár, oppo-

with the barbarians to the east was funneled through its customs posts. But its position brought problems. Exposed as it was to barbarian attack, the settlement suffered serious devastation during the Marcomannic wars (167–180). From the middle of the third century onwards, as barbarian pressures built up, the inhabitants must have been in constant fear for their safety. By the end of the first decade of the fifth century, the last remnants of the population had moved away to safer homes in the depths of the countryside.

GREECE

The first century B.C. was a period of devastation and decline in Greece. In 45 B.C. a friend of Cicero could write, "At sea...I was looking at the shores round about. Astern lay Aigina, before me Megara, on my right Piraeus, on my left Corinth; all once teeming cities—and now they lie in ruin and wreck before our eyes." During the long period of peace which was to follow, all this changed and urban life revived under the patronage of the philhellene emperors.

The owl, sacred symbol of Athena, adorns this silver coin of the city of Athens, minted between 460 and 450 B.C. during Greece's golden age. The city reached a population of about 300,000 at this time and became the ruling city-state of Greece. Although Athens lost this political position around 400 B.C., it remained a center of art and learning for the Romans and was an important university town.

To many Romans Greece was something of a curiosity—a place to visit in order to savor the culture of its past. Sparta, for example, was visited by hordes of tourists who enjoyed the museum-like atmosphere of the place: they could also, if they wished, enliven their visit with a trip to the theater to watch boys being flogged in contests to test their endurance!

The great sanctuaries at Epidauros, Delphi, and Eleusis were a constant source of interest to tourists, as were the Olympic games. Nero particularly enjoyed the literary competitions and games. In 66–67 he toured the principal cities to take part in contests, specially

Classical Greek sculpture: the Caryatid Porch from the Erechtheum shrine on the north side of the Acropolis in Athens, built 421–406 B.C.

Below: Hadrian initiated several construction projects in Athens, including the Corinthian-style library in the new (Roman) Agora to the north of the Acropolis.

probably continued in use as a teaching center until A.D. 529, when the university was finally closed down by the emperor Justinian.

Athens could also boast several libraries. One, built just south of the Stoa of Attalus was erected soon after A.D. 100. The building inscription records that the benefactor, Titus Flavius Pantainos, together with his son and daughter, gave "the outer colonnades, the peristyle, the library with its books, and all the decorations at their own expense." Another inscription from the building lays down the hours of opening and states that books may not be borrowed. A far more impressive building, the Library of Hadrian, was erected a few years later to the east of the Agora. Its vast colonnaded courtyard, once adorned with a "hundred splendid columns" (according to Pausanias), gave access to a massive block of rooms containing the library proper, which appears to have been closely modeled on the library at Pergamum. The library was just one of the buildings erected under Hadrian to improve

reprogrammed to coincide with his visit, and, delighted with his inevitable victories, he rewarded the province by conferring upon it immunity from taxes.

Apart from being an essential place for tourists to visit, Athens was renowned throughout the world for its famous university, where young men of good family could spend a year or two attending classes on Roman and Greek literature, Roman law, Greek philosophy, and of course the art of public speaking. Greeks were also prepared to educate girls, and indeed women could even become professors at the Athenian Academy. By the end of the

fourth century we hear of student troubles: groups of students of particular persuasions were apparently trying to induce newly arrived pupils to join them by force, and the civic authorities found it necessary to appoint special magistrates with jurisdiction over the gymnasia.

One of the gymnasia, built at the beginning of the fifth century A.D., lay in the center of the Athenian Agora. It was entered through a portico dominated by four colossal figures (the Stoa of the Giants) and consisted of a series of colonnaded courtyards with adjacent suites of rooms and baths, all set in a secluded walled garden. The building

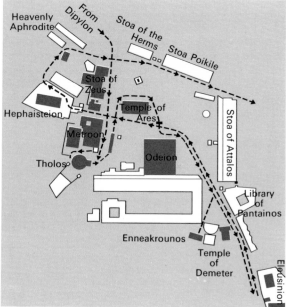

and beautify the city he so loved. Before becoming emperor, Hadrian had been a chief official (*archon*) of the town in 112, and had stayed there for extended periods during his eastern journeys in the winters of 124–125, 128–129, and 131–132. During this time he not only built the library, but completed the temple to Olympian Zeus, begun by Peisistratos. He also added a new quarter to the city divided from the old city by an elegant gate inscribed, "This is Athens, City of Theseus." But as one passed the other way from the ancient city to the new quarter, the reverse inscription read, "This is the City of Hadrian, not of Theseus."

Hadrian was not the only benefactor. Augustus had built a new market center, and his friend Agrippa had been responsible for the erection of the odeum in the Agora. There were also Greek millionaires like Herodes Attilus, who wished to beautify their homeland. Besides mere architectural embellishment, other attempts were made to revive the glories of Greece. Hadrian went so far as to reinstitute the Panhellenic games and the Panhellenic as-

172–167 B.C. The third Macedonian war. After the defeat of Perseus (168), Macedon was divided into four separate states ruled by a federal council.

149–146 Further involvement in Greece and Macedon. Andriscus claims the throne of Macedon. Rome sends troops (148) and annexes Macedonia as a province. Trouble among the Achaean League in the Peloponese leads to Roman military involvement in Greece, which culminates in the destruction of Corinth (146). The autonomous city governments were now placed under the supervision of the governor of Macedon.

87–84 The Mithridatic War. Sulla lands on the coast of Epirus (87) and proceeds to Athens, which is besieged and taken the next year.

49–30 The Civil Wars. Many campaigns fought between the various contenders in Greece and Macedon. Corinth refounded as a *colonia* by Caesar (46).

267 Athens devastated by the invading Herulians.

sembly, held annually and attended by deputies from all the cities of Greece and all those which could prove their Greek origin. But although the institution appears to have thrived, it was already too late. The spirit of ancient Greece was dead. All that remained was a picturesque shell—a gigantic museum—to amuse and interest tourists, scholars, and visiting emperors alike.

Praeneste (now Palestrina), near Rome. This model of its sanctuary shows the influence of Lindos. Built in the second and first centuries B.C., the structure introduced innovations while still reflecting a Greek flavor.

Lindos, on the east coast of Rhodes. Model reconstruction of its acropolis sanctuary as in the third century, with the small Temple of Athena at top. Its influence on Roman architecture was significant, as can be seen at Praeneste.

Left: Homer, foremost of the Greek poets (eighth century B.C.), and Pythagoras the mathematician and philosopher (late sixth century B.C.). The cultural legacy of Greece, which had done so much to awaken Roman interest in the arts during the Republic, remained a vital influence on Rome for centuries thereafter. Well-to-do Romans, trained by Greek tutors at home or in the universities of Athens and Rhodes, studied Greek authors in the original language.

Left to right: Figures in the Greek philosophical tradition. Socrates (ca. 470–399 B.C.), whose thought is known through the writings of his disciple, Plato. Heraclitus, a pessimistic metaphysician, sixth–fifth century. Smiling portrait bust of Democritus, greatest of the Greek natural philosophers, who lived around the year 400 B.C.

Solon *(directly above)*, Athenian ruler and poet, who lived around 638–559 B.C., instituted economic and constitutional reforms. Diogenes *(second from right)*, the fourth-century cynic philosopher. Sophocles the tragedian (496–406), author of 120 plays including the Oedipus cycle and *Electra.*

Below: The Athens Acropolis, already a relic and a tourist site by the second century A.D. One Herodes Atticus, a wealthy Greek from Marathon, launched many building projects at this time, including an odeum at the foot of the Acropolis. A scholar as well, he tutored Antoninus's adopted son, the future Marcus Aurelius.

257

ASIA MINOR

Asia Minor was a country of great cities—traditionally there were five hundred of them—mainly clustering along the fertile coastal regions of the west and south. Many were founded in the great colonization period of the tenth and ninth centuries B.C. by settlers from Greece, but additional settlements soon sprung up as the

original communities outgrew the confines of their first cities. Following Alexander's conquest, new royal capitals and garrison towns were created. The cities of Asia Minor all enjoyed a degree of autonomy, though they developed in the shadow of great empires—Persia, the Hellenistic kingdoms, and Rome—and were from time to time caught up in the conflicts which pervaded the region. But once peace had been established by Augustus, city life, freed from political stress, blossomed.

The journey of the Christian apostle Paul from Macedonia to Jerusalem, in the first century A.D., gives a vivid idea of the significance of coastal Asia Minor to the traveler. The boat trip from Philippi to the Troad took five days; thence Paul went to Assos and across to Mitylene. From Mitylene it was a day's trip to Chios, a day to Samos, and from there another day's journey took them to Miletus. Paul had

deliberately bypassed the obvious port-of-call of Ephesus, no doubt because of the tense political situation there, and after briefly dealing with some business, he set off once more via Rhodes, Patara, and Cyprus to Tyre and finally on to Jerusalem. His journey hopped from island to island, barely touching the mainland; such would have been the normal route for a man with no particular interest in the mainland cities.

A little earlier, however, Paul had decided to concentrate his efforts on Ephesus, where he began the daunting task of seeking converts among the cosmopolitan urban population. It was on this occasion that the famous riot took place. A silversmith, Demetrius, who made his living making trinkets for worshippers to offer at the nearby shrine of Diana, objected to the spread of Christianity which he saw as a threat to trade. Feelings ran high and an angry mob gathered in the theater chanting, "Great is Diana of the Ephesians." But tempers were cooled when the rioters were reminded of their precarious position in the law, and it was made clear to them that by their unruly behavior they were leaving themselves open to punishment.

The incident is a fascinating one for the impression it gives of the excitable population of these great cities where ethnic groups of very different religious beliefs lived and worked side by

The famous Diana of Ephesus, portrayed as a many-breasted fertility figure, in a style that contrasts sharply with Greek classicism. Museo Nazionale, Naples.

Far left: The Temple of Hadrian in Ephesus. Beside this ornate second-century A.D. temple stood a fountain in honor of Trajan.

Right: Impressive fragments of the temples and other Roman buildings in Ephesus date back to the first and second centuries A.D.

side. There was always tension, particularly between the Greek and the Jewish communities, and the smallest incident could spark off violence.

Ephesus was the principal town of the province of Asia and was the place where the governor of the province resided. "The city," said Strabo, "grew richer every day." Indeed it could hardly fail to do so. It was admirably sited on the sea at the mouth of the River Cäyster and served by a fine harbor. Trade routes from the extremely fertile Meander valley to the south and, overland, ultimately from the Euphrates, converged upon it. Moreover, close by, was the sacred location where Artemis (Diana) the Earth Mother, goddess of Anatolia, was worshipped. So revered was the sanctuary that it became a repository for treasures from all over the ancient world.

The actual location of the city had changed from time to time. The original settlement, founded by the Ionian Greeks about 1000 B.C., or just before, lay on the slopes of Mount Pion. Croe-

St. Paul *(above)* carried the Gospel through Asia Minor and finally to Rome, where he was martyred by Nero (A.D. 67.) This deed, and Nero's persecution of Christians, made the emperor (portrayed as a god on the coin at right) a particular villain to the Christians of Asia Minor.

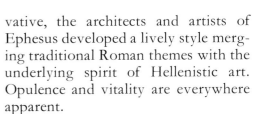

sus, king of Lydia in the sixth century, reestablished it close to the shrine of Artemis, but two centuries later Lysimachus, one of Alexander's generals, moved it once more to approximately its present position down by the now-silted harbor. It is this city in its developed state, the city of the first and second centuries A.D., that the visitor now enjoys. Its great buildings, the library of Celsus, built in memory of the governor of Asia in 106–107, the temples of Domitian and Hadrian, the fountain of Trajan, and a host of other elaborate structures, emphasize the wealth and exuberance of the community. Although always slightly conser-

vative, the architects and artists of Ephesus developed a lively style merging traditional Roman themes with the underlying spirit of Hellenistic art. Opulence and vitality are everywhere apparent.

By the fourth century Ephesus was in decline. Great physical changes were taking place along the western coast of Asia: harbors were becoming clogged with silt and the wide inlets were now fast filling with sediments. Ephesus, robbed of its harbor and surrounded by swamps, sank into poverty.

To the south of Ephesus lay the valley of the River Meander graced by the cities of Miletus and Priene. Here too,

Roman relief of a legionary with his Parthian captive, from the Arch of Septimius Severus and Caracalla in Rome (A.D. 203). Prisoners from Asia Minor fed the Empire's active slave trade and proved important to the Roman economy.

The bearded Mesopotamian nobles and the elegantly attired lady in this grave mosaic from Edessa (late third—early fourth century) exemplify the wealth and luxury of this area.

Ormizd II, an early fourth-century king of the Sassanid dynasty in Persia, is shown attacking and disarming his enemy, on this stone relief from Persepolis (now in Iraq). The Sassanids consistently menaced Roman power in Asia.

The legend of Nero Redivivus—Nero returned to life—was an article of faith to many in the Jewish-Christian sect that prevailed in Asia Minor in the first and second centuries. A manuscript illustration from a medieval Apocalypse *(left)* shows John, its author, on the isle of Patmos, where he states that he wrote the prophetic book (Chapter 1, verses 9–10). He supposedly fled to Patmos to escape Roman persecution. Bibliothèque Nationale, Paris.

Asia Minor, or modern Turkey *(below)*, proved important in the early history of Christianity, as the New Testament's Pauline epistles demonstrate. In the Book of Revelation, moreover, John refers to the "Seven Churches of Asia," the Christian communities of Ephesus, Smyrna, Pergamum, Thyatira, Sardis, Philadelphia, and Laodicea.

the processes of silting can clearly be discerned.

Priene, a medium-sized town of some quality, was, in the third century B.C., lapped by the sea; but by the time that Strabo was writing at the beginning of the first century A.D. it was already eight kilometers from open water. Having lost its economic significance by the Roman period, the community could not afford to engage in expensive building programs. As a result, their city, though continuing to be occupied, remained virtually unchanged and survives as a perfect example of an integrated Hellenistic building program. Miletus, further towards the sea, lasted longer, but by the time of Paul's visit it had already become something of a cultural backwater.

Ephesus, Miletus, and Priene, then, demonstrate, in brilliant clarity, different stages of urban development each fossilized by economic decline. This very fact is a reminder that econom-ically, and to some extent politically, each city retained a high degree of autonomy. Although they all belonged to the Roman province of Asia, each was ultimately responsible for its own livelihood.

Tiridates I *(left)* went to Rome in A.D. 66 and was crowned King of Armenia by Nero in the Forum Romanum. King Mithridates VI of Pontus *(above)* was an implacable enemy of Rome in the first century B.C.

192–189 B.C. War with Antiochus of Syria. The Roman armies force Antiochus out of Greece, and at Magnesia in Asia Minor, defeat him (190). Campaign against the Galatians (189).

133–128 The Kingdom of Pergamum becomes Roman. Attalus III bequeaths his kingdom to Rome.

105–63 Troubles with Mithridates of Pontus. Mithridates annexes Paphlagonia (105) and Cappadocia (96) and invades Bithynia (88). Sulla campaigns in Asia (85–84) and imposes terms on Mithridates. Between 75 and 63 Pompey campaigns in Asia with conspicuous success. Bithynia annexed, 74; Pontus, Cilicia, and Syria in 64. The rest of Asia Minor and Armenia now under Roman protection.

22–19 Augustus in the east. Settlement with Parthia and Armenia (20).

A.D. 57–113 Campaigns in Armenia. Army under Corbulo in Armenia. Settlement reached in 65. Further troubles during reign of Trajan lead to annexation of Armenia in 113.

161–165 Parthians invade Asia. Vologeses invades Armenia and Cappadocia (161), but situation restored by 165.

THE EAST

Amid the barren deserts
of Arabia, a few cultivated spots
rise like islands out of
the sandy ocean. The name of Palmyra...
denoted a multitude of palm-trees....

Edward Gibbon

The narrow coastal strip, often barely fifty miles wide, which lay between the eastern shores of the Mediterranean and the deserts and wastes of Syria and Arabia was a turbulent and somewhat troublesome region, partly no doubt because of its ethnically mixed population of Greek, Arab, and Semitic stock. Yet it provided a vital interface for Mediterranean trade with the east. Virtually all the major caravan routes from Arabia, India, and beyond, ended at the cities lining the desert fringe, whence an exotic range of luxury goods was transported to the great ports of Antioch and Caesarea for transshipment to Rome.

The destruction of the weakened Seleucid kingdom by Pompey in 64 B.C. effectively brought under Roman control not only Syria but the whole of the Levantine coast as far south as Egypt. With such a prize, Rome was now in a position to dominate the enormously valuable trade upon which the wealth of the region was based—perfumes from Arabia, spices and rare woods from India, and silk from China. Two principal routes were at this time in use: from the east, entrepreneurs would travel up the Euphrates, perhaps as far as Dura Europus, thence across the Syrian desert in camel train to the coast, stopping over at the great oasis city of Palmyra. Those using the southern route from Arabia, or via the Red Sea, would pass through Petra en route either for the coastal ports of Gaza and El Arish, or northwards along the Royal Road which flanked the desert edge through Gerasa, Bostra, and Damascus to Tyre or Antioch.

To the east of the River Jordan lay the land of an Arab tribe called the Nabataeans who remained on friendly relations with Rome until A.D. 106, when their territory was absorbed into the Empire to become the province of Arabia. Their principal city, Petra, carved out of the sandstone hills of the Jordanian steppe, had long dominated the trade route from the southeast, but by the end of the first century A.D. trade was in decline. Merchants had discovered and mastered the monsoons of the Indian Ocean and had now begun to bring the riches of the east across the sea to new ports which had developed on the Egyptian coasts of the Red Sea. It was in this time of change that the Nabataeans created a new center at Bostra, carefully sited on the natural routeway of the Wadi Sirhan to capture and control the perfume trade of central Arabia.

A street in Gerasa (Jerash). Incorporated in the Roman province of Syria after its conquest by Pompey in 63 B.C., Gerasa became a prosperous commercial city until the mid-third century.

Opposite: Outside Palmyra, in the Syrian desert, stand remains of ancient tower tombs which pre-date the Roman occupation of this once important oasis city.

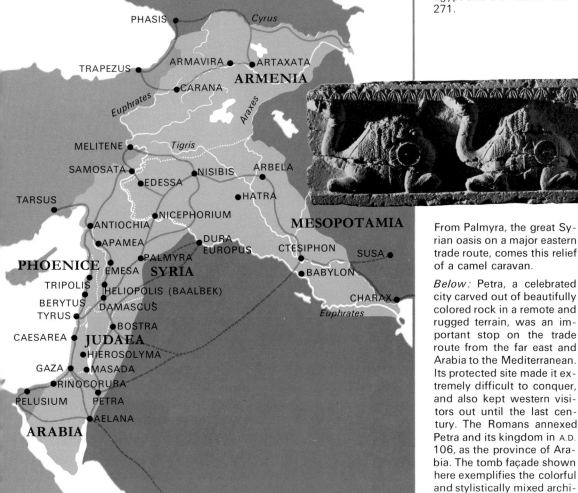

From Palmyra, the great Syrian oasis on a major eastern trade route, comes this relief of a camel caravan.

Below: Petra, a celebrated city carved out of beautifully colored rock in a remote and rugged terrain, was an important stop on the trade route from the far east and Arabia to the Mediterranean. Its protected site made it extremely difficult to conquer, and also kept western visitors out until the last century. The Romans annexed Petra and its kingdom in A.D. 106, as the province of Arabia. The tomb façade shown here exemplifies the colorful and stylistically mixed architecture of the ancient city.

known when Antony attacked it in 41 B.C., the city grew to considerable proportions during the early Empire until, in the third century, it was to form a bulwark between the declining power of Rome and their powerful eastern enemies, the Persians.

In 259 the Roman emperor Valerian was captured by the Persians. The Palmyrenes now took firm control of the situation, under the leadership of their king Odaenathus and his queen Zenobia. So powerful had he become that the emperor Gallienus was prepared to recognize him as co-regent of the East. After the death of Odaenathus, Zenobia maintained friendly relations with Rome until, encouraged by her delusions of grandeur, she set out to invade Egypt. Aurelian was forced to intervene and finally, in 273, to attack and devastate Palmyra. Thereafter the city became little more than a military post set in the midst of the desert.

The story of Palmyra dramatically demonstrates the power which could accrue to a community capable of monopolizing the luxury trade upon which the civilized Mediterranean world had become so dependent.

The fourth century saw a breakdown into smaller and weaker units as the power of the Persians continued to threaten the Roman east. With constant military upheavals, the old caravan routes were displaced and gradually ceased to be used, as the local populations took to a more nomadic way of life. Inevitably the more precariously located caravan cities declined and decayed. The rise of Christianity, however, gave a fresh boost to the intellectual life of some of the coastal centers which flourished, until the spread of Islam in the seventh century, effectively put an end to Roman culture.

Among the many exotic substances imported from the east, pepper from the Malabar coast was particularly prized. Pliny the Elder writes:

It is quite surprising that the use of pepper has come so much into fashion... pepper has nothing in it that can plead as a recommendation to either fruit or berry, its only desirable quality being a certain pungency; and yet it is for this that we import it all the way from India. Who was the first to make trial of it as an article of food? And who, I wonder, was the man that was not content to prepare himself by hunger only for the satisfaction of a greedy appetite?

Under Roman domination, however, it was Palmyra, spectacularly located in the middle of the Syrian desert, that was to become rich by exploiting its monopoly of trans-desert trade. Little

Baalbek, in modern-day Lebanon: interior wall of the cella in the so-called Temple of Bacchus, completed in the mid-second century A.D. The ornately carved Corinthian temple stands amid a sanctuary to Jupiter (associated with the eastern god Baal) which included several temples.

333–323 B.C. Alexander the Great in the east. The battle of Issus (333) and the fall of Persepolis (330) mark the beginning and the end of Alexander's campaigns of conquest in the east. After Alexander's death in Babylon (323), his empire is split between his generals, Seleucus taking control of Syria and founding a dynasty.

64–63 Pompey conquers Syria and Palestine. Syria is annexed in 64 B.C. In 63 Pompey marches on Jerusalem. Thenceforth Palestine is supervised by the governor of Syria.

A.D. 66–73 The first Jewish revolt. Vespasian and later Titus systematically reduce the Jewish strongholds culminating in the siege of Masada. Jerusalem destroyed.

106 Trajan annexes Arabia. The territory of the Nabataeans, in what is now Jordan, is annexed to become the province of Arabia Petraea.

114–117 Trajan's eastern campaigns. Campaigns in Mesopotamia (114–115). Ctesiphon taken but lost again in 117. On Trajan's death Hadrian gives up newly annexed eastern territories.

132–135 The second Jewish revolt. Hadrian founds a *colonia* in Jerusalem, thus sparking off the revolt of Bar-kokbar.

164–165 Invasion of Mesopotamia. The growing power of the Parthians causes Rome to intervene in the east. Ctesiphon captured (165) and Media invaded.

Mithras and Ahuramazda, the principal Iranian gods, hand a crown to King Ardashir II, who ruled Persia from 379 to 383. This tomb relief is from Taq-i-Bustan, late fourth century. Mithras, shown with sun rays, was adopted in Roman religion.

Right: Rising above the west coastline of the Dead Sea, the rock of Masada was a natural military redoubt. Jewish rebels withstood a long Roman siege here but were finally overcome in A.D. 73–74, after legendary resistance. The Romans, who had built eight forts for the conduct of their siege, occupied Masada until some time after 111.

ROME IN RETREAT

The decline of Rome was the natural and inevitable effect of immoderate greatness... as soon as time or accident had removed the artificial supports, the stupendous fabric yielded to the pressure of its own weight. The story of its ruin is simple and obvious; and instead of inquiring why the Roman empire was destroyed, we should rather be surprised that it had subsisted so long.

Edward Gibbon

Barbarian invasions, fragmented and ineffectual government, economic decline, and manpower shortage, heaping problem upon problem, culminated, in the early fifth century, in the collapse of the civilized western world. The statue shown above (from the Vatican Museum) represents a northern barbarian, one of the peoples who were pressing Rome's neighbors and Rome herself. The city of Constantinople, the successor to Rome in the east, is personified in an ivory relief (right) of the late fifth century. Kunsthistorisches Museum, Vienna.

A.D. 140–180   The beginnings of the barbarian inroads. Troubles along the British and Dacian frontiers under Antoninus Pius. A group of Caucasian horsemen, the Alani, invade Armenia. Parthia invades Armenia and Cappadocia (161). The army of Marcus Aurelius campaigns successfully in the east, but soldiers bring back plague to the west (166). Marcomanni and Quadi (two German tribes) invade the Danube provinces (166). Marcus Aurelius campaigns extensively in barbarian Europe.

180–235   The end of the old order. In the struggle for power following death of Commodus (193), Septimius Severus emerges. His strong rule culminates in extensive campaigning in Scotland which is completed by his son and successor, Caracalla. Thereafter increasingly weak government exacerbates widespread frontier crises.

235–284   Fifty years of anarchy. Many emperors emerge and fall. Problems with barbarians including Franks, Alamanni, and Goths in the north and Parthians in the east. Dacia is abandoned.

284–305   The reforms of Diocletian. Strong government combined with thorough reforms of civil administration and the army bring comparative peace. The Empire is now divided into two administratively separate parts—East and West.

305–337   Constantine. Diocletian's reforms enable Constantine to maintain a stable government in spite of internal dissentions. Christianity is legalized in 313.

337–ca. 450   Decline and collapse. Increasing frontier problems culminate in the invasion and ultimately the settlement of barbarians within the Western Roman Empire—Goths, Vandals, Germans, and Huns. Rome is sacked in 410. In the Eastern Empire Constantinople assumes leadership of the remnants of the Roman world.

THE BARBARIAN THREAT

The Lombard King Agilulf is shown *(left)* in a seventh-century relief commemorating a victory. *Above:* Merovingian horseman, in gilded bronze. Seventh century.

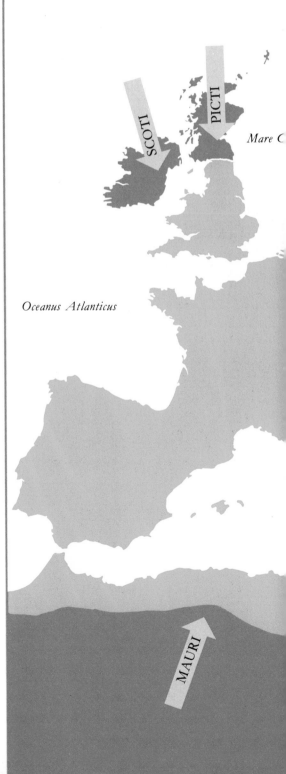

Taking a broad perspective, it could be said that the Roman Empire was merely an interlude, a temporary respite, in the inexorable expansion of northern peoples, from the north European plain and from Scandinavia, southwards towards the Mediterranean—a movement at times quickened by pressures created by new folk movements erupting from the Pontic steppes and beyond. The Roman Republic had experienced the potential power of the northern barbarians on several occasions; first the southerly migration of the Celts in the fourth century B.C., next the spectacular advances of the Cimbri and Teutones at the end of the second century B.C., and later the build-up of Germanic pressure which caused the Helvetii to move from their homeland and gave Caesar his opportunity to conquer Gaul on the assessment, no doubt largely accurate, that if Gaul had not been taken over by Rome it would have been swamped by the Germans. The campaigns of Augustus between the Rhine and the Elbe temporarily subdued the German threat, but in a century and a half it was to erupt again with violence.

The first signs of trouble came in 166, when under strong pressure from their northern neighbors, hordes of Langobardi and Marcomanni crossed into the province of Pannonia to ask for land on which to settle. The Roman response was to refuse permission and to drive them back. The incident passed off with little trouble, but shortly afterwards a vast band of Marcomanni, Quadi, and Iazyges broke through the frontier once more, this time with violence, some bands penetrating as far south as Aquileia—dangerously close to the heart of Italy. The emperor Marcus Aurelius responded immediately and after a series of successful campaigns drove the invaders back and pen-

etrated far into barbarian territory. His intention was to found two new provinces, *Marcomannia* in the area of Bohemia and *Sarmatia* in the re-entrant between Pannonia and the western border of Dacia. Extensive preparations were made: garrisons were placed in strategic places and large numbers of dispossessed Germans and Sarmatians were transported, some to serve as auxiliary troops, others to be settled within the northern provinces. Before the newly won territories could be organized, however, the emperor was forced to put down a revolt in Syria, and by the time he was free to return to the northern frontier the situation had deteriorated once more. The struggle continued for two more years until his death at Vindobona in A.D. 180, whereupon his successor, Commodus, abandoned all claim to the new territories.

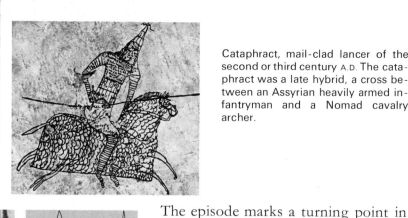

Cataphract, mail-clad lancer of the second or third century A.D. The cataphract was a late hybrid, a cross between an Assyrian heavily armed infantryman and a Nomad cavalry archer.

This late fourth-century mosaic portrays a Vandal riding forth from his village. From Carthage; now in the British Museum.

Wotan the war god, from an eighth-century Germanic gravestone. *Below right:* A Frankish warrior, a Dacian *(center)*, and a West Goth.

The episode marks a turning point in Roman history. Marcus Aurelius had approached the problem of the northern frontier in the same spirit as his predecessors would have dealth with it— by aggressive campaigning and by attempted territorial expansion. He did, indeed, gain some degree of success, but it was, of necessity, a temporary success. Campaigns might reduce the native population by slaughter and by transportation and resettlement, but they could not stamp out the root cause of the problem—the gradual build-up of population resulting partly from natural demographic factors and partly from folk movement from outside.

The Germanic peoples of northern Europe occupied a cul-de-sac. Along their northern and western flanks lay the sea and the bleak and inhospitable zone of coniferous forest; to the south was the frontier of the Roman Empire; while to the east lay the approaches to the Pontic steppe whence hordes of horse-riding nomads poured forth from time to time, forced on by population pressures building up behind them further to the

The Parthians *(above)*, in the east, were formidable opponents, and the only people Rome did not call "barbarians."

Opposite, bottom: Pen-and-ink sketch of an Arab rider attacking; tenth century.

Time is like a river made up of events,
and its current is strong;
no sooner does anything appear than
it is swept away,
and another comes in its place,
and will be swept away too.

Marcus Aurelius

east. The Sarmatians—the Iazyges (against whom Marcus Aurelius fought), and the Roxolani—were such a people. They had migrated west from the Caucasian steppe beyond the Don in the first century B.C. and first century A.D., eventually settling on either side of the Dacians; the Iazyges occupied the Hungarian plain between the Danube and the eastern boundary of Dacia; while the Roxolani took up their position between the Dneistre and the Danube. In Tacitus's view:

Plunder and not war is their passion.... [They are] a band of freebooters determined to ravage the country...in an onset of the cavalry they are impetuous, fierce, and irresistible. Their weapons are long spears or sabers of enormous size which they wield with both hands. The chiefs wear coats of mail formed with plates of iron or the tough hides of animals.

These, then, were the people who were moving into Europe during the early Empire, forced on westwards by their own aggressive neighbors the Alani, to occupy territories into which the Germans might otherwise have expanded. The sudden incursion of Germans and Sarmatians, which thrust through the Danube frontier during the reign of Marcus Aurelius, was the inevitable result of these two ethnic groups, under enormous pressures, erupting along the line of least resistance—south into the Roman world.

Of the Germans in the second and third centuries we know comparatively little. Most of the old tribal grouping of the first century, described by Tacitus, had all but disappeared and in their stead new confederacies had come into existence; the Franks and the Saxons in the west, the Birymedians on the middle Rhine, and the Alamanni between the Rhine and the Danube. While behind

The emperor Aurelian (270–275), a century after Marcus Aurelius, has left the so-called Aurelian Wall as the legacy of a brief but highly successful reign. A soldier rather than a philosopher, he won brilliant victories in the troubled border areas, particularly against Palmyra in the east. The wall he planned and initiated was completed by his successors; considerable portions survive today.

them to the north were the Vandals and the Lombards. A more northern group, the Goths, who had originally lived in the lower Vistula, had, by the beginning of the third century, migrated across northern Europe to take up a new position on the north shore of the Black Sea, thus adding to the pressures on their new neighbors, the Sarmatians. The emergence of new confederations, folk movements, the colonization of coastal territories, and the growth in size of settlements all speak of a fast-growing population and of increasing social and economic tension. The campaigns of Marcus Aurelius had temporarily alleviated the problem, but a few years later the storm was to gather once more.

In 215 the Alamanni broke into Upper Germany but were repulsed without much difficulty. So long as the Roman army was firmly controlled the frontier could be held, but as soon as internal problems led to the breakdown of centralized command the situation rapidly deteriorated. Soon after 250 the crisis broke and the frontier collapsed. Franks poured into Gaul penetrating as far as the Pyrenees. Alamanni thrust down the Rhône towards Italy, eventually reaching Milan where they were beaten in pitched battle; while the Ostrogoths (eastern Goths) crossed the Danube to run riot through Thrace and Macedonia, slaughtering a reputed 100,000 inhabitants of the city of Philippopolis (modern Plovdiv in Bulgaria). The situation was grim, not least because of the virtual anarchy which now pervaded the weakening Empire. The interminable power struggle among contenders for the throne meant that it took more than thirty years to restore a semblance of order. The Rhine-Danube frontier was finally re-established and regarrisoned, but it was now a very different world. Gone was

the province of Dacia; Ostrogoths were now living in Roman territory south of the Danube; and the fertile re-entrant between the Danube and the Rhine had become the preserve of the Alamanni. Once more a temporary peace had been established, but Rome was now in retreat.

The maintenance of the southern frontier posed fewer problems for Rome, not least because the boundaries of the Empire were ringed with mountain ranges and deserts. Even so, from the late second century, attacks on Roman territory became increasingly frequent. In Mauretania the desert tribes, in particular the Moors, became active during the reign of Hadrian, and in about 168, groups had crossed the Straits of Gibraltar and were raiding in Spain. However Commodus seems to have temporarily stabilized the situation by constructing towers and forts along the Mauretanian frontier, and there is evidence from Numidia that desert forts were being built and occupied in the early third century. By the middle of the third century much of the African frontier was under constant pressure from the desert tribes, though, apart from a raid by the Belmmyes in the late third century, Egypt seems to have remained secure.

Beyond the Syrian and Arabian deserts Rome confronted the powerful imperial state of Parthia, against which Trajan had fought in the early second century and which required further intervention by Marcus Aurelius and Septimius Severus. Rome maintained a healthy respect for the Parthian Empire, for not only did they control the

overland trade routes with India and China, but they were also a military force to be reckoned with. Early in the third century the old fragmented Parthian state was overthrown by the new centralized monarchy of the Persian Sassanids: this provided a far more serious threat to Rome and was to require active attention throughout much of the third century. During this period there were three major wars. The first, involving the emperors Severus Alexander, Gordianus III, and Philip the Arabian, ended with the Romans buying peace; the second, in the mid-250s, saw the Sassanians ravaging the provinces of Syria and Cappadocia and even assuming control of Antioch; in the third war, ca. 260, the emperor Valerian was personally captured by the Sassanid king, Shapur, while the Sassanian armies were once more pillaging Syria and southern Asia Minor. Rome was now little able to cope, and had the Palmyrenes not stepped into the power vacuum, the eastern provinces might well have succumbed to the Sassanian advance. Fortunately for Rome, however, Palmyra, under Odaenathus and Zenobia, was able to hold off further advances until 272, when the Roman armies led by Aurelian were once more strong enough to assume firm control. By this time, however, the Sassanid monarchy was now more concerned with its own eastern frontiers and had lost interest in the west.

The middle years of the third century (ca. 238–268) saw the barbarians on all sides breaking through the frontiers and thrusting into Roman territory. When Philip the Arabian celebrated the millennium of Rome in A.D. 247, the Empire must have seemed to be doomed; yet fifty years later a new stability was established and many regions were set for a period of prosperity greater than any they had yet experienced.

THE SUCCESSION OF POWER
A.D. 161–268

The brief period from the accession of Marcus Aurelius in 161 to the murder of Severus Alexander in 235 saw a dramatic reversal in the fortunes of Rome. At the beginning the Roman world was at peace, the economy was comparatively healthy, and the orderly succession of power was assured. Yet by the end, the northern and eastern frontiers had more than once been overrun and the barbarians were again massing, the economy was in a disastrous state, and the Roman world was about to embark upon a period of near anarchy.

The reasons for this sudden reversal were complex and interwoven. Rapid population increases among the barbarians, decline in population at home, and the exhaustion of silver mines were among the more obvious causes. But there were others. Hadrian's policy of dividing civil career structures from military ones meant that many senior officers were now totally without administrative experience—a dangerous situation, particularly when such men aspired to the throne, and one which increased to serious proportions the isolation of the army.

When Marcus Aurelius decided to abandon precedent and return to the principle of hereditary succession, appointing his unsuitable son Commodus as consort, he was unwittingly hastening the political collapse of the Empire. Commodus was soon removed, opening the way once more for aspiring military commanders to attempt to grab the throne. That one of them, Septimius Severus, was strong enough and sufficiently unscrupulous to be able to hold the Empire together for nearly two decades, was a fortunate accident. The remaining members of his dynasty were a disaster for Rome, and with their passing, the way was now open for other commanders to make a bid for power irrespective of the interests of the Empire.

161–180 MARCUS AURELIUS

Marcus Aurelius, adopted son of Antoninus, was a scholar whose philosophical works, *Meditations*, reveal a man intensely self-critical and bowed down by the responsibility of government. Realizing the enormity of his task, he immediately appointed Antoninus's second adopted son, Lucius Verus, as consort, clearly intending that Verus should undertake the military leadership of the state.

Soon after his succession the Parthians invaded Armenia and Verus, as supreme commander, was sent to restore the situation. The triumphant army, however, returning to Rome, brought with them a plague which caused widespread deaths in Rome itself and the countryside about.

It was at this moment (166) that the northern barbarians broke through the frontier. The emperor

180–193 COMMODUS

193–211 SEPTIMIUS SEVERUS

responded by taking personal command using Carnuntum as his headquarters. From here he first cleared the provinces of invaders and then campaigned deep into enemy territory (Verus, who was with him, died in 169). Apart from troubles in Syria which required him to spend some time in the east, Aurelius was fully engaged on the northern frontier problem until his death at Vienna in 180. Although he had not achieved his apparent aim of annexing new territories north of the Rhine-Danube frontier, by transporting and resettling vast numbers of Germans and Sarmatians within the provinces he had taken pressure off the frontier and had at the same time done much to counter the problems of manpower shortage and depopulation at home.

At home his policies were philanthropic, but a deepening economic crisis forced him to devalue

the coinage. His attitude to the succession is difficult to understand: rejecting the policy of Trajan and Hadrian, he decided not to appoint the best-suited heir to succeed him but instead nominated his own son, Commodus.

The famous equestrian statue of Marcus Aurelius, on the Capitoline Hill.

Above: *Coin showing Marcus Aurelius and Lucius Verus, who ruled together from 161 to 169.*

Commodus, who succeeded to the throne at the age of nineteen, immediately concluded a peace with the northern barbarians and abandoned all claim to his father's northern conquests.

At home his unpopular rule led to several assassination attempts, after each of which there were savage reprisals. Finally, after an attempt to poison him failed, he was killed by a hired gladiator.

Roman relief of Hercules performing one of his twelve labors. Commodus, like Emperor Caligula long before him, tried to imitate Herculean feats and apparently believed himself the reincarnation of the demigod.

In the chaos which followed the assassination of Commodus several contenders for the throne emerged. The first to be appointed was *Pertinax*, but he was murdered after three months in office, for failing to indulge the Praetorian Guard.

Next a senator, *Didius Julianus*, was elevated only to be replaced by *Septimius Severus*, a nominee of the Pannonian legions who marched on Rome and took control of the city.

Severus was an African from Leptis Magna whose native language was Punic: indeed it is said that he spoke Latin with a foreign accent throughout his life. He was above all a soldier and a man of violent reactions.

His claim to the throne did not pass uncontested. In the east Pescennius Niger, supported by the army on the Euphrates, staked a claim but was overwhelmed and the city of Byzantium, which had supported him, was destroyed (194). Meanwhile the governor of Britain, Clodius Albinus, crossed to Gaul, where he raised a large army to support his own claim. However, near Lyons he was defeated and the city was sacked (197). Severus now held absolute power.

His firm autocratic rule greatly weakened the position of the Senate. The emperor was now in sole control of financial matters and assumed the right to appoint

provincial governors, but the reforms which he introduced in the administration of justice were to have far-reaching and beneficial effects particularly for the poorer members of society.

Troubles in the east in 197 required an expedition deep into Parthian territory. The campaign was rapid and successful. More serious matters were, however, demanding attention along the northern frontier of Britain where, in the chaos following Albinus's attempt at the throne, barbarians had caused widespread damage.

The emperor and his sons left for Britain in 209, and in a series of brilliant campaigns succeeded in beating back the Picts, penetrating far into the north of Scotland. The campaigns were arduous and in 211 the emperor died in York. Severus's rise to the throne and the toughness of his reign marked a significant turning point in Roman history. Power and legitimacy could be acquired by brute

Entrance to the oversized forum which Septimius Severus erected as part of a vast construction program to edify his native city of Leptis Magna on the Libyan coast.

Left: *Pertinax, the first "soldier emperor," ruled for only three months in the year 193.*

force. Edward Gibbon sums up the situation thus:

273

211–217 CARACALLA

217–218 MACRINUS

218–222 ELAGABALUS

On his deathbed Severus is reported to have told his sons: "Stick together, give money to the army, and ignore everyone else."

Severus's two sons, Caracalla and Geta, succeeded their father in 211, but within a year Geta had been murdered at his brother's instigation and immediately afterwards (it was claimed), Caracalla had twenty thousand potential opponents massacred on suspicion.

The conflict between the two brothers was an inevitable result of their dominant characters. At one time, plans were made for dividing the Empire between them: Caracalla ruling the west from Rome, while Geta was to control the east from Antioch or

Alexandria, but Geta's murder intervened, saving the Empire from the prospect of another bloody civil war.

The only significant act of Caracalla's despotic rule was the conferment of citizenship on all freeborn inhabitants of the provinces —an act which may have been encouraged by the need to increase taxation revenue (from inheritance tax, to which only citizens were liable) in order to fill the depleted imperial exchequer. Enthralled by the exploits of Alexander the Great, Caracalla appears to have planned a massive campaign of conquest in the east; but before it could get properly under way, he was murdered by his Praetorian prefect, Macrinus, who now became emperor.

Marcus Opellius Macrinus was one of Caracalla's Praetorian prefects. His rise to power, following the emperor's assassination, marks a significant turning point in Roman history, since he was the first man to become emperor who was not a member of the Senate. The Senate accepted the position without opposition. Macrinus was, however, unpopular with the army, not least because they had been devoted to Caracalla and it was necessary for him to pretend that the emperor had died a natural death and to persuade an unwilling Senate to agree to Caracalla's deification. The army became increasingly rebellious, particularly after Macrinus brought the Parthian war to a rapid and inconclusive end.

Macrinus's rule was short-lived. While he was away in the east, a plot to extend the Severan dynasty was developed by a powerful woman, Julia Maesa, the sister-in-law of Septimius. Without sons of her own, she was intent to place her two grandsons Elagabalus and Alexander Severus on the throne. Using her not inconsiderable powers of leadership, supported by her fortune, she managed to defeat Macrinus. Thus Elagabalus became emperor. Elagabalus was an eastern fanatic deeply involved with the worship of the Syrian Sun god, a cult of which he was the high priest.

"In a magnificent temple raised on the Palatine Mount, the sacrifices of the God of Elagabalus were celebrated with every circumstance of cost and solemnity. The richest wines, the most extraordinary victims, and the rarest aromatics, were profusely consumed on his altar." Edward Gibbon

His exotic, oriental style of despotic government offended Roman society, and within a few years he was murdered by the Praetorian Guard.

Coin depicting Julia Domna between her sons Caracalla and Geta. Aureus minted by Septimius, A.D. 202.

Right: The Praetorian Guards, depicted in this relief from the second century B.C. Macrinus was the first Praetorian prefect who managed to become emperor.

Detail of a relief from the Arch of Septimius Severus showing a battering ram in use in the war against the Parthians.

The emperor Elagabalus, born in Syria, named himself after that country's sun god, shown on a relief from Asia Minor (Turkey).

Severus Alexander was proclaimed emperor by the Praetorian Guard on his cousin's death. As he was only thirteen at the time, the first part of his reign was executed under the control of a carefully chosen committee of sixteen senators. During this time a number of reforms were enacted in an attempt to control the economic crisis which was fast gathering force, but the overall result was to place far greater burdens and responsibilities on local officials, with the inevitable result that men became reluctant to accept office.

In the east the Sassanid dynasty had now gained control and had begun to threaten the eastern provinces. The emperor's attempts to stem the attacks were largely ineffectual. Meanwhile there were further troubles on the

On the death of Severus Alexander power was immediately grabbed by a Thracian soldier, Maximinus, an uneducated man who had risen from the ranks of the army of Septimius Severus. He was hated by the Senate and never bothered to visit Rome.

A first-class soldier, he spent most of his time campaigning on the Rhine against the Alamanni and along the middle and lower

The Gordians' reign was short-lived. After only three weeks Gordianus II was killed by the imperial governor of Numidia and Gordianus I committed suicide. The Senate responded by using their constitutional power to appoint their own emperors. In the event, two men were chosen—Balbinus and Pupienus, both competent old men with distinguished military and civil careers

At Ctesiphon (above) the Parthians under the Persian king Ardashir I opposed Rome both militarily and philosophically in the worship of Zarathustra (below).

Right: *The dominance of the so-called soldier emperors began with Maximinus, who in 235–238 issued this coin showing his son and successor.*

Rhine, to which the emperor responded by attempting to buy off the invaders. In March 235 he and his mother were murdered by his thoroughly disillusioned troops. Thus ended the dynasty of the Severans.

Septimius had clawed his way to power, and through strength and achievement had managed to establish his right, and that of his family, to rule in a semblance of traditional legitimacy. The death of Severus Alexander heralded the beginning of a period of anarchy that was to last for fifty years.

Danube against Sarmatians and Dacians, basing his headquarters at Sirmium (in Yugoslavia). Senatorial opposition to him came to a head in 238, exacerbated by his fiscal measures which imposed a considerable tax burden on the upper-middle classes. In that year a group of African nobles appointed the aging governor, Marcus Antonius Gordianus, as emperor, supported by his son. Evidently the Roman Senate were aware of what was planned and immediately approved, setting up a commission of twenty ex-consuls to remove Maximinus, who was now declared to be a public enemy.

behind them. Upon receiving the news, Maximinus decided to invade Italy, but the city of Aquileia resisted his progress and his officers, uneasy about the plan, rebelled and murdered him.

Meanwhile in Rome the Praetorian Guard were growing dissatisfied, not least because the Senate had not consulted them in their recent appointments. Finally they marched on the palace, captured the two old men, Balbinus and Pupienus, and dragged them naked through the center of Rome to the Praetorian camp where they were killed: thus ended the Senate's involvement in emperor-making.

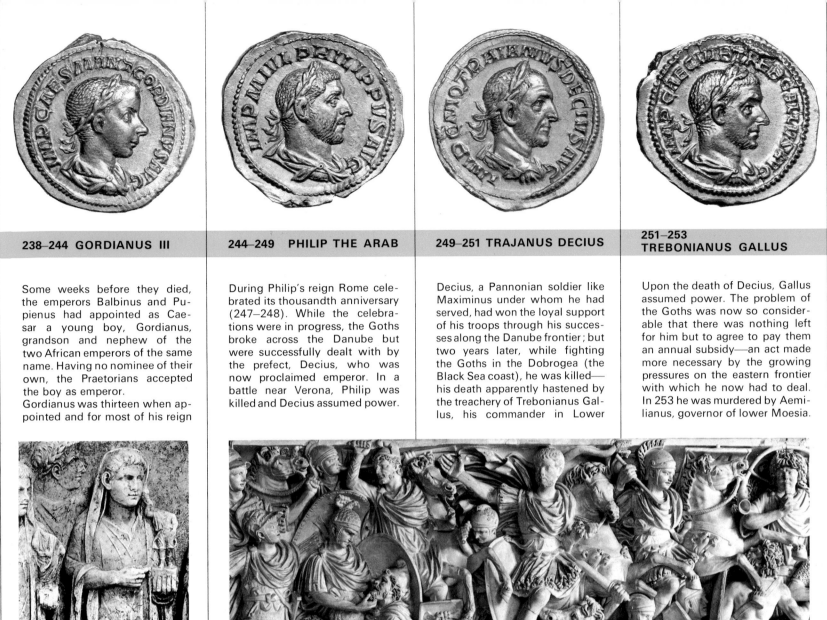

238–244 GORDIANUS III	244–249 PHILIP THE ARAB	249–251 TRAJANUS DECIUS	251–253 TREBONIANUS GALLUS

Some weeks before they died, the emperors Balbinus and Pupienus had appointed as Caesar a young boy, Gordianus, grandson and nephew of the two African emperors of the same name. Having no nominee of their own, the Praetorians accepted the boy as emperor.

Gordianus was thirteen when appointed and for most of his reign

During Philip's reign Rome celebrated its thousandth anniversary (247–248). While the celebrations were in progress, the Goths broke across the Danube but were successfully dealt with by the prefect, Decius, who was now proclaimed emperor. In a battle near Verona, Philip was killed and Decius assumed power.

Decius, a Pannonian soldier like Maximinus under whom he had served, had won the loyal support of his troops through his successes along the Danube frontier; but two years later, while fighting the Goths in the Dobrogea (the Black Sea coast), he was killed— his death apparently hastened by the treachery of Trebonianus Gallus, his commander in Lower

Upon the death of Decius, Gallus assumed power. The problem of the Goths was now so considerable that there was nothing left for him but to agree to pay them an annual subsidy—an act made more necessary by the growing pressures on the eastern frontier with which he now had to deal. In 253 he was murdered by Aemilianus, governor of lower Moesia.

Detail from the Altar of the Vicomagistri. The vicomagistri, *or street supervisors, ensured proper religious observances in honor of the lares and the emperor. By the third century it became their function to hunt out Christians.*

was under the control of able advisers. One of them, Timesitheus, a highly competent soldier, accompanied the emperor to the east where a series of notable victories were won against the Persians. He died in 243 and was replaced by another general, Philip, the son of an Arab nobleman. Philip immediately set about securing his own position and finally persuaded a conspiracy of soldiers to murder the emperor and to appoint him in his stead.

Coin issued by Philip in celebration of Rome's millenary in the year 247–248 (the traditional founding date was 753 B.C.).

Moesia. The Gothic menace which he had had to face was extremely serious. Vast hordes of Ostrogoths had broken through the Danube frontier and were ravaging Thrace and Macedonia. They had taken the town of Philippopolis (Plovdiv in Bulgaria) and, it was said, had slaughtered 100,000 of its inhabitants.

Above: *Sarcophagus of Hostilianus, son of Trajanus Decius: relief of a violent battle between Romans and barbarians.*

New swarms of barbarians... spread devastation through the Illyrian provinces, and terror as far as the gates of Rome. The defense of the monarchy, which seemed abandoned by the pusillanimous emperor, was assumed by Aemilianus.

Edward Gibbon

Valerian the Caesar came against us with seventy thousand men...
and we fought a great battle against him,
and we took Valerian the Caesar with our own hands...
and the provinces of Syria, Cilicia, and Cappadocia we burnt with fire,
we ravaged and conquered them,
taking their people captive.

Sassanian document

253–260 VALERIAN and 253–268 GALLIENUS

In 253 Publius Licinius Valerianus, a senator who at the time was governor of Raetia, became emperor. Realizing that the problems of the Empire were too much for one man to cope with, he immediately appointed his son Gallienus to rule with him. Gallienus remained in the west while Valerian went east to deal with the problems posed by the Persian

ern provinces would have been lost altogether.
Meanwhile in the west the situation was also deteriorating: the province of Dacia had succumbed to the Goths while raiding parties were attacking Athens and Ephesus; the Alamanni had broken through the frontier and had thrust down the Rhône valley into Italy; and the Franks had

Gauls" with its capital of Trier. The new "Empire" was successful in beating the barbarians back beyond the Rhine, but Roman territory in the Neckar district—the Agri Decumates—was lost for good.
Gallienus undertook sweeping army reforms, principal among which was the creation of a major cavalry corps which was station-

emperor and although he was beaten and killed by Gallienus, Gallienus was himself assassinated in the latter stages of the uprising. The reigns of Valerian and Gallienus marked a turning point in the fortunes of Rome. The barbarian threat had reached its peak: henceforth the Empire was to take the initiative under a succession of able military leaders.

During Valerian's reign, Pope Sixtus II died as a Christian martyr. The Pope, shown on painted pottery, had reconciled the churches of Rome and North Africa.

The reign of Valerian saw two critical events. In 254 occurred the first division of the Empire: Valerian was to rule in the east, his son Gallienus in the west. A second

major event was the capture of the emperor himself by an enemy. The relief above, from Naqsh-i-Rusta, Iran, shows King Shapur I of Persia and his prisoner Vale-

rian, captured in the year 260. He died in captivity. With them is Philip the Arab.

invasion. But the situation worsened and eventually Valerian was captured by the Persian king Shapur (260). Thereafter the Roman command of the east collapsed, and had it not been for the activity of the Palmyrene king Odaenathus in setting his semi-independent kingdom against the Persians, it is likely that the east-

crossed the lower Rhine and were ravaging Gaul as far south as the Pyrenees. Gallienus managed to win a considerable victory over the Germans near Milan (258), but in the far west he was too weak to prevent the commander of the Rhine garrison, Postumus, from proclaiming himself emperor of the independent "Empire of the

ed at Milan. The new force, with its considerable flexibility was designed to protect Italy from barbarian attacks, its central location enabling it to strike in any direction with equal facility. One disadvantage was that it could offer a power base for any aspiring leader. Indeed, its first commander, Aureolus, rebelled against the

In 269 Claudius II brought peace to the Danube provinces by destroying a vast army of Goths. In 273 Aurelian was driving the Persian raiders from the eastern provinces and restoring Roman rule once more in place of Palmyrene protectionnism. Rome had weathered the storm.

The missorium of Emperor Theodosius I, a silver plate found in Badojoz which commemorated the emperor's decennial in 388. Beside him are seated the two younger "Augusti," Ariadius and Valentian II: a sign of the administrative reforms enacted by Diocletian and Constantine.

In 284 the Praetorian Guard appointed Diocletian as emperor. This man, who was born in Illyria of humble parents and who had risen in the ranks through sheer ability, was to rule the Roman world for twenty years—and live to enjoy a gentle retirement on the shores of the Adriatic. During his reign the anarchy was brought to an end, firm rule established, and the machinery of government totally overhauled.

In spite of his simple origins, Diocletian enjoyed the majesty of Rome. He respected the Senate, at least nominally, championed the old religious cults, and is reputed to have dressed grandly in purple robes and diadems, demanding that those who wished to address him remained standing. But for all this he was a man of the times whose brilliantly sharp insight and firm resolve enabled him to carry out sweeping reforms unfettered by a nostalgia for the past. When Diocletian had finished with Rome, it looked more like the Byzantine world it was to become, than the classical Empire it had once been.

Diocletian had to face three major problems, all closely interrelated: the economic crisis; the need to reorganize the army; and the restructuring of the antiquated administrative machinery of the Empire. To each he brought sound judgment supported by experience gained during the period of anarchy.

The economic plight of the Empire was now serious. The ravages of the barbarian invasion, the colossal expense of supporting the army, depopulation and underproduction, the loss of the Dacian silver and gold mines, and a complete inability of the Roman administration to understand economic theory—all combined to create a dizzy spiral of inflation. Trajan had debased the *denarius* to 85 percent of its face value; Marcus Aurelius allowed it to fall to 75 percent; by the time of Septimius it had reached 60 percent. Worse was to

follow. In Egypt 30 liters of wheat cost less than one *drachma* in the second century, between 12 and 20 in the early third century, and by the time of Diocletian it had reached 120,000. Other estimates suggest that in the third quarter of the third century prices rose by nearly 1000 percent.

Faced with these staggering problems, Diocletian issued a new sound coinage hoping to stabilize prices. But the immediate response of the public was to buy goods with the lower denominations, forcing prices to rise even more steeply than before, and to hoard the silver and gold, which exchanged hands according to weight and not at face value. Clearly his measures had failed and there was nothing left to do but to take the ultimate and novel step of introducing a firm Prices and Incomes Policy. Accordingly, in 301–302 Diocletian issued his famous Edict on Prices in which were listed the maximum prices allowable for a wide range of commodities and for workers' wages, to apply throughout the whole Empire. Failure to observe them would be punished by death. Unfortunately the result was simply that goods ceased to be offered for sale on the open market and inflation continued—a pound of gold worth 50,000 *denarii* in 301 was valued at 300,000 twenty-three years later. There was now a serious danger that the money economy would collapse altogether and trade revert to barter, but the Edict had been set out in terms of the old *denarius* and this in itself did much to keep the idea of money alive.

Nevertheless taxes in kind were becoming a common occurrence in the third century. The *annona militaris*, irregular payments of food, raw materials, and other goods, demanded of local communities for the support of the army, had imposed considerable hardships on

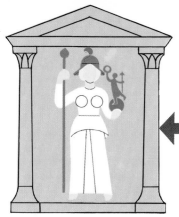

The Emperor

The governmental reorganization enacted by Diocletian created a virtual

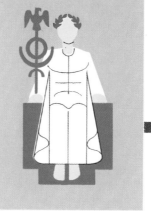

monarchy with centralized bureaucratic power and a harsh limitation of personal freedom in favor of the interests of the state.

Rome and Constantinople

Imperial power was now divided, to correspond to the two major geograph-

ical spheres of influence. The Empire's division into Latin and Greek sectors was to prove permanent.

The Chamberlain

The *praepositus sacri cubiculi* (director of the imperial bedroom) was responsible for the running of the emperor's household.

Finance Minister

The finance minister *(comes rerum privatarum)* was the supreme chief of administration of the imperial estates.

Chancellor

The *magister officiorum* (master of the imperial chancellery) had the direction of various departments (*scrivia*, cabinets).

Overseer of the Palace

The *quaestor sacri palatii* had functions approximating those of a minister of justice.

Master of the Treasury

The master of the treasury *(comes sacrarum cargitionum)* had the task of paying gifts from imperial monies.

Military Commanders

The two military commanders *(magistri militum)* were responsible directly to the emperor. Under Constantine, for the first time in Rome's thousand-year history, the civil and military administrations were separated.

The Army

The military consisted of the field army *(comitatenses)*, the border troops *(limitanei)*, and the emperor's body guard *(candidati)*. Friendly natives *(foederati)* in frontier areas also assisted with border patrol. Diocletian's military reforms did not alter the policy of subordinating officers and troops to the authority of provincial governors. The late Roman emperors had to struggle more and more with the unwillingness of the population to serve in the army. Therefore the army was obliged to muster increasing numbers of barbarians with the result that the military units no longer had the patriotic fervor of former days.

The People

The population found its lot in no way improved by the administrative and fiscal reforms of the fourth century. The rural population, in particular, was mercilessly exploited by the government, and relations between the ruling class and the populace were hostile. This social climate was perhaps the most severe antagonism that had yet existed in the Western Empire. It was to contribute to the downfall of the Empire, in part by making it difficult to raise the necessary revenues for the maintenance of an adequate army.

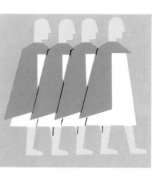

The Prefects

The entire Empire had been divided into four prefectures—Oriens, Illyricum, Italia, and Gallia. At the head of each prefecture stood the *praefectus praetorio* (Praetorian prefect). Constantinople, Sirmium, Milan, and Trier were their seats. These four prefectures embraced 14 dioceses, divided into a total of 117 provinces.

Provincial Governors

It became the main task of the provincial governors, as time went on, to raise essential tax revenue. The late Roman Empire was essentially a civil service state, and it would be an exaggeration to call all the officials corrupt or inefficient. The government had a well-trained police force at its disposal, to assist the officials in maintaining law and order. The bureaucracy remained reactionary. The Western Empire was too poor to support its ministerial officials adequately—the more reason for their taking advantage of every occasion for gain.

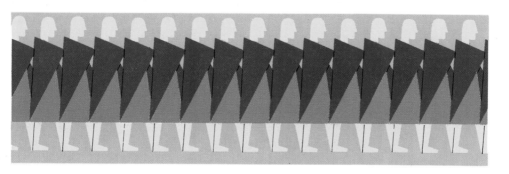

The two Caesars, or younger adjutant emperors, appointed by Diocletian in 296 are shown in coins at left. Galerius *(far left)* governed Illyrium, Macedonia, and Greece; he succeeded as emperor in the East in the year 305.

Constantine Chlorus *(left)* is portrayed entering London in the year 296; as Caesar he was responsible for Spain, Gaul, and Britain. He became emperor of the West in 305 and was the father of Constantine the Great.

the provinces by the very uncertainty of the tax. Now Diocletian regularized the situation by assessing all provinces according to their productive land and requiring his state officials to estimate the needs of the army in advance so that the provincial governors could be forewarned of the year's levy. In this way an annual budget was introduced into the Roman economy for the first time. When confidence in money returned under Constantine, many communities preferred to pay their *annona* in cash, thus revitalizing the money economy once more.

One of the problems underlying the Empire's precarious economic state was depopulation, accentuated by the desire of many people, tenants, small farmers, and traders alike, to give up their responsibilities in the face of crushing taxation. They might join larger estates as serfs, migrate to the towns, or, in cases of desperation, add to the growing number of bandits who were infesting the countryside. The trend had by now reached alarming proportions, and had it been allowed to continue, complete economic breakdown would have ensued. Diocletian and his successors took the only course open to them: in a series of edicts men were bound by law to their professions; artisans were forced to remain in their craft guilds, tenants were compelled to work the estates to which they were attached, and it was only a matter of time before sons were made to follow their father's profession. Harsh and repressive though these measures were, they slowed down the rate of disintegration and paved the way for the comparative prosperity of the fourth century.

The barbarian inroads of the third century demonstrated beyond dispute that the imperial army was no longer adequately structured to cope with frontier problems. Gradually new tactics

evolved which led to the total reshaping of the fighting force. The experience gained during this period was crystallized in the army reforms introduced by Diocletian. The old concept of a single army strung out evenly along a frontier line was now drastically modified—it had, after all, proved to be totally ineffective against the sudden surges of the highly mobile barbarian hordes. Under the reforms the army was now divided into two categories—the frontier troops *(limitanei)* and the field army *(comitatenses)*.

The *limitanei* were based in forts and fortlets along the frontier, where they were expected to remain throughout their lives, living in close proximity to their families and working land in the

By every available means, the Tetrarchs tried to demonstrate complete unity. This porphyry marble pillar shows Diocletian and Maximian embracing. It comes from the five-columned monument now in the Vatican Museum.

vicinity of their base. Since sons of soldiers were now required by law to enter the army, what emerged was essentially a sedentary militia rooted to the locality by ties of property and family. Many of these frontier units protected the territories in which they were recruited, while others were composed of barbar-

ians from beyond the frontier who had been allowed to cross into Roman territory and settle in return for military service. The *comitatenses*, on the other hand, were a highly mobile field force stationed some distance from the frontier line and ready to move with speed as soon as the enemy appeared. They too, were now composed largely of barbarian recruits not infrequently under the command of officers of the same nationality.

Thus by the beginning of the fourth century the army had been transformed. Old distinctions between citizen legionaries and *auxillia* had virtually disappeared, and instead the Empire was now defended largely by foreigners.

The financial and military reforms which Diocletian initiated created the need for a vast and cumbersome bureaucracy. After all, an army of 600,000 supported on a complex tax system could not otherwise be maintained. Indeed, it was an often repeated exaggeration that under Diocletian the Empire contained more tax gatherers than tax payers. To cope with the changed situation, Diocletian restructured the administrative framework of the Empire. Realizing that no one man could efficiently control so large a territory, in 286 he appointed Maximian as co-Augustus, entrusting to him the government of the western half of the Empire, while he himself moved to Nicomedia in Asia Minor to govern the east. Seven years later two subordinate partners, Constantius and Galerius, were nominated. The Empire was now divided into four, as a tetrarchy: Diocletian took the eastern provinces; Galerius the Danubian and Balkan regions; Maximian retained Italy, Spain, and Africa; while Constantius took over Gaul and Britain.

The four regions, each governed by a *prefect*, were divided into a number of

In his governmental reforms, Diocletian in 286 made the Empire into a Tetrarchy (four-man rule), led by two Augusti, himself in the East and Maximian in the West, and two Caesars; slightly younger men who would later succeed the Augusti (whereupon two new Caesars would be appointed, and so on). The Tetrarchy is shown in this carving of about A.D. 300 on the façade of St. Mark's in Venice: Diocletian and Maximian, the Augusti, at right; the two Caesars, at left, Galerius and Constantine Chlorus.

dioceses controlled by a *vicarius*, and each of the dioceses was in turn divided into provinces (of which there were now more than one hundred) under governors. The chain of command was essentially civil, each provincial army now becoming the responsibility of a military commander called a *dux*. The new scheme thus formalized the separation between the army and the civilian administration: it allowed a high degree of military flexibility, while at the same time preventing the build-up of power in the hands of any individual governor. The overall effect of the reform was to increase the efficiency of the state, but in doing so the civil service had grown to colossal proportions, putting an even greater strain on the decreasing percentage of the population who were actually engaged in productive activities.

The creation of the Tetrarchy (the rule of four) was a deliberate attempt to ensure peaceful succession within the Empire. Diocletian and Maximian, as Augusti, were to rule for twenty years while the two Caesars, Constantius and Galerius, served in junior capacities. When the Augusti retired, the Caesars would take their places, appointing Caesars of their own. The principle was sound, and on 1 May 305 Diocletian and Maximian abdicated according to plan. But almost immediately dissension set in among the potential successors. A weaker man might have been encouraged to reassume power, but not Diocletian: he had made up his mind and for the remaining nine years of his life he lived in peace in his palace.

His achievements were considerable. He was not a great innovator, but his power to see a problem clearly and to select the most effective of the possible solutions, arrested for the time being the destructive forces which were tearing the Empire apart.

DIOCLETIAN'S PALACE

This head from a marble statue has been found in one of Diocletian's residences, in Nicomedia. The identification is uncertain but a comparison with coins showing Diocletian reveals striking similarities.

The grandiose Palace of Diocletian in Yugoslavia, built for the emperor's retirement in A.D. 305, was a fortresslike rectangular structure some two hundred meters long. Its outer walls enclosed four principal buildings plus ancillary structures. The main entrance included an elaborate vestibule, still well preserved today *(above and opposite)*, built in a style that looked forward to Byzantine architecture.

Diocletian was born near the Dalmatian town of Salona in 246, and it was nearby at Spalato (Split) in the early years of the fourth century that he built a palace for his retirement. Enclosed in a massive defensive wall and protected by square and octagonal towers, the building has the appearance of a fort, and like a contemporary fort, the internal streets divide the enclosed area into three blocks.

The two blocks which together comprise the northern half of the palace, each contained large residential buildings arranged around courtyards and divided from the streets by colonnaded walks. One part of the palace contained the emperor's mausoleum which faced a small temple, probably dedicated to Jupiter (Diocletian's favorite deity), while occupying the entire southern side of the enclosure, lay the main residential range—a series of halls, apartments, and baths all linked together by a continuous loggia which ran the full length of the range and looked out across the Adriatic.

The palace is a fascinating mixture of styles and ideas. Fort-like in plan, it may well have been inspired by the palace built by Valerian in the 250s on an island opposite the city of Antioch, but its details reflect styles from all parts of the Empire. The mausoleum and the audience chambers look to Italy; arches springing from colonnades were widely employed at Leptis Magna during the rebuilding under Severus; while the decorative use of arches and lintels to enliven wall faces embodied skills and techniques widespread in Syria and Asia Minor.

The palace is a truly cosmopolitan building, its remote grandeur and defensive permanence perfectly matching the personality of the emperor and the spirit of the age which he did so much to mold.

CONSTANTINE THE GREAT

Head from the colossal statue of Constantine the Great, Palazzo dei Conservatori, Rome. The entire statue of the seated emperor had been about ten meters high. It was discovered in the fifteenth century in the Basilica of Maxentius in Rome. It was probably completed in the year 313.

The statue of Constantine the Great *(below)* stands on the balustrade of the Capitol in Rome.

The abdication of Diocletian and Maximian in 305 brought to an end the reality of the Tetrarchy. Then followed a period of confusion during which, at one time, in 308, the Roman Empire was ruled by no less than seven Augusti. Gradually, however, the picture cleared: after 313, for more than a decade, a semblance of the old idea of the Tetrarchy once more evolved with Licinius ruling the East and Constantine the West, each supported by Caesars. In 324 Constantine finally reunited the Empire and was to rule as sole Augustus until his death in 337. Even so, the division between East and West was maintained, since for much of the time the Empire was divided between two of Constantine's sons, Constantine II and Constantius II, serving in their capacity as Caesars. After Constantine's death the division was to continue at the level of Augusti.

Constantine, the eldest son of Constantius and a barmaid called Helena, was born at Niš in Yugoslavia in 290. On the abdication of Diocletian and Maximian in 305, he joined his father who was about to embark on an expedition to Britain, and in the next year at York was proclaimed Augustus by the army when his father died. Thus began the remarkable career of this ambitious young man. In two great battles, at Milvian Bridge just outside Rome (312) and at Chrysopolis not far from Byzantium (323), he defeated his two main opponents; first Maxentius, after which he was recognized as Senior Augustus by the Senate, and then Licinius, which left him undisputed master of the Roman world.

Strangely, the two battles are directly associated with the two major events of his reign. Just before Milvian Bridge it is said that he saw the cross superimposed on the sun, a phenomenon which led him to proclaim toleration of Chris-

tianity throughout the Empire in 313. At Chrysopolis he became aware of the great potential of the site of the old Greek city of Byzantium where he was

to found the new city of Constantinople. It is upon these two acts that Constantine's justifiable fame is based.

His conversion to Christianity is a curious and confused affair. Brought up in the court of Diocletian during the height of the persecutions, he would have become thoroughly aware of the nature and the strength of Christian be-

In this detail from a Byzantine miniature, Constantine pursues Maxentius across the Milvian Bridge in Rome. Christian symbols dominate the picture: Constantine, for example, is shown with a halo.

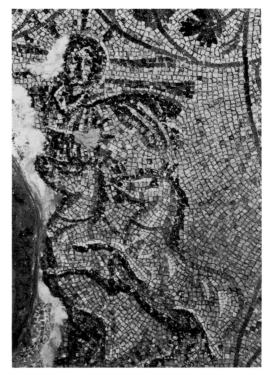

lief and it is indeed possible that his mother was a convert. Yet in his early life he was evidently a worshipper of Sol Invictus (the Unconquered Sun) and he seems to have continued for some while to believe that the sun and the Christian God were one and the same. Even as late as 318 he was still issuing coins with the legend *Sol Invictus Comes Augusti*, and the wording of his edict enforcing Sunday as a day of rest gives the firm impression that he believed that the Christians reserved the day in honor of the sun.

Yet in spite of the confusion in his own mind, he was prepared to put the full power of his office behind his convictions and to assume an active part in trying to solve the sectarian rifts which rent the Church. Writing to the vicar of Africa, he could say, "What higher duty have I in virtue of my imperial office and policy than to dissipate errors and repress rash actions and so cause all to offer to Almighty God true religion, honest concord, and due worship." Clearly he believed himself to be a servant of God and as such to be responsible for the well-being of the Church. For its part the Church in all its factions was content to accept his domination.

Throughout his reign Constantine showered favors on individual Christians and Christian communities alike, thus considerably swelling the ranks of the converted. At first his attitude towards paganism was one of toleration, allowing the old gods to be worshipped and even protecting them from Christian molestation, but in later life his attitudes hardened; temples were closed, treasures commandeered, and finally pagan sacrifices were banned. That the first emperor to be converted to Christianity also decided to found a new capital at Byzantium was a remarkable coincidence which was to totally change the direction of the civilized world. Henceforth old Rome—pagan, Latin speaking, and rooted in western tradition—began its slide into obscurity while the new center, Constantinople—Christian, Greek, and with a strong flavor of the Orient—emerged to lead the civilized world for another thousand years.

From the Arch of Constantine, relief showing the battle against Maxentius at the Milvian Bridge. This victory in the year 312 was not a defeat for the Tetrarchy, for at the Conference of Carnuntum the Tetrarchs had agreed that Maxentius's usurpations had to be corrected. Even if the tetrarchic system was not completely destroyed in this victory, nevertheless Constantine had been brought a step closer to his goal of supreme power.

THE CITY OF CONSTANTINE

On 18 September 324 Constantine, having just beaten his rival Licinius on the hills above Chrysopolis, crossed the Bosphorus to receive the submission of the town of Byzantium. Two years later, on 4 November 326, the emperor personally traced out the line of a new city wall and thus initiated the foundation of New Rome or Constantinople as it came to be called. On 11 May 330, in a ceremony in the hippodrome, the new city which had sprung up in the intervening period was formally dedicated.

The choice of Byzantium as the new center of the Roman world was thoroughly sound. Well protected on three sides by the Sea of Marmara and the Golden Horn, the peninsula guarded the most convenient crossing between Europe and Asia. The value of the site had long been realized: the first city to occupy the position was founded by colonists from the Greek city of Megara in the seventh century B.C. It had de-

The cisterns of Constantinople were constructed around 520 during Justinian's reign. They comprise 336 pillars, arranged in 12 rows of 28 pillars each. The cisterns give the impression of a gigantic basilica.

The splendor and beauty of Constantinople have inspired numerous artists to capture its likeness. The views of the city shown here *(left and below)* are details from a miniature contained in a Persian historical text written by Nashu as-Shilahi in 1537.

veloped, not without incident, until A.D. 196 when, in a fit of rage for its having supported a rival, Septimius Severus had had the walls torn down, the inhabitants massacred, and the buildings reduced to a smoldering heap. A few years later, however, realizing his mistake in leaving so strategically important a site unprotected, he rebuilt the city once more, this time on an enlarged scale.

By choosing Byzantium as his new capital Constantine was demonstrating a truth which had for some while been implicit, that the center of gravity of the Roman world had finally shifted. Constantinople was admirably sited, not only with respect to its own defensive qualities, but by virtue of the fact that from it both the European and the eastern frontiers could easily be reached.

Although Constantine's city grew rapidly, it was rarely used as an imperial residence until the time of Theodosius I (379–395), both Constantius II and Valens preferring to live at Antioch. To

begin with, it had none of the constitutional benefits enjoyed by Rome, but Constantius II (no doubt jealous of his younger brother ruling from Rome) decided to provide his capital with the full panoply of state officialdom—a senate of some three hundred, magistrates, and a prefect. Thus on 11 December 359 Constantinople gained constitutional parity with Rome.

The city continued to grow, soon outstripping the walls which Constantine had laid out. Valens built an aqueduct to improve the water supply, and in about 388 Theodosius I constructed a magnificent monumental approach to the city, the Golden Gate, on the road that led west to Dyrrachium. Later, in the early fifth century, the gate was incorporated in a colossal system of defenses built at the instigation of Theodosius II after the West had fallen to the barbarians. These walls were to hold out until 13 April 1204, when the Christian Crusaders broke through and pillaged the city unmercifully.

THE RISE OF CHRISTIANITY

In A.D. 49, twenty years after the death of Christ, a council of leading Christians held in Jerusalem decided to admit Gentiles to the Church. This single act, masterminded by Paul of Tarsus, was to prove decisive for, by taking this momentus decision, the Christian community had broken away from Judaism and was now offering itself to the world. In the euphoria of missionary zeal which followed, Paul and his supporters set about creating Christian enclaves in many of the principal ports and route centers of the ancient world, including Ephesus, Corinth, and Philippi, so as to spread their teaching throughout the Mediterranean.

For the most part the Roman world was tolerant of Christianity (all except for the Jews, who were bitterly hostile to it) and by A.D. 59 Christian communities had become well established in Rome. But toleration did not mean ready acceptance. Christians were unpopular partly because their rites were

Mosaic of Christ *(top)* from Hagia Sophia. Peter and Paul, on a bronze medallion. At right, the Christian emperor Valentinian I, from Barletta.

The opposition between Christianity and Roman power. The condemnation of Christ *(above)* by the Roman governor Pontius Pilate is the first act. Manuscript miniature from the Codex Purpureus, sixth century.

With the spread of Christianity, its threat came to be seen in both a religious and a political light. Christians refusing to worship the emperor died as martyrs, as in this ivory relief of the freezing to death of forty Christians in Asia Minor.

Persecution served to prove and harden the Christians' powers of resistance. The catacombs *(above)* offer a dramatic contrast to the lavish ecclesiastical buildings that followed the recognition of the Christian religion by Constantine.

widely misunderstood—they ate the flesh and blood of a son of God—but mainly because they were atheists. Their arrogant and impious behavior towards the old gods offended men as it must have angered the gods themselves. Thus natural disasters such as earthquakes and fires, sent by the gods, were the fault of the Christians. It was quite natural for the great fire of Rome (A.D. 64) to be blamed on these people and for the mob to wish to see retribution. Tacitus gives a detailed account of Nero's conduct of the affair.

First, Nero had self-acknowledged Christians arrested. Then, on their information, large numbers of others were condemned — not so much for incendiarism as for their anti-social tendencies. Their deaths were made farcical. Dressed in wild animals' skins, they were torn to pieces by dogs, or crucified, or made into torches to be ignited after dark as substitutes for daylight. Despite their guilt as Christians, and the ruthless punishment it deserved, the victims were pitied. For it was felt that they were being sacrificed to one man's brutality rather than to the national interest.

Persecution on this scale was unusual. A few decades later Pliny the Younger, then governor of Bithynia, had to face

the problem of how to deal with accusations made against Christians by informers. After investigating matters, he concluded:

I found nothing but a degenerate sort of cult carried to extravagant lengths.

Christianity spread mainly among the urban lower and middle classes, particularly in the Greek-speaking east. The rural population and the upper classes remained largely pantheistic, but by the second century the trend towards a vague monotheism can begin to be detected. Some believed that the sun symbolized the supreme unconquered god (as did Constantine before his conversion). Others of a more philosophical nature, turned to an updated version of Platonism which upheld the Idea of the Good and regarded the legends and myths surrounding the old gods as allegories to help people understand simple underlying truths. It was in this atmosphere of philosophical revival (neoplatonism), which flourished in Alexandria in the late second and early third centuries, that a Christian philosophy began to take shape and converts began to be found among the more educated classes.

During the third century when the Empire was plunged into chaos and the gods seemed to be wreaking vengeance on the civilized world, it was only natural that the impious Christians should be blamed. In 250 Decius demanded that all citizens should sacrifice to the gods and should obtain a certificate to the effect—failure to do so meant execution: seven years later Valerian confiscated Church property and exiled the clergy. But these were short-lived and comparatively minor persecutions, and for the remainder of the century a more tolerant attitude prevailed until Diocletian initiated the last, and in many ways the most sav-

age, attempt to suppress the cult—a measure perhaps of the strength it had now attained.

The "conversion" of Constantine brought persecution to an end, but it did more than that—it put the full power of the Empire behind the religion. It could even be argued that but for the dominant role played by Constantine, the Church would have torn itself apart with internal dissensions and rivalries.

The Christian revolution. Emperors, during the height of Roman power, had assumed divine attributes: Claudius (above) is portrayed in a statue as Zeus. After the triumph of Christianity, however, the late emperors are no longer worshipped. In the mosaic from Haghia Sophia (right), two Christian emperors are shown making offerings to Christ and Mary: Justinian, at left, presents the Church, while Constantine offers the city of Constantinople.

ART IN TRANSITION

Just before the anarchy of the third century temporarily halted artistic development within the Empire, a hint had been given of the new age to come. This first indication did not

come from Rome but from North Africa, in the city of Leptis Magna. Here the emperor Septimius Severus (193–211) decided virtually to rebuild the city of his birth. To do so he employed masons and sculptors from the east, many of them coming probably from Aphrodisias in Asia Minor. The styles which they adopted were well rooted in classical tradition, but showed a spirit that was plainly anti-classical. In relief sculpture, their deep drilling and steep undercutting produced harsh shadows emphasizing the simple black and white patterning of carved foliage; arches sprang in surprising baroque from colonnades. These were not novel characteristics, but here at Leptis the anti-classicism was allowed to become far more blatant than ever before. This style contrasts with the delicate restraint of the Ara Pacis. The most striking manifestation of the

new spirit was reserved for the treatment of a procession depicted on the Arch of Septimius erected in about A.D. 200. Here the emperor and his sons loom large over their attendants and all face the viewer in rigid serried ranks. Perspective is now unimportant; it is the rhythm of frontality, learned from Parthian art of the east, that now dominates.

When stability once more returns under the Tetrarchy, the new spirit has taken root. The emperors immortalized in hard Egyptian porphyry are now squat and solid, and stare out with lentoid eyes at the viewer, their strength emphasized by the squareness of their stylized features.

A little later Constantine might still build a traditional, almost archaic, tri-

The new style that dominated the late Empire is shown in the fourth-century relief from Constantine's Arch *(left)*: flatness, figures facing forward, and unrealistic proportions. Coins also reveal the new emphasis on frontality: Emperor Licinius Pater, A.D. 323–324 *(far right)*, contrasts with the earlier profile portraits (Caesar, first century B.C.).

umphal arch in Rome, but the friezes which his own artists carved are in the style of the new age: the emperor sits in opulent central splendor, his supporters providing a balanced regularity to the composition. It is but a short step from this to the base of the Theodosian obelisk in Constantinople, which belongs not to the Classical Age but to the Byzantine.

Far left: Eastern influences, as early as A.D. 200, can be detected in the Arch of Septimius Severus in Leptis Magna.
The relief offers an interesting contrast to classical works such as the late first-century B.C. Ara Pacis (shown on page 113), for the postures are now less varied, and the figures look straight ahead, as if frozen in a ceremonial and spiritual awesomeness.

Above left: By 388, with the obelisk of Theodosius (in Constantinople), these new traits have become fully dominant and the classical age of Augustus seems to have faded from memory.

All motion has stopped, and the human figures are reduced to geometrically uniform patterns. Frontality is elevated to a rigorous principle, and the only distinctions between figures are those of scale: the emperor is larger than the minor members of his court.

Above: Eastern influences played a role in the evolution of Roman art.
This Parthian rock relief (from Naqsh-i-Rusta), showing the triumph of King Shapur I, shares some traits with late Roman sculpture: the squarish heads are also seen in the reliefs of Constantine's Arch.

THE ECONOMIC CRISIS

Below: A shepherd, detail from a fifth-century sarcophagus. For centuries Rome had depended for its food supply, and other needs, on imports from all parts of the Empire. When the East was cut off and governed separately, the Western Empire felt the loss of important natural resources and entered a period of crisis.

Slavery had been an essential part of the Roman economy throughout the early Empire, but with the end of expansion, slaves were less easily and less cheaply acquired than before. The medallion *(right)*, a slave badge, contains an inscription: "Hold me lest I flee, and restore me to my master."

Throughout the first half of the fourth century there was a distinct improvement in the economic well-being of the Empire. The strong and forceful leadership of the House of Constantine cut internal strife to a minimum and allowed the frontiers to be policed in strength, while the stability of the money economy was to some extent maintained by a high-quality gold coinage, the issue of which was made possible by the confiscation of treasure from the pagan temples. Another factor which undoubtedly added strength to administration was that East and West still functioned together and for considerable periods were ruled by the same individual. All this ceased with the death of Julian in 363: the dynasty of Constantine had ended, barbarian raids were once more gathering strength, and henceforth East and West went their own separate ways.

The spectacular decline which the Western Empire was about to experience, was the result of a morass of interrelated causes, many of them firmly embedded in the very fabric of the Empire. Crucial to our understanding is the nature of the Roman economy. From the very beginning it was dependent upon the consumption of slaves to provide the energy necessary to fuel the productive processes. A ready supply of slaves under the Republic and the early Empire allowed an expanding economy, but at the same time rendered unnecessary any form of real technological progress: experiment and innovation were deadened by inertia. All the time that the Empire was expanding and was thus in a position to harvest new resources both of manpower (slaves) and of raw materials (food, metals, and so on), the nonproductive core of the Empire (which must include both the parasitic urban poor and the conspicuous consump-

tion of the rich), could be maintained. But by the early second century the boundaries of the Empire had been stretched to their limits: the edges of the natural Mediterranean-based region had been reached. Beyond lay unproductive deserts, mountain ranges, and forest zones. These areas could be penetrated, but they did not support the type of economy to which the Roman world was used, nor had the Empire the inventive and technological skills to exploit them. Thus further expansion would have been useless—a realization formalized in Hadrian's frontier policy.

Now a new factor intruded—the land frontiers of the Empire were of colossal length; all had to be continuously manned by an essentially nonproductive force which by the early fourth century had reached 600,000. Expansion provided surplus, part of which could be used to feed, cloth, and pay this body, albeit indirectly. Once the frontier had been stabilized, it was the Empire alone which now had to provide for itself—to feed its poor and its army, to satisfy the excessive desires of the wealthy, and to maintain the vast administrative structure.

The end of expansion also meant the end of a cheap and ready supply of

slaves—the very fuel upon which the Empire ran. Slaves could still be obtained, but at a price. It was at this moment that a new and totally unexpected factor suddenly appeared. In 166 the armies returning from the east introduced plague into the Western Empire, a disaster which was to recur for the next two decades, drastically reducing urban and rural populations alike. From this time forwards, manpower shortage became a problem of increasing seriousness.

The middle of the second century was therefore a turning point in the fortunes of Rome. It was a time when the economy needed to be drastically remodeled to suit the new situation. But this was not to be. The reforms of Hadrian and Antonius were little more than cosmetic. Perhaps the momentum of the Roman economy was now too great for anyone to arrest. At any event, the solutions which Marcus Aurelius was forced to attempt were traditional in the extreme—debasement of the coinage and a reversion to the policy of territorial expansion—but his increasing reliance on the use of barbarian troops in the army, itself the formalization of an earlier incipient trend, was to introduce a new force of considerable significance.

The scene was now set for the final act. The continued decrease in the rural population, hastened by the barbarian invasion of the third century and the accompanying anarchy, totally undermined the economic basis of the western part of the Empire. Depopulation was met by an increase in the tax load, which led inevitably to impoverishment. In spite of harsh legislation, people left the land in droves. While the owners of the large rural estates could benefit from this, acquiring new land at very low prices and making use of the cheap labor of the now-landless

Below: Statuette of a black slave cleaning a boot. In the breakdown of order in many provinces in the late Empire, slaves were becoming more difficult to control and to keep, since they could escape and quickly join roaming bands of outlaws.

peasants to run their greatly inflated establishments, the situation was one of increasing instability. Brigandage reached alarming proportions, particularly in Gaul where bands of Bagaudae (the free ones) roamed the countryside, their numbers swelled by deserters from the army and by groups of Germans infiltrating from the north. To counter these problems the administration of the Western Empire relied more and more upon German manpower. By the mid-fourth century the army was thoroughly Germanized. Moreover, abandoned land within the Empire was being settled by German communities with the active encouragement of the government. Small groups *(laeti)* were placed under provincial control, while larger groups *(foederati)* were left to govern themselves.

Until the middle of the fourth century the situation was fully controlled by the Roman administration, but from the 360s, for the next hundred years, matters began to get out of hand. As controlled settlement gave way to uncontrolled, so the Western Empire fell apart. In spite of the strong reaction which flared up against German commanders (leading to the execution of the highly successful Vandal general Stilicho), it was too late—the Western Empire had already disintegrated.

Yet the East remained strong. The reasons for this are difficult to untangle. It may be that the newly founded capital at Constantinople with its Graeco-Oriental culture was able to generate an energy and an enthusiasm which was now totally lacking in Rome. But another factor of great importance was that Constantinople controlled Asia Minor, which was still, at this time, a very considerable reservoir of manpower and wealth. So long as the Empire was governed as one, that surplus could be divided and would help to alleviate the economic crisis of the West; but as soon as the division gained a formal rigidity, as it began to do in the closing decades of the fourth century, the wealth of Asia Minor became the sole preserve of Constantinople. Its concentration in the East not only enabled the Byzantine Empire to develop its own rich culture, but it also added another nail to the coffin of the Roman West.

THE GOTHS AND THE ALANS

When Tacitus was describing the peoples of Germany at the end of the first century A.D., he made brief mention of a tribe called the Goths who occupied a territory on the Baltic shores and were under the strict rule of kings. Early in the third century the Goths moved south, in about 250 capturing the city of Olbia on the Black Sea and thereafter establishing a state of their own. One group, the Ostrogoths, settled around the Sea of Azov, their territory extending as far west as the Dnieper. The others, the Visigoths, took over the now abandoned province of Dacia.

At the time of the Gothic migration, the area from Moldavia to the Caspian Sea was occupied by a semi-nomadic people called the Alans. According to the historian Ammianus Marcellinus, they lived on meat and milk, occupied covered wagons, and drove their cattle and horses from place to place as the availability of good pasture dictated. "They take pride in killing any man whatever and as glorious spoils of the slain they tear off their heads,

then strip off their skins and hang them upon their war-horses as trappings."

The southward movement of the Ostrogoths split the homeland of the Alans into two, the western group concentrating in Moldavia, the eastern group between the Don and the Volga. This was the situation when, in the middle of the fourth century, a Mongoloid tribe called the Huns, who had previously occupied the region of the Altai Mountains, moved westwards towards Europe.

By about 355 the Huns were attacking the eastern Alans, forcing them to migrate south and west: by 370 they were defeating the Ostrogoths and a little later, having outflanked the Visigoths on the Dniester, they had taken possession of a vast territory stretching from the Caspian to the Hungarian plain. In the chaos which ensued, hundreds of thousands of dispossessed Goths and Alans poured

south to the Danube to seek permission to be allowed to cross the frontier into the Roman world.

At this moment (the winter of 375–376) Valens, the emperor of the East, was engaged in Syria, but seeing a chance to strengthen the frontier zone at no cost, he readily gave permission for the Visigoths to cross. Evidently his intention was to split them into detachments to serve in the eastern army and to settle the rest in Thrace; but gross mismanagement by the Romans, and a desire among the Visigoths to remain together, led to serious disturbance during which hordes of Ostrogoths crossed the Danube. Confusion reigned for two years.

Finally in May 378 Valens reached Constantinople and without waiting for reinforcements marched against the Goths. On 9 August the Roman army was defeated and the emperor killed: it was a disastrous moment for Rome. Gratian, the emperor of the West, immediately appointed a young Spanish general, Theodosius, to take charge

Emperor Valentian I *(above left)* was brought to power by the army in the year 364. He was to be the Western Empire's last truly dynamic emperor. Valentian divided the government with his brother Valens, whose Eastern Empire was overrun by West Goths. His Eastern successor was Theodosius I *(above right)*, who allowed Goths to settle within the Empire. After ten years' rule in the East, he took over the entire Empire in 388.

Examples of Roman and barbarian coexistence. Stilicho *(left)*, the son of a Vandal leader who had joined the Romans, became commander-in-chief of the army under Theodosius.
Alaric, a Goth, served with the Romans but changed sides when he failed to receive a high military command in 395. Galla Placida *(above right)*, was first married to Alaric's successor Ataulphus (414) and then to Constantius III.

The Saxon village of Warendorf, a sixth-century settlement, was excavated in the years 1951–1959. The evidence that was found enabled archaeologists to make a reconstruction of the village. It was from villages such as this that the Saxons who invaded Britain came.

Eagle-brooch, of gold, glass, and colored stones, barbarian workmanship of the fifth century. In this period (fifth-sixth centuries) Goths and Lombards in considerable numbers penetrated into Italy as far as Tuscany. They settled more or less permanently. Evidence of their craftsmanship has been found throughout the area.

and gradually order was restored—the Ostrogoths were forced back beyond the frontier, while the Visigoths were allowed to settle south of the lower Danube.

The situation was, however, desperately unstable. When some years later Theodosius employed Visigoths in his successful campaign against a western usurper, Maximus, they refused to return home, instead they preferred to roam through Macedonia pillaging the province. "The barbarians have left their own territory," wrote the Bishop of Constantinople in 392, "and many times have overrun huge tracts of our lands, setting fire to the countryside and seizing the towns. Instead of returning to their homes, like drunken revelers, they mock us."

When Theodosius died in 395, the Visigoths, under their newly elected leader Alaric, went completely out of control. Skillful maneuvering by the eastern politicians, however, turned Alaric's energies against the western general Stilicho and eventually, after pillaging southern Greece and narrowly

Attila, king of the Huns, between 433 and 453, attacked Gaul in 451 but was repelled, only to invade Italy a year later.

Odoacer (above right) became the ruler of Italy (476–493) at the head of a barbarian force. After maintaining a puppet emperor for a time in Rome, he abolished the reduced Western Empire altogether.

evading capture, Alaric was officially recognized as military chief of the northwest Balkans.

As the collapse of the western world approached, the political confusion deepened. In 401 Stilicho managed to beat back the Visigoths who were intent on invading Italy. A few years later, however, he was enlisting Alaric's help, but events elsewhere prevented collaboration. Alaric immediately demanded, and received, a huge sum in compensation (407). Having tasted the riches of Italy, Alaric decided once more to invade and, throughout the winter of 408–409, settled down to besiege Rome itself. When, by 410, it was clear that no ransom was forthcoming, the city was taken and sacked. It was a dreadful blow to the morale of east and west alike. St. Jerome could write: "When the brightest light of the whole earth was extinguished, when the Roman Empire was deprived of its head...when the whole world perished in one city, then 'I was dumb with silence, I held my peace even from God, and my sorrow was stirred.'" Yet for all the stark horror of the event, the fall of Rome had little military significance. The emperor

and government were now safely in Ravenna, and its commanders were involved with far more serious problems elsewhere.

The story of the end of the Visigoth migration can be briefly told. A rapid march to southern Italy in an attempt to reach the cornfields of Africa came to nothing—it was at this stage that Alaric died—and the horde moved north again; this time to Gaul where they championed the Empire from time to time against other bands of invaders. In 415 they were moving through Spain as allies of Rome, exterminating groups of Germans who had already penetrated the area. Finally in 418, having returned to Gaul, they were settled in Aquitania as federates with Toulouse as their capital.

The history of the Alans, the other tribe ousted from the steppe by the Hunnic advance, was no less remarkable. In 378 they played a significant role in the defeat of Valens at Adrianople, and two years later, together with the Ostrogoths and a detachment of Huns, they had settled in Pannonia. In 401, however, this time in concert with the Vandals, they crossed into Noricum, their settlement being recognized by Stilicho in return for services against the Visigoths.

The arrangement with Rome ended in 406 when the majority of the Alans joined the hordes of northern barbarians who had just crossed the Rhine, and together they thrust through France. Two years later they had entered Spain where, in Lusitania, they settled down for a decade until 417 when they were routed by the Visigoths (working as confederates of Rome). Thereafter they joined forces with the Vandals, whose king assumed the title *Rex Vandalorum et Alanorum*, and marched with them on their remarkable trek to Carthage.

Rome saved by the Pope: In 452, after Attila invaded northern Italy and destroyed Aquileia, Pope Leo I personally interceded with the barbarians and persuaded them to withdraw north of the Alps. The Pope later (455) kept the Vandal chieftain Genseric from destroying the city. Painting by Raphael, from the Vatican.

The barbarian migrations and invasions of the Empire. The map suggests the irresistibility of their movement against Rome. It nevertheless remains true that many of the peoples were more capable of assimilation and coexistence than the Romans believed, and that the change could have occurred less violently.

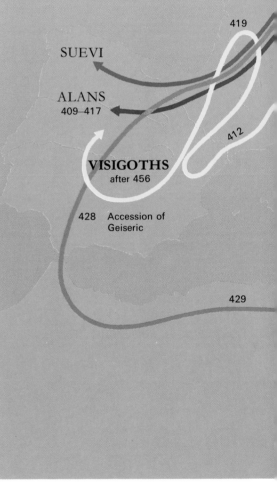

SUEVI

ALANS
409–417

419

412

VISIGOTHS
after 456

428 Accession of
Geiseric

429

Thus in a brief period of forty years vast hordes of barbarians from the east, dislodged by the Huns from their homelands and carefully deflected from the Eastern Roman Empire, had swept across Europe creating panic and confusion in their wake. It was little wonder that the crumbling authority of the West found it difficult to cope.

THE VANDALS

From the mid-fourth century the Western provinces had come under increasing pressure from the Germans. Julian had gained spectacular successes against German war parties in the 350s, for the most part rounding them up and forcing them back across the Rhine. And when in 367 barbarian hordes swept through Britain, the government of Valentinian I was able to restore the situation within two years. Valen-

tinian's successor, Gratian, was, however, far less satisfactory and in 383 he was killed in an army revolt led by Magnus Maximus. Maximus was a competent soldier who, for the next four years, having set up his base in Trier, was to campaign widely in Gaul and Spain, restoring a degree of order to the provinces. But delusions of grandeur led him to march on Italy where Theodosius I, emperor of the East, defeated and killed him. After eight years of uncertain government in the West, Theodosius I who had been holding the Empire together, died and was succeeded by his sons, Arcadius in the East and Honorius in the West. Both young men showed little ability and were thoroughly dependent on their military advisers.

Honorius, only ten years old on his accession, was dominated by his guardian and commander-in-chief Stilicho,

a Vandal by origin, who remained in virtual control of the West for the next thirteen years. Towards the end of Stilicho's command, in the winter of 406–407, the Rhine frontier collapsed and hordes of Vandals and Suebi together with groups of Alans broke through and began to rampage through Gaul. The event, shocking in the

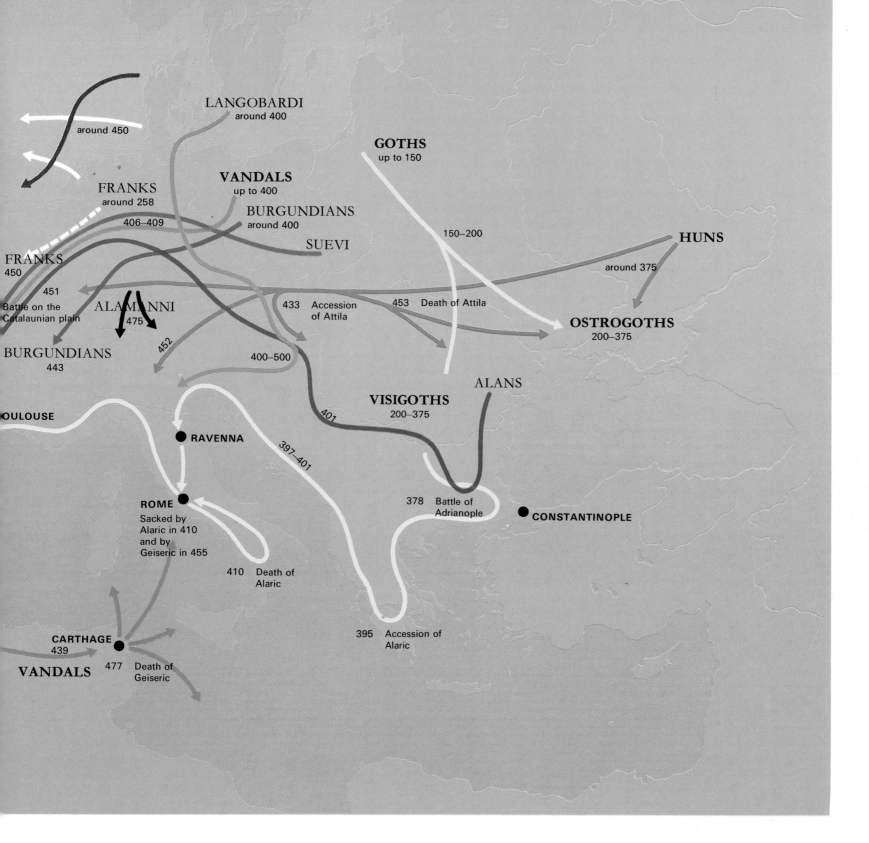

LANGOBARDI
around 400

GOTHS
up to 150

VANDALS
up to 400

BURGUNDIANS
around 400

SUEVI

HUNS

around 375

FRANKS
around 258

around 450

406–409

150–200

OSTROGOTHS
200–375

FRANKS
450

451
Battle on the
Catalaunian plain

ALAMANNI
475

452

433   Accession
of Attila

453   Death of Attila

400–500

BURGUNDIANS
443

ALANS

VISIGOTHS
200–375

401

OULOUSE

RAVENNA

397–401

378   Battle of
Adrianople

CONSTANTINOPLE

ROME
Sacked by
Aleric in 410
and by
Geiseric in 455

410   Death of
Alaric

395   Accession of
Alaric

CARTHAGE
439

VANDALS   477   Death of
Geiseric

extreme, had widespread repercussions. In Britain an obscure army officer, Constantine III, was thrust to power and immediately crossed to the continent, where, from his base at Arles, he created a new Gallic Empire in southern Gaul and Spain. From here he was able to maintain a degree of internal security until the winter of 409, when the Vandals, Suebi, and Alans finally broke through the Pyrenees and ravaged Spain. His temporary empire fell apart and in 411, after a period of utmost confusion, he was defeated by the imperial army from Ravenna and executed. The Suebi and the Vandals now controlled the northwest of Spain, but under continuous pressure from the Romans and the confederate Visigoths (who by now were settled in Aquitania), they eventually decided to move south. In 429, led by Gaiseric, they crossed the Straits of Gibraltar into Africa. Six years later Mauretania and Numidia were conceded to them and in 439 they had taken Carthage.

THE DISINTEGRATION OF THE WEST

The rich and extensive lands of the great Empire were a natural target for displaced or nomadic peoples. Military defense of the Empire required unprecedented revenues, which had to be raised from new sources. The administrative and economic changes required by the new challenges led eventually to the division of the Empire in 395. At left, medallion showing a Sarmatian rider, from Bulgaria.

The Roman Empire in A.D. 117, under Trajan, at its fullest expansion.

In 395, the Empire was divided; the borders of the East and West are indicated above.

The great migratory movements of the Visigoths, Alans, Suebi, and Vandals across the length and breadth of the Roman world shattered the fragile unity of the west. In a brief period of fifty years or so from the first appearance of the Visigoths on the Danube in 375, the West disintegrated. Africa was lost to the Vandals, the Suebi occupied parts of Spain, Visigoths were settled in southern Gaul, Britain had been swamped by the Saxons and in Germany and the north and east of Gaul, Franks, Alamanni, and Burgundians were being allowed to settle.

For a while the freebooting general, Aëtius, upheld the semblance of Roman rule in central and northwestern Gaul, but it was an unstable interlude. He was, however, strong enough to defeat an onslaught of Huns led by Attila in a pitched battle near Troyes in 451. Attila moved against the west again, the next year, this time descending on Italy, but was forced to retire and

died in 453. Aëtius did not survive him for long: he was assassinated at the instigation of Valentinian III in 454 and with his death Gaul was lost. Meanwhile the Visigoths had greatly extended their territory, penetrating into Spain and annexing most of the peninsula.

Thus as the last quarter of the century of collapse approached (450–475) little

of the Western Empire remained. Emperors of a kind continued to be nominated. But when the last of them, Romulus Augustulus, was deposed in 476, the general who removed him let the Eastern government know that there was really no need to appoint a replacement since he could look after the remnants of the West himself. Just over 1200 years from its traditional date of foundation, Rome had ceased to exist.

The Lex Romana Visigothorum, the vernacular legal system of the West Gothic king Alaric II, A.D. 506, was also valid for Roman subjects. At left, a West Gothic lord; beside him stands a representative of the Roman Church. Despite its legislative limitations, the Lex Romana Visigothorum played an important role in the legal history of southwestern Europe in the Middle Ages. In southern France it was used for five hundred years after the end of the West Gothic rule. It was not until the thirteenth century that the influence of the Justinian law code (Corpus Iuris Civilis), the most important of the late Roman codifications, reached France by way of Italy, and replaced the Visigoth code.

Last of the emperors. The historians of the Renaissance considered the year 476— in which puppet emperor Romulus Augustulus was discharged—as the end of the Roman Empire. This event was merely one of many important points in late Roman history, but it does represent a culmination of the general trend of Germanization in the West. Portrait of Emperor Romulus Augustulus on a Roman coin.

Under Emperor Justinian, the Eastern Empire rose to a powerful position. The Eastern Empire was tempted to seek to reconquer Italy, but no firm foothold in the West was henceforth possible, even though various short-lived campaigns were sometimes undertaken after 526. The portrait of Justinian is a detail of a mosaic from San Vitale in Ravenna.

Bottom: Ruins of the Forum Romanum, by G. B. Piranesi (d. 1778).

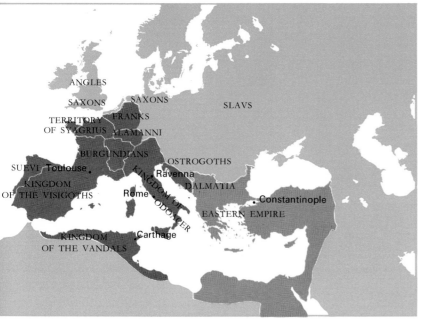

In 476, occurred the dissolution of the Western Roman Empire, under Romulus Augustulus.

By 526, during the reign of Justinian the Great in Constantinople, the West was entirely in barbarian hands.

CONSTANTINOPLE

While the West suffered the torment of dismemberment, the Eastern Empire remained largely unscathed. Behind its massive defensive walls and lulled by the long and stable reign of Theodosius II, the city of Constantinople prepared itself to become the center of the civilized world.

Elegant churches sprang up. On the site of the first Haghia Sophia (dedicated by Constantius II in 360 and burned down by a mob in 404), Theodosius completed a new church in 415—five years after Rome was sacked by the Goths. A generation later a local citizen, Studius, founded another church, St. John the Baptist, which was to become the most powerful monastery in the Byzantine Empire. It was dedicated in 462—seven years after Rome was sacked a second time, by the Vandals. Thus as Rome died, Constantinople sprang into vigorous life.

But the real glories were yet to come. In 527 Justinian ascended to the throne. Son of a peasant and married to an actress of dubious reputation, in the thirty-eight years of his reign he was to transform not only his city but his Empire. Surrounded by brilliant men, he proceeded to win back much of the old Empire. Italy, Africa, and parts of Spain were reunited once more under one emperor, while at Constantinople he erected buildings of a quality the world had never seen, culminating in the staggering achievement of the church of Haghia Sophia—Divine Wisdom.

Procopius wrote:

The church presents a most glorious spectacle, extraordinary to those who behold it and altogether incredible to those who are told of it. In height it rises to the very heavens...
It is distinguished by indescribable beauty excelling both in its size and the harmonies of its measures.

The church of Theodosius had been destroyed during mob violence in 532. Justinian decided to rebuild it immediately, "regardless of expense gathering together skilled workmen from every land." Anthemius of Tralles, a mathematician, was appointed to take charge, assisted by Isidorus of Miletus. Their church was opened five years later—but almost immediately an earthquake caused it to collapse. Reconstruction began once more and finally the great church—substantially the building that remains today—opened its doors. As the sun rose on Christmas day, 563 the now aging emperor entered.

And when the first glow of light, rosy-armed, leapt from arch to arch, driving away the dark shadows, then all the princes and people with one voice hymned their songs of praise and prayer; and as they came to the sacred courts it seemed as if the mighty arches were set in heaven.

Paul the Silentiary

It is perhaps ironic that the death blow to the great city should be struck in the name of the Christian Church. On 13 April 1204 the Latin armies of the Fourth Crusade broke through the walls and in an orgy of avarice and destruction removed everything of value, leaving only a ruin. One of the devastated participants wrote:

Of holy relics I need only say that it contained more than all Christendom combined; there is no estimating the quantity of gold, silver, rich stuffs and other valuable things....It is [my belief] that the plunder of this city exceeded all that had been witnessed since the creation of the world.

Above: Justinian and his wife Theodora, from the famous San Vitale mosaic. The couple assumed exclusive power in Constantinople on 1 August 527.

Right: Vast interior of Hagia Sophia in Constantinople, from an engraving by Fossati. The church, erected between 532 and 537, was a marvel of engineering.

ROME'S LEGACY

While this (theological war) was being waged in Jerusalem, terrible news arrived from the West. We learnt how Rome had been besieged, how her citizens had purchased immunity by paying a ransom, and how then, after they had thus been despoiled, they had been beleaguered again, to forfeit their lives after having already forfeited their property. At the news my speech failed me, and sobs choked the words that I was dictating. She had been captured—the city by whom the whole world had once been taken captive.

Saint Jerome, quoted by Toynbee in *A Study of History*

Thus, for instance, the Pantheon... (has)...so won my whole heart, that I scarcely saw anything besides (it). But, in truth, can man, little as man always is, and accustomed to littleness, ever make himself equal to all that

here surrounds him of the noble, the vast, and the refined?
As it happened to me in the case of natural history, so goes it with me here also; for the history of the whole world attaches itself to this spot, and I reckon a new-birth day—a true new birth from the day that I entered Rome.

Johann Wolfgang von Goethe, *Travels in Italy*

Among the innumerable monuments of architecture constructed by the Romans, how many have escaped the notice of history, how few have resisted the ravages of time and barbarism!... And yet even the majestic ruins prove that those countries were once the seat of a polite and powerful empire. Their greatness alone, or their beauty, might deserve our attention; but they are rendered more interesting by two important circumstances, which connect the agreable history of the arts with the more useful history of human manners. Many of those works were erected at private expense, and almost all were intended for public benefit... If the emperors were the first, they were not the only architects of their dominions. Their example was universally imitated by their principal subjects, who were not afraid of declaring to the world that they had spirit to conceive, and wealth to accomplish, the noblest undertakings.
...All the quarters of the capital, and all the provinces of the empire, were embellished by the same liberal spirit of public magnificence, and were filled with amphitheaters, theaters, temples, porticos, triumphal arches, baths, and aqueducts, all variously conducive to the health, the devotion, and the pleasures of the meanest citizen. The boldness of the enterprise, the solidity of the execution, and the uses to which they were subservient, rank the aqueducts among the noblest monuments of Roman genius and power.

Edward Gibbon,
The Decline and Fall of the Roman Empire

Classical Roman legal thought, the object of study in universities of northern Italy since the twelfth century, is a magnificent legacy still valid today. Our illustration from the *Corpus Iuris Civilis* shows an extract from the XXIXth book of the Digest, "The Soldier's Testament."

Right: Rome, Porta Appia, in the background the Arc of Drusus.

Roman civilization lived on in unique splendor with the Western Goths in Spain and with the Eastern Goths of Italy, less securely with the Burgundians of Gaul, and almost stunned with the Franks. Nowhere, however, did it disappear completely and forever, for the simple reason that it lived on in the thinking and piety of the Church, in the taste and knowledge of scholars, in the meditations of Christian philosophers and in legal institutions.

William Seston, *Propyläen Weltgeschichte*

The Empire was vastly superior to all other monarchies and was, indeed, the only one worthy of the name, in spite of its imperfections. It is not a question of whether monarchies are desirable, but rather, of whether the Romans had, or had not, fulfilled their design of containing the old cultures and of spreading Christianity.... Without the Roman Empire there would have been no continuity in learning.

Jacob Burckhardt, *Weltgeschichtliche Betrachtungen*

Far left: Roman street in Aleppo, Syria.

Below: The Pantheon in Rome.

Right: The hippodrome of Aphrodisias, Turkey.

The Romans arrived at universal
monarchy not only by the arts of war,
but likewise by their wisdom, their
perseverance, their passion for glory,
and their heroic love for their country.

> Montesquieu,
> *Grandeur and Declension of the Roman Empire*

Rome is the fallen civilization which
is closest to our own in terms of
time and which has had by far the
greatest influence on it, since it has
given us an endless wealth of testimony in stone and marble, in gold and
iron, in clay and glass, and in books
of law, history, philosophy and poetry.

> Golo Mann, Preface to M. Grant's
> *The Decline and Fall of the Roman Empire.*
> German edition.

Others, for so I can well believe, shall
hammer forth more delicately a
breathing likeness out of bronze, coax
living faces from the marble, plead
causes with more skill, plot with their
gauge the movements in the sky, and
tell the rising of the constellations.
But you, Roman, must remember that
you have to guide the nations by your
authority, for this is to be your skill.

> Virgil, *The Aeneid*

Rome did not invent education,
but she developed it on a scale unknown before,
gave it state support,
and formed the curriculum that persisted till our harassed youth.
She did not invent the arch, the vault, or the dome,
but she used them with such audacity and magnificence
that in some fields her architecture has remained unequaled;
and all the elements of the medieval cathedral
were prepared in her basilicas.
She did not invent the sculptural portrait,
but she gave it a realistic power rarely reached by the idealizing Greeks.
She did not invent philosophy,
but it was in Lucretius and Seneca
that Epicureanism and Stoicism found their most finished form.
She did not invent the types of literature,
not even the satire;
but who could adequately record the influence of Cicero on oratory,
the essay, and prose style, of Virgil on Dante, Tasso, Milton,
...of Livy and Tacitus on the writing of history,
of Horace and Juvenal on Dryden, Swift, and Pope?
Her language became, by a most admirable corruption,
the speech of Italy,
Rumania, France, Spain, Portugal, and Latin America;
half the white man's world speaks a Latin tongue.
Latin was, till the eighteenth century,
the Esperanto of science, scholarship,
and philosophy in the West;
it gave a convenient international terminology to botany and zoology;
it survives in the sonorous ritual
and official documents of the Roman Church;
it still writes medical prescriptions, and haunts the phraseology of the law.
It entered by direct appropriation,
and again through the Romance languages
to enhance the wealth and flexibility of English speech.
Our Roman heritage works in our lives
a thousand times a day.

> Will Durant, *Caesar and Christ*